A World Survey of Religion and the State

This book delves into the extent of government involvement in religion (GIR) between 1990 and 2002 using both quantitative and qualitative methodology. The study is based on the Religion and State dataset (RAS), which includes 175 governments across the globe, all of which are addressed individually in this book. The forms of GIR examined in this study include whether the government has an official religion, whether some religions are given preferential treatment, religious discrimination against minority religions, government regulation of the majority religion, and religious legislation. The study shows that GIR is ubiquitous, that GIR increased significantly during this period, and that only a minority of states, including a minority of democracies, have separation of religion and state. These findings contradict the predictions of religion's reduced public significance found in modernization and secularization theory. The findings also demonstrate that state religious monopolies are linked to reduced religious participation.

Jonathan Fox (Ph.D. in government and politics, University of Maryland, 1997) has published more than 40 articles on religion and government in publications such as *Comparative Politics, Comparative Political Studies, International Studies Quarterly,* and *Journal of Peace Research.* He has also published three books: *Bringing Religion into International Relations* (2004) (with Shmuel Sandler); *Religion, Civilization, and Civil War: 1945 Through the New Millennium* (2004); and *Ethnoreligious Conflict in the Late Twentieth Century: A General Theory* (2002). Fox has received a grant from the Israel Science Foundation and has given guest lectures at universities around the world. He is an Associate Professor of Political Studies at Bar Ilan University, Israel.

Cambridge Studies in Social Theory, Religion, and Politics

Editors

David C. Leege, *University of Notre Dame*
Kenneth D. Wald, *University of Florida, Gainesville*

The most enduring and illuminating bodies of late nineteenth-century social theory – by Marx, Weber, Durkheim, and others – emphasized the integration of religion, polity, and economy through time and place. Once a staple of classic social theory, however, religion gradually lost the interest of many social scientists during the twentieth century. The recent emergence of phenomena such as Solidarity in Poland; the dissolution of the Soviet empire; various South American, Southern African, and South Asian liberation movements; the Christian Right in the United States; and al Qaeda have reawakened scholarly interest in religiously based political conflict. At the same time, fundamental questions are once again being asked about the role of religion in stable political regimes, public policies, and constitutional orders. The series Cambridge Studies in Social Theory, Religion, and Politics will produce volumes that study religion and politics by drawing upon classic social theory and more recent social scientific research traditions. Books in the series offer theoretically grounded, comparative, empirical studies that raise "big" questions about a timely subject that has long engaged the best minds in social science.

Titles in the Series:

Joel S. Fetzer and J. Christopher Soper, *Muslims and the State in Britain, France, and Germany*
Anthony Gill, *The Political Origins of Religious Liberty*
Pippa Norris and Ronald Inglehart, *Sacred and Secular: Religion and Politics Worldwide*

A World Survey of Religion and the State

JONATHAN FOX

Bar Ilan University, Israel

CAMBRIDGE
UNIVERSITY PRESS

CAMBRIDGE UNIVERSITY PRESS
Cambridge, New York, Melbourne, Madrid, Cape Town, Singapore, São Paulo, Delhi

Cambridge University Press
32 Avenue of the Americas, New York, NY 10013-2473, USA

www.cambridge.org
Information on this title: www.cambridge.org/9780521707589

First published 2008

Printed in the United States of America

A catalog record for this publication is available from the British Library.

Library of Congress Cataloging in Publication Data

Fox, Jonathan, 1967–
   A World survey of religion and the state / Jonathan Fox.
      p. cm. – (Cambridge studies in social theory, religion, and politics)
   Includes bibliographical references and index.
   ISBN 978-0-521-88131-9 (hardback) – ISBN 978-0-521-70758-9 (pbk.)
   1. Religion and state – History – 20th century. 2. Religion and politics – History – 20th century.
3. World politics – 1989– I. Title. II. Series.
BL65.S8F69 2008
322'.109049–dc22   2007031307

ISBN 978-0-521-88131-9 hardback
ISBN 978-0-521-70758-9 paperback

To my parents, Jack and Barbara Fox. Without their love and support this book would not have been possible.

Contents

Acknowledgments

I would like to thank R. Scott Appleby, Robert Barro, Jay Demerath, Eliezer Don-Yehiyia, Tanja Ellingsen, Ted R. Gurr, Pat James, Rachel McCleary, Shmuel Sandler, Shlomo Shpiro, Bernard Susser, and numerous anonymous referees, all of whom provided useful advice and criticism at some point in this project. I would especially like to thank Ken Wald and David Leege for their time and efforts in bringing this book to publication. I also acknowledge the hard work by the research assistants who collected the data for the RAS project, including Hana Bagelman, John Daley, Rifka Dzodin, Aaron Ettengoff, Dalia Ganz, David Yisroel Halevi, Oren Keston, Tamara Lafair, Marcelle Last, Rebecca Scharbach, Doni Schuman, Valeria Schefter, Hagai Stern, Donna Susser, and Shira Traison. All errors of fact or interpretation that remain are mine alone. This research was supported by the Israel Science Foundation (Grant 896/00) and the Sara and Simha Lainer Chair in Democracy and Civility.

I

Introduction

This study asks a seemingly simple set of questions. What is the extent of government involvement in religion (GIR) between 1990 and 2002 across the globe? Has the extent or nature of this involvement changed during this period? What social and political factors can explain the variation over place and time in GIR? How is GIR otherwise related to important social and political phenomena?

The answers to these questions are not so simple. The intersection between religion, state, and society is complex and not fully understood. This is reflected in the current state of the scholarship on the topic. The first element of the basic problem in this field of scholarship can be illustrated by the legend of the Oracle at Delphi, who was once asked who was the smartest person in the world. The answer she gave was Socrates. When he heard about this, Socrates was at first confused because he felt that he knew nothing. Upon reflection, Socrates reasoned that the Oracle had declared him the smartest person in the world because although he knew nothing, at least he knew that he knew nothing. The rest of the people in the world believed that they knew something but their supposed knowledge was incorrect or inaccurate. Thus, while Socrates' knowledge could be said to be zero, everyone else's knowledge was less than nothing.

I am not suggesting that the current scholarship on the intersection between religion, politics, and society is worth less than nothing. Nothing could be further from the truth. Yet this field is colored to a great extent by what we do not know. All studies on the topic, including this one, are subject to several limitations. First, none of them are able to look at the entire religious economy for the entire world. The term religious economy is defined here as all of the religious activity that occurs within a given society.

It is possible to study the entire religious economy of a single state or small number of states and there exist excellent global surveys of various aspects of the religious economy. However, no study to my knowledge has encompassed the entire global religious economy nor is it likely that any study will do so in the near future – even simply to present the nature of the global religious economy for a single point in time, much less to track its evolution over time. There is too much we do not know. Thus, at least at our present level of knowledge, social science studies of religion will be somehow limited in their scope.

Second, even when limiting the scope of a study to something manageable, there are aspects of religion that are easier to study than others. As social scientists, we study human behavior either by individuals or groups. Behavior can be measured. For instance, if we want to know how often someone attends religious services or if that person believes in God, we can ask that person. Many studies of religiosity are based on survey data using exactly these types of questions.

These types of questions can elicit how people behave, but do not touch on why people behave in this way. Why does one attend religious services? Why does one believe in God? The issue of motivation is essential to understanding religion's impact on society. We can elicit some information on motivations through studies that examine the correlation of other variables, such as up-bringing or economic status, with attendance at religious services or belief in God. Yet these studies rarely provide complete statistical explanations and in any case are based on the assumption that correlation implies causation. We can also ask the individuals surveyed but this assumes that these individuals fully understand their own motivations and are willing and able to communicate them.

Measuring the intersection between religion and government raises similar issues. For instance, it is easy to measure whether a government has arrested religious leaders belonging to a minority religion. However, the motivation for those arrests might be unclear. It can be part of a campaign motivated by purely political concerns to repress a minority. The arrests may be due to suspicion of illegal activities, such as supporting terrorism. They may be part of a government effort to restrict the growth of a minority religion in the state. There can be any number of other motivations. The context of the arrests and, if available, government declarations of why this action was taken can shed some light on the government's motivations but more often than not the true motivation for the arrests will remain at least partially obfuscated. For example, even in a blatant case of religious leaders supporting terrorism, those leaders and their advocates rarely fail to claim they are innocent and that their arrest is purely religious or political discrimination. Conversely, governments that arrest religious leaders for political reasons will often accuse these leaders of crimes such as supporting terrorism as a pretext. In most cases, the government's motivations are not clear and different rational individuals can, and do, come to significantly different conclusions regarding the motivations for those arrests. Furthermore, many government activities in the realm of religion have a potential set of motivations that are arguably far more complex and difficult to discern than the motivations discussed in this example.

In short, measuring actions is easier than measuring motivations. An essential element of collecting events-based data – the type of data that is the focus of this study – is inter-coder reliability. This means that two individuals looking at the same information would code the same variable in the same way. While inter-coder reliability is rarely 100 percent for actions taken by governments, it is nearly impossible to achieve a level of acceptable agreement with regard to issues of motivations.

The third element of the basic problem, as implied above, is that even when measuring something objective, such as government actions, information is often imperfect. A good illustration of this is the number of deaths in a conflict, a classical variable often measured by political scientists. Setting aside issues of whether the number includes just combatants killed, or also includes collateral civilian casualties and deaths due to the disease and famine often caused by war, this is still a difficult variable to code. For instance, the estimates for the deaths in Rwanda during the early 1990s range from a few hundred thousand to over one million. While the number of people who died is an exact number, the chaos of the situation makes it difficult to ascertain that number. Furthermore, the two sides in a conflict, as well as third parties, often have motivations to overestimate or underestimate the number of deaths. Thus, just because a fact is ascertainable in theory, does not mean that it can be ascertained in practice.

In addition, despite the fact that information on events around the world is becoming increasingly available and detailed, the coverage is never 100 percent and it is likely that some events that would influence the coding of events-based variables are not recorded anywhere. Also, when collecting such data, resource limitations restrict the amount of time that can be devoted to any one case and thereby limit the number of sources on that case that can be checked. So it is more than likely that some events that are recorded somewhere are also not uncovered and therefore are not included in the codings of the data.

All studies of events data are subject to this type of problem. The only question is the extent to which it is an issue in a particular study. The only way to deal with it is to make a good faith effort to collect the data based on the best information available and based on the assumption that if the data is not 100 percent accurate, it is sufficiently close to the reality on the ground to be the basis for a meaningful study.

Fourth, there is little agreement on how the various parts of the religious economy fit together. This is true of both the relationship between these parts and their relative importance. For example, one theory has it that, for a number of reasons (discussed in more detail in Chapters 2 and 11), religious monopolies cause people to become less religious. This theory is controversial and the empirical tests of the theory produce mixed results. This debate is just one among many regarding the interaction between religion's various facets.

An interrelated issue is the question of which part of the religious economy is most important. Returning to the example of the link between religiosity and religious monopolies, is government policy the driving force behind this particular relationship or is the driving force the religiosity of the population? It is unlikely that this relationship is unidirectional so the answer is likely both. Even so, this leaves open the question of which influences the other more. This question gets even more complicated when one adds to the equation additional elements of the religious economy such as religious institutions, religious lobby groups, religious political parties, the religious beliefs of policy makers, and of those who influence these policy makers.

Based on all of this, if I were to describe our current state of knowledge on the intersection between religion, politics, and society as a puzzle, I would do so as follows. It is a puzzle with many of the pieces missing. Many of the existing pieces are discolored from an imperfect printing process and misshapen from an imperfect cutting process. Furthermore, the pieces overlap so their shape is of little use. Our ability to place them correctly into the larger picture is limited to our use of the pictures on the pieces. To make matters worse, some of the pieces are made on a scale that is too large or too small for the true scale of the puzzle. Finally, we do not have the box so we have no guide for the completed picture and must rely on the pieces of the puzzle itself in order to put it together. Of course, this can be said to be true of many fields of academic endeavor, but it is particularly true of this one.

This study focuses on one piece of this puzzle in a limited time frame – the intersection between religion and state between 1990 and 2002. Thus, it can be said that the goal of this study is to take a single piece of this puzzle, clarify its shape and picture, and hopefully place it better within our imperfect and incomplete puzzle. This goal is both a limited and ambitious one. On one hand, this study cannot provide a final picture of the entire religious economy. On the other hand, the information included in the Religion and State (RAS) dataset is more complete and comprehensive than previous studies with regard to its portion of the puzzle. This includes how much information is collected for an individual country and how many countries are included in the dataset. As is discussed in detail in Chapter 3, some previous studies do match the scope of countries included in the RAS dataset, but no large-n quantitative study on this topic contains as much information on GIR.

Nevertheless, while this study arguably brings more clarity to this piece of the puzzle, it cannot be considered the final word for two reasons. First, while the amount and detail of information included in the RAS dataset is superior to that of previous studies, future studies will no doubt improve upon this one. Second, this study is subject to all four of the limitations on this type of study that I have just discussed. Thus, to return to the legend of Socrates and the Oracle at Delphi, we likely know more than nothing but we must question everything that we know as our knowledge is certainly imperfect and incomplete.

THE RELIGION AND STATE DATASET, GIR, AND SEPARATION OF RELIGION AND STATE

This study is based primarily on an analysis of the Religion and State (RAS) dataset, which includes 62 variables each of which measures a particular way a government can become entangled in religion. Each of these variables can be placed into one of five broader categories of GIR and is coded yearly for 175 governments for the 1990 to 2002 period. These variables are discussed in Chapter 3 and the countries included in the study, as well as their codings on these variables, are listed in Chapters 5 through 10.

Before discussing the details of the RAS dataset it is important to address two central and interrelated concepts, which are the basis upon which the RAS data was developed: GIR, and separation of religion and state (SRAS). There is no real agreement in the academic literature as to what constitutes SRAS either in theory or in practice. Yet, as this study is based on an analysis of data on the extent of GIR and SRAS for 175 governments, it is essential to create a working definition of GIR and SRAS.

This study defines SRAS as the absence of any government support for religion as well as the absence of any government restrictions on religion or regulation of religion. Any government support for religion, restrictions on religion, or regulation of religion is considered GIR. This operational definition of SRAS is stricter than the definition most academics would use, as is discussed in more detail in Chapters 3 and 4. Other definitions of SRAS allow some GIR without a violation of SRAS. In order to differentiate the concept of SRAS used to develop the data from other concepts of SRAS, I designate it as absolute-SRAS.

Basing variables on this definition of GIR and absolute-SRAS has a number of advantages. It allows for the measurement of GIR without any philosophical or theoretical bias. A government either takes an action, such as declaring an official religion or legislating some aspect of religious law, or it does not. This sets aside questions of whether the particular action taken combined with the government's other actions with regard to religion are of a sufficient magnitude and nature to violate some theoretical or philosophical concept of SRAS. The information is simply collected and coded systematically. The resulting variables are sufficiently versatile to then use them to operationalize multiple standards of SRAS and examine how many states meet those standards. This analysis is provided in Chapter 4.

The RAS dataset provides measures of this nature that look at five aspects of GIR. *Official GIR* measures the official relationship between religion and state. This includes whether the state has an official religion and, if not, the exact nature of the government's relationship with the various religions that exist within its borders. *Official restrictions* measures whether the government treats different religions differently. *Religious discrimination* is defined as restrictions on the religious practices of religious minorities. It does not include other forms of political, social, or economic discrimination against religious minorities. Of course such nonreligious discrimination against religious minorities is deplorable, but it does not strictly constitute government support, restrictions, or regulation of religion. This variable consists of 16 types of religious discrimination, which are measured individually. *Religious regulation* measures the extent of government regulation of the majority religion or all religions. This is measured separately from the previous variable because the

motivations and implications of regulating all religions or the majority religion
are potentially very different from the motivations for restricting the practice of
a minority religion. This variable consists of 11 types of regulation, each of
which is measured individually. *Religious legislation* measures the extent to
which the government legislates various aspects of religious law. It includes
33 types of legislation, each of which is coded individually.

These variables are described in detail in Chapter 3, which includes a full
listing of the component variables of the *religious discrimination, religious
regulation,* and *religious legislation* variables as well as the reasoning and intellectual history behind the development of these variables.

SOME LIMITATIONS AND QUALIFICATIONS

These variables, despite covering a broad range of government laws, policies,
and actions in the realm of religion, are also limited in certain ways, as just
described. It is important, however, to emphasize that one of the primary
limitations is that the RAS data examines the objective laws, policies, and
actions of a government or its representatives but not the motivation behind
those actions. In a sense this constitutes measuring what we can measure in the
hope of using that to obtain insights on what we would actually like to study. In
the end, religion resides to a great extent in individual and collective psyches
and consciousnesses, a realm that is notoriously difficult to measure.

Yet it also exists in actions taken by individuals, groups, institutions, and
governments. These actions in and of themselves are worthy of study. This is
not just in order to better understand motivations, though this is an important
goal. The act of accurately and systematically describing the ways in which
governments become involved in religion and under what circumstances they
do so is a difficult and important task. Furthermore, this must be done in a way
that allows the actions of one government easily to be compared to those of
another, and, as well, allows the collective actions of groups of governments to
be correlated with other social, economic, and political variables. In the best of
all worlds the RAS data would include detailed variables on motivations.
However, accurately coding government actions, laws, and policies in such
a way that these codings are not significantly subject to dispute strains the
limits of the current level of knowledge, methodology, and available resources.

Despite all of this, motivations color every aspect of this study. For instance,
the findings provided later in this study show that there has been a rise in GIR,
especially government support for religion. But what does this mean in the
larger context? Are governments supporting religion in order to help preserve
it in the face of declining individual religiosity? Are they supporting it because
their populations are becoming more religious? If the latter is the case, is this in
order to better reflect the population's wants and needs or is it a cynical attempt
to maintain power by co-opting the political power of religion? Similar questions come up when trying to explain a rise in religious discrimination against
minorities. Is this because of a desire to support the national religion by

repressing minority religions? Or perhaps it is due to increasing religious militancy among some religious minorities, which the government sees as a threat.

This documented rise in GIR is certainly part of a more complicated set of trends in the religious economy. GIR may be increasing, but this is at least in part due to decreases in the importance of religion in other aspects of the religious economy. For instance, as is discussed in more detail in Chapter 2, modernity places many pressures on religion causing its influence in many aspects of society to decrease. Many have argued that these modern processes will result in religion's decline or even demise as a significant social and political force.

Yet, as the findings of this study show, religion is, among other things, a resilient social phenomenon, capable of adjusting and evolving in an ever-changing environment. A fuller picture of the world's religious economy would show secularization – the reduction of religion's influence in society – occurring in some parts of the religious economy, and sacralization[1] – the increase of religion's influence in society – occurring in other parts.

A second important limitation on the RAS data is that it covers only the 13-year timespan of 1990 to 2002. This limited timespan is not sufficient to answer some of the seminal questions asked in the social science study of religion including, but not limited to, whether or not religion is in a state of decline. However, the RAS data can provide information on whether one aspect of religion has declined for this limited time segment. Of course, any rise or fall in GIR does not imply that there has been a rise or fall in the entire religious economy but it can provide some insight into this larger question. It can also measure the extent to which GIR exists in recent times, which also has implications for some important debates in the field. Yet, as noted, the same action taken by a government can have different implications for the rise or fall of religion depending on the context and motivation for that action. Thus, even if the timespan covered by the RAS dataset was one of centuries rather than years, it would be insufficient to come to any final conclusions regarding the rise and fall of religion in the larger religious economy, though it would likely improve our ability to reach such conclusions.

While this is more of a definitional issue than a limitation of the variables, it is important to note that GIR is only one aspect of the intersection between religion and government. GIR covers government actions that influence religion. There are also a number of ways in which religion can influence the government. For instance, the religious beliefs of policy makers can influence their decisions. The religious beliefs of populations can also influence the decisions of policy makers. Many states have official and unofficial religious lobbies and some have religious political parties.

Be that as it may, I argue in Chapter 12 that this rise in GIR between 1990 and 2002, while only part of the larger picture for a limited time segment, is sufficient to show that some aspect of religion remains important. That is, there

---

[1] This term is borrowed from Demerath (2001), who makes an argument similar to the one made here.

is no reasonable interpretation of these findings that does not result in the conclusion that religion, in some form, remains a potent and influential part of modern society and politics.

RELIGIOUS ECONOMIES AND SUBECONOMIES

It cannot be emphasized often enough that GIR measures only one aspect of a complex, multifaceted, and interrelated religious economy. Yet even a single religious subeconomy such as the one measured by GIR has a considerable level of complexity that exists along two dimensions.

The first dimension is levels of analysis. The most basic unit of analysis of the RAS dataset is that of the 175 governments included in the dataset. Each of these governments has a unique system of GIR that is at least a little bit different and often more than a little bit different from that of the most similar state. Thus, no generalization about GIR can be fully accurate as there are usually exceptions to every rule. Even if there are few exceptions, the specific manifestations of most generalizations will play out differently from state to state. For instance, one finding of this study is an increase in the extent of religious legislation between 1990 and 2002. However, this is not true of all states and while there are certain types of religious legislation that increased more than others, the exact types of new religious laws passed during this period varied from state to state. Thus, underneath a common trend found at the global level of analysis there is a rich and complex diversity at the state level of analysis.

To make matters more complex, a number of factors – religious tradition, world region, economic development, regime type – all influence the extent of GIR in a given state. While groupings of states based on these intermediate-level variables are more homogeneous than the larger population of states, there is still considerable diversity within them. Also, controlling for all of these factors, as well as others, does not provide anything close to a complete explanation for the level of GIR in a particular state. Thus, either there is some critical variable not included in the study or local and state-level explanations explain at least as much of the variance as this set of variables.

Yet a global analysis that uses these variables is the only practical way to systematically analyze the commonalities and differences in GIR across the world. Using the comparative approach to look at 175 governments is extremely difficult at best. It is also subject to Karl Deutsch's classic criticism of such studies:

Introspection, intuition [and] insight [are] processes that are not verifiable among different observers. . . . But even though we can understand introspectively many facts and relations which exist, it is also true that we can understand in our fertile imagination very many relations that do not exist at all. What is more, there are things in the world that we can not understand readily with our imagination as it is now constituted, even though we may be able to understand them . . . in the future, after we have become accustomed to the presuppositions of such understanding. We can, therefore, do nothing more than accept provisionally these guesses or potential insights. . . . If we want to take them seriously, we must test them. We can do this by selecting . . . data, verifying them [and] forming explicit hypotheses as to what we expect to find. . . . And we then finally test these explicit hypotheses by confrontation with the data. . . . In the light of these tests we revise our criteria of relevance, we get new and revised data and we set up new methods of testing.[2]

This is especially true of large-n studies, such as this one, which include particularly large amounts of cases and information. Human minds, or at least most human minds, are not capable of objectively assimilating this amount of information in a systematic and reproducible manner. Thus, despite its many flaws, the large-n quantitative approach is better able to handle this scope of information than the unaided human mind.

That being said, the results from this type of approach cannot be considered complete unless they are then applied to more specific contexts using the comparative approach. It is the comparative approach that is the source of the theories tested using the quantitative method and the end goal of the quantitative method is to provide us with a better understanding of what is occurring in individual states. The goal is that the interplay between the large-n quantitative approach and the comparative approach will produce results superior to those that could be gleaned from either approach alone.

The second dimension of complexity in the GIR subeconomy of religion is the scope of the types of GIR that exist. The RAS data measures five distinct aspects of GIR. Yet each of these distinct forms of GIR are interrelated. While it is not possible or desirable to discuss all of these interrelationships at this point, a basic example of this is that states with official religions are more likely to treat some religions differently from others, discriminate against religious minorities, regulate the majority, and legislate religion. This becomes even more complex when one adds to the mix that the individual parts of this subeconomy interact collectively and individually with the larger religious economy and with other aspects of politics, economics, and society.

The question of how the religious economy, the subeconomy defined by absolute-SRAS and GIR, and the individual parts of that subeconomy fit into the larger picture is a central focus of this study. As this varies based on intermediate- and state-level factors, this is not a simple question to answer.

TAKING IT ALL INTO ACCOUNT

This study tries to provide an improved and more accurate picture of GIR in the world between 1990 and 2002 and to place that picture within the larger religious economy. Chapter 2 examines the existing literature and theories on the changing role of religion in modern times. It also develops the basic argument

---

[2] Deutsch (1963: 53).

that modernity is causing a decline in some parts of the religious economy, as has been predicted by many in the social sciences, but that other parts of the religious economy are reacting to compensate. These include both religious fundamentalism and GIR. Chapter 2 also examines theories regarding specific aspects of the religious economy and their potential influences on GIR. This includes religiosity, regime type, and specific religious traditions.

Chapter 3 provides a discussion of previous attempts to measure GIR as well as other parts of the religious economy. It also describes the RAS variables in detail, how those variables were influenced by previous attempts to measure religion, and how the RAS variables differ from previous variables.

Chapter 4 provides the global analysis of the RAS data. This includes an analysis of the absolute levels of the various RAS variables and the extent to which they changed between 1990 and 2002, controlling for religious traditions. It addresses the question of how many states have SRAS based on multiple definitions of the concept. It also provides a multivariate analysis of the impact of such factors as religious tradition, economic development, regime, and demographics on GIR. All of this is intended, among other things, to test the prediction described in Chapter 2 that modernity will lead to the decline or even the demise of religion as a significant political and social force.

Chapters 5 through 10 examine the state level of analysis. Each chapter focuses on a specific world region: Western democracies, the former Soviet bloc, Asia, the Middle East–North Africa region, sub-Saharan Africa, and Latin America. These chapters provide descriptions of GIR for each country in the study as well as the country codings on each of the 62 RAS variables. Each chapter also provides a discussion of regional trends in GIR, including how each country fits into a basic taxonomy of GIR, which is developed in these chapters.

Chapter 11 examines several factors at the intermediate level of analysis. This includes a study analyzing which of the 60 types of religious discrimination, religious regulation, and religious legislation increased and decreased, controlling for religious tradition and world region. It also further examines the intersection between GIR and both individual religiosity and regime type.

Chapter 12 accomplishes two goals. First, it places all of the diverse findings of this study into a more comprehensive framework. Second, it makes the argument that while this study focuses on one aspect of the religious economy, the evidence presented here is sufficient to argue that religion remains an important social and political force. This is not to say that religion is monolithically becoming more important or even maintaining the same level of importance. Rather, religion is a dynamic social phenomenon that is evolving in an ever-changing environment. Some aspects of the religious economy are becoming more influential at the same time as other aspects are becoming less influential. Put differently, while secularization can be said to be occurring in some parts of the religious economy, sacralization is occurring in others. Thus, the evidence presented here contradicts the predictions by many secularization theorists of an overall and monolithic drop in religion's influence.

In all, this study does not fully answer most of the questions asked in this chapter. Because of all of the limitations described here it is not really possible to do so. However, this study can be described as similar to the never-ending quest for perfection. The goal is never reached but in striving to achieve it, we can come closer to our goal. This study does not constitute the final word on even the limited topics of the extent of SRAS and GIR in the world. However, it does provide some new insights and new information that significantly adds to our knowledge of the topic.

2

The Question of Religion's Role in Politics and Society

Modernization, Secularization, and Beyond?

Modernization and secularization theory – the argument that religion is becoming less important as a political and social factor in modern times – have had a far-reaching influence on the study of religion in the social sciences. Exactly how far-reaching this influence has been is a topic of debate that is beyond the scope of this study. It is sufficient to say that a large plurality of the scholars familiar with the topic would likely agree with the following. First, this body of theory, at the very least, was among the most prominent theories on the role of religion in politics and society for much of the twentieth century. Second, some have claimed that it reached the point of a paradigm that was nearly unquestioned in some circles. By this I mean that it is a fact that some have made this claim, not that all would agree with it. Third, by the late twentieth century, among social scientists, the level of acceptance of this body of theory has decreased and the study of religion has increased. While modernization theory and secularization theory are two distinct, but related, bodies of theory, when discussing them as a whole I refer to them as modernization-secularization theory.

Among those who support or describe this body of theory there is little agreement on secularization's definition, including how much of a decline in religion constitutes secularization. Most who have addressed the topic in recent years feel that it is a limited concept, usually defining it as some form of decline of religion or its public influence. This has many variations including arguments that people are becoming less religious, that religion's influence on public institutions is diminishing, and that religion is moving from the public sphere to the private sphere.

However, there are still some who would define modernization-secularization theory in more absolute terms. In some cases this is because they believe the argument, but in many cases it is likely part of an attempt to set up a straw man to knock down.

That being said, the discussion in this chapter is ordered by the types of arguments presented in the debate rather than by the extent to which these arguments are taken. The discussion here is intended to present the variety of opinions on the topic rather than take any stand on the issue of how much secularization must occur for it to be called secularization.

The discussion is further complicated by religion's multifaceted nature. That is, different scholars focus on different aspects of religion's intersection with politics and society. As each of religion's many facets is unique, the facet on which a particular study focuses influences its conclusions. This makes for a dissonant literature that in some ways resembles the Tower of Babel: apparent disagreements in the nature and extent of secularization can often be traced to the fact that different scholars are talking about different things. As discussed in more detail in Chapter 11, these conclusions are also influenced by geography, religious tradition, and regime. Yet, the role of religion in society and politics can vary among different states within the same geographic region, belong to the same religious tradition, and have similar regimes.

Because different scholars are focusing on different aspects of religion in different contexts, one can be accused of mixing apples and oranges. Nevertheless, such a discussion is necessary. To return to the Tower of Babel analogy, that different scholars are essentially speaking different languages certainly makes it more difficult to complete the task at hand but, unlike the task of those ancient builders, the task presented here is neither impossible nor fraught with hubris. Despite the difficulty in finding a common language nearly all of the literature discussed in this chapter addresses the same issue or at least interrelated facets of the same phenomenon. Thus the discussion in this chapter does, of necessity, mix apples and oranges. However, every attempt is made to properly identify apples and oranges as such so that later they can be separated out.

It is important to note that the purpose of this chapter is limited. It is intended to review the arguments present in the literature surrounding this debate, the intellectual heritage of this literature, and how it has influenced the study of religion, politics, and society. Put differently, along with the discussion of quantifying religion in Chapter 3, it is intended to set the stage for the analyses in subsequent chapters. A basic argument made in this chapter is that while there is no consensus as to whether there has been an overall decline or increase in religion's influence, it is becoming increasingly clear that the influence of some facets of religion has decreased while the influence of other facets has increased. Thus, secularization and sacralization are occurring simultaneously in different aspects of society but religion, while evolving, does not seem to be disappearing. In addition, what aspect of religion's influence is secularizing and what aspect is sacralizing differs from society to society. As is discussed in more detail in Chapter 12, all of this is inconsistent with the predictions of modernization-secularization theory.

IS THE WORLD BECOMING MORE SECULAR?

The seminal social thinkers who founded the social sciences all believed that modernization would lead to a gradual decrease in religion's influence in society and politics. While there may have been disagreement among such thinkers as Freud, Marx, Comete, Durkheim, Weber, and Toennies as to the particulars of this reduced role for religion, they all agreed that processes within modernity would cause it to occur.[1]

In order to understand this downgrading of religion as a significant social and political force, it is important to understand its historical context. These thinkers were among the torchbearers for the Enlightenment. An important element of the Enlightenment was the promotion of rationalism, reason, and science as a basis for guiding government, society, and human behavior. Religion, at least in its then current reactionary and conservative form, was seen as a threat to the society they aspired to create. Accordingly, they all found ways to marginalize it in their theories. Government was to be guided by scientific and rational principles. Individual behavior was to be understood through this lens of science and reason. This included replacing religious criteria for proper behavior with rational scientific criteria as well as using the social science of psychology to understand human behavior. That being said, the views held by these thinkers on the topic were not in all cases unidimensional. Many of them recognized that religion had a significant social influence, which they expected to decline but not disappear due to modernity. However, they did agree on three things: "First, religion is based on its social context; thus the truth of religion is relative rather than universal. Second, society was experiencing a crisis of religious belief. Third, industrialization was breaking the hold of religion on society."[2]

This general theme of religion as a tool that serves a function in society was central to predictions of religion's decline. Religion can serve certain functions in society including acting as the social cement that binds society together and suppresses conflict between social groups. It can be used as a form of social control. It is a source of legitimacy for society and its institutions. It is a source of identity. It provides a means for emotional expression and dealing with the difficulties of life. This includes providing answers for those unanswerable questions of why people suffer and die, why bad things happen to good people, and so on. It also provides an explanation for the existence of the physical universe and how it functions.[3]

This approach both explained how an irrational phenomenon like religion survived and why it was expected to decline. It had remained central in many societies until the Enlightenment because it had a rational basis – to serve these functions. But as rational, scientific phenomena and institutions began to serve these roles in society, the need for religion would diminish.

Bryan Wilson's book *Religion in Sociological Perspective* provides one of the best descriptions of this set of predictions. He argues that this replacement of

---

[1] For a review of these individual thinkers' views on religion, see Aldridge (2000), Bruce (1992), and Turner (1991).

[2] Fox (2002: 38).

[3] Turner (1991: 109), Wilson (1982: 26–35).

religion with rational and scientific bases for society has occurred. Religious criteria for proper behavior have been replaced by laws that focus on "overt acts likely to disturb social relations" rather than morality. Also, technical solutions have replaced moral attitudes in solving social problems. For instance surveillance technology creates a rational basis for obeying laws, making morality obsolete as a force for social control.[4]

Similarly, modern states no longer rely on religion for legitimacy. State power tends to be self-justified or legitimated by the will of the people, national identity, or other secular bases for identity. Often the modern state's capabilities for coercion and communication make transcending legitimation unnecessary. That is, the governing systems of many states are based on the assumption that man can manufacture conditions for social order.[5]

Religion is also being challenged or replaced in other arenas of life. Science provides understanding of the physical universe. The media and entertainment industry influence moral attitudes and people's emotional lives. The social science of psychology largely defines how to measure and achieve emotional health. In a way, it also provides an answer to the question of why evil exists, by redefining evil as a result of psychological pathologies that can be understood and controlled with therapy, medical treatments and, if necessary, incarceration. However, some existential issues, such as the question of what happens to us after we die, still remain within the purview of religion or some other non-rational set of beliefs, at least for those who are unwilling to accept that life ends with death.

While this brief description of secularization theory – the sociological paradigm for marginalizing religion – does not do justice to the extensive literature on the topic, it is sufficient to present the paradigm's central claim and the basic reasoning behind that claim. In short, the functions that religion served in the past are in modern times being fulfilled by more rational scientific institutions, which do a superior job at fulfilling these functions. Consequently, religion's influence will decline or perhaps move from the public sphere to the private sphere.[6]

Modernization theory, the political science paradigm on the topic, takes a different approach. Rather than focusing on the clash between reason and religion, it posits that a set of processes inherent in economic modernization will inevitably lead to the decline of religion as a relevant social factor. Urbanization was expected to undermine the traditional community, which was one of the strongholds of religion. Small, homogeneous, close-knit communities where religion is a central element of politics and social life simplify socialization and enforce religious norms. When people move to big cities they are, ironically, more isolated and can choose between diverse social

---

[4] Wilson (1982: 38–44).
[5] Wilson (1982: 39–40, 54).
[6] For a survey of the secularization literature, see, among others, Beckford (1985), Cox (1965), Glasner (1977), Martin (1978), and Wilson (1966; 1976).

networks, some of which are based on religion but many of which are not. Being religious becomes a matter of individual choice and many choose to be less religious.

Increased literacy rates give the masses access to information that was once available only to elites and in some cases only religious elites. This allows individuals to read and interpret religious texts for themselves and exposes them to a broader range of ideas, both religious and secular. Mass education and communications technology, including most recently the Internet, has further increased this empowerment and the free flow of ideas.

Science undermines religion's role in explaining the world. For example in the Judeo-Christian world the concept of the seven days of creation was once unopposed but now this idea competes with the big bang and evolution. Science has also replaced religion as a source of solutions to problems. In the past social, physical, and spiritual problems as well as definitions of proper social order were the purview of the clergy. Today, most people in modern societies see a doctor when they are physically ill and see a mental health professional when they have psychological problems. Science has also directly undermined aspects of traditional morality by giving people options that were not previously available. For example, birth control technology has allowed people to engage in sex with less risk of pregnancy.

Nationalism and other bases for identity are said to be replacing religion as the source of identity. Political ideologies, generally somehow linked to the will or interests of the people as a basis for governing – something common to diverse ideologies including liberalism, socialism, communism, and fascism – are replacing religion as the basic guides for a just society. Modern secular political and social institutions are replacing religious ones. Government bureaucracies are both defining and enforcing a new secular morality that is replacing religious morality. Secular social institutions are filling roles formerly filled by religious institutions. Also, the mass entertainment industry is propagating a set of values that many call antireligious.[7]

Despite this coherent set of reasons setting out why religion had a declining influence on politics, the most important trend in political science was that religion was simply not considered central to the discipline by most of its practitioners, at least until the 1980s. Perhaps the strongest indication that this was the case was that the relevant political science literature focused primarily on ethnicity, not religion. Religion was treated as a side issue or as an additional phenomenon that would decline in modern times. Of course, there were always scholars who studied religion but their work on religion was not considered central to the discipline. In the political science literature on conflict and violence, for example, until the events of Waco, Texas, in 1993 few political

---

[7] For a survey of the modernization literature, see Almond (1960), Apter (1965), Deutsch (1953), Foster-Carter (1985), Halpern (1964), Kautsky (1972), Rostow (1959), Donald Smith (1970; 1974), and Sutton (1968).

scientists considered religiously motivated violence in the West as anything other than a thing of the past.[8]

It is arguable that international relations theory more profoundly discounts religion than do political science and sociology. This is because, unlike these two disciplines, international relations has no theory explaining why religion is not important, it is simply taken for granted that it is not. A survey of major international relations journals between 1980 and 1999 shows that articles in these journals almost never consider religion an important influence on international relations.[9] In those few instances where religion could not be ignored, it was generally placed into some other category, for example terrorism, institutions, civil society, culture, or civilizations. By doing this, international relations scholars can avoid using the term "religion." This trend in the international relations literature has declined but not disappeared since 9/11.[10]

A prominent example of this phenomenon is the "clash of civilizations" debate, based on Samuel Huntington's theory, which took place primarily during the mid to late 1990s, but still continues at the time of this writing. Huntington posits that in the post–Cold War era, most conflicts will be between several civilizations that, by his own admission, are primarily defined by religion.[11] This theory has sparked a considerable debate that is in many ways about religion but in which few participants actually use the term "religion." Huntington's critics focus on more seemingly secular types of criticisms. One such avenue is that some form of identity other than civilizations will be the primary basis for political groupings. While this, potentially, could include religious identities, it rarely does. Critics usually focus on groupings smaller than civilizations, such as the state, the nation, and ethnic groups, or on a unified world order. Others attack Huntington's methodology. Still others claim Huntington ignored some important secular factor in world politics that makes his theory irrelevant. These factors include conflict management, population and environment issues, the power of modernity and secularism, military and economic power, economic prosperity, information technology, and desires to emulate and align with the West.[12]

While it is likely that most social scientists would not wish to take the argument of religion's decline to its most extreme conclusion – that religion will disappear and become irrelevant – there are some who accuse social scientists, or at least elements among social scientists, of doing exactly this. For instance, Jeffrey Hadden argues that "few forecasts have been uttered with

---

[8] Kaplan (2002: 2).

[9] Of 1600 articles in four major international relations journals (*International Organization, International Studies Quarterly, International Security*, and *World Politics*), only six articles "featured religion as an important influence" (Philpott, 2002: 69).

[10] Fox & Sandler (2004).

[11] Huntington (1993; 1996).

[12] For a detailed discussion of Huntington's theory and its critics, see Fox (2004). For a more complete discussion of international relations theory and religion, see Hurd (2004), Fox & Sandler (2004), Philpott (2002), and Thomas (2005).

more unshakable confidence than sociology's belief that religion is in the midst of its final death throes," and that secularization theory "has not been subjected to systematic scrutiny because it is a doctrine more than it is a theory." Hadden believes that sociology and the other social sciences were born in context of tensions between religion and liberal culture in Europe. Social scientists saw themselves as engaged in a struggle against religion's monopoly on the mind and consciousness. Thus the founding generations of social scientists were not disinterested analysts. Rather, they were advocates for the science and reason they believed should and would crush the ignorance and superstition caused by religion. Hadden further argues that at the time he wrote the article, 1987, sociologists were recruited from those with a secular world view and those recruits that did not have such a world view were socialized to that view during the education process.[13]

Others echo Hadden's arguments. Helen Ebaugh claims that secularization theory was so central to the social sciences that it "displaced attempts to understand the actual meaning and organizational significance of religion in contemporary society." The few who studied religion published in journals that focused on religion and whose readership was mostly outside the mainstream. This included the minority of sociologists who focused their research on religion and were mostly people with strong religious affiliations, including former and current clergy.[14] Anthony Gill similarly laments that "if there ever were an award for the most durable, yet outdated, theoretical perspective in the social sciences, secularization theory would be the winner, or at least a close runner-up. ... Despite strong empirical evidence to the contrary ... this view persists among many political scientists."[15]

In all fairness, the extreme form of this type of claim – that social scientists allowed an antireligious ideology to cause them to ignore religion – overstates the case. However, it is also difficult to deny that the history of the study of religion provides these critics with enough ammunition to try to make such a case. It is also nearly impossible to sort out the exact pervasiveness and influence of modernization-secularization theory in the social sciences during the twentieth century, but it is possible to set some bounds.

On one side, this body of theory did exist and many subscribed to it. It is also fair to describe this body of theory as the dominant paradigm on religion in the social sciences for most of the twentieth century. On the other side, there were always social scientists who recognized the continuing influence of religion, as well as academic organizations that focused on the study of religion, but they were considered to be outside the mainstream. There also were a number of

---

[13] Hadden (1987).
[14] Ebaugh (2002: 387–9).
[15] Gill (2001: 119–20). For similar arguments see Marshall (1998), and Sherkat & Ellison (1999: 364). These accusations are also directed at non-academics including journalists, policy makers, political elites, the liberal intelligentsia, and diplomats. For more see Gopin (2000: 37–40), Luttwak (1994: 8–14), Marshall (1998), Rubin (1994: 20–1), and Stempel (2000).

antireligious biases among many of those who belonged to such organizations. The emphasis of their studies was often on weird and obscure groups. Many of these studies can be linked to a desire to show that "religion is rooted in fraud, foolishness, fakery, and perversion." There was a "greater antagonism toward groups to the extent that their members are highly committed" and believe in the supernatural. There also prevailed a "notion ... that the social scientific study of religion per se is necessarily coercive of faith."[16]

Those who focused on area studies were often at odds with the paradigm that religion was becoming an epiphenomenon. The concept that religion had a declining influence on the public sphere was especially difficult to justify among scholars of the Middle East. Yet even there, until the late 1970s, an argument could have been made that religion was declining in influence. Iran was becoming more secular under the Shah. Pan-Arab nationalism, a secular ideology that focused on ethnic rather than religious similarities, was popular. However, most Middle Eastern countries continued to have official religions and to enforce elements of these religions as law. Thus, secularization clearly had not taken place to the extent that many believed it had in the West.

In sum, where one stood to a great extent depended on where one sat. This was true of one's academic discipline, subdiscipline, and which area of the world one studied. The argument that religion was in decline can be said to have been influential and likely the most influential theory on the topic of religion's role in society for much of the twentieth century, but it was never universally accepted.

SECULARIZATION AND SACRALIZATION

Since around 1980, the modernization-secularization paradigm has been increasingly called into question, though the paradigm still has its defenders. World events since the late 1970s have called attention to religion's continued impact on society and politics. These events include the Iranian revolution and subsequent Islamic opposition movements throughout the Islamic world. There are also numerous clashes between Muslim and non-Muslim groups throughout the world including those in Bosnia, Chechnya, India, Nigeria, and the Sudan. The attacks of September 11, 2001, the increasingly international terror activities of Al-Qaeda, and the realization that many Muslims who live in Western states subscribe to radical Muslim ideologies have made it clear that this is also relevant to the West.

This increasing awareness of the power of religion is not limited to Islam. Ronald Reagan's rise to the presidency with the help of the religious right demonstrated the power of Christian fundamentalism in U.S. politics. The liberation theology movement in Latin America and increasing participation of Catholic clergy in Latin American opposition movements demonstrates

---

[16] Stark & Finke (2000: 18–20).

religion's continuing potency in that world region. There is no shortage of ethnoreligious clashes that involve groups other than Muslims, including those in Sri Lanka, Tibet, and the Sikh-Hindu tensions in India. It is also becoming clear that while there may be a decrease in attendance at worship in some Western countries, on a worldwide basis it is increasing.[17]

It would be simple to portray the ensuing debate as a black and white argument over whether religion is in decline. There are certainly some participants on the debate who argue along these lines and others who can be portrayed in this manner. However, the more accurate description of reality can be portrayed through a famous Talmudic story.

Beit Hillel and Beit Shamai were two rabbinic schools in pre-Talmudic times named after their founders Rabbi Hillel and Rabbi Shamai. While these two schools agreed on most aspects of Jewish law, they had a number of famous debates, the specifics of which are unimportant in this context. These debates were so intense and divisive that a "heavenly voice" called out to settle the debate. It said that both of them were correct but as the law must be settled one way or another, in all but a few cases that law would follow Beit Hillel.

The debate over modernization-secularization theory can be settled in the same way. Both secularization and its opposite, sacralization, are occurring. Religion is a dynamic, diverse, and multifaceted phenomenon, which exists in a society that is constantly changing and evolving. Consequently, religion must also constantly change and evolve, at least with respect to its relationship with society. Some aspects of religion's influence on society are increasing while others are decreasing, and while even others are changing in a way that has an indeterminate effect on the extent of religion's influence. From this perspective both sides of the debate can be correct.

However, if one must choose sides, those who disagree with secularization-modernization theory are probably more correct than the theories' defenders. Secularization-modernization theory predicts a monolithic decline in religion as a significant social and political force and, if taken to an extreme, its demise. The latter clearly has not yet happened and whether the former has occurred is debatable. Even if there has been an overall decline it is not clear whether the extent of that decline is sufficient to call it secularization. Drawing the line between what is and is not considered secularization is not a trivial task.

Two Views of Modernity and Religion's Persistence

Despite the overall argument presented here for the simultaneous increases and decreases in religion's influence, there is value in presenting the more basic form of the arguments that counter modernization-secularization theory. These arguments can be divided into two categories. The first is that religion has always been an influential factor but the prominence of modernization-secularization

---

[17] Norris & Inglehart (2004).

theory has caused many social scientists to ignore this. Furthermore, religion is not just present, it is among the basic elements of modern society. Historically, religion has been an intrinsic component of all major civilizations. It is an important component of "civilizational premises."[18] For example, Judaism and Christianity influence the West's "preference for legal and political, that is, nonviolent conflict resolution."[19] Religion is arguably among the bases for many nationalist ideologies in the West.[20] Also, the origin of the Westphalian state system can be traced to religious roots, even if those roots include the desire to regulate religion.[21]

Another version of this argument posits that religion has not disappeared but it has evolved. Religion constantly renews itself to survive in new social and political settings. Elites tend to desire more worldly religions to legitimate their worldly success, and pressure more established religions to become worldlier. However, many, especially those from the lower echelons of society, desire less worldly religions to provide solace for their lack of worldly success. This results in both movements to revitalize the faith of established religions and the formation of new religions or sects of the established religions. Thus, as one religion secularizes, another less secular one forms to take its place.[22]

Others point out that religion is evolving into alternative noninstitutionalized forms of belief in the supernatural and paranormal. These include beliefs in paranormal phenomena, occultism, mysticism, ESP, ghosts, telepathy, faith healing, astrologers, seances, dream interpretation, card reading, and divination. Since these forms of beliefs are not generally included in surveys of religiousness, recorded declines in religious belief can be misleading.[23]

The second explanation for the continuing presence of religion takes these evolutionary arguments a step further, positing that rather than causing religion's demise, modernization contributes to a "resurgence" or "revitalization" of religion. That is, the forces described in the modernization-secularization literature exist but, rather than disappearing, religious groups are defending themselves and evolving to become stronger. From this perspective urbanization, science, literacy, the increasing importance of legal and bureaucratic standards of behavior, and so on are having the influences that modernization-secularization theory predict. However, rather than causing the eventual decline of religion, these processes have caused religious groups and institutions to evolve in order to defend themselves against these modern processes and, as a result, religion is undergoing a process of revitalization.

A large part of this is a reaction to the erosion of traditional culture and morality by modern secular ideas. Hollywood and the Western entertainment

---

[18] Arjomand (1993: 37).
[19] Weigel (1992: 174).
[20] Anthony Smith (1999).
[21] Philpott (2000).
[22] Stark & Bainbridge (1985), Shupe (1990), Stark & Finke (2000).
[23] Canetti-Nisim (2003), Stark & Finke (2000).

industry are often blamed for undermining traditional values. These values include chastity and modesty (especially the modesty of women), as well as the concept that religion should play a significant role in defining public morality. In the non-West they are also blamed for imperialistically supporting Western culture and values including an undue emphasis on materialism and physical beauty at the expense of local values. This has led to increased efforts to counter these negative aspects of modernization.

Furthermore, religious groups use modern technologies and resources as well as modern organizational and political strategies and resources to fight what they perceive as the negative effects of modernization. This includes lobbying, use of the courts, links with political parties, mobilization, the use of modern communications networks and technology, and the use of the media and the Internet to influence public opinion and export their views. Also, their leadership often has advanced education from modern universities.[24]

In addition, modernization has allowed both the state and religious institutions to increase their spheres of influence, resulting in more clashes between the two.[25] Modern political systems have facilitated "the admission of the masses into politics and the recruitment of huge numbers of people into a broadened elite of professionals, business people, military officers, government bureaucrats, and teachers. ... Yet these changes also give upward mobility to the religious sectors of the population that have greater loyalty to a more narrow, religiously defined community."[26]

Another form of the argument that modernization is causing a resurgence of religion is exemplified by Mark Juergensmeyer. He argues that the resurgence of religion in the third world is due to a failure of modern secular ideologies like liberalism, communism, socialism, and fascism. After independence the majority of third-world states based their regimes on these ideologies, which all promise prosperity and social justice. Yet in almost all cases they failed to live up to these promises. Furthermore, these governments are accused of being the puppets of the West, thereby associating them with imperialism. This has led to a crisis of legitimacy for these secular ideologies and the governments guided by them, creating a legitimacy vacuum that religion is well suited to fill. Local religious traditions are seen as an authentic and indigenous alternative to the foreign and corrupt secular ideologies that have failed to provide a better life for the common man.[27]

Juergensmeyer's arguments have been echoed and expanded upon throughout the literature. While disagreeing in some specifics, these parallel arguments are generally consistent with the theme that the failures of third-world governments combined with the Western origin of most of today's political ideologies are contributing to a religious backlash. These failures include the failure to

[24] Jeff Haynes (1998: 7–8), Sahliyeh (1990: 13), Shupe (1990: 22).
[25] Shupe (1990: 23–6).
[26] Rubin (1994: 23).
[27] Juergensmeyer (1993).

produce sufficient economic development and truly democratic regimes. Another common theme is that religion is a traditional opposition ideology that is particularly suited to play the role of an anticolonial ideology.[28] These factors are also commonly used to explain the rise of political Islam. This literature also focuses on the West's support for corrupt, repressive governments in the Muslim world, the clash between Muslim and Western values, and the transnational nature of the political Islam movement.[29]

Many similarly describe the rise of religious fundamentalism as a direct consequence of modernity. Fundamentalism has been defined as "a specifiable pattern of religious militance by which self-styled true believers attempt to arrest the erosion of religious identity, fortify the borders of the religious community, and create viable alternatives to secular structures and processes."[30] In short, the goal of fundamentalism is to defend religion and religious identities against secularism. The common enemy of all fundamentalists is modernity, which they consider "humanity's revolt against God."[31]

In order to defend against modernity, fundamentalists try to create a separate social and political space with special behavior, language, music, body language, dress, and hairstyles to differentiate members from outsiders. They create a set of rules that are portrayed as a return to the religious values of the past but are perhaps better described as new creations to replace a lost tradition. This is because modernity has created a new environment in which religion must exist and fundamentalist interpretations of their religions must be innovative to function in modern times. This results in selective use of religious traditions and innovative interpretations of religious texts, which are in many ways unprecedented. In short, instead of returning to a past golden age of religion, fundamentalists are creating something that is new and unique to modernity, both original and derivative of traditional religion.[32]

Fundamentalists tend to take one of two options in order to defend against modernity. The first is to build a closed community into which the modern values which threaten religion cannot enter. These communities tend to be all-encompassing. Members are discouraged from interacting with outsiders, except to bring them into the community, and rules govern all aspects of life with little or no distinction between the public and private spheres.[33] The second option is to try to change their environment to fit their ideology. This is done by taking over or otherwise altering their state's regime through either peaceful political means or militant and violent strategies. Their agenda includes subordinating science and the economy to religious authority because

---

[28] Appleby (2000: 106), Jeff Haynes (1994; 1997; 1998), Sahliyeh (1990), Williams (1994: 803), Williamson (1990).

[29] Jeff Haynes (1994: 64–93), Monshipouri (1998), Nasr (1998), Philpott (2002: 83–90), Tibi (2000: 847).

[30] Appleby (2000: 86).

[31] Almond, Appleby & Sivan (2003: 37–8).

[32] Almond et al. (2003), Appleby (2000), Marty & Appleby (1991).

[33] Almond et al. (2003: 46–8).

both need the normative restraints of religion to function in a safe and just manner.[34] Fundamentalist militance can be traced to this desire to reform the world in their religion's image. When peaceful means fail to protect the community, it is easier to justify violent ones and the necessity of gaining political power in order to change surrounding society to be more like this "past."[35]

These movements are modern in several other ways. They tend to recruit mostly among young educated unemployed or underemployed males – those who in many ways most acutely feel left behind my modernity.[36] They use modern tools and strategies including modern communications, propaganda, mobilization, and organizational techniques as well as modern political institutions. Also, because of its tendency to be all-encompassing, fundamentalism has been compared to modern fascist-socialist and communist-nationalist ideologies in that all of these ideologies tend toward totalitarianism, seek to construct new collective identities and boundaries and use political action to realize them.[37]

In sum, whether religion is experiencing a resurgence or it has simply never gone away, it is clear that modernity has caused religion to evolve. This is not surprising because religion is a part of society and culture and when society and culture change, any element of them, including religion, cannot avoid changing with them. Thus, while the debate can be presented in the simplistic terms of whether religion is in decline, holding its own, or becoming more influential, to do so is an oversimplification.

The Debate Among Sociologists

While the description of the state of the literature up to this point in the chapter includes sociologists, it is important to emphasize that the majority of sociologists who address these issues have done so within the context of a separate debate. This debate revolves around the two questions noted at the beginning of this chapter: what is the definition of secularization? and is secularization occurring? This debate is somewhat complicated by the fact that the answer to the second question is heavily influenced by the answer to the first.

The central debate over the definition of secularization can be divided into two camps. The first defines secularization as the decline of religiosity. That is, secularization means people are becoming less religious. The second defines secularization as the decline in the influence of religion in the public sphere.

This debate is similar to the debate just described, but distinct in two ways. First, the debate is somewhat insular with its participants primarily addressing each other and not the wider literature. Second, there is a more distinct attempt to define secularization. This includes the issues of to what facet of religion the

---

[34] Kuran (1991), Mendelsohn (1993).
[35] Appleby (2000: 87–91).
[36] Appleby (2000: 87).
[37] Eisenstadt (2000: 601–5).

theory applies and to what extent religion must decline in order for it to be called secularization.

The arguments for why religiosity will decline have already been outlined. Recently there have been a number of counter-arguments positing that religiosity has not declined. First, the belief that religiosity is declining is at least in part based on "the myth of past piety." Yet evidence of a historical lack of religious participation suggests that people in the past were no more religious than they are today.[38]

Second, empirical results on changes over time in religiosity are mixed. Some studies show that church attendance in the USA has tripled over 150 years and that there is no demonstrable decline in church attendance in Europe.[39] Norris and Inglehart show that religiosity is declining only in countries that have "existential security" – places where the population does not need to worry about basic needs including physical safety, and access to adequate medical care, food, and shelter. However, overall religiosity in the world is increasing because most of the world's population does not have existential security and the populations that have low existential security – and are thus more religious – also have higher fertility rates.[40]

Third, many make arguments similar to those already described regarding the simultaneous secularization of some aspects of society and sacralization of other aspects of society.[41] Finally, Rodney Stark provides a particularly novel argument. He provides a list of quotes by noted social thinkers over a span of centuries, each predicting the imminent demise of religion. Stark argues that if they were correct, their successors would not have made similar predictions.[42]

The debate that focuses on whether there has been secularization in the public sector is basically about the privatization of religion. Thus, even those who argue that secularization is occurring in this arena generally admit that religion remains present in society. They just argue that it is becoming a private issue that has no place in the public sphere. This debate has two aspects: whether this privatization is in fact occurring, and how much privatization must occur before it is called secularization.

If one argues that any significant public influence of religion contradicts the predictions of secularization, it is easy to make the argument that secularization has not occurred. There is no shortage of examples of the continuing public influence of religion.[43] That being said, more nuanced views can interpret these manifestations of religion as less influential than they were in the past. Put differently, religion, which once had no rivals for its social functions, is now

---

[38] Stark (1999), Swatos & Christiano (1999).

[39] Stark (1999).

[40] Norris & Inglehart (2004).

[41] Demerath (2001), Stark (1999), Stark & Bainbridge (1985), Stark & Finke (2000), Swatos & Christiano (1999).

[42] Stark (1999).

[43] Sherkat & Ellison (1999), for example, make this type of argument. For additional examples, see Chapters 5 through 10 of this book.

rivaled by some element of modern secular society on every front.[44] Given this, the question of whether secularization has occurred in the public sphere depends to a great extent on how much secularization must occur before it meets the predications of modernization-secularization theory.[45]

There are a number of sociologists who argue that the public influence of religion is declining and that this process of privatization is sufficient for it to be consistent with the predictions of secularization for several reasons. First, religion – once a dominant aspect of the social system – has become one of many competing influences.[46] Second, there has been a decline in the "scope of religious authority." Religious authority can be defined as "a structure that attempts to enforce order and reach its ends by controlling the access of individuals to some desired goods, where legitimation of that control includes some supernatural component, however weak." As most societies, at the very least, place limits on such authority, secularization is occurring.[47] Third, modernity has caused religions to become worldlier than before. Fourth, religion is now an individual choice, not an aspect of society.[48] Fifth, the evolution of religion into new forms has weakened its societal influence.[49]

These arguments are countered by arguments that there has not been sufficient privatization for it to be called secularization and that secularization and sacralization are occurring simultaneously in the religious economy. Both arguments have been described in more detail already.

This review reveals some interesting trends among the sociological literature. While there is certainly some debate over the facts on the ground, the primary debate seems to be one of interpretation. Specifically, how much must religion's public influence decline in order for it to be called secularization? This issue is hotly debated but there seems to be an agreement that modernity has altered religion's public role and most, but not all sociologists, seem to agree that there has been some decline in religion's public influence. None of those participating in the debate are claiming that religion has disappeared or even that it will disappear. There is disagreement over whether there have been shifts in the level and nature of religiosity but no one claims that the religious individual is an endangered species. The same is true for religion's influence in the public sphere.

A general criticism of this debate is that most of those involved focus only on the West. While it is arguable that religion has declined in the West, it is more difficult to make this argument in the non-West. Nearly every study that surveys the non-West finds little evidence that religion is in decline.[50]

---

[44] Lambert (1999).
[45] For similar arguments see Beyer (1999) and Voye (1999).
[46] Dobbelaere (1999), Lechner (1991).
[47] Chaves (1994).
[48] Dobbelaere (1999).
[49] Lechner (1991).
[50] See, for example, Jeff Haynes (1998), Juergensmeyer (1993), and Norris & Inglehart (2004).

In fact, much of the literature discussed here that posits that religion is experiencing a resurgence focuses on the non-West. Thus, geography is an important element of this debate, even if it is rarely explicitly acknowledged.

This debate is complicated by a literature that has recently emerged in the sociology of religion literature, known alternatively as the rational choice, supply-side, or economic theory of religion. The basic argument in this literature is that the extent to which a state supports a religion is inversely proportional to the proportion of that state's population that is religious.

The theory is based on the assumption that religiosity is influenced by market-like forces. People, or "religious consumers," engage in maximizing behavior in their interactions with the divine. Accordingly, choosing a religion involves a cost-benefit analysis. The costs of religious participation usually include one's time, restrictions on behavior, and monetary costs, including dues and the expectation to give charity. The benefits include social benefits, expected rewards in an afterlife, moral justification, and feelings of spiritual well-being. Religious "producers" have a similar interest in maximizing their number of congregants and, consequently, an interest in "marketing" their religion to consumers. This is balanced against other potential interests, for example gaining support from the government, or other "goods" that increase institutional success, as well as theological issues. All of this behavior in a free religious market results in a dynamic where consumers have a choice of religions and are more likely to find a religion that is attractive to them than would be possible in a market with a state-supported religious monopoly.[51]

In a religious monopoly – where the religious market is limited to one or a small number of religions – there are several structural factors that tend to reduce religious participation. First, religious institutions are supported by the government and assured of congregants through their monopoly. This gives them less incentive to actively meet the needs of congregants. Second, states with religious monopolies often enforce aspects of the religion. This can cause resentment against the religion. Third, in restricted religious markets, religious institutions tend to be controlled by professional clergy who seek increased rewards for their profession and lower professional obligations. These obligations include mandatory religious behavior. As the rewards begin to outweigh the costs, religious motives become less important among those entering the clergy. Fourth, in a monopoly market, consumers who wish to belong to another religion must support their own movement and pay religious taxes either directly or through their general taxes to a government that financially supports the state religion.[52]

It is also important to note several factors that influence this dynamic. First, the ability of a religion "to monopolize a religious economy depends upon

---

[51] Iannaccone (1995a; 1995b), Stark & Finke (2000).
[52] Finke (1990), Stark & Finke (2000), Madeley (2003b), R. Stephen Warner (1993).

the degree to which a state uses coercive force to regulate the religious economy."[53] Second, even an unregulated market is not fully fluid. Under normal circumstances, people do not switch religions or denominations. Those who switch tend to switch to religions similar to their current religion and this switching often occurs in the context of mixed marriages. Thus, shifts in the religious economy often occur over generational time scales and this can cause a time-lag in the influence of shifts in government regulation of religion. Third, this theory applies mostly to membership in religious organizations and attendance at religious services, ceremonies, and events but general belief in religious concepts, such as God, are less affected. The general demand for religion remains relatively constant over time but may not be fully satisfied in monopoly economies.[54]

This debate is particularly important because it specifically argues that secularization in one aspect of society is directly linked to sacralization in another. Thus, if one accepts this theory, and not all do, it becomes impossible to treat the change in religion's influence in society and politics as unidirectional.

Many sociologists criticize this theory for a number of reasons. The theory is very formal, rigid, and oversimplifies a complex phenomenon. It tries to apply the concept of rational choice to a nonrational phenomenon. People's religious choices are stable. There are often strong social benefits for staying in a religion and strong social sanctions for leaving it. For example, religion is often correlated with ethnicity, thereby creating significant costs for switching religions.[55] Religious behavior is usually based on "socialization, institutionalized custom, and ingrained habit," all of which are factors that resist change.[56] Religious "producers" tend to target groups and social networks for conversion to their religions more often than they target individuals.[57] This theory is based in part on a nonsociological approach that is not appropriate for understanding this aspect of human behavior.[58]

The empirical evidence on this theory is mixed. The majority of studies on the topic compare religiosity to some measure of religious diversity with some studies supporting the theory and others not.[59] Some argue that any correlation found between religious diversity and religiosity is due to the fact that the religious diversity variables used are mathematically associated with religious participation.[60] Chapter 11 includes an analysis of this theory that correlates

---

[53] Stark & Finke (2000: 199).
[54] For a more detailed description of this theory see Stark & Finke (2000). For some comparative studies that argue that this theory explains the levels of religiosity in the USA, Europe, and Latin America, see Finke (1990), Finke & Iannaccone (1993), Froese (2004), and Stark & Iannaccone (1994).
[55] Ellison (1995).
[56] Demerath (1995).
[57] Williams (1994: 788–9).
[58] Demerath (1995: 105).
[59] Norris & Inglehart (2004: 95–9).
[60] Voas, Olson, & Crockett (2002).

religiosity with the RAS variables and provides results consistent with the theory.

The dependence of this theory on the Western experience becomes apparent when we examine a country such as Saudi Arabia. It is exclusively Muslim by law, the only exception being for visitors, diplomats, and some foreign workers. It also has the highest level of government support for religion of any country in the world with a religious market that is correspondingly less free than any other state. Yet, contrary to rational choice models of religion, arguably it has a population that is *more* religious than any Western country. This can easily be explained by the homogeneous culture, active state enforcement of the religion, and the fact that all citizens are educated in the religion as well as socialized into it. Thus, it seems that the supply-side theory assumes a Western or Western-like political and social setting.[61]

The larger debate among sociologists raises some important questions. While the extent of religiosity in the world is not a central question of this book, I do focus on the public influence of religion in the form of government involvement in religion (GIR). There seems to be a considerable dispute over the extent of this public influence and how much of a decline in this public influence is necessary for it to be called secularization. While to what extent religion's public influence must decline before it is called secularization is a subjective issue, the question of the actual level of GIR that exists in the world is one that this study is designed to evaluate.

SPECIFIC RELIGIOUS TRADITIONS

A number of scholars, as well as anecdotal evidence, suggest that specific religious traditions influence the role of religion in society. This type of argument has several different variations. For example, Norris and Inglehart argue that "the distinctive worldviews that were originally linked with religious traditions have shaped the cultures of each nation in an enduring fashion." This is true even of nonreligious people because in modern times "these values are not transmitted primarily by the church but by the educational system and the mass media."[62]

Perhaps the most famous version of this argument can be found in Max Weber's book, *The Protestant Ethic and the Spirit of Capitalism.*[63] Weber's arguments linked religious attitudes toward accumulation of wealth with economic success. Many picked up on Weber's theme that the doctrines and culture associated with specific religions would influence patterns of economic

---

[61] Proponents of the supply-side theory would likely argue that these seemingly high levels of religiosity in Saudi Arabia are in fact covering up for the fact that many belong to the state religion but do not actually wish to be religious. That is, state religions tend to artificially inflate their numbers (Stark & Finke, 2000; Stark & Iannaccone, 1994).

[62] Norris & Inglehart (2004: 17–18).

[63] Weber (1930).

development and, by association, secularization. One of the most detailed versions of this type of argument is presented in David A. Martin's book, *A General Theory of Secularization*. While he briefly notes that Christian societies will secularize before non-Christian societies, most of his discussion focuses upon the difference between Protestant, Catholic, and Orthodox Christian countries. To be clear, for Martin, all paths lead to secularization but religious traditions influence the specific path that leads to secularization.[64]

Many argue that secularization does not occur in Islamic societies. A number of factors are cited to explain why this is the case. In Islam, secular law is superseded by divine law and most regimes in Muslim countries accept this principle or at least pay lip service to it. Islam has no clergy, making all believers equidistant from God.[65] It also tends to focus on the local level, thereby increasing participation, as well as the feeling that one has a personal connection to the religion and its institutions. It has been an important source of identity, which has been especially important in the context of the struggle against colonialism.[66]

Survey research by Norris and Inglehart both confirms and falsifies some of these theses regarding specific religions. There is more support among Muslims for a religious role in society and for religious authorities. Catholics and Muslims tend to be more traditional on issues related to religion such as abortion, suicide, and euthanasia. Catholics, not Protestants, tend to have a stronger work ethic among Christians, but Muslims have an even higher work ethic. Thus if the influence of Weber's Protestant work ethic ever existed, based on this evidence it no longer does.[67]

There are also a number of empirical studies that examine the influence of specific religions on a wide variety of political and social factors. These studies are discussed in more detail in Chapter 3.

CONCLUSIONS

The past prominence of modernization-secularization theory can easily place any discussion of the changing role of religion in modern times into a simplistic format where secularization is occurring or it is not. Yet, there seems to be a growing realization that this dichotomy does not reflect reality. Religion is, among other things, a complicated multifaceted social phenomenon that is constantly changing, evolving, and adapting to an ever-changing environment.

---

[64] Martin (1978) also notes a number of additional factors that influence the pace of secularization which are similar to those discussed earlier in this chapter. It is also important to note that Martin's use of secularization is non-ideological – it is simply what happens to religion as it ages and adapts.

[65] While in practice Imams often fill roles that would be typically filled by clergy in the West, they are not officially clergy. Officially, all Muslims are equidistant from God.

[66] Gellner (1992: 6–20).

[67] Norris & Inglehart (2004).

Thus some aspects of religion in some places are secularizing but other aspects of religion in other places are becoming more powerful and influential.

As is the case with religion itself, the literature on the role of religion in modern society and politics is multifaceted. There are a multitude of opinions and perspectives on the topic which are not fully reconcilable with each other. Yet it can be said that over the past 25 to 30 years there has been considerable change in the social science scholarship on religion. Political scientists since the early 1980s have increasingly included religion in their discussions. Since 9/11, this has also been true of international relations theorists. Sociologists began seriously questioning secularization theory in the late 1980s, a trend that picked up steam through the 1990s.

Thus, the past few decades have seen a continuously increasing interest in the role of religion in society and politics. Whether this reflects a shift in religion's actual role or just a paradigm shift is unclear. One reason for this ambiguity is a lack of systematic, comprehensive, empirical cross-national data on the topic. In fact, it is arguable that much of the debate over this topic is due to the fact that different researchers focus on different parts of the world and different aspects of politics and society. Thus, simply collecting the proper information in the proper manner can shed light upon what is actually occurring, which, in turn, can settle at least some aspects of this debate.

3

Quantifying Religion

Empirically examining the role of religion in social phenomena requires accurate measures. This chapter has three purposes. First, it describes the variables used in this study to measure government involvement in religion (GIR).[1] Second, it describes and critiques the types of variables used to measure religion in previous studies, as well as how they influenced this study's variable design. Unfortunately the discussion of past attempts is a short one because until recently religion has rarely been included in cross-national empirical studies of social and political phenomena. When it is included, the measures are often limited, crude and indirect. Third, this chapter reviews many of the empirical findings that correlate religion with social and political phenomena.

PAST MEASURES OF RELIGION

Past measures of religion generally use one of four methods, each of which measures a different aspect of religion. First, many measure some aspect of religious identity – whether individuals or populations are nominally members of specific religions. Second, some focus on religious diversity within a state. Third, many use survey data to measure religiosity – the extent to which individuals are religious. Fourth, some measure the involvement of social and political institutions and groups, including governments, in religion. I will discuss each of these types of variable.

Identity-based Variables

The majority of religion variables used by cross-national quantitative studies are identity-based variables. They measure religious identity in a number of ways. Some measure whether individuals, groups, or states belonging to one religious tradition are somehow different from those belonging to another

---

[1] This chapter is an updated and expanded version of Fox & Sandler (2003).

religious tradition. A number of such studies compare Islam to other religions. Some of these studies focus on whether Islamic states are disproportionally autocratic and find that Muslim states tend to be autocratic.[2]

Many studies that compare religious traditions focus on conflict. For example, one study finds that between 1988 and 2002, Islamic groups perpetrated the majority of terrorist incidents.[3] Another examines differential levels of conflict participation and violence in domestic conflict between 1945 and 2001. It found that Muslims participate in less conflict than Christians but when one takes into account that there are approximately twice as many Christians as Muslims in the world, proportionally Muslim groups are more conflict prone. Also, on average, conflicts involving Muslims are not disproportionally violent but the level of violence of these conflicts increased significantly in the 1990s.[4]

Survey-based studies similarly link religious identity to a wide variety of phenomena. These include domestic violence, how individuals deal with conflict, attitudes toward abortion, issues of morality and tolerance, support for liberalism, support for particular political parties in the USA, and a wide range of additional factors discussed later in this chapter.[5]

Norris and Inglehart examine the link between religious identity and a number of political and social phenomena in a multi-country study. Muslim attitudes toward democracy are similar to those of other religions but there are sharp differences between attitudes in Islamic and Western countries on social issues. Muslims are more likely to support a religious role in society. Muslim societies score the highest on work ethic variables. Catholics and Muslims are more traditional on issues of abortion, suicide, and euthanasia. Jews tend to be more left wing, Protestants, Hindus, and Buddhists more right wing, and Catholics the most right wing.[6]

A second type of identity-based variable measures whether the two groups involved in a conflict belong to different religions. In a previous study I found that the majority of domestic conflicts between 1945 and 2001 are not interreligious. However, since 1980, among separatist conflicts, those that involve religious identity differences are the most violent. International interventions by foreign governments in ethnic conflicts are more likely in interreligious conflicts and nearly 80 percent of these interventions are on behalf of minorities religiously similar to the intervening state.[7]

---

[2] Fisch (2002), Midlarsky (1998).

[3] Ben-Dor & Pedahzur (2003).

[4] Fox (2004: 46–67).

[5] For domestic violence see Cunradi, Caetano, & Schafer (2002), Nason-Clark (1997; 2001); for individuals and conflict see Polkinghorn & Byrne (2001); for abortion see Hayes (1995); for morality and tolerance see Jelen & Wilcox (1990), Miller (1996), Wald (1987: 267–9); for support for liberalism see Karpov (2002); for US political party support see Jelen (1993); for political activities see Beyerlein & Chaves (2003: 229).

[6] Norris & Inglehart (2004).

[7] Fox (2004).

Most studies in the genre show that religious identity differences influence conflict. This is true of domestic conflict[8] and international conflict. One study found that religious identity differences between leaders rather than populations made international conflicts in the Middle East more likely.[9] However, a study of domestic and international territorial conflicts found no connection between religious identity and conflict.[10] A series of studies on terrorism in the past few decades found that the majority of terrorist acts and new terrorist groups have been religious ones but others argue that even so, this terrorism is primarily motivated by nationalism.[11]

A third type of identity-based study examines which groups are fighting. For example, such a study might ask whether the majority of conflicts involving Muslims are against other Muslims or against non-Muslims. Generally, these studies find the majority of conflicts to be intrareligious.[12]

Finally, when addressing religious identity it is difficult to avoid the clash of civilizations debate. As discussed in Chapter 2, Huntington predicted that in place of the East-West conflict of the Cold War era, most conflict in the post–Cold War era would be between several civilizations that are for the most part religiously homogeneous.[13] As it happens, the vast majority of relevant empirical tests contradict the theory, but the purpose of this discussion is to illustrate the types of variables that are used to measure religious identity. The majority of these studies simply ask if civilizational conflicts are more common or violent than other conflicts. This is analogous to studies that examine whether interreligious conflicts are different from intrareligious conflicts.

Most of these studies find that intercivilizational and intracivilizational conflicts are not substantially different from each other.[14] One study did find that civilizational variables had an impact on international conflict, though less of an impact than that of a number of other factors.[15] Similarly, studies that compare the impact of religious identity and of civilizational identity found that while civilizational identity does have an impact on domestic conflict, the impact of religious identity is stronger.[16] This implies that civilization variables are really surrogate variables for religious identity and that the religion variables are more accurate. Some studies focus on an aspect of civilization other than conflict. For example, one study found that mediation between states of

----

[8] Roeder (2003).

[9] Lai (2006).

[10] Pearce (2004).

[11] Weinberg & Eubank (1998), Weinberg, Eubank, & Pedahzur (2002); with Pape (2003) arguing for nationalist motivation.

[12] See, for example, Fox (2004), and Tusicisny (2004).

[13] Huntington (1993; 1996: 45–8) divides the world into eight major civilizations, all of which, with the exception of African civilization, include religion in their definitions. For a detailed discussion of the overlap between religious and civilizational identity see Fox (2004).

[14] Chiozza (2002), Ellingsen (2000), Henderson (2004; 2005), Henderson & Singer (2000), Henderson & Tucker (2001), Russett, Oneal, & Cox (2000), Tusicisny (2004).

[15] Henderson (2004).

[16] Fox (2004), Roeder (2003).

different civilizations was more effective than mediation between states of the same civilization and another that civilizational affinities do not explain UN General Assembly voting behavior.[17]

In all, identity-based religion variables can produce interesting results but are subject to a major shortcoming – the results based on them can show difference but not causality. For example, these studies often show religious-identity conflicts to be different from other conflicts but cannot show that these differences are because of religious factors. That religion is a cause of these findings is inferred, not proven. While this can be said of any correlation based on the adage that correlation does not necessarily mean causation, religious identity is a general categorization that can overlap with several political, social, cultural, racial, and economic factors. Thus, even studies that control for many of these potentially intervening factors can rarely control for all of them and, therefore, cannot exclude the possibility that some factor that is not included in the equation is the true explanation.

An even more serious problem with this type of variable is that it might be a specific religious factor rather than religious identity that is the real reason for the correlation. Measuring religious identity but not the more specific religious factors with which it is at least partially covariant is similar to judging one car as superior to another based solely on which one won a race. Certainly, we would expect the car that wins to be the better car, at least as far as speed is concerned, but this does not tell us what aspect of the engineering made it better. Or perhaps the difference was not in the car itself and rather was due to a better driver or pit-crew.

One example of this problem is related to a finding that among separatist conflicts those that involve religious identity are, on average, more violent. Further examination shows that the primary explanation for this is that the cases where the religious minority experienced discrimination and publically expressed complaints were particularly violent. This more specific religious factor is most likely the reason for much, but not all, of the increased violence among religious separatist minorities.[18]

Identifying specific religious factors as variables (which I will discuss in more detail) also partially addresses the issue of whether the findings attributed to religion variables are really due to some overlapping factor. Detailed and specific variables reduce the chance that some unmeasured concurrent factor may explain the finding. Of course, this problem can never be fully eliminated from quantitative studies, or from non-quantitative studies for that matter, but the more specific religion variables are superior to religious identity variables in this respect.

Given this, why do so many studies use religious identity variables? One reason is that they are simple to collect. This is not to accuse those who use this type of variable of laziness. Rather, more detailed variables require

[17] See, for mediation, Leng & Regan (2002); and, for UN voting behavior, Ellingsen (2002).
[18] Fox (2004).

considerable resources to collect. This can include hundreds or thousands of research hours. In the case of survey-based studies this can be even more expensive because cross-national data entails separate surveys in multiple countries. Also, the empirical study of the impact of religion on social and political phenomena is a relatively new field. This warrants the use of these relatively simple variables to provide preliminary results and guidance into what should be the future research agenda.

Religious Diversity

Religious diversity variables, like religious identity variables, are based on demographics, but employ demographics in a different manner. They in some way measure the extent to which a location, usually a state, is religiously diverse. There are several types of diversity variables. Some simply measure how many religious groups above a certain size reside within a country.[19] The Herfindahl index gives the probability that two randomly drawn individuals in a country are from different religious groups.[20] Other variables use complex equations that are sensitive to the size of the various religious populations in a state.[21] There are also several studies that include religious diversity as part of general diversity variables.[22] Many studies using religious diversity variables examine religion's role in conflict. Most of them link religious diversity to the onset, intensity, and incidence of ethnic conflict and civil war but some find no link between religious diversity and conflict.[23] There are also a large number of sociological studies that link religious diversity to a wide range of social phenomena.[24]

The religious diversity variables, are subject to the same criticisms as the religious identity variables, except in some sociological studies where the factor that is being studied is religious diversity.

Survey-based Variables

Survey-based variables measure the extent to which individuals are religious. They are based on questions such as:

• How often do you attend your place of worship?
• How often do you pray?
• How often do you study the Bible?

---

[19] See, for example, Rummel (1997).
[20] See, for example, Fearon & Laitin (2003).
[21] See, for example, Reynal-Querol (2002).
[22] See, for example, Sambanis (2001), and Vanhanen (1999). Both use a measure, created by Vanhanen (1999: 59), which combines ethnic and religious diversity.
[23] For those that find a link, see Reynal-Querol (2002), Rummel (1997), Sambanis (2001), Vanhanen (1999); for those finding no link, see Fearon and Laitin (2003).
[24] For a sampling of these studies see the discussion of the supply-side theory of religion in Chapters 2 and 11.

- Do you participate in religious voluntary organizations?
- Do you believe in God? Heaven? Hell? An afterlife? The soul? Sin? The supernatural?
- Do you consider yourself religious?
- Do you believe religion is important for raising children?

The vast majority of these studies are sociological and focus on single states or some group within a single state. The examples discussed here are meant to be illustrative rather than an exhaustive discussion of all such research.

One of the more popular of these variables is church attendance, and many consider it the best measure of religiosity.[25] One common line of study links it to lower levels of self-reported domestic violence.[26] Another links it to "such diverse political activities as voting turnout and choice, lobbying elected officials, engaging in collective communal action, and participating in protests."[27] Survey-based studies can also address religion by asking people their opinions on political issues related to religion, such as attitudes toward protecting a country's religious heritage, the involvement of religious leaders in politics, abortion, and prayer in public schools.

Several survey-based scales have also been developed to measure more specific aspects of religion. Most of these scales use a set of statements, usually 10 to 40, with which the respondent agrees or disagrees. One scale measures whether people are conflicted over the issue of religion.[28] Another differentiates between "whether religion is considered an end itself (intrinsic) or as a means to some other end (extrinsic)."[29] A third scale, called the "Quest" scale, measures those aspects of religion that are neither intrinsic nor extrinsic.[30] A fourth measures whether individual's faith is mature.[31] A fifth measures the level of an individual's Christian Orthodoxy.[32] These scales, and others, focus on individual religiosity. They tend to be applied in surveys taken in only one state, most often in the USA, and are not intended to examine cross-national differences.

However, there exist survey-based studies of religion that include respondents from many countries in the same analysis. Some also analyze each country individually and compare the results. One of the most comprehensive of such studies is Norris and Inglehart's book, *Sacred and Secular*.[33] In brief, this study uses data from the World Values Surveys (WVS), which were taken from 1981 to 2001 and include data from 76 countries (though not all 76 in any given

---

[25] Argyle (1959: 6).
[26] See, for example, Cunradi et al. (2002), Ellison & Anderson (2001), Ellison, Bartkowski, & Anderson (1999), Fergusson et al. (1986).
[27] Beyerlein & Chaves (2003: 229).
[28] See, for example, Funk (1967).
[29] Nielson & Fultz (1995).
[30] For a complete description of this scale see Batson & Schoenrade (1991: 431).
[31] See, for example, Erickson (1991: 137).
[32] Hunsberger (1989: 361–2).
[33] Norris & Inglehart (2004).

year). These surveys ask questions similar to those just listed and Norris and Inglehart analyze all of these variables in relation to a number of political and social factors. Their analysis focuses primarily on secularization (I discussed in detail in Chapter 2) and whether a dominant state religion influences religiosity.

Another study based on this data tests several aspects of Huntington's clash of civilizations theory using a combination of religiosity and religious identity variables and finds a number of differences between Muslims and non-Muslims on issues of sexual tolerance, child rearing, attitudes toward religion and the role of women in society.[34] Some studies based on this type of data simply survey the cross-national results of the religiosity data and do not correlate this data with any other social or political phenomena.[35]

Robert Barro and Rachel McCleary take another approach to using the cross-national survey data. They use data from the WVS and the International Social Survey Program for the 1980s and 1990s to calculate national averages for religiosity. They then compare those scores to social and economic variables such as per capita GNP. In this way they convert individual-level religiosity variables into state-level indicators that can be compared to many traditional state-level economic and political measures.[36]

The overall utility of this type of variable is mixed. It is the most appropriate type of variable for studies that focus on the individual, but the use of the data for creating state-level variables is more problematic. This type of data is available for some countries and not others, introducing some selection bias by overrepresenting the West. Moreover, because the WVS is not centrally funded and is done only in states where local researchers are able to obtain funding for the survey, this further biases the sample in favor of wealthier states and states with more developed academic institutions. Apart from these biases, it is difficult to obtain data in some states for a number of reasons. Autocratic regimes may not allow such surveys or may induce participants to give answers that will please their government. Some states include large undeveloped areas where taking a survey is difficult at best. In countries experiencing unrest or civil war, fielding a survey is not practical. As a result of these barriers, the WVS, the most widespread global religious survey, still includes less than half of the world's states.

The states that are excluded are often exactly those that most need to be studied. For instance many studies focus on regime, conflict, and development. Given this, any set of data that is likely to systematically exclude states that tend to be on one side of the scales that measure these phenomena (the most autocratic, underdeveloped states, currently experiencing violent conflict) is problematic. This is not to say that such studies are useless. They are of value and can produce important results, but they are based on a flawed case selection

---

[34] Esmer (2002).
[35] See, for example, Campbell & Curtis (1994), and Sigelman (1977).
[36] Barro & McCleary (2003), McCleary & Barro (2006a; 2006b).

process and, consequently, the results drawn from them cannot be considered definitive.

Another issue with this type of data involves levels of analysis. A connection between this type of variable and state-level variables assumes that examining the opinions of individuals can explain group-level or state-level behavior. While certainly collective opinions can influence state-level phenomena such as national policy decisions, this is not always the case. It is well known that even in democratic states the opinions of the majority do not always translate into policy. Sometimes a vocal minority has more influence than a less-vocal majority. Furthermore, such polls can only show what individual respondents answered to a series of questions. These polls provide no evidence as to whether this is translated into group-level behavior. Of course, this translation from the individual level to the group level can and often does happen, but this type of variable does not account for this factor.[37]

Nevertheless, this type of variable is potentially useful. It can provide a fairly accurate measure of popular attitudes toward religion in a particular locale, usually a state. Thus, where data is available, religiosity variables can provide a more direct connection between religion and other social and political phenomena than can be provided by identity-based variables.

Government, Group, or Institutional Behavior

A final type of variable used to measure religion focuses on a group, governmental, or institutional behavior or characteristic. One of the simplest examples of this type of variable is presented in the *World Christian Encyclopedia* (*WCE*)[38] and measures whether states have a "religious philosophy." The *WCE* did not systematically analyze the data but others have used the data. One analysis showed an increase in state support for religion between 1980 and 2000 in Europe.[39] Another series of studies found several other important results. First, state religions are less common in religiously heterogeneous states and communist states. Second, when there is little regime change, there is also little change in the presence or absence of a state religion. Third, this variable is linked to several aspects of religiosity.[40] This variable is available for over 200 states but is problematic because the *WCE* never defines what is meant by "religious philosophy." A comparison with the analogous Religion and State Project (RAS) variable shows that this "religious philosophy" does not coincide exactly with whether the state has an official religion.

However, the idea of measuring the official relationship between religion and the state government has merit. In previous studies I link a simple yes or no

[37] Other individual level variables used to explain group-level phenomena include variables based on relative deprivation theory. These variables are subject to similar criticisms. For more, see Rule (1988: 200–23).
[38] Barret, Kurian, & Johnson (2001).
[39] Madeley (2003a; 2003b).
[40] Barro & McCleary (2005), McCleary & Barro (2006a; 2006b).

version of this variable with the formation of ethnic grievances. It also influences discrimination against ethnic minorities and rebellion by ethnic minorities.[41] Based on this, collecting a more detailed variable, such as the *official GIR* variable (which I discuss later in this chapter), seems like a potentially fruitful avenue of investigation.

However, this type of variable has two major limitations. First, having an official religion can mean different things in different states. It can be the result of historical inertia, with little practical impact, or it can represent the fact that the state is a religious state. For example both the UK and Iran have official religions. Clearly the role of religion in the two states is very different. Other states, for example Greece, fall in the middle with a substantial entanglement between government and religious institutions but falling far short of being a theocracy. (I will discuss this dynamic in more detail in the comparative analyses in Chapters 5 through 10.)

Second, state support for religion is only one aspect of GIR. Another aspect is state policy toward religious minorities. Some states with official religions, Andorra, Malta, and Liechtenstein, for example, place no restrictions on the religious practices of minorities, while others, such as Saudi Arabia, make it illegal for a citizen to be a member of minority religions. An additional aspect of GIR is the extent to which the state legislates religious precepts. While even Western democracies do this to a considerable extent, the amount of legislation in such states is not comparable to that of states like Iran and Saudi Arabia, which essentially declare that state law is religious law. Finally, official sponsorship of a state religion does not necessarily mean that the state is involved in the day-to-day affairs of religious institutions. Some states, like Argentina, declare an official religion but do not otherwise influence the internal workings of the relevant religious institutions. Others, like Morocco, monitor mosques, Koranic schools, and Islamic organizations to ensure that they adhere to approved doctrine and that their activities do not become political in nature.

Another strategy for measuring state involvement in religion is to measure a number of more specific ways governments can become involved in religion. Fearon, Laitin, and Mecham collected this type of list of variables for 163 countries.[42] The variables they collected include:

- There is a state religion that is constitutionally recognized.
- The state gives added resources to adherents/elites of any religion not available to others.
- The state allows, in general, free practice of religion.
- The state requires religious groups to get approval for religious activities from a state ministry.

---

[41] Fox (2002; 2004).

[42] I obtained the information on these variables directly from James Fearon in a document entitled "Religious Grievances Coding Sheet," January 19, 2001.

- The state regulates the practice of missionaries, beyond the normal bureaucratic processing for nonreligious organizations or for foreign organizations (when missionaries are foreigners).
- The state singles out a religion or sect of the population for harassment or discrimination, or permits through inaction civilians harassing members of that religion. This discrimination must be such as not justified by the rule of law.

While this list is relatively short, it was collected for most countries and across a large time period with data points from 1949 to 1999, something that cannot be said of most similar examples of this type of data collection.

A series of studies takes an approach similar to that of Fearon, Laitin, and Mecham. This research path began with studies by Mark Chaves and some colleagues[43] with a list of 13 variables for 18 European states. These variables were then collected for Latin American states.[44] Finally, Norris and Inglehart expanded the original 13 variables to the following 20.[45]

- "The constitution limits freedom of religion.
- The constitution does not recognize freedom of religion.
- A single official (established) state church exists.
- The state favors one religion.
- Religious organizations must register with the state or be designated by it to operate legally, or the government imposes restrictions on those organizations not registered or recognized.*
- The state issues legal permits for religious buildings.*
- The state appoints or approves church leaders, church leaders appoint or approve government officials, and/or church leaders have specific positions in the government.
- The state pays church salaries directly.*
- The state subsidizes some/all churches.*
- The state provides tax exceptions for some/all churches.*
- The state bans clergy from all or some specified religions from holding public office.*
- The state owns some church property and buildings.*
- The state mandates some religious education in state schools, even though students can be exempted from this requirement with a parent's request.
- There are reports of forced religious conversions.
- The state restricts some denominations, cults, or sects.
- The state restricts/bans some missionaries from entering the country for proselytizing purposes.

---

[43] Chaves & Cann (1992), Chaves, Schraeder, & Sprindys (1994).

[44] Gill (1999).

[45] Norris & Inglehart (2004) are unclear on how many states are coded on this scale but two tables in their book note that it is coded for 22 "postindustrial societies" and 21 countries in "post-Communist Europe."

- The state restricts/censors some religious literature entering the country or being distributed.*
- The state imprisons or detains some religious groups or individuals.*
- The state fails to deter serious incidents of ethno-religious conflict and violence directed against some minority groups.
- The state is designated a country of particular concern for freedom of religion by the U.S. Department of state."

Adding all of these measures together can create a GIR scale based on state behavior rather than just on whether the state has an official religion. This arguably provides a more accurate picture of GIR than the official religion variables. Studies based on these variables found that state regulation of religion is correlated with lower church attendance among Christians and lower participation in the Hajj among Muslims but there is no significant correlation between these variables and several survey-based measures of religiosity.

However, this particular set of measures is problematic because it does not sufficiently distinguish between different types of government action. This manifests in two ways. First, the combined scale does not differentiate between officially designating a religion, more specific ways of supporting a religion, legislating religion as law, regulating religion, and restricting religious minorities. Yet each of these types of GIR has different motivations and implications.

Second, many of the individual items do not differentiate between treatment of the majority and minority religions. For instance, is the state detaining or imprisoning members of the majority or minority religions, or perhaps of both? The implications for the state attitude toward religion posed by this question are considerable. This example is part of a more general principle where states can support some religions while restricting others. This list of variables includes some that specifically measure this as well as others that confound this effort by grouping state treatment of majority and minority religions into the same variable. Eight of these variables, those marked with asterisks, are subject to this criticism. This mixing of apples and oranges may be the reason the composite variable based on these items does not correlate with religiosity.

However, combining different aspects of GIR is not necessarily inappropriate and, as I will argue, doing so can create a measure that is in some ways superior. This is best done by starting with a set of variables, each of which distinctly measures a specific aspect of GIR, and then combining them. This simplifies the sorting of the apple from the oranges.

There are several other problems with this particular set of variables. They do not measure the magnitude of the government behavior. Detaining or imprisoning members of minority groups, for example, can be done occasionally, for a few days, or involve mass detentions that continue for years. Similarly whether "the state restricts some denominations, cults, or sects" can mean anything ranging from the most minor of restrictions of a few religions to the outright banning of all of them. Another problem is that whether the state does or does not fail "to deter serious incidents of ethno-religious conflict and violence directed against some minority groups" is not necessarily dependent on religious issues at all. The motivations for both the attacks and the state response to them can involve political or economic issues as well as issues of the state's ability to maintain order within its borders.

There are several other studies that collect this category of variable. A recent study by Grim and Finke codes 15 variables for 2003, 5 in each of the following categories: government regulation of religion; government favoritism of religion; and social regulation of religion. While this set of variables is in some ways better than those previously discussed they are still problematic. Each variable is coded from 0 to 2, so the variables take severity into account. The data is limited to a single year. Some of the components of these variables, such as "Government interferes with individual's right to worship," suffer from the problem of whether they apply to minorities or the majority group.[46]

Minkenberg codes a variable that focuses on a more specific and less ambiguous aspect of GIR – the role of religious parties in government. He measures the following factors:

- the existence of religious political parties;
- the existence of other parties with ties to religious groups;
- the existence of party platforms that have explicit religious content;
- whether religious cleavage is salient in voting;
- whether religious parties have been the part of government within the past 20 years.

He finds that the most restrictive abortion policies in Western countries are in those states where religion's political impact is limited.[47]

Price focuses on a specific set of government behavior for 23 Muslim states and 23 non-Muslim states. He measures the influence of religious law in the following spheres:

- personal status;
- economics;
- social customs;
- crime and punishment;
- governance.

Price also builds a scale for "authenticity," which measures the comparative acceptance of religious and secular concepts for guiding government and society. This scale is as follows:

0–2: Non-religious concepts, technologies, and institutions are accepted without reference to religion.

3–5: The above are accepted by claiming compatibility with religion.

[46] Grim & Finke (2006).
[47] Minkenberg (2002).

6–8: The above are accepted but are believed to be enhanced by religious ones.

9–11: The above are accepted because they are "traced" to religious roots.

12–15: The above are rejected.

This variable is in some ways similar to the *WCE*'s "religious philosophy" variable, but is clearer as to the criteria for measurement.[48]

The variables of Price and Minkenberg are useful in that they are more specific about the aspects of government they measure. However, each only measures a few specific aspects of GIR, only part of the larger picture.

Some studies focus on how religion influences the behavior of non-governmental groups. Several such studies focus on ethnic minorities using a variable available in the Minorities at Risk dataset to measure religious grievances among ethnic minorities.[49] This variable measures whether an ethnic minority publicly expresses grievances over religious issues. One study finds that this variable does not affect ethnic protest in 40 Middle Eastern and Asian states.[50] Another finds a correlation between religious grievances and ethnic rebellion.[51]

In previous studies I developed more detailed variables for religious discrimination and religious grievances for use with the Minorities at Risk dataset. The religious discrimination variable measures the following types of discrimination against 105 ethnic minorities worldwide:

- restrictions on the public observance of religious services, festivals, and/or holidays;
- restrictions on building, repairing, and/or maintaining places of worship;
- forced observance of religious laws of other group;
- restrictions on formal religious organizations;
- restrictions on the running of religious schools and/or religious education in general;
- restrictions on the observance of religious laws concerning personal status, including marriage and divorce;
- restrictions on the ordination of and/or access to clergy;
- restrictions on other types of observance of religious law.

Each of these variables was coded on a scale of 0 to 2 based on the severity of these restrictions. I also coded a religious grievances variable that focused on complaints expressed over these types of discrimination as well as a category for general grievances expressed over religious discrimination. Each item was coded on a scale of 0 to 3 based on the intensity of these grievances. Both of

---

[48] Price (1999; 2002).

[49] For more on the Minorities at Risk dataset, see Gurr (1993; 2000) and the project website at www.cidcm.umd.edu/inscr/mar.

[50] Sahliyeh, Sinha, & Pillai (2002).

[51] Laitin (2000).

these sets of variables were modeled after similar discrimination and grievance variables included in the Minorities at Risk dataset measuring political, cultural, and economic discrimination and grievances.

I also coded three additional variables. The first measures demands for additional religious rights by ethnic minorities that are unconnected to complaints over discrimination. It is coded on the following scale:

1. None.
2. The group is demanding more religious rights.
3. The group is seeking a privileged status for their religion which offends the religious convictions of the dominant group.
4. The group is seeking to impose some aspects of its religious ideology on the dominant group.
5. The group is seeking a form of ideological hegemony for its framework which will affect some of the dominant group.
6. The group is seeking a form of ideological hegemony for its framework which will affect most or all of the dominant group.

The second measures the level of organization of the group's religious institutions on the following scale:

1. No religious institutions exist.
2. Informal institutions exist (e.g. lay-person led prayer meetings).
3. A formally ordained clergy exists but there are no established houses of worship.
4. Formal houses of worship exist but they are not organized under a formal unified ecclesiastical structure (e.g. mosques in most Muslim states).
5. Formal houses of worship are organized under a formal unified ecclesiastical structure (e.g. the Catholic Church).

The third variable measures the religious legitimacy, as described earlier in this chapter.

These variables are linked to a number of aspects of ethnic conflict, including political, economic, and cultural discrimination, the formation of grievances, mobilization, protest, and rebellion.[52] They have the advantage of focusing on specific aspects of religious involvement in group behavior. They are also specific as to which groups are being coded. Unfortunately these variables have limited compatibility with datasets other than the Minorities at Risk dataset because they are coded for 105 specific politically active ethnic minorities, which is a unit of analysis exclusive to that dataset.

The *WCE* codes two religious discrimination variables for over 200 countries. These variables focus on a religious minority, rather than an ethnic one. The first is the Christian Safety Index, which measures treatment of Christians

---

[52] For a discussion of these variables and results based on them see Fox (2002; 2004).

in a state on a scale of 0 to 100.[53] The second measures state support or suppression of Christianity on the following scale:

1. The state propagates Christianity.
2. Massive state subsidies to churches.
3. Limited state subsidies to churches.
4. The state subsidizes religious schools only.
5. Complete state non-interference in religion.
6. Limited political restrictions.
7. There is discrimination against minorities.
8. State interference and obstruction.
9. State hostility and prohibition.
10. State suppression and eradication.

Open Doors[54] codes a similar measure for discrimination against Christians based on the following questions:

- Does the constitution and/or national laws provide for freedom of religion?
- Are individuals allowed to convert to Christianity by law?
- Are Christians being killed because of their faith?
- Are Christians being sentenced to jail, labor camp or sent to a psychiatric hospital, because of their faith?
- Do Christians have the freedom to print and distribute Christian literature?
- Are Christian publications censured/prohibited in this country?
- Are Christian meeting places and/or Christian homes attacked because of anti-Christian motives?

These variables are useful if one wants to study the role of Christianity in states but, as they focus on Christianity alone, they are not as useful for examining the general treatment of religious minorities or the general role of religion.

Freedom House developed a measure of religious freedom that ranges from 1 to 7, but only for 74 countries.[55]

BUILDING BETTER VARIABLES

Of necessity, all variables that measure some political, social, or economic aspect of religion have two limitations. First, they focus on some aspects of religion but not others. Second, they focus on how religion manifests politics and society rather than the essence of religion itself, which arguably resides in the individual soul or psyche, depending on one's perspective on certain existential questions. The methodology I use to measure religion for this study attempts to make virtues of these necessities.

---

[53] Barret et al. (2001).
[54] See the Open Doors website at http://www.opendoorsuk.org/wwl.php.
[55] The project has since moved to the Hudson Institute. For more details see http://colf.huson.org.

The strategy is to collect variables that are as detailed as possible in order to measure several aspects of GIR and separation of religion and state (SRAS). For the purposes of these variables, absolute-SRAS means no government support for religion and no government interference or restrictions on religion. Of course, there are other definitions of SRAS (which I will discuss in detail later in this chapter and in Chapter 4), but this definition is the one that guides the variables, discussed here. I chose this definition because it is the simplest to operationalize and the variables used to measure it can also measure the other definitions.

Consequently, these variables effectively measure government involvement in religion (GIR), which can be described as any government support for religion, or any government regulation or limitations placed on religion, the opposite of absolute-SRAS. Accordingly, absolute-SRAS is set at 0 for all of these variables and they increase in value as GIR increases. I measure the following five types of GIR:

- the official role of religion in the state;
- whether the state restricts or gives preferential treatment to some or all religions;
- restrictions placed on minority religious practices;
- regulation of all religion or the majority religion;
- whether the state legislates religion.

I also collect information on religious identity and diversity.

I use this multifaceted approach because religion is a complex phenomenon that can manifest in multiple ways. The RAS project focuses on the influence of religion on state behavior. Even in this limited arena religion has several potential influences. Also, measuring each influence separately, and then combining them increases accuracy and transparency. Both separate and combined measurements are essential in understanding any findings that these variables produce.

This methodology brings to mind the parable of the three blind men feeling an elephant. One feels the trunk and thinks it is a snake. Another feels a leg and thinks it is a tree. The third feels the tail and thinks it is a mouse. Yet anyone who can see would realize that it is an elephant. In a way we are blind men trying to determine the shape of an elephant and need to feel as many parts as possible to form an accurate picture.

Accordingly, this study uses five separate categories of variables with three of these categories consisting of multiple separate variables which are combined to create a composite scale. I do not believe that any variable or set of variables can be 100 percent accurate in measuring religion, but this methodology allows us to build variables that are sufficiently accurate to be useful for the purposes of this study.

All of the variables described below, except for the demographic variables, are coded yearly for the 1990 to 2002 period. The data was collected for

175 governments. In most cases this refers to the government of a state, but in some cases governments with only limited recognition, such as the government of Turkish Cyprus, were coded if they had effective control of a specified territory. This includes all states with populations of 250,000 or more as well as several less populous states. (For a listing of the countries included in the dataset as well as the codings for the variables described here, see Chapters 5 through 10. For more information on data collection and reliability see the Appendix.)

The Official Role of Religion in the State

The *official GIR* variable is a modified version of a variable developed, but never collected, by Cole Durham.[56] It measures the official role of religion in the state on the following scale:

0. Hostile: Hostility and overt prosecution of all religions (e.g. the former USSR).
1. Inadvertent insensitivity: There is little distinction between regulation of religious and other types of institutions.
2. Separationist: Official SRAS, and the state is slightly hostile toward religion.
3. Accommodation: Official SRAS and a benevolent or neutral attitude toward religion.
4. Supportive: The state supports all religions more or less equally.
5. Cooperation: The state falls short of endorsing a particular religion but certain religions benefit from state support more than others. (Such support can be monetary or legal.)
6. Civil religion: While the state does not officially endorse a religion, one religion serves unofficially as the state's civil religion.
7. The state has more than one official religion.
8. The state has one official religion.

For many of the analyses I divided this variable into two variables because essentially two different things are being measured: hostility to religion, and support for religion. Also many of the statistical tests I use assume linear relationships. Thus, dividing this variable into two separate ones simplifies many of the analyses performed here. The first of these variables is *official support* and is coded as follows:

0. No support (accommodation or lower on the *official GIR* variable)
1. Supportive
2. Cooperation
3. Civil religion

---

[56] Durham (1996). I added a category for states that have more than one official religion. I also renamed his "endorsed churches" category as civil religion.

4. The state has more than one official religion.
5. The state has one official religion.

It is important to emphasize that this variable is ordinal and not categorical. Each category is a higher level of establishing a religion than the previous one. Establishing a religion is certainly higher in this respect than singling out a single religion but not making it the official state religion (civil religion). The civil religion category is closer to establishing a religion than giving preferential treatment to more than one religion. Similarly, giving preferential treatment to some religions is closer to establishing a religion than supporting all religions equally. Finally, giving support is more GIR than maintaining SRAS.

The second is *official hostility*, which is coded as follows:

0. No hostility (accommodation or higher on the *official GIR* variable)
1. Separationist
2. Inadvertent insensitivity
3. Hostile

Like the previous variable this one is also clearly ordinal. Overt hostility to religion is more intensely directed at religion than the regulation of religion in the context of the regulation of other institutions. Both of these are more intense than a tendency to be hostile to religion in the context of SRAS.

It is important to note that these measures focus on the treatment of the majority religion. That is, it is possible for a state to support some religions while being hostile to others, but these variables do not reflect this. I argue that states that support any religion are not hostile to the concept of religion. This is a critical distinction, which differentiates states such as Saudi Arabia, which supports Wahabbi Sunni Islam and is hostile to all other religions, and states such as the former USSR, which was hostile to all religions. I assess the treatment of minority religions in a separate variable.

It is also important to note that the term "civil religion" is used here to mean precisely "while the state does not officially endorse a religion, one religion serves unofficially as the state's civil religion," and does not refer to uses of the term by others such as Robert Bellah.[57]

State Restrictions and Preferential Treatment for Some or All Religions

This variable, *general restrictions*, has no real precedent in the literature. It measures whether some religions get preferential treatment compared to others. The word "other" is in parentheses because while states that prefer one religion will restrict other religions, states that are generally hostile to

[57] Bellah (1978).

religion will restrict all of them. The variable is measured on the following scale:

0. No (other) religions are illegal and there are no significant restrictions on (other) religions.
1. No (other) religions are illegal but some or all (other) religions have practical limitations placed upon them or some religions have benefits not given to others due to some form of official recognition or status not given to all religions.
2. No (other) religions are illegal but some or all (other) religions have legal limitations placed upon them.
3. Some (other) religions are illegal.
4. All (other) religions are illegal.

Unlike the *official hostility* variable, which measures whether states are hostile to all religions, the *general restrictions* variable measures whether the state is hostile to any religion. Thus, it examines the concept of hostility to religion from a different perspective.

Restrictions on Minority Religious Practices

The *religious discrimination* variable focuses on the extent of restrictions placed on minority religious practices. I argue that this is the best method for examining the role of religion in discrimination against religious minorities because it is possible, and even likely, that political and economic restrictions placed on a minority may have nonreligious motivations. In contrast, there is a greater likelihood that restrictions placed on religious practices are motivated by religion. Also, even if such restrictions have secular motivations, they would still constitute GIR.

It is important to emphasize that this variable measures restrictions that are placed only on minorities. Those placed on all religions in a state, including the majority religion, are included in the *religious regulation* variable.

I use the methodology I developed in my previous studies to measure *religious discrimination.*[58] While my earlier scale included only eight items, the one used here includes 16 specific types of restrictions on minority religions, each coded separately. This list of restrictions includes all of those on my previous scale and is as follows:

- restrictions on public observance of religious services, festivals, and/or holidays, including the Sabbath;
- restrictions on building, repairing, and/or maintaining places of worship;
- restrictions on access to places or worship;
- forced observance of religious laws of another group;
- restrictions on formal religious organizations;

[58] Fox (2002; 2004).

- restrictions on the running of religious schools and/or religious education in general;
- arrest, continued detention, or severe official harassment of religious figures, officials, and/or members of religious parties;
- restrictions on the ability to make and/or obtain materials necessary for religious rites, customs, and/or ceremonies;
- restrictions on the ability to write, publish, or disseminate religious publications;
- restrictions on the observance of religious laws concerning personal status, including marriage, divorce, and burial;
- restrictions on the ordination of and/or access to clergy;
- restrictions on conversion to minority religions;
- forced conversions;
- restrictions on proselytizing;
- requirement for minority religions (as opposed to all religions) to be registered;
- restrictions on other types of observance of religious law.

Each of these components is assessed on the following scale:

0. Not significantly restricted for any.
1. The activity is slightly restricted for some minorities.
2. The activity is slightly restricted for most or all minorities or sharply restricted for some of them.
3. The activity is prohibited or sharply restricted for most or all minorities.

The results are then totaled to produce a composite variable that ranges between 0 and 48.

It is important to emphasize that I weight each of the components in this measure equally (and do the same for several other measures) not because I posit that each is equally important. Rather, it is because there is unlikely to be any consensus as to exactly what weight should be given to each of these 16 measures. Given this, weighting each equally is the most transparent alternative. As each of these component variables is coded separately, other researchers who wish to weight them differently will be able to do so. I will discuss this reasoning in more detail.

Regulation of All Religion or the Majority Religion

The *religious regulation* variable measures the extent to which the government monitors, restricts, and regulates the majority religion or all religions in a state. This is substantively different from *religious discrimination* because the motivations for restricting a minority religion and for regulating a majority religion are potentially different. The former can be motivated by a desire to maintain the dominance of a majority religion while the motivations for *religious regulation* can be more complicated. It can reflect a government fear or dislike for all religion. It can be because the state government is so deeply involved in the workings of the majority religion that in effect it regulates the religion. It can also reflect a state preference for certain strains of the majority religion and/or fear or hostility toward religious organizations that are associated with the majority religion but are outside the state sphere of influence. That is, sometimes a religion will have multiple and parallel sets of institutions, some supported by the state and some opposed by the state. Restriction on alternative religious institutions of the majority group are coded on this variable.

Whatever the motivation for regulating a majority religion, doing so clearly constitutes GIR. From this perspective motivations are less problematic.

While there is no direct precedent for this variable, several of the items included in the 11 types of *religious regulation* are similar to items included in previous measures of religion. The *religious regulation* variable is coded using the same principle as the *religious discrimination* variable and includes the following items:

- restrictions on religious political parties;
- arrest, continued detention, or severe official harassment of religious figures, officials, and/or members of religious parties;
- restrictions on formal religious organizations other than political parties;
- restrictions on the public observance of religious practices, including religious holidays and the Sabbath;
- restrictions on public religious speech including sermons by clergy;
- restrictions on access to places of worship;
- restrictions on the publication or dissemination of written religious material;
- arrest of people for religious activities;
- restrictions on religious public gatherings that are not placed on other types of public gathering;
- restrictions on the public display by private persons or organizations of religious symbols, including religious dress, nativity scenes, and icons;
- other religious restrictions.

Each of these components is assessed on the following scale:

0. No restrictions.
1. Slight restrictions including practical restrictions or the government engages in this activity rarely and on a small scale.
2. Significant restrictions including practical restrictions or the government engages in this activity occasionally and on a moderate scale.
3. The activity is illegal or the government engages in this activity often and on a large scale.

The results are then totaled to create a composite variable that ranges between 0 and 33. I weight each of these items equally for the same reasons I weight the items on the *religious discrimination* scale equally.

Religious Legislation

The *religious legislation* variable measures whether the government legislates religion. While there is no direct precedent for this variable many of the individual types of legislation are similar to items in the variables included in previous measures of religion. This list includes diverse topics including legislation of religious law as state law, financial support for religion, religious education, and the commingling of religious and political positions. All of these types of government behavior, as well as the others on the list, have in common that they are different ways the government can legislate religion and clearly constitute GIR.

The types of religious legislation included in this variable are:

- dietary laws (restrictions on producing, importing, selling, or consuming specific foods);
- restrictions or prohibitions on the sale of alcoholic beverages;
- personal status defined by clergy;
- laws of inheritance defined by religion;
- restrictions on conversions away from the dominant religion;
- restrictions on interfaith marriages;
- restrictions on public dress;
- blasphemy laws, or any other restriction on speech about religion or religious figures;
- censorship of press or other publications on grounds of being anti-religious;
- mandatory closing of some or all businesses during religious holidays including the Sabbath or its equivalent;
- other restrictions on activities during religious holidays including the Sabbath or its equivalent ("blue laws");
- standard but optional religious education in public schools;
- mandatory religious education in public schools;
- government funding of religious schools or religious educational programs in secular schools;
- government funding of religious charitable organizations;
- government collects taxes on behalf of religious organizations (religious taxes);
- official government positions, salaries, or other funding for clergy;
- funding for religious organizations or activities other than those listed above;
- clergy and/or speeches in places of worship require government approval;
- some official clerical positions made by government appointment;
- presence of an official government ministry or department dealing with religious affairs;
- certain government officials are also given an official position in the state church by virtue of their political office;
- certain religious officials become government officials by virtue of their religious position;
- some or all government officials must meet certain religious requirements in order to hold office;

- presence of religious courts that have jurisdiction over some matters of law;
- seats in legislative branch and/or cabinet are by law or custom granted, at least in part, along religious lines;
- prohibitive restrictions on abortion;
- the presence of religious symbols on the state's flag;
- religion listed on state identity cards;
- religious organizations must register with government in order to obtain official status;
- presence of an official government body that monitors "sects" or minority religions;
- restrictions on women other than those listed above;
- other religious prohibitions or practices that are mandatory;

While there are 33 components to this variable, the optional and mandatory religious education components are mutually exclusive. Thus, when totaled, this measure ranges from 0 to 32. I weight each of these items equally for the same reasons I weight the items on the *religious discrimination* scale equally.

General GIR

General GIR is a composite measure of these five variables. It provides an approximate measure of the overall relationship between religion and state. I re-scaled each of the variables to measure from 0 to 20. For example, the *religious legislation* variable, which ranges from 0 to 32, is divided by 32 then multiplied by 20. I included the *official GIR* variable by including the *official support* and *official hostility* variables separately (but these measures cannot both be greater than 0 at the same time). I added the re-scaled measures to form a scale of 0 to 100. I weight each of these measures equally for the same reasons that the individual components of the *religious discrimination* variable are weighted equally.

The purpose of this variable is to create a general measure of GIR that includes all of the ways governments can become entangled in religion. As I have noted, to some extent this is mixing apples and oranges. In other words, it is arguably problematic to combine measures of several different aspects of GIR into a single measure due to the qualitative differences between the phenomena they measure. While this objection clearly has some validity, I argue that the advantages to using this measure outweigh the disadvantages. Each individual measure looks at a different aspect of GIR and does not present the entire picture. Combining these diverse measures creates a variable that arguably represents the overall GIR in a state.

This variable is less vulnerable to the apples and oranges criticism than those I criticized when describing the "past measures of religion" because this variable has a greater level of transparency. Specifically, this variable is made of five general variables that include a total of 62 distinct and individually coded components. It is clear what these components are, what they measure, and how they are combined. Furthermore, the data is designed so that any of these 62 individual components, or any combination of them, can be examined separately. In contrast, many of the variables described as "past measures of religion" are unclear on whether they are coding regulation of the majority religion or restrictions on religious minorities. For example, it is unclear whether Norris and Inglehart's measure for imprisonment or detention of "some religious groups or individuals" refers to "groups or individuals" from the majority religion, the minority religion, or both.[59]

Thus, some of Norris and Inglehart's variables can be described as mixing orange juice and apple juice. Once they are mixed they are nearly impossible to separate. In contrast, the RAS composite variable mixes whole oranges and apples, which can be easily separated at a later date. Put differently, as long as it is clear what is being measured, how it is being measured, and there is an ability to separate out all of the individual components of a measure, creating a composite measure has certain advantages. It allows the creation of a global measure for GIR that can be compared and contrasted with its individual components. Thus even those who object to the use of such a variable are able to evaluate the impact of individual components and whether the results produced by doing so diverge from those produced by the composite variable. The majority of the tests performed in this study do exactly this.

Comparing the Variables

While each of these variables measures a different aspect of GIR, they are related. For example, states with official religions are more likely to have religious legislation. It is therefore important to assess the extent to which these variables in fact overlap. Table 3.1 presents the correlations between the RAS variables used in this study.[60]

Excluding the correlations involving *general GIR*, which is constructed from the other variables, there are a total of 14 correlations. All but one of them is significant, though nine of them have a correlation of less than 0.5 and the highest correlation is 0.693. This means that while there is a significant overlap between the variables, they are by no means identical. This supports the argument that the best methodology for measuring GIR is to measure several different aspects of the phenomenon.

Some Further Comments on Methodology

First, as I have previously noted, when combining variables I weight all of the components equally for purposes of transparency. This decision requires some

---

[59] Norris & Inglehart (2004).

[60] For a brief discussion of the use of statistical significance tests in analyses that include an entire population rather than a sample of a population, see Chapter 4.

TABLE 3.1. *Correlations Between Separation of Religion and State Variables,*
2002

	General restrictions	Religious discrimination	Religious regulation	Religious legislation	General GIR
Official support	.348***	.372***	.090	.693***	.731***
Official hostility	.219**	.230**	.475***	−.154*	.166*
General restrictions	—	.690***	.474***	.520***	.801***
Religious discrimination	—	—	.505***	.607***	.801***
Religious regulation	—	—	—	.314***	.565***
Religious legislation	—	—	—	—	.810***

Correlations are two-tailed Pearson correlations.
* = Significance < .05
** = Significance < .01
*** = Significance < .001

further comments. In the course of the RAS project I have been asked by colleagues to single out individual items on the list for special attention or to give them extra weight in my codings because a colleague considers the indicator in question to be of particular importance or influence. However, there is no agreement as to which variables should be singled out in this manner. In other words, when I present this data to colleagues,[61] I usually get suggestions of this nature but the specific variable I am asked to single out is rarely the same. About half of the RAS variables have been singled out in this manner. Based on this, I conclude that it is not feasible to achieve agreement over which of the RAS variables should be weighted or singled out and that giving all of them equal weight is likely the most transparent and least controversial option available. As the data is designed so that other researchers can combine and weight the component variables separately, those who feel differently will be able to use the data as they feel is best. It is also possible to recombine the measures by either dropping some of them from the existing composite measures or even creating new composite measures based on the 62 component variables. This can be done based on intuition and knowledge of the topic, as was done here, or based on statistical methodologies such as factor or cluster analysis.

Second, the methodology used in the RAS project is based on the methodology used for a similar and successful project that focuses on ethnic conflict – the Minorities at Risk (MAR) project[62] – which also used the intuitive approach for building many of its composite variables. Tests for the appropriateness of the composite variables used here are available in the Appendix.

Finally, the number of indicators in the RAS data is higher than in previous data collections but the potential exists for even more detailed data. If I were to begin collecting this data today, based on suggestions by colleagues, research assistants, and the process of collecting the data, I'd likely construct a new

[61] I estimate that since 1999 over 100 colleagues have commented on the RAS data.
[62] Gurr (1993; 2000).

coding scheme that included many more items. This detailed approach has several advantages. It is easier to delete or simplify an existing variable or set of variables than to expand one. It allows researchers to focus on specific aspects of the data. For instance someone interested in religion in education would be able to focus on the relevant component variables in the *religious legislation* category. Further, as there is little agreement on which of these is more "important," making all of them available has obvious advantages.

Religious Identity

The RAS project also collected variables for religious demographics. The percentage of each country's population that belongs to each of the following religions was coded separately: Roman Catholic, Protestant Christian, Orthodox Christian, Other Christian,[63] Sunni Islam, Shi'i Islam, Other Islam,[64] Buddhism, Hinduism, Judaism, Animism, and other. From this information the following variables were constructed.

Majority religion measures the religion to which the majority of the country's population belongs. It includes the categories just listed as well as general Islam and general Christianity. These two variables were coded when the majority of a country was Muslim or Christian but no single sect of these religions dominated, or in cases where there was not sufficient information available to determine to which sect the majority belonged.

Majority percentage measures the proportion of the population that belongs to the majority religion.

Minority religions measures the number of minority religions that constitute at least 5 percent of the population.

The RAS project's population estimates are based on the *WCE*, the *CIA World Factbook*,[65] and country-specific sources. In general, an average of all available sources was used, weighted for estimated reliability of the various sources. For the most part, this weighting was based on a general impression that the *WCE* tends to be optimistic in its estimate of the number of Christians in some states, as suggested by the fact that in most cases the *WCE* counts more Christians than do other sources. Unlike the other variables in this study these variables were coded only once because demographic figures change slowly over time.

ALTERNATIVE DEFINITIONS OF SRAS

These variables are based on a strict definition of SRAS: no government support for religion, no government interference in religion, and no government

---

[63] This category includes Christian sects that do not fit into the other categories and cases where it is unclear to which Christian sect the Christians in question belong.

[64] This category includes Muslim sects that do not fit into the other categories and cases where it is unclear to which Muslim sect the Muslims in question belong.

[65] Barret et al. (2001); the *CIA World Factbook* is available at http://www.cia.gov/cia/publications/factbook.

regulation of religion. This definition of SRAS, which I designate absolute-SRAS, is the definition that is used throughout this study unless otherwise noted. Other definitions are always identified by more specific terms.

There is some debate over the definition of the term "SRAS." The literature differentiates between two different concepts of SRAS. Both of these standards are part of a more general liberal ideal that the state should be separate from religion, which is an ideological manifestation of secularization.[66] While these definitions are more recent developments, they are based on classical liberal thought.

The first, "neutral political concern," requires that the state neither help nor hinder one particular ideal more than another. This definition allows government support and/or interference in religion, as long as it is equal for all religions. The variables used here can also measure this. For a state to have a level of SRAS consistent with this definition it would need to be coded as "supportive" or lower on the *official GIR* variable because all of the higher codings involve preferential treatment for some religions. The state must also engage in low levels of *religious discrimination* to remain consistent with the principle of equal treatment. It would be preferable that such a state had few of the items on the lists for *religious regulation* and *religious legislation* coded but as these variables do not directly measure equal treatment, this is not necessary. However, it is arguable that if too many of these items are coded this would at least indirectly indicate support for a specific religious tradition.

The second definition of SRAS, "exclusion of ideals," requires that the state should not base its actions on a preference for any particular way of life. This definition focuses on intent rather than outcome. Since the RAS variables focus on outcome, there is no real way to directly test this definition using them, but it is fair to argue that when a state engages in substantial GIR, it is unlikely that the intent to maintain SRAS exists. States with official religions certainly do not have SRAS under this definition. Nor do those that in law or practice give preference to some religions over others ("supportive" or higher on the *official GIR* measure) or engage in substantial levels of *religious discrimination*. It is also arguable that the following items on the list of *religious legislation* imply the legislation of a specific religious tradition, thus indicating that "ideals" are involved in this legislation:

- dietary laws;
- restrictions or prohibitions on the sale of alcoholic beverages;
- restrictions on conversions away from the dominant religion;
- restrictions on public dress;
- mandatory closing of some or all businesses during religious holidays including the Sabbath or its equivalent;

[66] I use the descriptions provided by Madeley (2003a) of these definitions of SRAS but it should be noted that Madeley's discussion is based on Joseph Raz, *The Morality of Freedom* (Oxford University Press, 1986).

- other restrictions on activities during religious holidays including the Sabbath or its equivalent;
- some or all government officials must meet certain religious requirements in order to hold office;
- prohibitive restrictions on abortion;
- the presence of religious symbols on the state's flag;
- presence of an official government body that monitors "sects" or minority religions.

While this operational definition is not exact, it approximates the "exclusion of ideals definition of SRAS." In Chapter 4 these two definitions are used as the basis for more specific operational definitions of SRAS, which are then examined based on the data.

CONCLUSIONS

Measuring religion is a difficult task no matter what aspect of religion one is trying to measure. Furthermore the science of building state-level religion variables is relatively underdeveloped in the social sciences. This is likely due to the popularity of modernization-secularization theory until recent decades. Attempts to measure religion's influence on government, while increasing since the early 1990s, have been relatively scarce. The variables described in this chapter constitute to my knowledge the most detailed set of measurements of GIR to date.

Despite being more detailed and comprehensive than previous measures, the RAS variables are by no means perfect. This is true for the epistemological reasons noted in Chapter 1. There are additional reasons this is true, and these reasons, while overlapping with the discussion in Chapter 1, require additional discussion.

First, while the 62 measures in the RAS dataset constitute a significant increase in detail and comprehensiveness, it is always possible to add more measures. This would include measures on different types of GIR as well as providing more detail on some of the types that are covered. For example, in retrospect, the diversity of state policies toward religious education in public schools and the funding of religious private schools calls for measures far more detailed than the three items in the *religious legislation* measure used here.

Unfortunately, this issue is inevitable in this type of research. In order to collect the data, it is necessary to finalize a coding scheme before the collection process begins. This is because of limited resources, which must be used as efficiently as possible when collecting this type of data. It is almost always the case that during the data collection process, factors that in the best of all worlds should have been included in the coding scheme are uncovered but the project is too far into the data collection process to go back over all of the ground that has already been covered. Thus, any such collection of data is usually incomplete, but with each round of coding, the mistakes of the previous one are corrected and new ones are made. The search for a complete set of variables to measure religion is in this way much like seeking spiritual perfection, a never-ending process that can result in considerable improvement over time but never actually reaches its goal.

A second problem with the data is that it is open to another of the same criticisms I make against previous attempts to measure religion – that it measures what is easiest to measure. The RAS data measures how governments behave, not why they behave as they do. This has some serious implications for the analysis, especially because the same government action can have multiple motivations.

This is particularly true for the *religious regulation* variable. Some governments may regulate religion in the process of supporting it while others may regulate it in order to suppress it. For instance a government might regulate and monitor speeches given by clergy in order to make sure that the clergy remain in line with the state religion's official doctrine or because they fear that the clergy might criticize the government. The RAS data does not make this distinction and in this manner is subject to the criticism of mixing apple juice and orange juice. Motivations for establishing an official religion are similarly complex. It can be the result of historical inertia, a desire to control religion because the government fears the power of religion, or due to a genuine desire to support a particular religion. Passing *religious legislation* can be motivated by any of these larger concerns as well as more specific ones related to the particular type of legislation in question. *Religious discrimination* against religious minorities is perhaps the least subject to this type of criticism because the restriction of minority religious practices in a way that is not done for the majority religion is less likely to have a motivation other than to maintain the dominance of the majority religion. However *religious discrimination* can still be motivated by other factors including a general desire to suppress a minority, especially if it is an ethnic minority that is in conflict with the government.

That being said, this type of problem with the data is somewhat inevitable. What a government does is simply a less problematic measure to collect than what motivates its actions. Government actions are factual. Though these facts may sometimes be in dispute, in the end the government either did or did not take a particular action or pass a particular law. In contrast, I am not certain that accurately measuring motivations is even possible. Certainly one can ascribe motivations to governments, but this is an area of scholarly endeavor in which there is generally much disagreement with goodwilled scholars often ascribing vastly different motivations, for the same action. This means that in many, if not most or all cases, any coding of any variable measuring motivations to the satisfaction of all experts on the topic, or even a majority of them, would likely be impossible. This is even true in those cases where a government or its leaders openly admit their motivations, because it would be impossible to determine whether these are their true motivations or political pretexts.

Thus, the RAS data sacrifices measuring motivations, an important but possibly an impossible factor to accurately measure, for the values of transparency and accuracy. That being said, the unmeasured motivations behind the actions actually measured by the RAS dataset are important and I try to address them in the analysis presented in this book. For better or for worse, some variables are better addressed using qualitative rather than quantitative methodology.

Finally, it is important to keep in mind that the RAS variables measure only one facet of religion's impact on society – the continuum between absolute-SRAS and GIR for 1990 to 2002. Thus, any results based on this data are only a part of the larger picture for a particular segment of time. I address how these results fit into the larger picture in Chapter 12. That being said, no dataset or study of this type can cover all aspects of religion for all time. Based on the scope of previous studies, the data presented here arguably has a scope that is well above what seems to be the minimum necessary for legitimate academic endeavor and certainly meets the standards of the discipline.

In all, the RAS data has considerable potential to add to our knowledge of the role of religion in politics and society. It is by no means perfect or all-encompassing but it is arguably an improvement over the previous generation of data, and therefore part of the next logical step in the continuing effort by academics to measure and analyze a particularly complicated and multifaceted· topic.

4

Global GIR from 1990 to 2002

The purpose of this chapter is to provide a basic analysis of the Religion and State (RAS) dataset on the global level.[1] In doing so it specifically examines shifts over time in government involvement in religion (GIR) as well as the causes or correlates of GIR. The term "global" has two meanings in this context. First, the analysis includes all 175 countries in the RAS dataset. Second, it focuses on the six composite variables described in Chapter 3 and not their individual components. Put differently, this chapter concentrates on the overall trends in GIR from 1990 to 2002. Subsequent chapters will examine more specific aspects of GIR.

The analysis here revolves around several interrelated issues. What is the extent of GIR across the globe? What change, if any, has there been over time in the extent of GIR and separation of religion and state (SRAS)? What basic factors can explain the variation in GIR from country to country? Two factors that are given particular attention in this respect are economic development and religious traditions.

This analysis tests the modernization-secularization theory (described in detail in Chapter 2), which predicts the decline or possibly the disappearance of the public influence of religion in the modern era. If this body of theory is correct, we would expect three outcomes: that the extent of GIR would be relatively low in the 1990–2002 period; that there would be a drop in GIR between 1990 and 2002; and that more economically developed countries would have less GIR. The results presented here run counter to these expectations and, accordingly, can be interpreted as falsifying modernization-secularization theory with respect to GIR during the 1990 to 2002 period.

However, these results cannot be taken as definitive evidence of any changes in the overall influence of religion in the world for several reasons. First, the 13-year period analyzed here is not long enough for us to make any decisive judgments about long-term trends, though it can be taken as indicative of those

---

[1] An earlier version of some of the analyses in this chapter is presented in Fox (2006).

trends. Second, religion is multifaceted and GIR is only one aspect of this influence.

Third, GIR and other aspects of religion's influence on society and politics have complex interrelationships. For example, according to the supply-side theory of religion, a rise in GIR would cause a decrease in individual religiosity. An analysis of this relationship (presented in Chapter 11) shows that for some measures of religiosity this inverse relationship does exist.

Fourth, the RAS variables measure what governments do, not the motivations behind those actions. For example, the arrest or harassment of religious leaders can be due to a general hostility toward all religion, or because a government looks upon religion favorably as long as religion is kept out of politics. It can also mean that a state genuinely supports a state religion and represses factions of that religion that are not fully in line with the official religious doctrine.

Fifth, GIR, as defined here, can include both government support for religion and government hostility to religion. There are obvious differences in the implications of these two possibilities in assessing the overall trend in religion's influence in society and politics.

Based on all of this, the analysis of general trends in GIR is best evaluated at this point as no more than what it means on its face. A rise or drop in GIR simply means that there has been a rise or drop in GIR. In Chapter 12, I place these and other findings in the larger context and argue that there is no reasonable interpretation of the continuing presence and rise in GIR during the 1990–2002 period that does not in some way falsify some basic predictions of modernization-secularization theory. That being said, in order to properly assess the meaning of the overall trend in GIR within the context of the larger picture, it is first necessary to establish the overall trends in GIR. Thus, the analysis in this chapter is a logical starting point.

To recall, GIR is defined here as the extent to which a national government or plurality of local governments in a state becomes involved in religious issues through legislation, policy, or consistent action. More formally this involves five types of GIR, each of which is measured by a separate variable: the official role of religion in the state including whether there is an official religion; whether the government generally restricts some or all religions; whether the government restricts the religious practices of minority religions; whether the government regulates the majority religion or all religions; and whether the government legislates religion. Put differently, GIR can be described as the opposite of absolute-SRAS.

In the context of this analysis, the term absolute-SRAS means the absence of any government interference, regulation, or support for religion. However, this chapter also includes an analysis of how many states can be said to have SRAS based on other definitions of SRAS that are discussed both here and in Chapter 3. Unless otherwise noted, the term SRAS refers to absolute-SRAS and other definitions of the term are identified with more specific qualifiers and terms.

Finally, the analysis in this chapter is based primarily on quantitative methodology. Of course this type of analysis is well complemented by anecdotes and examples that illustrate the findings. (Case descriptions can be found in Chapters 5–10.)

The analysis in this chapter proceeds in several stages. The first set of analyses simultaneously examines whether the extent of GIR changed between 1990 and 2002 and whether the patterns of GIR differ between different religious traditions. As explained in Chapter 2, both in theory and in practice these two sets of questions are interrelated.

This study divides all states into five groups based on religious traditions: Catholic, Orthodox Christian, other Christian, Muslim, and other states. These evaluations are based on the majority population in a state. This is not an ideal division. First, these groupings can put significantly different religious traditions into the same category. Second, it contains no category for Protestant Christians. However, this categorization is the best that can be accomplished in practice. A meaningful statistical evaluation is not possible unless each category has a minimum number of states. The smallest category, Orthodox Christian, which contains 12 states, is borderline in this respect. This requirement makes it impossible to include separate categories for Shi'i Muslims as well as for other major world religions such as Buddhism and Hinduism. Thus having a single category for all Muslim states, and one for states that are neither Christian nor Muslim is not intended to dismiss or overlook the diversity both between and within these religious traditions. Rather, it is an artifact of the limitations of statistical analysis.

The "other Christian" category is especially problematic. In addition to all Christian states that are not Catholic or Orthodox, it includes Christian majority states where no one Christian tradition has a majority as well as states where information on denomination is unclear. It also does not differentiate between those states with Protestant majorities and those without. This is primarily because in practice it is difficult to discern whether many Christian groups should be considered Protestant. Some consider Protestant any Christian group that is not Catholic or Orthodox. Yet there are many denominations of Christianity that likely do not fit the definition of Protestant. For instance Middle Eastern Christian sects such as the Copts predate the Protestant reformation by over a millennium. Other Christian churches, such as the Anglican Church, are sometimes called Protestant and sometimes not. Accordingly, I deem it less problematic on operational grounds to include Protestant states in the "other Christian" category.

Despite these limitations, the results based on this categorization of religious traditions are still relevant and important. While there may be diversity within the categories used here, it is clear that there are significant commonalities among the states within each category which make them substantially different from the states in other categories. The Catholic and Orthodox Christian categories represent distinct traditions within Christianity that are different from the other traditions. The "other Christian" category represents states that are Christian but are not fully within the Catholic or Orthodox traditions of Christianity. Muslim states are clearly distinct from non-Muslim ones. Finally, the "other" category includes a wide variety of religious traditions but these traditions are different from Christianity and Islam.

Thus, while these categories can easily be seen as an oversimplification, they are still sufficiently different to determine whether GIR differs between religious traditions. Any difference between religious traditions shown to be present in the analysis is likely a small part of a larger and more complicated set of influences by religious traditions on GIR. In any case, as is discussed in Chapter 3, there is ample precedent for using this type of categorization of religion in statistical analyses by social scientists. Thus, these categorizations all meet the standard of current practices in the field.

The analysis of the change in GIR over time includes two parts. The first examines the mean level of GIR for each religious tradition as well as for the entire world on a yearly basis. This includes an analysis of the six RAS variables that were discussed in Chapter 3: *official support;*[2] *general restrictions; religious discrimination; religious regulation; religious legislation;* and *general GIR*.

The analysis evaluates the significance of these results in two ways. First it performs a t-test for the difference in the means for each possible pairing of religious traditions for each year. Second, it performs a test for changes over time in GIR. This is presented in a separate table that uses the information from the original means tests as follows. It sets the level of GIR in 1990, or the earliest year for which data is available for a state as a baseline of 1. It then evaluates the change between the baseline and the magnitude of GIR in subsequent years. Thus, if between 1990 and 2002 the mean measures of one of the GIR variables rose from 1.0 to 1.1 this would be presented as a 10 percent rise in GIR. As 1995 is the first year for which data is available for all 175 states in the RAS dataset, this set of tables presents the results from 1995 to 2002. The statistical significance of the results is tested by comparing the mean for 1990 (or the earliest available year) to the mean for the year in question using a t-test.

The second part of the analysis of changes over time in GIR examines GIR from a different perspective that focuses on absolute levels of GIR. That is, on a given variable, how many score one, how many score two, and so on. This is especially important with regard to how many score zero and how many score above zero. This is because the difference between not engaging in GIR and engaging in GIR is a difference that is arguably more important than the difference in the extent of GIR among states that engage religion in an official capacity. This difference is also important because the absence of GIR clearly

---

[2] The companion variable to this one, *official hostility*, is not included in these tests because in any given year between 1990 and 2002 between 13 and 16 states were coded as higher than zero on this variable. Thus there is insufficient variation on this variable to obtain meaningful results.

constitutes absolute-SRAS but there is no clear consensus on whether low levels of GIR violate the concept of SRAS. This section of the analysis also presents the percentage of states that fall into various levels on the various GIR variables.

The next step of the analysis examines whether or not states have SRAS. Accordingly, I use the definitions of SRAS discussed in Chapter 3 to develop several operational definitions of SRAS and to determine how many states meet these operational definitions.

The multivariate analysis uses OLS multiple regressions to examine the impact of religious tradition, economic development, and a number of other factors on GIR. The specific control variables used in this analysis are discussed in the multivariate analysis section of this chapter.

In order to fully understand this analysis it is important to note that the analysis presented here uses the entire universe of cases and not a sample taken from a larger population. This means that any differences found are real differences. Thus, measures of statistical significance are measures of the strength of the findings. This phenomenon is analogous to the difference between an election poll and an actual election. In a poll a number of voters are surveyed in order to predict the results of an election. The assumption is that the voters who are surveyed are representative of the larger population, but there is a margin for error and statistical significance is a measure of the likelihood that the results of the survey actually represent the larger population. However, in an actual election, a difference of a single vote is enough to determine the winner, even if the number of voters is in the millions.

In studies that contain the entire population of potential cases, some scholars contend that measures of statistical significance are inappropriate.[3] This study nevertheless uses tests of statistical significance for two reasons. First, the contention that such tests are inappropriate is controversial. Second, the standard of the discipline in political science is to use measures of statistical significance in order to measure the strength of the findings.

BIVARIATE ANALYSIS

The bivariate analysis includes three sections. The first examines the mean level of change in GIR over time. The second examines the absolute level of GIR. The final section examines the question of how many states can be said to have SRAS based on several operational definitions of the term.

Change Over Time and Differences Between Religious Traditions

The first section of this analysis examines the levels of GIR on a yearly basis between 1990 and 2002 controlling for religious tradition and also examines the extent of change in GIR over time for this period. In this section I first present all of the results then discuss the implications of these results.

---

[3] See, for example, McCloskey (1987).

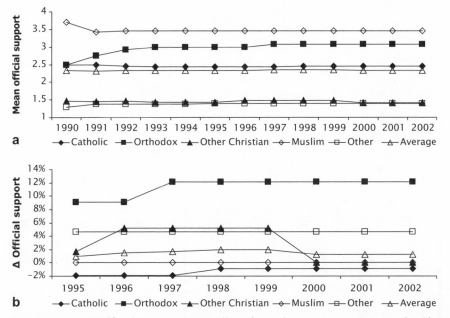

FIGURE 4.1. (a) Official Support Controlling for Religion, 1990 to 2002; (b) Change Between 1990 and 2002 in Official Support. (In cases where data was not available for 1990, the first available year was used.)

The results presented in Figures 4.1a and 4.1b and Table 4.1 show measurable differences in *official support* between religious traditions. Muslim majority states score the highest, followed by Orthodox Christian states, then Catholic states. The mean score for states in the "Other Christian" and "Other" categories is nearly the same for most years in this study but "Other Christian" states consistently score slightly higher. Many of these results are statistically significant. All of them are consistent over the entire 1990–2002 period.

There was a slight overall increase of 1.2 percent in *official support* over time. The largest increase in *official support* was a 12 percent increase in Orthodox states. It also rose 4.7 percent in "Other" states. In "Other Christian" states it rose by as much as 5.2 percent during the 1990s, but by 2002 was at the same level as 1990. In Muslim states there was no change during this period. Finally, in Catholic states it dropped by 0.9 percent. None of these results have statistical significance. This change represents 9 states changing their level of *official support* with 7 increasing the extent of *official support* and 2 decreasing it. Consequently, the most accurate description of these results is that the level of *official support* remained relatively stable over this period with a slight tendency to increase.

The results for *general restrictions*, presented in Figures 4.2a and 4.2b and Table 4.2, are similar to those for *official support*. Muslim states score the highest followed, in turn, by Orthodox, Catholic, "Other," and "Other Christian" states. Many of these results are statistically significant.

TABLE 4.1. *Significance Scores for Figure 4.1a*

Religion	Differences between means													Significance (t-test) of difference between this religion and marked religion for marked year		
	1990	1991	1992	1993	1994	1995	1996	1997	1998	1999	2000	2001	2002	<.05	<.01	<.001
Catholic	gkn	hjn	gjn	hkn	hkn	hkn	gkn	gkn	hkn	hkn	hkn	hkn	hkn	a	b	c
Orthodox	—	gm	hn	io	io	io	io	io	io	io	io	io	io	d	e	f
Other Christ.	l	bdl	ael	bfl	bfl	bfl	afl	afl	bfl	bfl	bfl	bfl	bfl	g	h	i
Muslim	bio	aio	aio	bio	bio	bio	bio	bio	bio	bio	bio	bio	bio	j	k	l
Other	bl	bdl	bel	bfl	bfl	bfl	bfl	bfl	bfl	bfl	bfl	bfl	bfl	m	n	n

TABLE 4.2. *Significance Scores for Figure 4.2a*

Religion	Differences between means													Significance (t-test) of difference between this religion and marked religion for marked year		
	1990	1991	1992	1993	1994	1995	1996	1997	1998	1999	2000	2001	2002	<.05	<.01	<.001
Catholic	l	flm	flm	flm	flm	flm	flm	flm	flm	flm	flm	flm	flm	a	b	c
Orthodox	—	ch	ch	ci	ci	ci	ci	ci	ci	ci	ci	ch	ch	d	e	f
Other Christ.	l	el	el	fln	fln	fln	fln	fln	fln	fln	flm	eln	eln	g	h	i
Muslim	cim	cim	cim	cim	cim	cim	cim	cim	cim	cim	cin	cim	cim	j	k	l
Other	j	aj	aj	ahj	ahj	ahj	ahj	ahj	ahj	ahj	agk	ahj	ahj	m	n	n

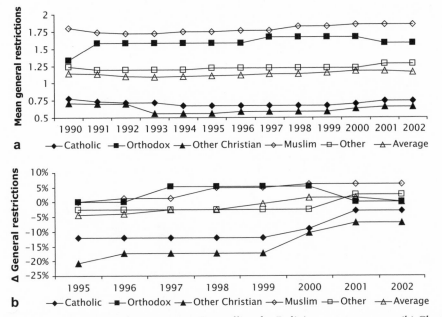

FIGURE 4.2. (a) General Restrictions Controlling for Religion, 1990 to 2002; (b) Change Between 1990 and 2002 in General Restrictions. (Significance of change since 1990 (t-test) < .05 for "Average" in 1995 to 1997. In cases where data was not available for 1990, the first available year was used.)

The mean level of *general restrictions* was the same in 2002 as it was in 1990 but it was not stable over the 1990 to 2002 period. It was as much as 4.4 percent lower than 1990 during the 1990s and in 2000 and 2001 was 1.5 percent higher than in 1990. This pattern of *general restrictions* dropping then rising again was present in "Other Christian," Catholic, and "Other" states. Conversely *general restrictions* increased by as much as 5.3 percent in Orthodox states during this period, but by 2000 was at about the same level as 1990. *General restrictions* rose steadily among Muslim states. None of the changes between 1990 and 2002 were statistically significant.

Overall the coding of this variable changed for 20 states, with 8 lowering the level of *general restrictions* and 12 increasing it. The average level remained stable because those that lowered their level did so by an average of 1.75 points and those that increased the level did so by an average of 1.42 points. Thus, despite the fact that 11.4 percent of the states in this study changed their policy with regard to *general restrictions*, there is no overall trend in these changes.

The results for *religious discrimination* are presented in Figures 4.3a and 4.3b and Table 4.3. Muslim states again score the highest, followed in turn by Orthodox, "Other", "Other Christian," and Catholic states. The results are somewhat stable over time with a few exceptions. First, between 1990 and 1991 there is a steep increase in *religious discrimination* due to the addition of several Orthodox states to the data. After that, the level of *religious discrimination*

A World Survey of Religion and the State

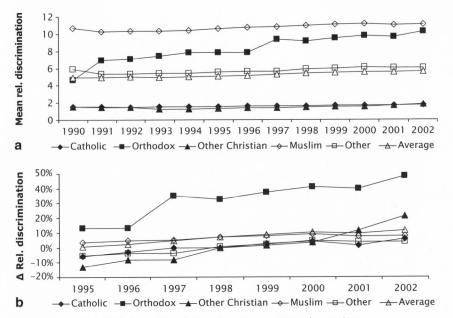

FIGURE 4.3. (a) Religious Discrimination Controlling for Religion, 1990 to 2002; (b) Change Between 1990 and 2002 in Religious Discrimination. (Significance of change since 1990 (t-test) < .05 for "Orthodox" in 1997 to 2000, and 2002, for "Muslim" in 1998 to 2002, and for "Average" in 1998 to 2001. Significance of change since 1990 (t-test) < .01 for "Average" in 2002. In cases where data was not available for 1990, the first available year was used.)

consistently increases among Orthodox states, slowly closing the gap between them and Muslim states. Second the average level of *religious discrimination* in "Other Christian" states is slightly lower than those for "Other" states until 2001.

Between 1990 and 2002, the average level of *religious discrimination* increased by a statistically significant 11.6 percent. It also increased in each of the individual religious traditions. The 48.2 percent and 7.9 percent increases among Orthodox and Muslim states were statistically significant. The average level of *religious discrimination* in Catholic and "Other Christian" states followed the pattern of dropping then rising that was present in these states for the *general restrictions* variable, but the scores for 2002 were higher than those for 1990. The coding for *religious discrimination* changed in 72 (41.1 percent) states between 1990 and 2002, decreasing in 17 states and increasing in 55. This is better than a 3 to 1 ratio of increases versus decreases.

The results for *religious regulation* are presented in Figures 4.4a and 4.4b and Table 4.4. Muslim states again score the highest, followed in turn by "Other" states and Orthodox states. Catholic and "Other Christian" states have about the same level of *religious regulation* throughout this period, with Catholic states scoring higher until 1995 and "Other Christian" states scoring higher from 1996. Many of these results are statistically significant.

TABLE 4.3. *Significance Scores for Figure 4.3a*

Religion	Differences between means													Significance (t-test) of difference between this religion and marked religion for marked year		
	1990	1991	1992	1993	1994	1995	1996	1997	1998	1999	2000	2001	2002	<.05	<.01	<.001
Catholic	ln	elm	fln	fln	fln	fln	fln	fln	fln	fln	fln	fln	fln	a	b	c
Orthodox	—	bh	ci	ci	ci	ci	ci	ci	ci	ci	ci	ci	ci	d	e	f
Other Christ.	ln	el	fln	fln	fln	fln	fln	fln	fln	fln	fln	fln	fln	g	h	i
Muslim	cim	cim	cim	cim	cim	cim	cim	cim	cim	cim	cim	cim	cim	j	k	l
Other	bhj	ahj	bhj	bhj	bhj	bhj	bhj	bhj	bhj	bhj	bhj	bhj	bhj	m	n	n

TABLE 4.4. *Significance Scores for Figure 4.4a*

Religion	Differences between means													Significance (t-test) of difference between this religion and marked religion for marked year		
	1990	1991	1992	1993	1994	1995	1996	1997	1998	1999	2000	2001	2002	<.05	<.01	<.001
Catholic	ln	ln	ln	ln	ln	ln	ln	dln	dln	dln	dln	dlo	dlo	a	b	c
Orthodox	k	j	j	j	j	j	j	aj	aj	ak	ak	ak	ak	d	e	f
Other Christ.	lo	lo	lo	lo	lo	ln	ln	ln	ln	ln	ln	ln	ln	g	h	i
Muslim	cei	cdi	cdi	cdi	cdi	cdi	cdi	cdi	cdi	cei	cei	cei	cei	j	k	l
Other	bi	bi	bi	bi	bi	bh	bh	bh	bh	bh	bh	ch	ch	m	n	n

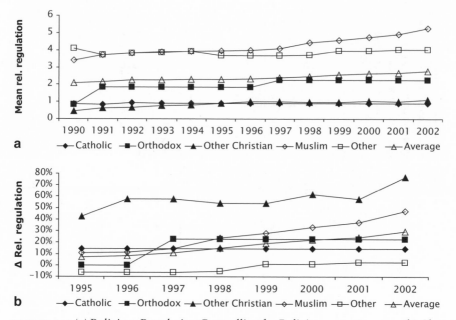

FIGURE 4.4. (a) Religious Regulation Controlling for Religion, 1990 to 2002; (b) Change Between 1990 and 2002 in Religious Regulation. (Significance of change since 1990 (t-test) < .05 for "Other Christian" in 2002, for "Muslim" in 1997 and 2000 to 2002 and "Average" for 1996. Significance of change since 1990 (t-test) < .01 for "Muslim" in 1995, 1996, 1998, and 1999, and "Average" in 1997 to 1999. Significance of change since 1990 (t-test) < .001 for "Average" in 2000 to 2002. In cases where data was not available for 1990, the first available year was used.)

On average, *religious regulation* increased by a statistically significant 29.8 percent between 1990 and 2002. It also increased steadily for each of the individual religious traditions with the exception of "Other" states. In "Other" states the mean level of *religious regulation* decreased by as much as 6.3 percent during this period but by 2002 was 2.4 percent higher than it was in 1990. The 76.9 percent and 47 percent increases among "Other Christian" and Muslim states were statistically significant. The 22.7 percent and 14.7 percent increases among Orthodox and Catholic states were not. The coding for *religious regulation* changed in 49 (28 percent) states between 1990 and 2002 decreasing in 8 states and increasing in 41. This is better than a 5 to 1 ratio of increases versus decreases.

The results for *religious legislation* are presented in Figures 4.5a and 4.5b and Table 4.5. Muslim states again score the highest. In fact the score for Muslim states on *religious legislation* of an average of 12.5 laws in 2002 is more than double that of any other religious tradition. All of the other traditions score between 4.4 and 5.3; thus there is comparatively little difference between them. Accordingly it is not surprising that the difference between Muslim states and each of the other four religious traditions is statistically

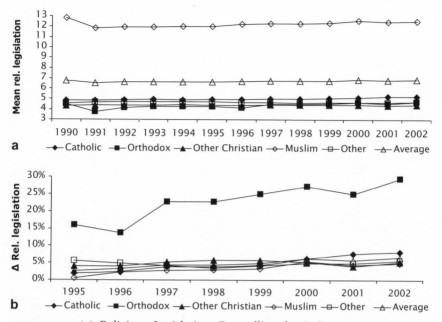

FIGURE 4.5. (a) Religious Legislation Controlling for Religion, 1990 to 2002; (b) Change Between 1990 and 2002 in Religious Legislation. (Significance of change since 1990 (t-test) < .05 for "Catholic" in 2000, for "Orthodox" in 1997 to 2002, and for "Muslim" in 1996 to 1998. Significance of change since 1990 (t-test) < .01 for "Catholic" in 2001 and 2002, for "Muslim" in 1999, and for "Average" in 1995. Significance of change since 1990 (t-test) < .001 for "Muslim" in 2000 to 2002 and for "Average" in 1996 to 2002. In cases where data was not available for 1990, the first available year was used.)

significant, but the differences between the six possible pairings between the other four religious traditions are not.

The average level of *religious legislation* increased by a statistically significant 6.5 percent between 1990 and 2002. It also increased for each of the religious traditions. The 29.5, 8.1, and 4.8 percent increases among Orthodox, Catholic, and Muslim states were statistically significant. The 5.6 and 2.5 increases among "Other" and "Other Christian" states were not. The coding for *religious legislation* changed in 67 (38.3 percent) states between 1990 and 2002 decreasing in 14 states and increasing in 43. This is better than a 3 to 1 ratio of increases versus decreases.

The results for *general GIR* are presented in Figures 4.6a and 4.6b and Table 4.6. Muslim states again score the highest, followed in turn by Orthodox, "Other", Catholic, and "Other Christian" states. These differences are consistent across the 1990 to 2002 period and many of them are statistically significant.

The average coding for *general GIR* increases a statistically significant 3.8 percent between 1990 and 2002. However, the average level of *general GIR*

TABLE 4.5. *Significance Scores for Figure 4.5a*

Religion	Differences between means													Significance (t-test) of difference between this religion and marked religion for marked year		
	1990	1991	1992	1993	1994	1995	1996	1997	1998	1999	2000	2001	2002	<.05	<.01	<.001
Catholic	—	—	—	—	—	—	—	—	—	—	—	—	—	a	b	c
Orthodox	—	—	—	—	—	—	—	—	—	—	—	—	—	d	e	f
Other Christ.	—	—	—	—	—	—	—	—	—	—	—	—	—	g	h	i
Muslim	cfio	cfio	cfio	cfio	cfio	cfio	cfio	cfio	cfio	cfio	cfio	cfio	cfio	j	k	l
Other	—	—	—	—	—	—	—	—	—	—	—	—	—	m	n	n

TABLE 4.6. *Significance Scores for Figure 4.6a*

Religion	Differences between means													Significance (t-test) of difference between this religion and marked religion for marked year		
	1990	1991	1992	1993	1994	1995	1996	1997	1998	1999	2000	2001	2002	<.05	<.01	<.001
Catholic	gl	dgl	egl	ehl	egl	egl	egl	fgl	fgl	fgl	fgl	fhl	fgl	a	b	c
Orthodox	l	aik	bik	bik	bik	bik	bik	cij	cik	cik	cik	cik	cik	d	e	f
Other Christ.	alm	afln	afln	bfln	afln	afln	afln	afln	afln	afln	afln	bfln	afln	g	h	i
Muslim	cio	ceio	ceio	ceio	ceio	ceio	ceio	cdio	ceio	ceio	ceio	ceio	ceio	j	k	l
Other	gl	hl	gl	hl	hl	hl	hl	hl	hl	hl	hl	hl	hl	m	n	n

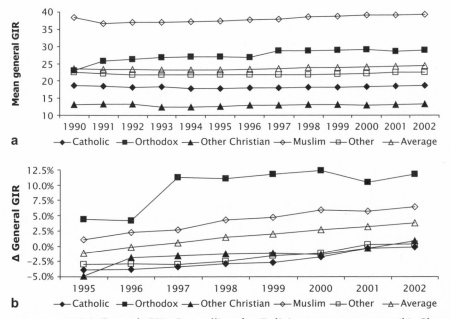

FIGURE 4.6. (a) General GIR Controlling for Religion, 1990 to 2002; (b) Change Between 1990 and 2002 in General GIR. (Significance of change since 1990 (t-test) < .05 for "Catholic" in 2000, for "Orthodox" in 1995, 1997, 1998, and 2000, for "Muslim" in 1995, and for "Average" in 2001 and 2002. Significance of change since 1990 (t-test) < .01 for "Muslim" in 1996 to 1999. Significance of change since 1990 (t-test) < .001 for "Muslim" in 1999 to 2002. In cases where data was not available for 1990, the first available year was used.)

follows the pattern of dropping before rising, with a drop of as much as 1.1 percent during the mid-1990s. Catholic, "Other Christian," and "Other" states follow this pattern but only Catholic states show an overall drop (0.1 percent). The level of *general GIR* rose by 11.8 percent in Orthodox states and a statistically significant 6.4 percent in Muslim states.

The coding for *general GIR* changed in 115 (65.7 percent) states, decreasing in 29 states and increasing in 86. This is nearly a 3 to 1 ratio of increases, versus decreases. The results for religious traditions are equally straightforward. As presented in Table 4.7, the various religious traditions can be clearly ranked on their levels of GIR on each of the 6 variables measured here. As is summarized in Table 4.8, many of these differences are statistically significant. In fact, the difference of each of the 10 possible pairings of religious traditions is statistically significant for at least 1 of the variables. Also, when comparing the scores of Muslim states to the other 4 religious traditions for all 6 variables, a total of 24 comparisons, the difference between Muslim states and the other religious traditions are statistically significant for 20 of these comparisons.

The results for changes over time are more complicated. On one hand, the overall results clearly show that GIR increased on all 6 composite RAS

TABLE 4.7. *Summary of Ranking of Scores Between Religious Traditions in 2002*

	Official GIR	General restrictions	Religious discrimination	Religious regulation	Religious legislation	General GIR
Catholic	3	3	5	5	2	4
Orthodox	2	2	2	3	3	2
Other Christian	4	5	4	4	5	5
Muslim	1	1	1	1	1	1
Other	5	4	3	2	4	3

TABLE 4.8. *Summary of Significant Differences Between Religious Traditions*

	Orthodox	Other Christian	Muslim	Other
Official support				
Catholic	na	1990–2002	1990–2002	1990–2002
Orthodox		1991–2002	na	1991–2002
Other Christian			1990–2002	na
Muslim				1990–2002
General restrictions				
Catholic	1991–2002	na	1990–2002	1991–2002
Orthodox		1991–2002	na	na
Other Christian			1990–2002	1993–2002
Muslim				1990–2002
Religious discrimination				
Catholic	1991–2002	1992–2002	1990–2002	1990–2002
Orthodox		1991–2002	na	na
Other Christian			1990–2002	1990–2002
Muslim				1990–2002
Religious regulation				
Catholic	1997–2002	na	1990–2002	1990–2002
Orthodox		na	1990–2002	na
Other Christian			1990–2002	1990–2002
Muslim				na
Religious legislation				
Catholic	na	na	1990–2002	na
Orthodox		na	1990–2002	na
Other Christian			1990–2002	na
Muslim				1990–2002
General GIR				
Catholic	1991–2002	1990–2002	1990–2002	na
Orthodox		1991–2002	1990–2002	na
Other Christian			1990–2002	1990–2002
Muslim				1990–2002

TABLE 4.9. *Summary of Changes Over Time in RAS Variables Between 1990* and 2002*

	Official GIR (%)	General restrictions (%)	Religious discrimination (%)	Religious regulation (%)	Religious legislation (%)	General GIR (%)
Catholic	−0.9	−3.0	+5.7	+14.7	+8.1[b]	−0.1
Orthodox	+12.0	0.0	+48.2[a]	+22.7	+29.5[a]	+11.8
Other Christian	0.0	−6.9	+21.3	+76.9[a]	+5.2	+0.9
Muslim	0.0	+6.1	+7.9[a]	+47.0[a]	+4.8[c]	+6.4[c]
Other	+4.7	+2.5	+3.7	+2.4	+6.0	+0.3
Average	+1.2	0.0	+11.6[a]	+29.8[c]	+6.5[c]	+3.8[a]

a = Significance (t-test) of change over time < .05.
b = Significance (t-test) of change over time < .01.
c = Significance (t-test) of change over time < .001.
* In cases where data was not available for 1990, the first available year was used.

variables examined here. On the other hand the details show a considerable diversity in a number of ways. First, the extent and significance of this rise over time varies from variable to variable. As summarized in Table 4.9, *official support* and *general restrictions* show relatively low levels of change over the 1990 to 2002 period that do not reach the level of statistical significance, but all the other variables show larger increases that are statistically significant.

This is particularly interesting because the first set of variables, *official support* and *general restrictions*, measures the overall structural relationship between religion and the state, while the second set, *religious discrimination*, *religious regulation*, and *religious legislation*, measures the more specific minutiae of policy. A change in the first set of variables would require structural changes in the relationship between religion and state on the level of a change in political regimes, constitutional changes, or at least major policy shifts. In contrast, a change in a specific law or policy is sufficient for a change in the second set of variables.

Given this, the overall pattern of change between 1990 and 2002 can be described as follows. The basic structural relationship between religion and state in the world is relatively stable over this period with perhaps a slight increase with time. However, within this structural stability, there is a strong trend toward higher GIR due to significant changes in government policies.

Second, while overall GIR rose, it did remain stable or fall in many states. The coding of at least one of the six variables examined here changed in 116 of 175 (66.2 percent) states. The codings for at least one of the 62 component RAS variables increased in 103 states but at least one of these codings also decreased in 45 states. This includes 32 states where some codings increased and some decreased. In 59 states there was no change at all, in 13 there were only decreases in the GIR codings, and in 71 there were only increases. Thus, in this diversity, increases in GIR outweighed the decreases.

Third, overall rise in the GIR variables between 1990 and 2002 was not always linear. Both *general restrictions* and *general GIR* showed an overall pattern of dropping during the mid-1990s then rising again by 2002 to levels higher than the 1990 levels.

Fourth, the patterns of change differed across religious traditions. In some, GIR rose steadily and in others it fell during the middle of the 1990 to 2002 period but had risen by 2002 to be as high or higher than the 1990 levels. The only aspect of GIR that increased steadily and significantly for all religious traditions was *religious legislation*.

That being said, even in this diversity the results consistently show at the very least an absence of an overall decrease in structural GIR (the *official support* and *general restrictions* variables) and an overall rise in GIR on the *religious discrimination*, *religious regulation*, and *religious legislation* variables. It is arguable that the nonstructural variables are more sensitive to change than are the structural variables, which might suggest that the trend of an increase in GIR is the actual trend and that, given more time, it will be reflected also in changes in the structural variables. This would seem to indicate that the preponderance of the results presented here is consistent with the contention that factors inherent in modernity caused a resurgence of religion between 1990 and 2002, at least with respect to GIR.

Yet it is not possible to get away from the finding that this rise is not a monolithic one. Because of this it is perhaps most accurate to say that secularization is occurring in some times and places in some aspects of religion's multifaceted relationship with politics and society, but sacralization is also occurring in others. How these results fit into the picture of the larger religious economy is discussed in Chapter 12.

Absolute Levels of GIR

An analysis of the absolute levels of GIR provides a different perspective on the RAS data. One of the key pieces of information that can be gleaned from this type of analysis is the difference between states that do and do not engage in GIR.

The results for *official GIR*, presented in Table 4.10, show little change over time in the extent of GIR. However, there were some small changes that, overall, have statistical significance. For instance, the number of states that were coded as "accommodation" – the category of this variable that most closely represents absolute-SRAS – increased from 39 (22.3 percent) to 41 (23.4 percent) in 2002. This means that, based on the standard of *official GIR*, over three-quarters of states do not have absolute-SRAS. Also, the number of states with one official religion dropped from 45 to 44 between 1990 and 2002. The number of states that support religion increased by two, and the number of states that are hostile to religion ("Separation" and lower) dropped by four.

These results confirm the findings of the means-tests that the extent of GIR varies between religious traditions. There is also some support for the finding

TABLE 4.10. *Values for Official GIR in 1990* and 2002*

	Catholic (%)	Orthodox Christian (%)	Other Christian (%)	Muslim (%)	Other (%)	All states (%)
1990*						
One official religion	18.6	16.7	9.8	57.4	12.5	25.7
Multiple official religions	0.0	0.0	4.9	0.0	0.0	1.1
Civil religion	41.9	50.0	7.3	12.8	6.3	20.0
Cooperation	14.0	16.7	24.4	10.6	25.0	17.7
Supportive	4.7	8.3	2.4	0.0	3.1	2.9
Accommodation	11.6	0.0	46.3	12.8	28.1	22.3
Separationist	9.3	8.3	4.9	6.4	3.1	6.3
Inadvertent insensitivity	0.0	0.0	0.0	0.0	12.5	2.3
Hostile	0.0	0.0	0.0	0.0	9.4	1.7
2002						
One official religion	16.3	16.7	9.8	57.4	12.5	25.1
Multiple official religions	0.0	0.0	4.9	0.0	0.0	1.1
Civil religion	41.9	58.3	7.3	12.8	6.3	20.6
Cooperation	18.6	25.0	24.4	10.6	28.1	20.0
Supportive	2.3	0.0	2.4	0.0	3.1	1.7
Accommodation	14.0	0.0	48.8	10.6	31.3	23.4
Separationist	7.0	0.0	2.4	8.5	3.1	5.1
Inadvertent insensitivity	0.0	0.0	0.0	0.0	12.5	2.3
Hostile	0.0	0.0	0.0	0.0	3.1	0.6
n	43	12	41	47	32	175

* In cases where data was not available for 1990, the first available year was used.
Significance (Chi-squared) for both cross-tabulations = .000.
Significance (Chi-squared) of difference between 1990* and 2002 = .000.

that Muslim states have the highest levels of GIR. In both 1990 and 2002, the percentage of Muslim majority states that declare an official religion is 57.4. In contrast, the other categories of religious traditions range between 9.8 and 18.6 percent on this statistic. However, if we focus on how many states support religion in general, Muslim states are not as unique. In 2002 all majority Orthodox states supported religion. Only 79.8 percent of majority Muslim states supported religion. This is not much more than for Catholic states, 79.1 percent of which supported religion. Thus, whether Muslim states have more GIR than other religion traditions on the *official GIR* variable depends on how one looks at GIR.

Among all the religious traditions, the "Other Christian" category has the highest level of absolute-SRAS, with nearly half of these states coded as having "accommodation." Almost a third of "Other" states are also coded as having "accommodation." The highest level of hostility to religion ("Separation" or lower) is the 18.6 percent of states in the "Other" category that are coded as being hostile to religion in 2002.

TABLE 4.11. *Values for General Restrictions in 1990* and 2002*

	Catholic (%)	Orthodox Christian (%)	Other Christian (%)	Muslim (%)	Other (%)	All states (%)
1990*						
No limitations	37.2	0.0	56.1	12.8	31.3	31.4
Practical limitations	48.8	41.7	26.8	23.4	31.3	33.1
Legal limitations	14.0	58.3	7.3	44.7	18.8	24.6
Some illegal	0.0	0.0	9.8	14.9	18.8	9.7
All illegal	0.0	0.0	0.0	4.3	0.0	1.1
2002						
No limitations	37.2	0.0	58.5	10.6	25.0	30.3
Practical limitations	51.2	41.7	24.4	21.3	37.5	33.7
Legal limitations	11.65	58.3	9.8	44.7	21.9	25.1
Some illegal	0.0	0.0	7.3	19.1	15.6	9.7
All illegal	0.0	0.0	0.0	4.3	0.0	1.1
n	43	12	41	47	32	175

* In cases where data was not available for 1990, the first available year was used.
Significance (Chi-squared) for both cross-tabulations = .000.
Significance (Chi-squared) of difference between 1990* and 2002 = .000.

The results for *general restrictions*, presented in Table 4.11, also show little overall change between 1990 and 2002. Yet there are enough changes for the difference between the two years to be statistically significant. This is because while 11.4 percent of the states in this study changed their policy with regard to *general restrictions*, there is no overall trend in these changes. Regardless of these shifts, in both 1990 and 2002 less than one-third of states are coded as placing "no limitations" on religion, which means that more than two-thirds do not have absolute-SRAS on this variable.

The results for *general restrictions* confirm the findings of the means-tests that the extent of GIR varies between religious traditions. They also support the finding that Muslim states have the highest levels of GIR. In 2002, percentage of Muslim states that ban at least one religion was 23.4. This is by far the highest score for that statistic. Furthermore, no non-Muslim states ban all religions other than the state religion. However, while only 10.6 percent of Muslim states are coded as placing "no limitations" on religion, all Orthodox states place at least some limitations on religion, but no Orthodox states actually ban any religions. Thus, for this variable also, whether Muslim states have the most GIR depends on how one wants to look at the issue. "Other Christian" states can be said to have the highest levels of absolute-SRAS because a majority of them are coded as placing "no limitations" on religion.

The results for *religious discrimination*, presented in Table 4.12, confirm the results of the means-tests and show an increase in GIR between 1990 and 2002. The number of states that engage in no *religious discrimination* dropped from

TABLE 4.12. *Values for Religious Discrimination in 1990* and 2002*

	Catholic (%)	Orthodox Christian (%)	Other Christian (%)	Muslim (%)	Other (%)	All states (%)
1990*						
0	44.2	8.3	43.9	12.8	28.1	30.3
1	14.0	8.3	22.0	4.3	9.4	12.0
2	14.0	0.0	12.2	10.6	18.8	12.6
3	11.6	16.7	4.9	8.5	3.1	8.0
4 to 5	11.6	0.0	9.8	4.3	12.5	8.5
6 to 10	4.7	33.3	7.3	8.5	9.4	11.3
11 to 15	0.0	16.7	0.0	29.7	0.0	9.3
16 and higher	0.0	0.0	0.0	17.0	18.8	10.2
2002						
0	37.2	0.0	39.0	10.6	21.9	25.1
1	23.3	0.0	22.0	2.1	9.4	13.1
2	11.6	0.0	17.1	8.5	15.6	12.0
3	9.3	16.7	4.9	10.6	12.5	9.7
4 to 5	9.3	16.7	7.3	8.5	15.6	10.3
6 to 10	9.3	33.3	14.6	8.5	9.4	9.1
11 to 15	0.0	8.3	2.4	25.5	6.3	9.1
16 and higher	0.0	25.0	0.0	25.5	15.6	11.4

* In cases where data was not available for 1990, the first available year was used.
Significance (Chi-squared) for both cross-tabulations = .000.
Significance (Chi-squared) of difference between 1990* and 2002 = .000.

53 to 44. Furthermore, this increase occurred in each of the five categories of religious tradition examined here.

These results show considerable variation between religious traditions. The results presented in the table indicate that Orthodox states, and not Muslim ones, have the highest levels of GIR. No Orthodox state scores below a 3 on this variable but a significant number of Muslim states score 2 or lower. Also, about the same percentage of Muslim and Orthodox states score in the highest category of *religious discrimination* shown in the table. However, what the table does not show is that no Orthodox state scores higher than 20 on *religious discrimination* but 17 percent of Muslim states do, with the highest score being 38, nearly double that of the highest scoring Orthodox states. Thus, also for this variable, which religious tradition has higher levels of GIR depends on how one looks at GIR.

The results for *religious regulation*, presented in Table 4.13, confirm the results of the means-tests and show an increase in GIR between 1990 and 2002. In fact a pivotal change occurred during this period where in 1990 a majority of 56 percent of states engaged in no *religious regulation* but in 2002 a majority of 53.7 percent did engage in *religious regulation*. This rise in *religious regulation* occurred in all five religious traditions. Furthermore, this

TABLE 4.13. *Values for Religious Regulation in 1990* and 2002*

	Catholic (%)	Orthodox Christian (%)	Other Christian (%)	Muslim (%)	Other (%)	All states (%)
1990*						
0	76.7	50.0	75.6	31.9	40.6	56.0
1	4.7	8.3	14.6	14.9	3.1	9.7
2	2.3	0.0	2.4	6.4	6.3	4.0
3	14.0	8.3	2.4	6.4	12.5	8.6
4 to 5	0.0	33.3	0.0	12.8	12.5	8.0
6 to 10	0.0	0.0	4.9	19.1	12.5	7.4
11 to 15	2.3	0.0	0.0	8.5	9.4	4.6
16 and higher	0.0	0.0	0.0	0.0	3.1	0.6
2002						
0	72.1	33.3	63.4	19.1	34.4	46.3
1	4.7	8.3	17.1	12.8	3.1	9.7
2	7.0	8.3	4.9	2.1	9.4	5.7
3	11.6	16.7	7.3	6.4	12.5	9.7
4 to 5	2.3	33.3	0.0	17.0	15.6	10.3
6 to 10	0.0	0.0	4.9	25.5	12.5	9.1
11 to 15	2.3	0.0	2.4	14.9	9.4	6.9
16 and higher	0.0	0.0	0.0	2.1	3.1	1.1

* In cases where data was not available for 1990, the first available year was used.
Significance (Chi-squared) for both cross-tabulations < .01.
Significance (Chi-squared) of difference between 1990* and 2002 = .000.

shift was not just a shift from no *religious regulation* to minimal *religious regulation*. Rather, many states substantially increased the extent of *religious regulation* in which they engage.

The results show considerable variation across religions. They also show Muslim states as having the highest levels of GIR. Only 19.1 percent of Muslim states did not engage in *religious regulation*, which is by far the lowest score on this statistic, and 42.5 percent scored six or higher, which is by far the highest score on this statistic.

The results for *religious legislation*, presented in Table 4.14, show that religious legislation is ubiquitous. In 1990, 4 states legislate none of the 33 categories of *religious legislation* included in the RAS dataset. This drops to 1 state, the USA, in 2002. Furthermore, in both 1990 and 2002 very few states have less than 2 of these categories of laws on the books. Thus, looking at the lowest scores of *religious legislation* is not helpful in determining if the extent of *religious legislation* increased between 1990 and 2002. However, when looking at the highest scores, 40.5 percent of states scored 6 or higher in 1990 and this rose to 44.5 percent in 2002.

As is the case with several of the other variables, Muslim states stand out as having the highest levels of GIR. In 2002 61.7 percent of Muslim states had on

TABLE 4.14. *Values for Religious Legislation in 1990* and 2002*

	Catholic (%)	Orthodox Christian (%)	Other Christian (%)	Muslim (%)	Other (%)	All states (%)
1990*						
0	0.0	8.3	4.9	2.1	0.0	2.3
1	0.0	8.3	9.8	0.0	6.3	5.1
2	0.0	16.7	14.6	8.5	21.9	12.0
3	18.6	25.0	17.1	6.4	25.0	16.6
4	18.6	8.3	22.0	6.4	12.5	14.3
5	14.0	16.7	4.9	6.4	12.5	9.7
6 to 7	32.6	8.3	9.8	4.3	9.4	14.3
8 to 10	7.0	8.3	17.1	6.4	6.3	9.1
11 to 15	0.0	0.0	0.0	27.7	3.1	8.0
16 and higher	0.0	0.0	0.0	31.9	3.1	9.1
2002						
0	0.0	0.0	2.4	0.0	0.0	0.6
1	2.3	8.3	7.3	0.0	3.1	3.4
2	2.3	0.0	14.6	6.4	25.0	10.3
3	14.0	16.7	14.6	8.5	18.8	13.7
4	18.6	25.0	9.5	4.3	12.5	14.3
5	20.9	16.7	9.8	6.4	15.6	13.1
6 to 7	30.2	25.0	17.1	6.4	12.5	17.1
8 to 10	11.6	8.3	14.6	6.4	6.3	9.7
11 to 15	0.0	0.0	0.0	23.4	6.3	7.4
16 and higher	0.0	0.0	0.0	38.3	0.0	10.3

* In cases where data was not available for 1990, the first available year was used.
Significance (Chi-squared) for both cross-tabulations < .05.
Significance (Chi-squared) of difference between 1990* and 2002 = .000.

the books at least 11 of the 33 laws measured by the RAS dataset. Other than 6.3 percent of states in the "Other" category, no state in another category of religious tradition scored higher than 10 laws.

The results for *general GIR*, presented in Table 4.15, do not obviously reflect the slight rise in GIR that was shown in the means-tests. However, these results do show that no state other than the USA scored zero on this variable both in 1990 and in 2002.[4] In 2002 a majority of 78.3 percent scored higher than 10 and a majority of 54.9 percent scored higher than 20. Furthermore, within each religious tradition a clear majority scored higher than 10 and for each religious tradition except the "Other Christian" category a majority scored higher than 20.

There is a clear variation across religious traditions. Which religious tradition has the highest level of GIR depends on the criteria one uses. On one hand

[4] The USA's uniqueness as the only state in the RAS dataset to have no GIR is discussed further in Chapters 5 and 11.

TABLE 4.15. *Values for General GIR in 1990* and 2002*

	Catholic (%)	Orthodox Christian (%)	Other Christian (%)	Muslim (%)	Other (%)	All states (%)
1990*						
0	0.0	0.0	2.4	0.0	0.0	0.6
0.001 to 5	9.3	0.0	31.7	6.4	21.9	15.4
5.001 to 10	9.3	0.0	4.9	4.3	6.3	5.7
10.001 to 15	11.6	16.7	9.8	6.4	3.1	8.6
15.001 to 20	18.6	16.7	26.8	10.6	21.9	18.9
20.001 to 30	39.5	25.0	22.0	4.3	15.6	20.6
30.001 to 40	11.6	41.7	2.4	12.8	12.5	12.0
40.001 to 50	0.0	0.0	0.0	29.8	12.5	10.3
50.001 and higher	0.0	0.0	0.0	25.5	6.3	8.0
2002						
0	0.0	0.0	2.4	0.0	0.0	0.6
0.001 to 5	11.6	0.0	36.6	6.4	15.6	16.0
5.001 to 10	7.0	0.0	2.4	2.4	12.5	5.1
10.001 to 15	7.0	0.0	9.8	4.3	6.3	6.3
15.001 to 20	18.6	25.0	24.4	8.5	15.6	17.1
20.001 to 30	51.2	16.7	22.0	8.5	18.8	24.6
30.001 to 40	4.7	50.0	4.4	12.8	12.5	10.9
40.001 to 50	0.0	8.3	0.0	25.5	15.6	10.3
50.001 and higher	0.0	0.0	0.0	31.9	3.1	9.1

* In cases where data was not available for 1990, the first available year was used.
Significance (Chi-squared) for both cross-tabulations = .000.
Significance (Chi-squared) of difference between 1990* and 2002 = .000.

no Orthodox state scores below 15, while a minority of 13.1 percent of Muslim states score below 15. On the other hand, 57.4 percent of Muslim states score higher than 40, as opposed to only one of the 12 Orthodox states.

The overall results of this section provide a different perspective on the data than does the analysis in the previous section. Simply put, a minority of these states engage in no GIR on any one of these variables and only one state, the USA, engages in no GIR on all of them. However, when examining shifts from no GIR to GIR and vice versa, there is some indication that the changes go in both directions, but states that began engaging in GIR outnumber those that ceased to engage in GIR. The ratio of states that began to engage in GIR to those that stopped engaging in GIR was 2 to 1 for *official GIR*, 6 to 4 for *general restrictions*, 14 to 5 for *religious discrimination*, 19 to 2 for *religious regulation*, and 3 to 0 for *religious legislation*. This scarcity of absolute-SRAS and the shift away from absolute-SRAS is inconsistent with the predictions of modernization-secularization theory.

The results with regard to religious traditions are similar to those from the analysis in the previous section but with a key difference. States with religious traditions do show different patterns of GIR, but the results with regard to the finding that Muslim states have the highest levels of GIR are less clear. For some variables whether Muslim or Orthodox states engage in more GIR depends on one's perspective, but for others Muslim states clearly engage in more GIR.

HOW MANY STATES HAVE SRAS?

The question of how many states have SRAS is a complicated one because there is no single definition of SRAS and many existing definitions are difficult to operationalize. Two basic definitions of SRAS were discussed in Chapter 3. The first, "neutral political concern," requires that the state neither help nor hinder any particular ideal more than others. The second, "exclusion of ideals," requires that the state should not base its actions on a preference for any particular way of life.

Both of these definitions are somewhat difficult to operationalize. In the case of the "neutral political concern" definition, it is hard to draw the line between what constitutes helping or hindering religion. For this reason I develop three alternative operationalizations of this concept. These and all other operationalizations of SRAS used in this study are presented in Table 4.16. Any operationalization of SRAS based on the "neutral political concern" definition should allow the "separationist," "accommodation," and "supportive" codings of *official GIR*. "Accommodation" is absolute-SRAS, "supportive" represents equal support for all religions and hence can be said to be neutral toward religion. "Separationist" implies a general hostility to religion in the context of a regime that formally respects the concept of SRAS but does not necessarily single out a particular religion for this hostility. "Inadvertent insensitivity" also does not necessarily imply that any particular religion is singled out for government hostility, but it does constitute a sufficient level of hostility that many might argue it should not be included in any definition of SRAS. It is therefore included in one of the alternative operationalizations of the "neutral political concern" definition but not the others.

It is also unclear how to include the other RAS variables into the operationalization of the "neutral political concern" definition. It is arguable that any coding above zero on any of these variables may constitute a violation of government neutrality toward religion. Yet it is also arguable that such an operationalization of the "neutral political concern" definition is overly strict because a government may have a few laws or policies that constitute GIR without really infringing on a more general regime of SRAS.

This is especially true of the *general restrictions* variable. While no restrictions at all is clearly SRAS, it is arguable that the "practical restrictions" coding is also within the bounds of SRAS because there is no legal regime of SRAS. Accordingly, in some of the operationalizations of the "neutral political concern" definition of SRAS, "practical restrictions" is considered to violate SRAS and in others it is not.

It is clear that *religious discrimination* violates the "neutral political concern" definition because it represents unequal treatment of religious minorities.

TABLE 4.16. *Criteria for SRAS Based on Seven Alternate Definitions*

	Official GIR	General restrictions	Religious discrimination	Religious regulation	Religious legislation	General GIR
Absolute SRAS	Accommodation only	None	None	None	None	0 Only
Near-SRAS 1	Accommodation only	None	Up to 3	Up to 3	Up to 3	Up to 5
Near-SRAS 2	Separationist and accommodation	None	Up to 5	Up to 5	Up to 5	Up to 10
Neutral political concern 1	Separationist, accommodation, & supportive	None	None	Up to 3	Up to 3	Up to 10
Neutral political concern 2	Separationist, accommodation, & supportive	Practical limitations	Up to 3	Up to 5	Up to 5	Up to 15
Neutral political concern 3	Inadvertent insensitivity, separationist, accommodation, & supportive	Practical limitations	Up to 5	Up to 10	Up to 5	Up to 20
Exclusion of ideals	Hostile, inadvertent insensitivity, separationist, accommodation, supportive, & cooperation	Practical & legal limitations	Up to 10	Up to 10	See list in Chapter 3	Up to 30

For this reason one operationalization of the "neutral political concern" definition requires that this variable be coded as zero. The others adopt a more lenient stance based on the argument that a limited amount of *religious discrimination* does not necessarily violate a larger framework of SRAS.

The operationalizations of the "neutral political concern" definition of SRAS allow for low to medium levels of *religious regulation*. This is because this variable measures the regulation of all religions or at least of the majority religion. However, at some point this regulation gets to the point where it is difficult to argue that the government is actually neutral on the issue of religion.

The inclusion of the *religious legislation* and *general GIR* variables in the "neutral political concern" definition of SRAS is also based on these principles. Neither of these variables directly implies that the government is favoring a particular religion over others. However, as the codings for these variables increase, it is more difficult to argue that this favoritism is not occurring.

The "exclusion of ideals" definition of SRAS is more difficult to operationalize because it involves intent rather than action. As long as the government does not base its activities on any particular religious ideal, an activity that constitutes GIR is not a violation of SRAS. Based on this, and the fact that this study uses other stricter alternative operationalizations of SRAS, the operationalization of the "exclusion of ideals" definition presented here is a very broad one.

Any coding of *official GIR* that does not constitute the tacit or official endorsement of a specific religion or religions is not considered to violate the "exclusion of ideals" definition. The "legal limitations" coding of *general restrictions* is allowed because these restrictions may have nonreligious motivations. The line between SRAS and non-SRAS for *religious discrimination, religious regulation,* and *general GIR* is set at a level at which it is difficult to argue that religious ideals are not involved. Finally, legislating one of the specific types of *religious legislation* that are listed in Chapter 3 as violating the "exclusion of ideals" definition of SRAS is considered to violate this definition of SRAS here.

It is also possible to develop additional definitions and operationalizations of SRAS based on the RAS data. One such definition is the absolute-SRAS definition that is used in the discussion in most of this study. This standard is simply to operationalize with the coding for *official GIR* set at "accommodation" and for all other variables set at zero.

Another standard for SRAS can be called near-SRAS. This definition still holds to the ideal of no support or hindrance of religion, but acknowledges that states that generally have a regime of SRAS may for various historical, cultural, or political reasons violate absolute-SRAS in a few isolated incidents. There are two operationalizations of this standard with the first being stricter than the second.

Clearly, other than the absolute-SRAS standard, any of these standards can be operationalized in multiple ways. The seven operationalizations of these four standards for SRAS are representative of the other operationalizations and range from strict standards, like absolute-SRAS, to broader operationalizations of more lenient standards, like this study's operationalization of the "exclusion of ideals" definition.

Based on these operational definitions, determining how many states have SRAS is straightforward. Table 4.17 shows the proportion of states meeting each element of these seven operational definitions as well as the proportion of states conforming to all of the requirements for each operational definition. The results show that while many of the individual requirements of some of the definitions are met by a majority of states, few states meet every element of these definitions.

As one would expect, the absolute-SRAS standard is met by the lowest proportion of states. In fact, only the USA meets this standard, both in 1990 and 2002. More interestingly, all of the other operationalizations show that between 10.9 percent and 22.3 percent of states have SRAS. This is especially unexpected since these different operationalizations were intentionally developed to range from very strict operationalizations of SRAS to relatively broad and inclusive definitions. Thus, the debate over how SRAS should be defined and measured has a relatively limited impact on how many states are said to have SRAS with the exception of the absolute-SRAS definition.

The change between 1990 and 2002 was relatively small. The number of states with SRAS dropped slightly on four of the operationalizations, stayed the same on two of them, and rose slightly for one.

All of this strongly supports the argument that religion remains an important social and political factor. No matter how it is measured, a majority of at least 77.7 percent of states did not have SRAS in 2002. Based on this, religion somehow significantly influences regime structure and government behavior in a large majority of the world's states. This is true regardless of one's position on a number of issues, including how GIR fits into the larger religious economy and the nature of the government motivations behind this GIR. Both of these issues are discussed in more detail in Chapter 12.

As presented in Table 4.18, the finding that there is significant GIR in most states holds true across religious traditions. In 2002 no more than 36.6 percent of states belonging to any religious tradition have SRAS based on any of these operationalizations. Yet, there is also some clear variation across religious traditions. On six of the seven definitions no Orthodox states have SRAS. Excluding Orthodox states, Muslim states are the least likely to have SRAS on most of these operationalizations. Catholic states are the next least. "Other Christian" states are the most likely to have SRAS on these operationalizations.

This, combined with the results of the previous sections, means that Muslim states have a higher average level of GIR, but a larger proportion of Orthodox states have sufficient GIR that they do not have SRAS based on all operationalizations of SRAS used here, except for the operationalization of the "exclusion of ideals" standard. Put differently, if one were to place all states on a continuum between absolute SRAS and absolute GIR, all Orthodox states would fall in the area where states are not considered to have SRAS but few Orthodox states would be on the extreme GIR end of the scale. In contrast, Muslim states can be found from one extreme of the scale to the other, with

TABLE 4.17. *Proportion of States That Meet the Criteria for SRAS in 1990 and 2002*

	Official GIR (%)	General restrictions (%)	Religious discrimination (%)	Religious regulation (%)	Religious legislation (%)	General GIR (%)	All criteria for the definition (%)
1990*							
Absolute SRAS	22.3	31.4	30.3	56.0	2.3	0.6	0.6
Near-SRAS 1	22.3	31.4	62.9	78.3	36.0	15.4	14.9
Near-SRAS 2	28.6	31.4	71.4	86.3	60.0	21.1	16.6
Neutral political concern 1	31.5	31.4	30.3	78.3	36.0	21.1	14.3
Neutral political concern 2	31.5	64.5	62.9	86.3	60.0	29.7	20.6
Neutral political concern 3	33.8	64.5	71.4	93.7	60.0	48.6	21.7
Exclusion of ideals	53.2	89.1	82.7	93.7	20.0	69.2	11.4
2002*							
Absolute SRAS	23.4	30.3	25.1	46.3	0.6	0.6	0.6
Near-SRAS 1	23.4	30.3	59.9	71.4	28.0	16.6	10.3
Near-SRAS 2	28.5	30.3	70.2	81.7	45.4	21.7	16.6
Neutral political concern 1	30.2	30.3	25.1	71.4	28.0	21.7	8.0
Neutral political concern 2	30.2	64.0	59.9	81.7	45.4	28.0	18.9
Neutral political concern 3	32.5	64.0	70.2	90.8	45.4	45.1	22.3
Exclusion of ideals	53.1	89.8	79.3	90.8	18.3	69.7	10.9

* In cases where data was not available for 1990, the first available year was used.

TABLE 4.18. *Proportion of States That Meet the Criteria for SRAS Controlling for Religious Tradition, 2002*

	Catholic (%)	Orthodox Christian (%)	Other Christian (%)	Muslim (%)	Other (%)
1990*					
Absolute SRAS	0.0	0.0	2.4	0.0	0.0
Near-SRAS 1	9.3	0.0	31.7	6.4	18.8
Near-SRAS 2	14.0	0.0	31.7	6.4	21.9
Neutral political concern 1	14.0	0.0	24.4	6.4	18.8
Neutral political concern 2	18.6	8.3	31.7	10.6	28.1
Neutral political concern 3	20.9	8.3	34.1	10.6	28.1
Exclusion of ideals	7.0	33.3	12.2	4.3	18.8
2002					
Absolute SRAS	0.0	0.0	2.4	0.0	0.0
Near-SRAS 1	7.0	0.0	22.0	4.3	12.5
Near-SRAS 2	11.6	0.0	36.6	6.4	18.8
Neutral political concern 1	11.6	0.0	36.6	4.3	9.4
Neutral political concern 2	14.0	0.0	36.6	10.6	21.9
Neutral political concern 3	16.3	0.0	39.0	14.9	28.1
Exclusion of ideals	4.7	25.0	17.1	6.4	12.5

* In cases where data was not available for 1990, the first available year was used.

more states being closer to the extreme GIR end of the scale. Thus, based on all the evidence presented here, whether Orthodox or Muslim states have the most GIR depends on one's perspective on the meaning of SRAS.[5]

MULTIVARIATE ANALYSIS

The multivariate analysis uses OLS regressions to examine the impact of several factors on the RAS variables. The primary intent of this section of the analysis is to examine the impact of economic modernization on GIR. This is because economic modernization figures prominently in theories that predict religion's decline as well as theories that predict its resurgence. Of course the analysis includes other potential influences such as religious tradition and regime.

Research Design

Each of the six RAS variables used in the previous analyses in this chapter serve as dependent variables here and are examined independently for 1990, 1993, 1996, 1999, and 2002. This is in order to examine whether correlations revealed by the analysis hold true over time.

[5] For more discussion on the variance in GIR between Muslim states, see Chapter 11.

Economic modernization is measured using two separate variables: the log of per capita GDP, and infant mortality.[6] Both of these variables are standard variables used to measure economic modernization[7] and are available for most states. In order to understand the relationship between these economic variables and GIR it is important to note that log-per-capita-GDP is positively related to economic development, and infant mortality is negatively related to economic development. That is, a higher log-per-capita-GDP indicates more economic development but a higher infant mortality indicates lower economic development.

In order to control for the impact of specific religious traditions, four dummy variables are added – one each for Catholic states, Orthodox Christian states, "Other Christian" states, and Muslim states. Each of these variables is coded as 1 if the state belongs to the relevant religious tradition and otherwise is coded as 0. It is not necessary to add a variable for "Other" states as such a variable is effectively included because those states are coded as 0 on the other four variables.[8]

Two variables are included to control for religious diversity: the percentage of the population of the largest religious denomination in the state, and the number of smaller denominations that constitute 5 percent or more of the country's population estimates.[9] I include these variables because, as discussed in Chapter 3, several studies link religious diversity to political phenomena.

Another important control is the nature of the regime. I use two variables from the Polity dataset to control for this phenomenon. The first is the Polity measure that measures the extent of democracy or autocracy in a state. It ranges from −10 to 10 with −10 being the most autocratic and 10 being the most democratic. The variable is based on the regulation, openness, and competitiveness of executive recruitment, constraints on the executive, and the regulation and competitiveness of political participation.[10] The second variable taken from the Polity dataset measures how many years a regime has persisted

---

[6] The log of per capita GDP is generally used instead of the original form of the variable because the difference between $1,000 and $2,000 a year, for example, is considered more important than the difference between $20,000 and $21,000 a year. In tests not presented here, regressions using the original GDP variable, as well as transformations of the infant mortality variable (its log and square) were similar to these results presented here but weaker. The UN's Human Development Index (HDI) provides similar results. This measure, along with several others, was not used here because data is missing for a large number of states.

[7] The particular versions of these variables used here are taken from the UN Statistics Division website at http://unstats.un.org/unsd/default.htm. The per capita GDP variable is available yearly. The infant mortality variable is available for 1990, 1995, and 2000. The version of this variable closest chronologically but not from a subsequent year to the regression in question was used.

[8] Because of this, if a dummy variable for "Other" states was included, the statistical software would remove one of the variables for religious tradition. Selecting one not to include is a research decision because it allows for a more consistent comparison across regressions.

[9] For more details on the RAS project's population estimates, see note 2 in Chapter 5.

[10] For more details see Jaggers & Gurr (1995) and the Polity project webpage at http://www.cidcm.umd.edu/.

without a change in the Polity measure, which represents a regime's political stability. Both of these measures are available yearly.

Finally, I use the log of a state's population in order to control for population size. This is because it is possible that states with small populations will have different methods of organizing their governments than larger states.

Data Analysis and Discussion

Overall the results from the multivariate analysis are consistent with the findings from the bivariate analysis with regard to the influence of specific religious

TABLE 4.19. *Multiple Regressions Predicting Official Support*

Independent variables	Model 1				
	1990	1993	1996	1999	2002
Majority Catholic	−.034	−.031	−.060	−.052	−.029
Majority Orthodox	.018	.139	.105	.121	.125
Maj. other Christian	−.013	.014	−.004	.001	.000
Majority Muslim	.298***	.222*	.234*	.229*	.236**
% Largest religion	.498***	.509***	.478***	.476***	.482***
# Minority religions	.025	.018	.005	.009	.035
Polity	.035	−.124	−.041	−.079	−.100
Regime stability	.052	.036	.014	−.013	−.036
Log population	−.063	−.048	−.050	−.034	−.033
Log per-capita GDP	.129	.197*	.183*	.224**	.226**
df	155	173	174	174	174
Adjusted r-squared	.397	.386	.359	.370	.367
	Model 2				
Majority Catholic	−.046	−.031	−.054	−.050	−.032
Majority Orthodox	−.001	.094	.078	.085	.093
Maj. other Christian	−.003	.026	.012	.021	.017
Majority Muslim	.310***	.232**	.247**	.238**	.245**
% Largest religion	.474***	.479***	.453***	.449***	.451***
# Minority religions	−.002	−.021	−.028	−.028	−.005
Polity	.002	−.127	−.029	−.062	−.084
Regime stability	.045	.062	.038	.020	−.001
Log population	−.078	−.073	−.072	−.062	−.062
Infant mortality	−.221**	−.204***	−.175*	−.202**	−.208**
df	155	173	174	174	174
Adjusted r-squared	.425	.394	.362	.371	.370

All values in the table are Beta Values. Means were substituted for missing data. For all dependent variables o means full SRAS.
* = Significance < .05
** = Significance < .01
*** = Significance < .001

TABLE 4.20. *Multiple Regressions Predicting General Restrictions*

Independent variables	Model 1				
	1990	1993	1996	1999	2002
Majority Catholic	−.208	−.207*	−.242*	−.205*	−.113
Majority Orthodox	.015	.125	.080	.120	.133
Maj. other Christian	−.151	−.191*	−.211*	−.206*	−.163
Majority Muslim	.192	.132	.095	.138	.148
% Largest religion	.234	.242*	.243*	.217	.137
# Minority religions	.065	.079	.090	.105	.086
Polity	−.076	−.260**	−.320***	−.359***	−.456***
Regime stability	.040	.035	.030	.030	.007
Log population	.167*	.151*	.174*	.195**	.220***
Log per-capita GDP	−.032	.112	.159	.161	.170*
df	155	173	174	174	174
Adjusted r-squared	.178	.268	.311	.352	.368
	Model 2				
Majority Catholic	−.238*	−.233*	−.257**	−.222*	−.127
Majority Orthodox	−.020	.069	.030	.074	.097
Maj. other Christian	−.156	−.186*	−.198*	−.192*	−.151
Majority Muslim	.190	.131	.103	.142	.152
% Largest religion	.246	.226	.222*	.198	.113
# Minority religions	.089	.065	.069	.087	.061
Polity	−.123	−.292***	−.326***	−.359***	−.451***
Regime stability	−.011	.011	.017	.027	.017
Log population	.177*	.142*	.160*	.180**	.201***
Infant mortality	−.140	−.236**	−.245***	−.223**	−.202**
df	155	173	174	174	174
Adjusted r-squared	.192	.301	.341	.374	.381

All values in the table are Beta Values. Means were substituted for missing data. For all dependent variables 0 means full SRAS.

* = Significance < .05
** = Significance < .01
*** = Significance < .001

traditions on GIR. They also consistently show that economically developed states have higher levels of GIR.

The regressions presented in Table 4.19 show a strong positive relationship between *official support* and economic development. Log-per-capita-GDP is positively associated with *official support* in all five regressions and significantly so for all the regressions except the one for 1990. Keeping in mind that the measure is negatively related to economic development, infant mortality reaffirms the positive relationship between *official support* and economic development in all five regressions. In addition, the variables measuring Muslim

TABLE 4.21. *Multiple Regressions Predicting Religious Discrimination*

Independent variables	Model 1				
	1990	1993	1996	1999	2002
Majority Catholic	−.302**	−.223*	−.226*	−.215*	−.162
Majority Orthodox	−.053	.116	.086	.142*	.199**
Maj. other Christian	−.239*	−.195*	−.211*	−.217**	−.176*
Majority Muslim	.228*	.210*	.166	.171	.179*
% Largest religion	.089	.095	.099	.078	.073
# Minority religions	−.089	−.084	−.072	−.068	−.033
Polity	−.081	−.264***	−.338***	−.368***	−.452***
Regime stability	.034	.107	.100	.089	.072
Log population	.161*	.126	.153*	.178**	.196***
Log per-capita GDP	.087	.109	.143	.166*	.204**
df	155	173	174	174	174
Adjusted r-squared	.271	.328	.372	.400	.438
	Model 2				
Majority Catholic	−.323**	−.248**	−.238**	−.227*	−.174*
Majority Orthodox	−.081	.060	.044	.101	.161*
Maj. other Christian	−.233*	−.190*	−.199*	−.202*	−.161*
Majority Muslim	.237*	.209*	.174	.176*	.185*
% Largest religion	.075	.079	.081	.058	.044
# Minority religions	−.101	−.098	−.091	−.089	−.065
Polity	−.125	−.296***	−.342***	−.364***	−.443***
Regime stability	.010	.083	.093	.094	.091
Log population	.153*	.118	.140*	.161**	.172**
Infant mortality	−.223**	−.234**	−.211**	−.204**	−.223***
df	155	173	174	174	174
Adjusted r-squared	.304	.361	.394	.415	.451

All values in the table are Beta Values. Means were substituted for missing data. For all dependent variables o means full SRAS.

* = Significance < .05
** = Significance < .01
*** = Significance < .001

majority and the proportion of the country that belongs to the largest religion are also significantly and positively associated with *official support* in all ten regressions.

The regressions for *general restrictions*, presented in Table 4.20, show a positive relationship between economic development and GIR, but it is not as strong as the relationship between *official support* and economic development. Log-per-capita-GDP is significantly associated with higher levels of *general restrictions* only in the regression for 2002. Infant mortality shows a positive relationship between *general restrictions* and economic development in all of

TABLE 4.22. *Multiple Regressions Predicting Religious Regulation*

Independent variables	Model 1				
	1990	1993	1996	1999	2002
Majority Catholic	−.375***	−.256*	−.240*	−.234*	−.197*
Majority Orthodox	−.176*	−.072	−.106	−.072	−.047
Maj. other Christian	−.365***	−.248**	−.213*	−.235**	−.179*
Majority Muslim	−.106	−.077	−.098	−.034	.045
% Largest religion	.036	.061	.073	.014	.044
# Minority religions	−.103	−.075	−.055	−.066	−.023
Polity	−.114	−.355***	−.409***	−.417***	−.453***
Regime stability	−.005	.054	.025	−.016	−.058
Log population	.234**	.199**	.222***	.253***	.273***
Log per-capita GDP	.032	.019	.057	.103	.124
df	155	173	174	174	174
Adjusted r-squared	.191	.255	.266	.312	.375
	Model 2				
Majority Catholic	−.405***	−.307**	−.276**	−.266**	−.220*
Majority Orthodox	−.214**	−.138	−.161*	−.124	−.088
Maj. other Christian	−.364***	−.250**	−.211**	−.227**	−.170*
Majority Muslim	−.102	−.089	−.100	−.035	.047
% Largest religion	.035	.060	.068	.002	.026
# Minority religions	−.096	−.062	−.051	−.068	−.035
Polity	−.168*	−.418***	−.436***	−.430***	−.459***
Regime stability	−.049	−.022	−.029	−.049	−.070
Log population	.236***	.208**	.225***	.249**	.262***
Infant mortality	−.215*	−.266***	−.222**	−.227**	−.203**
Df	155	173	174	174	174
Adjusted r-squared	.226	.306	.300	.344	.396

All values in the table are Beta Values. Means were substituted for missing data. For all dependent variables 0 means full SRAS.
* = Significance < .05
** = Significance < .01
*** = Significance < .001

the regressions except the one for 1990. Catholic and "Other Christian" states have significantly lower levels of *general restrictions* in many, but not all, of the regressions. The Polity variable is significantly and negatively associated with *general restrictions* for all of the regressions from 1993 onward. This means that autocratic governments have more GIR than do democratic ones. Finally, countries with larger populations tend to have more GIR. This relationship is significant for all of the regressions for *general restrictions*.

The regressions for *religious discrimination,* presented in Table 4.21, show results similar to those for *general restrictions.* Log-per-capita-GDP is

TABLE 4.23. *Multiple Regressions Predicting Religious Legislation*

Independent variables	Model 1				
	1990	1993	1996	1999	2002
Majority Catholic	−.145	−.114	−.128	−.116	−.082
Majority Orthodox	−.081	−.019	−.075	−.044	−.036
Maj. other Christian	−.071	−.006	−.041	−.030	−.017
Majority Muslim	.520***	.424***	.439***	.459***	.499***
% Largest religion	.279**	.272**	.262**	.268**	.293**
# Minority religions	.022	.005	.017	.035	.092
Polity	−.088	−.280***	−.220***	−.234***	−.232***
Regime stability	.046	.011	.011	−.007	−.043
Log population	.122*	.143*	.150**	.171**	.176***
Log per-capita GDP	.287***	.372***	.347***	.371***	.381***
df	155	173	174	174	174
Adjusted r-squared	.525	.517	.508	.525	.540
	Model 2				
Majority Catholic	−.140	−.092	−.095	−.089	−.067
Majority Orthodox	−.084	−.078	−.099	−.077	−.067
Maj. other Christian	−.045	.017	−.009	.004	.012
Majority Muslim	.546***	.447***	468***	.478***	.516***
% Largest religion	.221*	.215*	.211*	.223*	.240*
# Minority religions	−.056	−.076	−.056	−.036	.016
Polity	−.108	−.258***	−.177**	−.190**	−.189**
Regime stability	.083	.094	.096	.083	.047
Log population	.083	.093	.103	.118*	.120*
Infant mortality	−.299***	−.280***	−.229***	−.239***	−.260***
df	155	173	174	174	174
Adjusted r-squared	.544	.495	.480	.489	.506

All values in the table are Beta Values. Means were substituted for missing data. For all dependent variables 0 means full SRAS.
* = Significance < .05
** = Significance < .01
*** = Significance < .001

significantly associated with higher levels of *religious discrimination* in the regressions for 1999 and 2002. Infant mortality shows a positive relationship between *religious discrimination* and economic development in all five of the regressions. Catholic and "Other Christian" states have significantly lower levels of *religious discrimination* in all of the regressions. Muslim states engage in higher levels of *religious discrimination* in six of the ten regressions. Autocratic states, as measured by the Polity variable, have significantly higher levels of GIR from 1993 onward. Finally, countries with larger populations tend to

TABLE 4.24. *Multiple Regressions Predicting General GIR*

Independent variables	Model 1				
	1990	1993	1996	1999	2002
Majority Catholic	−.260**	−.198*	−.222**	−.205*	−.141
Majority Orthodox	−.052	.083	.031	.072	.099
Maj. other Christian	−.226*	−.170*	−.188*	−.191**	−.160*
Majority Muslim	.262**	.199*	.185*	.211**	.241**
% Largest religion	.364**	.369***	.368***	.348***	.336***
# Minority religions	.012	−.003	.015	.026	.062
Polity	−.058	−.330***	−.336***	−.375***	−.443***
Regime stability	.063	.076	.056	.037	.005
Log population	.126	.117*	.139*	.168**	.185***
Log per-capita GDP	.112	.209**	.239**	.271***	.290***
df	155	173	174	174	174
Adjusted r-squared	.383	.468	.486	.527	.556
	Model 2				
Majority Catholic	−.288**	−.223**	−.230**	−.217**	−.156*
Majority Orthodox	−.091	.006	−.024	.013	.047
Maj. other Christian	−.218*	−.160*	−.167*	−.167*	−.138*
Majority Muslim	.274**	.203**	.200*	.220**	.250***
% Largest religion	.347**	.338***	.335***	.316***	.295***
# Minority religions	−.003	−.036	−.022	−.011	.016
Polity	−.117	−.363***	−.331***	−.364***	−.428***
Regime stability	.029	.066	.064	.056	.034
Log population	.116	.097	.114*	.138**	.150**
Infant mortality	−.297***	−.333***	−.296**	−.306***	−.308***
df	155	173	174	174	174
Adjusted r-squared	.443	.524	.519	.554	.578

All values in the table are Beta Values. Means were substituted for missing data. For all dependent variables 0 means full SRAS.
* = Significance < .05
** = Significance < .01
*** = Significance < .001

have more GIR. This relationship is significant for all of the regressions except those for 1993.

The regressions for *religious regulation*, presented in Table 4.22, show a pattern similar to those of *general restrictions* and *religious discrimination*. Log-per-capita-GDP is not significantly associated with *religious regulation* for any of the regressions but infant mortality shows a positive and significant relationship between economic development and *religious regulation* for all five regressions. Catholic and "Other Christian" states have significantly lower levels of *religious regulation* in all of the regressions. Orthodox Christian states

TABLE 4.25. *Number of Significant Relationships in Multiple Regressions, Tables 4.19 to 4.24*

	1990		1993		1996		1999		2002	
	−	+	−	+	−	+	−	+	−	+
Majority Catholic	7	—	8	—	8	—	8	—	5	—
Majority Orthodox	2	—	—	—	—	—	—	1	—	2
Maj. other Christian	5	—	8	—	8	—	8	—	6	—
Majority Muslim	—	8	—	5	—	5	—	5	—	8
% Largest religion	—	5	—	6	—	7	—	4	—	5
# Minority religions	—	—	—	—	—	—	—	—	—	—
Polity	1	—	9	—	9	—	9	—	9	—
Regime stability	—	—	—	—	—	—	—	—	—	—
Log population	—	6	—	6	—	9	—	10	—	10
Log per-capita GDP	—	1	—	3	—	3	—	4	—	5
Infant mortality	5	—	6	—	6	—	6	—	6	—

have lower levels of *religious regulation* in three of the regressions. Autocratic states, as measured by the Polity variable, have significantly higher levels of GIR in all of the regressions except for the 1990 regression for Model 1. Finally, countries with larger populations tend to have more GIR. This relationship is significant for all of the regressions for *religious regulation*.

The regressions for *religious legislation*, presented in Table 4.23, show a stronger relationship between economic development and GIR than do any of the other RAS variables. Economic development is positively and significantly associated with *religious legislation* for all ten regressions. States with a Muslim majority and states in which a larger proportion of the country belongs to the majority religion have significantly higher levels of *religious legislation* in all ten regressions. Autocratic states have significantly higher levels of GIR from 1993 onward. States with larger populations have significantly higher levels of *religious legislation* in seven of the regressions.

The regressions for *general GIR*, presented in Table 4.24, not surprisingly are consistent with the previous five sets of regressions. Log-per-capita-GDP is significantly and positively associated with *general GIR* for all of the regressions other than the one for 1990. The infant mortality variable reveals a significant and positive relationship between economic development and *general GIR* for all five regressions. Catholic and "Other Christian" states have significantly lower levels of *general GIR* in all of the regressions and Muslim states have significantly higher levels of *general GIR* in all of the regressions. Autocratic states have significantly higher levels of GIR from 1993 onward. Finally, states with larger populations have significantly higher levels of *general GIR* in seven of the regressions.

In order to compile all of the results from these regressions into an easier format to assimilate, in Table 4.25 I created a listing of how often each variable was statistically significant and whether these significant relationships were positive or negative ones. For each variable for each year there were a total of 12 regressions, except in the case of economic development, where there were 6 for each variable.

The results show that economic development is strongly associated with higher levels of GIR. However this relationship proves stronger when using infant mortality than when using log-per-capita-GDP. Infant mortality was significantly associated with GIR in all but one of 30 regressions. In contrast, log-per-capita-GDP was significantly associated with GIR in 16 of 30 regressions. Nevertheless there are no significant negative relationships between log-per-capita-GDP and the RAS variables and only in 1 regression was there a non-significant but negative relationship. Thus a conclusion that more economic developed countries tend to have higher levels of GIR is clearly supported by this analysis.

The results for specific religious traditions are consistent with those of the bivariate analysis. Muslim states have higher levels of GIR in 31 of 60 regressions. These results are especially strong for *official support, religious legislation,* and *general GIR.* Catholic states have lower GIR in 36 regressions, and "Other Christian" states have lower GIR in 35 of the regressions. Orthodox Christian states show 2 regressions with a negative significant relationship and three with a positive significant relationship. Overall, these results support the prediction that different religious traditions will have different levels of GIR. They also support the prediction that Muslim states will have higher levels of GIR. In nearly all of the regressions, either Muslim states have significantly higher levels of GIR or Christian states have lower GIR. In several regressions both of these relationships occur.

Interestingly, the results regarding Muslim majority states are linked to the proportion of a state's population that belongs to the majority religion. States with a larger percentage of the population belonging to the majority religion tend to have more GIR in 27 of the regressions. This is not particularly surprising because we would expect that states with more homogeneous populations would have less need for SRAS since there are fewer members of religious minorities to object to such GIR. However, this seems to be the case mostly for Muslim majority states. Of the 27 regressions where this factor is statistically significant, only 3 of them are states where Muslim majorities are not significantly associated with more GIR. Thus, a more exact conclusion based on these results is that the more homogeneously Muslim a state is, the higher are the levels of GIR.

However, there is a possibility that this particular relationship may have direction of causality issues. That is, it may be that Muslim states that have high levels of GIR are religiously homogeneous due to the high levels of GIR. Many Muslim states place extreme restrictions on minority religions, and there is ample anecdotal evidence that these restrictions often motivate non-Muslims to emigrate. In some cases, for example in Saudi Arabia and the Maldives, all non-Muslim religions are illegal, with some exceptions for foreign workers, visitors, and diplomats. Also, as is shown in Table 4.11, Muslim states are the most likely to criminalize membership in a minority religion.

Not surprisingly, democracies tend to have more SRAS and autocracies more GIR. One would expect the concept of civil liberties, including religious freedom, as well as the concept of SRAS to be stronger in democratic states. However, (as is discussed in Chapter 11) these results do not mean that democracies have no GIR, just less, on average, than autocratic states. This relationship is significant in 37 of the regressions.

Finally, states with larger populations tend to have significantly higher levels of GIR in 41 of the regressions.

CONCLUSIONS

Even when viewed narrowly as applying only to government behavior and structure, and assuming that the results do not in any way impact on conclusions regarding the motivation behind GIR, the results presented here support some important conclusions. The most important of these results are presented in Table 4.26, which is based on the predictions discussed in Chapter 2.

No matter one's perspective on the data, GIR remains ubiquitous throughout the world. No matter how one defines and operationalizes SRAS, a large majority of the world's states do not have it. Thus, as measured by the RAS variables, GIR remains a significant factor across the globe.

Yet, GIR is not a static phenomenon. Many aspects of GIR fluctuated in both directions between 1990 and 2002, but for the most part the overall direction of change was toward more GIR. That is, from 1990 to 2002 there are more states in which GIR increased than in which it decreased. Also, while there were temporary decreases in the average levels of some of the GIR variables, both in general and for specific religious traditions, in all cases the average levels of the RAS variables showed nearly the same level of GIR or more GIR in 2002 than in 1990.

Yet these fluctuations were complex ones. In 32 states some aspects of GIR increased while others decreased. The timespan covered by the RAS data is relatively small in the scheme of processes that likely take centuries to play out. Accordingly, it is possible that the shifts in the average level of GIR between 1990 and 2002 are part of a larger pattern that includes both ebbs and peaks in GIR. Put differently, while there is a documented rise in GIR during the 1990 to 2002 period, the argument that some aspects of the religious economy are secularizing and some aspects are sacralizing is more strongly supported by the data than any prediction regarding the overall increase or decrease in religion's influence, even when applied narrowly to GIR.

Be that as it may, the results presented here call modernization-secularization theory into serious question. The theories predict a significant and general decline in religion's influence in society and politics. Yet the results presented here show that religion remains a significant influence in at least one aspect of the religious economy. Even if one assumes that there has been a long-term decline in GIR and that much of the current GIR is a reaction against declining religiosity or government attempts to repress religion, the fact remains that very few states have no GIR. Furthermore, a large majority of them have sufficient GIR that their regimes cannot be said to have SRAS based on all of the definitions and operationalizations of the concept used in this study.

This study used seven separate operational definitions of SRAS. The strictest, absolute-SRAS, shows that only the USA has SRAS. However, some of these seven definitions allow states to become considerably entangled in religion before they are considered not to have SRAS. For example, based on the operationalization of the "exclusion of ideals" definition, a state can do all of the following and still be considered to have SRAS:

- give some religions more official recognition or support than others;
- place legal limitations on some religions;
- engage in the most severe forms of 3 of the types of *religious discrimination* listed in Chapter 3 against all minorities or in as many as 10 of less severe forms of these types of *religious discrimination* for some religious minorities;
- engage in the most severe forms of 3 of the types of *religious regulation* listed in Chapter 3 or as many as 10 of them in their less severe forms;
- legislate any or all of the 33 types of *religious legislation* listed in Chapter 3 except for the 10 types that are specifically listed as violating this definition of SRAS;
- score as high as 30 on the *general GIR* variable.

Most would consider a state that does all of this a state that does not have SRAS. Yet, in 2002 only 10.9 percent of states can be said to have SRAS based on this definition. Using the most lenient operationalization of the "neutral political concern" definition, which is actually stricter on all of the items except the one for *religious legislation* (it allows up to five laws from the list with no restriction on which laws), 22.3 percent of states can be considered to have SRAS.

Given this, it is unlikely that any operationalization of SRAS that would find acceptance even among a significant minority of scholars would show anywhere close to a majority of states having SRAS. Put differently, some of the operationalizations used here allow a considerable amount of GIR before a state is said not to have SRAS to the extent that many would consider them to be unrealistically tolerant of GIR. Even these definitions showed only a small minority of states as having SRAS in 2002.

Another related result is that economic development is linked to more GIR. However, it is possible to argue that this is because modernization causes people to become less religious and governments are reacting to protect this dwindling religiosity through the legislation of religious behavior that was once enforced by social norms. Then again, as is discussed in more detail in Chapter 12, this implies that even if religiosity is dropping, religion remains influential in other aspects of the religious economy. This continuing influence is inconsistent with the predictions of modernization-secularization theory.

TABLE 4.26. Review of Results as They Relate to Predictions Discussed in Chapter 2

Prediction	Result	Explanation
Predictions based on modernization and secularization theory		
There will be a significant and monolithic drop in GIR over time: structural level.	False	The structural-level variables – *official GIR* and *general restrictions* – were mostly stable over time but increased slightly between 1990 and 2002. This was mostly consistent across religious traditions. For a summary of these results see Table 4.9.
There will be a significant and monolithic drop in GIR over time: government policy level.	False	The policy-level variables – *religious discrimination, religious regulation,* and *religious legislation* – all rose significantly between 1990 and 2002. This result was fully consistent across religious traditions. For a summary of these results see Table 4.9.
There will be a significant and monolithic drop in GIR over time: general patterns.	False	*General GIR* increased significantly between 1990 and 2002. This was consistent across all religious traditions except Catholicism. In Catholic states *general GIR* dropped 0.1% – a negligible drop. For details see Figures 4.6a and 4.6b.
Economic modernization will result in lower GIR.	False	Economic modernization is significantly linked to higher levels of GIR. This relationship became stronger between 1990 and 2002. For a summary of these results see Table 4.25.
SRAS will be common.	False	No matter how the term SRAS is defined and measured a large majority of countries do not have SRAS. This result is consistent across religious traditions. For details see Tables 4.17 and 4.18.
Predictions based on religious denomination		
Religious tradition will have an impact on GIR.	True	Each religious tradition examined here had a unique pattern of GIR including scores on the various GIR variables and nuances in the patterns of change over time in these variables. For details see Tables 4.7 and 4.9.

Prediction	Result	Explanation
Predictions based on religious denomination		
Muslim countries will have more GIR than non-Muslim countries.	Mostly True	Based on mean scores Muslim countries consistently have the highest levels of GIR. The highest scoring countries on the GIR variables are mostly Muslim countries. However, Orthodox Christian countries are the least likely to be among the lowest scoring countries on the GIR variables. For details see Table 4.7.
Catholic states will have more GIR than "other Christian" states.	Mixed	This is true for *official GIR, general restrictions, religious legislation,* and *general GIR* but not for *religious discrimination* and *religious legislation.* For details see Table 4.7. ("Other Christian" states serve as a surrogate variable for Protestant states in this evaluation.)
Christian states will have less GIR then non-Christian states.	Mixed	Muslim states have more GIR. States that are neither Muslim nor Christian ("other" states) have less GIR than at least one category of Christian state on all variables other than *religious regulation.* For details see Table 4.7.
Other important findings not linked to predictions presented in Chapter 2		

Democratic states have less GIR. For a summary of these results see Table 4.25. (See Chapter 11 for further analysis showing that, while having lower mean levels of GIR, few democracies have SRAS based on any of the operationalizations of SRAS used in this study.)

GIR is more common in states with religiously homogeneous populations. This is true especially of Muslim majority states. For a summary of these results see Table 4.25.

States with larger populations tend to have significantly higher levels of GIR. For a summary of these results see Table 4.25.

The results also show that other factors, including religious tradition regime, and several demographic factors, have a significant impact on GIR. The results for religious traditions, as summarized in Table 4.26, are mixed with regard to the predications that exist in the literature.

These results also speak to the nature of democracy. On one hand, democracies are associated with lower levels of GIR, but, as is demonstrated in Chapter 11 GIR still exists in most democratic regimes. Also, we normally think of the 1990 to 2002 period as one characterized by democratization. These results demonstrate this period is also characterized by an increase in GIR. This implies that democratization has not necessarily meant liberalization in the religious sense. That is, states that have adopted democratic systems of governance do not necessarily have liberal policies toward the religious sector.

While the results presented here are significant, they are limited by a few factors. First, despite everything discussed to date, GIR is only one aspect of the religious economy, which includes complex and multifaceted intersections between religion on one hand and politics and society on the other. Second, the RAS variables are better at measuring what governments do than why they do it. Third, there is an incredible diversity in patterns of GIR. This diversity exists both within and between world regions and the world's major religious traditions. For instance, the relationship between the state and Islam differs considerably between regions. The patterns of GIR in Muslim majority states in the Middle East, for example, are very different from those in the former Soviet bloc. They are also different from state to state within these regions, even when looking only at Muslim states.

Based on all of this, no general analysis of the composite RAS variables can give us a full understanding the place of GIR in this religious economy. Yet, as noted at the beginning of this chapter, it is a good starting point for a full discussion on the topic. Chapters 5 to 10 examine the extent of GIR in each of 175 governments included in this study.

In all, this study has yet to paint the full picture of the role of GIR in the religious economy, assuming that a complete and accurate picture is even possible. However, a good canvas has arguably been created in a good frame. As is discussed in more detail in Chapters 2 and 12, the results presented here do fit into a larger picture that can be described in at least a general sense. In this larger picture some facets of the complex religious economy are becoming stronger, more common, and more influential while others are becoming weaker, less common, and less influential. This dynamic, vibrant, and evolving religious economy is not consistent with the predictions of secularization-modernization theory.

5

Western Democracies

The previous chapter provides an analysis of global trends in government involvement in religion (GIR) and separation of religion and state (SRAS). This chapter and the following five chapters are intended to provide a more detailed look at the relationship between religion and state. This includes an examination of each of the 62 types of GIR measured by the RAS dastaset for each of the 175 countries included in the dataset.

SOME GENERAL COMMENTS ON THE REGION BY REGION ANALYSIS

This chapter examines GIR and SRAS in Western democracies. The RAS project divides the world into six regions based on a previous division by a large-scale data collection project – the Minorities at Risk dataset, which focuses on ethnic conflict.[1] The following five chapters each focus on another of these world regions. This use of world regions is appropriate as the countries within each of these six world regions share many cultural traits and tend to have a common history.

The regional analysis in these chapters is intended to provide a snapshot of the extent of GIR for each world region in 2002 as well as for each of the 175 individual countries included in the RAS dataset. This includes a listing of each country's score on the *official GIR*, *general restrictions*, and *general GIR* variables and a listing of which countries engage in each of the 60 specific types of *religious discrimination*, *religious regulation*, and *religious legislation*. The population assessments are based on RAS project estimates, which make use of general sources as well as country specific sources.[2]

---

[1] For more on the Minorities at Risk project see the project website at www.cidcm.umd.ecu/.

[2] The RAS project's population estimates are based on Barrett, Kurian, and Johnson (2001), the *CIA World Factbook* (available at http://www.cia.gov/cia/publications/factbook/), and country-specific sources. In general, an average of all available sources was used, weighted for estimated reliability. This weighting was based on a general impression that Barrett et al. (2001) tends to be

This analysis also includes a brief description of the situation in each of the 175 countries included in the RAS dataset.[3] The purpose of these descriptions beyond their face value is twofold. First, in order to give the reader a better understanding of the facts behind the numbers they provide a brief overview of the raw information that was translated into the RAS variables analyzed in this study. Accordingly they cover the 1990 to 2002 period covered by the RAS dataset but are generally current through the end of 2004.[4] Second, the quantitative analyses in this study tend to focus on trends and similarities. Yet there is a considerable amount of diversity in state religion policies across the globe. These descriptions help to bring this out. These chapters also develop a taxonomy for the placement of states into categories based on the extent and nature of GIR in these states. This taxonomy helps to guide the discussion of SRAS and GIR in these states.

Space considerations make an analysis of change over time in the 62 specific types of GIR analyzed here impossible on a country by country basis. Chapter 11 includes an analysis of change over time controlling for world region and major religious traditions. This creates a framework for analyzing the data using three levels of analysis. The global picture provided in Chapter 4 focused on overall trends. Chapters 5 through 10 provide a more detailed examination of the diversity of the relationships between religion and state that exist in different states. The intermediate-level analysis in Chapter 11 identifies trends that are bigger than can be seen at the state level but are specific to certain groupings of states and, therefore, do not fully present themselves at the global level of analysis.

WESTERN DEMOCRACIES

For the purposes of this study, the Western democracies are Western Europe, North America, Australia, and New Zealand. This definition of the West is

optimistic in its estimate of the number of Christians in some states. This impression is based on the fact that in most cases Barrett et al. (2001) counted more Christians than do other sources, combined with the fact that the study focuses on Christianity. Additional information on religious demographics and religious congregations can be found at http://www.adherents.com/ and http://www.worldchristiandatabase.org.

[3] These descriptions are necessarily brief due to space considerations. They are based on more extensive reports that were prepared in a country by country basis by the RAS project's research assistants: Hana Bagelman, John Daley, Rifka Dzodin, Aaron Ettengoff, Dalia Ganz, David Yisorel Halevi, Oren Keston, Tamara Lafair, Marcelle Last, Rebecca Scharbach, Doni Schuman, Valeria Schefter, Hagai Stern, Donna Susser, and Shira Traison. These reports use general sources including US State Department reports, Barrett et al. (2001), reports by several human rights organizations, country-specific academic writings, and media reports taken mostly from the Lexis/Nexis database.

[4] Given the enormity of the task of properly updating the information for each of 175 countries, it was not possible to provide country by country descriptions more recent than this. For more details and more recent information on each country see the general sources noted in the previous note as well as Wood (2005) and Richardson (2003).

similar to other definitions, for example that of Samuel Huntington.[5] Basically it comprises those states that are commonly held to have a Western culture, were not part of the Soviet bloc during the Cold War, and that have established traditions of democratic government.

The evidence presented here shows that even though Western democracies share a certain level of homogeneity with regard to regime, culture, and history, there is a wide diversity of approaches toward religion. This diversity is reflected in the information presented in Tables 5.1, 5.2, 5.3, and 5.4. For example, most Western democracies have in common that they support religion to some extent, but the nature and extent of that support varies considerably. Of the 27 governments examined here, nine have official religions. An additional 13 governments support one or more religion and one state, France, has a tendency to regulate all religion. Thus, only four Western states neither endorse nor are hostile to religion based on the *official GIR* variable.

Sixteen Western governments place significant limitations on at least some minority religions. Of the 16 categories of restrictions included in the RAS data, 9 of them exist in at least one Western democracy. The most common, the requirement for minority religions to register with the government, exists in 12 Western states. This category was only coded if only minority religions are required to register or in cases where all religious groups must register but some or all minority groups have difficulty in registering. Six states place some form of restriction on formal religious organizations. Five states restrict proselytizing by some religions. Several other types of restrictions exist in from one to four Western democracies.

The only type of GIR that is relatively rare in Western democracies is government regulation of the majority religion. Of the 11 types of regulation examined by the RAS project, only 3 exist in Western democracies and 2 of these exist in only 1 state and the third in 2 states.

Religious legislation, in contrast, is common in Western democracies. Of the 33 types of religious legislation examined by the RAS project, 25 exist in at least one Western democracy. Also, with the exception of the USA where none of these types of legislation exist, all Western democracies have between 2 and 10 of these 33 types of legislation on the books with an overall average of about 6 per state. The most common form of *religious legislation* is financial support for religious education, which exists in all Western democracies other than the USA. In 22 of these states courses on religion are taught in public schools. Other forms of religious legislation that exist in at least 10 states are government collection of religious taxes, government funding of clergy, the presence in the government of a department dealing with religious affairs, and the requirement for all religions to register. There are also 16 additional types of legislation which exist in 9 or fewer states in the region.

---

[5] Huntington (1993; 1996).

TABLE 5.1. *Separation of Religion and State in Western Democracies in 2002, Basic Information*

Country	Maj. religion	% Maj. rel.	# Min. groups with 5% of population	Official GIR	General restrictions	General GIR
Andorra	Catholic	89.0	0	One official religion	No limitations	23.13
Australia	Christian	28.6	3	Accommodation	No limitations	2.50
Austria	Catholic	78.0	3	Cooperation	Legal limitations	24.25
Belgium	Catholic	80.9	1	Cooperation	Legal limitations	25.50
Canada	Christian	41.8	2	Accommodation	No limitations	3.52
Cyprus, Greek	Orthodox	78.0	1	Cooperation	Practical limitations	16.13
Cyprus, Turkish	Islam, Sunni	99.0	0	Cooperation	Practical limitations	16.96
Denmark	Protestant	86.3	1	One official religion	No limitations	26.04
Finland	Protestant	89.0	1	Multiple official religions	Legal limitations	32.88
France	Catholic	69.6	2	Separationist	Legal limitations	22.92
Germany	Christian	35.7	2	Cooperation	Practical limitations	19.88
Greece	Orthodox	93.0	0	One official religion	Practical limitations	33.31
Iceland	Protestant	99.0	0	One official religion	Practical limitations	29.79
Ireland	Catholic	92.0	0	Civil religion	No limitations	15.75
Italy	Catholic	85.0	1	Cooperation	No limitations	13.00
Liechtenstein	Catholic	80.0	1	One official religion	Practical limitations	27.50
Luxembourg	Catholic	97.0	0	Cooperation	No limitations	10.50
Malta	Catholic	91.0	0	One official religion	No limitations	25.63
Netherlands	Christian	34.5	3	Accommodation	No limitations	1.25
New Zealand	Protestant	62.6	3	Cooperation	No limitations	10.50
Norway	Protestant	95.2	0	One official religion	No limitations	25.83
Portugal	Catholic	97.0	0	Civil religion	Practical limitations	21.94
Spain	Catholic	99.0	0	Civil religion	Legal limitations	27.63
Sweden	Protestant	84.0	0	Cooperation	No limitations	12.17
Switzerland	Christian	46.1	1	Cooperation	Practical limitations	20.50
UK	Protestant	53.0	3	Multiple official religions	Practical limitations	27.67
USA	Protestant	61.8	3	Accommodation	No limitations	0.00

TABLE 5.2. *Religious Discrimination in Western Democracies in 2002*

Country	Build or repair places of worship	Access to places of worship	Forced observance	Formal orgs.	Publications	Clergy	Proselytizing	Register	Other	Total
Andorra										0
Australia										0
Austria				x				x		2
Belgium				x			x			2
Canada			x							1
Cyprus, Greek								x		1
Cyprus, Turkish								x		1
Denmark								x		1
Finland				x				x		2
France	x			x			x	x		4
Germany	x	x			x		x	x	x	6
Greece							x	x	x	3
Iceland								x		1
Ireland										0
Italy								x		1
Liechtenstein										0
Luxembourg										0
Malta										0
Netherlands										0
New Zealand										0
Norway	x	x								2
Portugal										0
Spain	x							x		2
Sweden									x	1
Switzerland				x	x	x	x	x		5
UK				x						1
USA										0
TOTAL	4	2	1	6	2	1	5	12	3	36

The following categories of religious discrimination were not included in this table because none of the Western democracies engage in these practices: public observance; schools and education; arrest, detention and harassment; materials; personal status; conversions; and forced conversions.

TABLE 5.3. *Religious Regulation in Western Democracies in 2002*

	Political parties	Public display	Other restrictions	Total
Andorra				0
Australia				0
Austria				0
Belgium				0
Canada		x		1
Cyprus, Greek				0
Cyprus, Turkish				0
Denmark				0
Finland				0
France				0
Germany				0
Greece			x	1
Iceland				0
Ireland				0
Italy				0
Liechtenstein				0
Luxembourg				0
Malta				0
Netherlands				0
New Zealand				0
Norway				0
Portugal	x		x	2
Spain				0
Sweden				0
Switzerland				0
UK				0
USA				0
TOTAL	1	1	2	4

The following categories of religious restrictions were not included in this table because none of the Western democracies engage in these practices: arrest, detention, and harassment; organizations and political parties; public observance; publications; speech; access to places of worship; arrest of nonleaders; and public gatherings.

This summary of the extent of GIR in Western democracies reveals a considerable diversity in the extent and nature of GIR. However, the summary is lacking in enough detail to fully answer several important questions: Why and how does religion persist in Western democracies? Is the relationship between religion and state similar in all of these states or does this relationship take different forms in different states – that is, are the differences between Western democracies differences in the extent of GIR or differences in the kind of GIR?

The rest of this chapter is devoted to examining these questions. In order to accomplish this I divide countries into categories of GIR and briefly examine the status of religion in each state based on two principles. The first is the official level of government support for the majority religion and the second is government treatment of minority religions.

The categories of GIR used here are based on the *official GIR* measure described in Chapter 3 but add more detail in order to differentiate between the types of official religions. I describe and define each of the particular categories of this taxonomy in the section in which the first government that fits into this category appears. The overall categorization of the states in this region is presented in Table 5.5.

ACTIVE STATE RELIGIONS

Among Western democracies there are six states with active state religions. The term active state religion is defined here as where the state has one or more official religions *and* the state actively promotes the state religion through legislating aspects of the religion, granting it control over some aspects of law, requiring religious education for members of the religion, funding the religion often through religious tax collection, and support for clergy and seminary education. In these cases, the state religion maintains a level of independence from the government and the government clearly sets national policy. Other than Malta, all of the Western democracies in this category also place some restrictions on minority religions.[6]

No Restrictions on Minorities

Malta

Chapter 1, section 2, of Malta's constitution makes Catholicism the state religion and mandates that the Church has "the duty and the right to teach which principles are right and which are wrong," and that state school compulsory education must include the study of the Roman Catholic Apostolic

---

[6] The following are used as general sources for the country reports presented in this and subsequent chapters: Morigi, et al. (2000); Amore (1995); Barret et al. (2000); U.S. Department of State International Religious Freedom Reports 2000–2006 and Human Rights Reports, 1994 to 2006; UN Abortion policies webpage at http://www.un.org/esa/population/publications/abortion/profiles.htm; "Abortion in Law History and Religion," *Childbirth by Choice Trust*, 1995, http://www.cbctrust.com/homepage.html; "Religious Freedom World Report," *International Coalition for Religious Freedom*, http://www.religiousfreedom.com/wrpt/Europe/ireland.htm; www.religioustolerance.org; "Freedom in the World," *Freedom House*, http://www.freedomhouse.org; www.religlaw.org; World Religions and Cultures: http://wrc.lingnet.org/; "Religious Freedom in the Majority Islamic Countries, 1998 Report," Aid to the Church in Need, http://www.alleanzacattolica.org/acs/acs_english/acs_index.htm; "Handbook on Religious Liberty Around the World," http://religiousfreedom.lib.virginia.edu/rihand. Subsequent notes refer to additional sources used in the marked country report.

TABLE 5.4. *Religious Legislation in Western Democracies in 2002*

	Personal status	Public dress	Blasphemy	Censorship	Close businesses	Blue laws	Optional education	Mandatory education	Fund education	Fund Rel. charity	Taxes	Fund clergy	Other rel. funding
Andorra							x		x			x	
Australia					x				x				
Austria							x		x		x		
Belgium		x			x		x		x	x	x	x	
Canada		x					x		x				x
Cyprus, Greek							x		x				
Cyprus, Turkish							x		x				x
Denmark						x	x		x	x	x	x	
Finland							x		x	x	x	x	
France		x							x	x			
Germany		x					x		x	x	x	x	
Greece				x			x		x	x	x	x	
Iceland							x		x				
Ireland			x		x		x		x				
Italy							x		x		x	x	x
Liechtenstein							x		x				
Luxembourg							x		x			x	
Malta							x		x	x	x		
Netherlands									x	x			
New Zealand					x				x				
Norway								x	x			x	
Portugal							x		x			x	
Spain		x					x		x		x	x	
Sweden	x							x	x		x		x
Switzerland		x	x				x		x		x		
UK			x				x		x	x		x	
USA													
TOTAL	1	6	3	1	4	1	20	2	26	9	11	12	4

	Some clergy appointed	Gov. rel. dept.	Rel. position for gov. official	Gov. position for religious official	Religious requirements	Rel. courts	Legislature or cabinet	Abortion	Flag	Registration	Sects	Other	Total
Andorra	x		x										5
Australia			x										4
Austria		x						x		x	x		6
Belgium								x		x	x		10
Canada													4
Cyprus, Greek									x	x			3
Cyprus, Turkish									x	x			5
Denmark		x			x								9
Finland	x	x							x	x			9
France		x								x	x		6
Germany										x	x		7
Greece	x	x			x				x				9
Iceland									x	x			7
Ireland												x	6
Italy								x		x	x		6
Liechtenstein	x							x					4
Luxembourg													4
Malta		x				x		x	x				8
Netherlands													2
New Zealand								x					3
Norway	x	x	x		x		x		x				8
Portugal		x											4
Spain										x			7
Sweden											(x)		6
Switzerland		x											8
UK	x	x	x	x	x		x	x	x	x			10
USA													0
TOTAL	6	10	4	1	4	1	2	7	8	11	6	1	160

The following categories of religious legislation were not included in this table because none of the Western democracies engage in these practices: dietary laws; alcohol; inheritance; conversion; marriages; approve speeches; identity cards; and women.

TABLE 5.5. *Taxonomy of Western Democracies*

Separation of religion and state	Type of restrictions on minorities			
	None	Low (1–2)	Moderate (3–5)	High (6+)
Religious state	—	—	—	—
Active state religion	Malta	Denmark Finland Greece Iceland Norway	—	—
State-controlled religion	—	—	—	—
Historical / cultural state religion	Andorra Liechtenstein	United Kingdom	—	—
Preferred treatment for some religions or support for a particular tradition	Ireland Italy Luxembourg New Zealand Portugal	Austria Belgium Cyprus, Greek Cyprus, Turkish Spain Sweden	Switzerland	Germany
General support	—	—	—	—
Moderate separation	Australia	Canada	—	—
Nearly full separation (2 or less on legislation)	Netherlands USA	—	—	—
Hostility	—	—	France	—

Faith.[7] Section 40 protects religious freedom and provides that compulsory Catholic education will not be imposed on non-Catholics. Since 1991 the government and the Catholic Church have participated jointly in a foundation that funds Catholic schools.

Those who marry under the auspices of the Catholic Church are regulated through religious law. Family issues for such couples can be brought to either church tribunals or civil courts. Divorce is banned in Malta. In 1991 the government granted all religions the same privileges as the Catholic Church

---

[7] Unless otherwise noted, the discussions of constitutions in this and subsequent chapters are based on the copies of constitutions contained in the International Constitutional Law database (ICL) at http://www.oefre.unibe.ch/law/icl/ or the Religion and Law Research Consortium at http://www.religlaw.org/. In the event that these databases did not include an English-language version of a constitution for a particular country, an internet search was performed and, if possible, the country's embassy was contacted. This process yielded sufficient information on 149 constitutions among the 175 countries included in this study. Unless otherwise noted, the constitutions discussed here are those that were in force in 2002.

including the right to own property and for their clergy to perform marriages and other functions.

Malta's flag includes a cross in the upper left-hand corner. Abortion is illegal in Malta under all circumstances.[8]

Low Restrictions on Minorities

Denmark

Section 4 of the Danish constitution declares the Evangelical Lutheran Church the state religion and, "as such, it shall be supported by the State." Section 66 states that "the constitution of the Established Church shall be laid down by Statute."

The government collects taxes on behalf of the state Church. No other religious body receives government money in this manner. The government subsidizes the state Church's clergy's salaries and pensions. The Ministry of Ecclesiastical Affairs provides "administration, supervision, advisory services" to the state Church. The government has enacted Sunday observance legislation and the state flag includes a cross. However, the constitution provides for full religious freedom and states that "no one shall be liable to make personal contributions to any denomination other than the one to which he adheres."

All schools, including religious ones, receive government support and the state religion is taught in all public schools though, on parental request, students may opt out of these courses. Religious organizations other than the state Church must register with the government. Other than Scientologists, the government has never refused registration requests. Scientologists continue to operate with few restrictions.[9]

Finland

Section 6 of Finland's 1999 constitution bans discrimination on the basis of religion. Section 11 protects religious freedom and the right to profess or not profess a religion. Section 76 states that "provisions on the organization and administration of the Evangelic Lutheran Church are laid down in the Church Act." The Act states that laws regarding the internal affairs of the Church are ratified by parliament but can only be proposed by the Church itself.

Finland maintains two state churches, the Evangelical Lutheran Church and the Orthodox Church. The state churches record births, deaths, and marriages on behalf of the government for church members, but these services are also provided by the government. The state collects taxes on behalf of these churches from all church members but citizens are allowed to opt out of these

---

[8] Joe Vella, "Malta: The Mouse that Roars, New Ways for Old," http://www.searchmalta.com/ezine/mouse/newways.shtml; Ministry of Justice Malta, "Marriage Legacies Law," September 7, 1831, last amended 1975, http://justice.magnet.mt/dir2-laws/.

[9] Royal Danish Ministry of Foreign Affairs website, http://www.um.dk/english/danmark/danmarksbog/kap1/1-14.asp; http://www.km.dk/publikationer/thechurch.htm.

taxes. The state churches receive 2 percent of the proceeds of community taxes and the government finances the education of clergy.

Minority religions must register but the requirements are minimal. Registration has only been refused once, in 1998 to Scientologists. Religious instruction is standard in public schools. Until recently it was only available in the state religions. Based on a 2003 law, instruction in minority faiths will be made available. Students can also take courses in "philosophies of life" in place of the religion course. The Finnish flag includes a cross.

Recently there has been a trend of disengagement between the state churches and the government. In 1997 local church officials ceased being government officials and the churches began being responsible for their salaries. In 2003, the President of Finland ceased to be the one to officially appoint bishops and archbishops of the Evangelical Lutheran Church.[10]

Greece

Article 3 of the 1975 Greek constitution establishes the Greek Orthodox Church as "the prevailing religion in Greece." It also guarantees the Church's autonomy, designates the "Holy Synod of Bishops and the Parliament Holy Synod which emanates from the former" as the Church's governing body, and that the "text of the Holy Scriptures shall be maintained unaltered" and cannot be translated without the Church's permission. The government also recognizes the Orthodox Church's canon law.

Articles 33 and 59 require that the president and members of parliament take religious oaths of office. This oath refers to the Greek Orthodox faith but parliament members of other religions may alter the oath to be compatible with their religion. No such provision is made for the presidential oath. Article 14 of the constitution allows the state to seize newspapers and other publications on a number of grounds including "an offence against the Christian or any other known religion." Article 16 states that "the development of national and religious consciousness" is part of the government's obligations with regard to education.

The government subsidizes the Orthodox Church, including maintaining church buildings and salaries for clergy. The government also pays the salaries of the three official Muslim Muftis of Thrace, who are selected by the government based on the advice of a government-appointed panel of Muslims.

Religious instruction is mandatory in public schools for Greek Orthodox students, but students of other religions are exempt. A 1939 law prohibits the

[10] Seppo (1998); Juha Seppo, "The Current Condition of Church-State Relations in Finland," The Evangelical Lutheran Church of Finland website, http://www.evl.fi/english/church_for_ the_people/seppo.htm; Library of Congress, *Finland – A Country Study* (Washington, DC: Library of Congress, 1988), http://lcweb2.loc.gov/frd/cs/fitoc.html; Council of Europe Human Rights, http://www.humanrights.coe.int/Minorities/Eng/FrameworkConvention/StateReports/ 1999/finland/Article_8.htm; Finland Ministry of Education website, http://www.minedu.fi/ minedu/ministry/church_affairs.html; Virtual Finland: *Religion and Churches in Finland*, 1998, http://virtual.finland.fi/.

functioning of private schools in buildings owned by non-Orthodox religious foundations. However, this law is not enforced. The Greek flag contains a cross.

Although Article 13 of the constitution guarantees religious freedom, minority religions clearly have an inferior status in Greece. Article 13 also prohibits proselytizing by all religions, including the Greek Orthodox religion, but this is only enforced with regard to minority religions, especially Evangelical Christians and Mormons, who are often arrested for proselytizing. Article 13 also states that "the ministers of all religions are subject to the same obligations towards the State and to the same state supervision as the ministers of the established religion."

Only the Orthodox Church and the Muslim and Jewish religions are considered public persons in the law. All other religious organizations must organize as private entities. Those that do not are sometimes harassed by government officials. Until a 1998 decision of the European Court of Human Rights, minority religions needed the approval of the local Orthodox bishop in order to build a house of prayer. In 2000 the Ministry of Education and Religion denied the Scientologists a permit to build a house of prayer on the grounds that Scientology is not a religion. Also, obtaining permits to build or enlarge minority religion places of worship is often a difficult bureaucratic process.

Turkic Muslims have a special status in Greece based on the 1923 Treaty of Lausanne, which gives the Muslim community of Thrace charitable and social organizations as well as Islamic muftis (judges) who receive government salaries. In 1980 the government placed control of the Islamic charitable trusts in the hands of the muftis, which upset many Muslims because, through its power of appointment, this gave the Greek government indirect control over the trusts. Thrace's Muslims also have the right to Turkish-language education.[11]

Iceland

Article 62 of Iceland's constitution declares the Evangelical Lutheran Church the state Church. Article 79 requires a referendum before changing the status of the state Church. All other religious associations must register with the government in order to gain recognition. Article 63 protects this right subject to good morals and public order. All citizens who are 16 years or older must pay an annual church tax. Article 64 allows members of other recognized religions to direct their church tax to the University of Iceland. The government provides additional funds to the state Church, pays the salaries of 146 ministers of the Church, who are considered public employees, and operates parish churches throughout Iceland. Article 64 also states that no one may lose their civil rights due to their religion but religion cannot exempt one from generally applicable civil duties. Article 65 protects against discrimination on the basis of religion.

[11] Pollis (2002).

All public schools have mandatory education in Christianity. Formally, only the Minister of Education has the power to exempt students from this but individual schools usually grant informal exemptions. The state Church runs all cemeteries in Iceland. Iceland's flag contains a red and white cross on a blue background.

There is some movement toward additional separation between Iceland's government and Church. A 1998 law transferred the power to enact church law from Iceland's parliament to the Church Assembly.[12]

Norway

Article 2 of Norway's constitution establishes the Evangelical Lutheran Church as the state religion, but also guarantees religious freedom. Article 4 requires that the King shall at all times profess, uphold, and protect the Evangelical-Lutheran religion. Article 12 requires that more than half of the Council of Ministers (akin to a cabinet) profess the state religion, and Article 27 states that any member of the Council who is not a member of the state Church "shall not take part in proceedings on matters which concern the State Church." These proceedings in the past have included the appointment of the Church's bishops, but this power was transferred to the diocesan during the 1990s. Article 16 states that the King "ordains all public church services and public worship, all meetings and assemblies dealing with religious matters, and ensures that public teachers of religion follow the norms prescribed for them." Article 100 excludes willful contempt of religion from the right to a free press.

The state financially supports the state Church and other registered religions proportional to population. Registration of minority religions is necessary only in order to receive state funds. Since 1995 all students are required to take a course called Religious Knowledge and Education in Ethics, which covers most world philosophies and religions but focuses on Christianity. Until 1995 these classes focused on the state Church. The government includes a Ministry of Cultural and Church Affairs. The minister must be a member of the state Church. Norway's flag has a blue and white cross on a red background.

While the government generally guarantees religious freedom, there is tension with some religious minorities. For example, Muslims have had difficulty in obtaining permits to build mosques in areas where they are concentrated.

In 2002 a report commissioned by the National Council of the Church of Norway recommended a loosening of ties between church and state. The government has appointed a state-church commission to review the issue. In 2006 the commission recommended "that the existing state-church system be abolished."[13]

---

[12] Karl Sigurbjornsson, "The Church of Iceland, Past and Present," http://www.kirkjan.is/?english/church_of_iceland.

[13] Boyle & Sheen (1997: 352); Ministry of Cultural and Church Affairs website, http://odin.dep.no/kkd/engelsk/index-b-n-a.html.

HISTORICAL OR CULTURAL STATE RELIGION

The countries in this category all have official state religions, but other than this official designation their governments take few or no steps to support the religion more than they support any other religion. Other than funding for religious education and perhaps some other minor funding of religion, their involvement in religion tends to be symbolic, ceremonial, and generally a result of historical momentum rather than any active support for religion. Among Western democracies in this category, only the UK places any significant restrictions on minority religions.

No Restrictions on Minorities

Andorra

Article 11 of Andorra's constitution "guarantees the Roman Catholic Church free and public exercise of its activities and the preservation of the relations of special co-operation with the state in accordance with Andorran tradition." It "recognizes the full legal capacity of the bodies of the Roman Catholic Church which have legal status in accordance with their own rules." It "guarantees the freedom of ideas, religion, and cult" and that people don't have to disclose their beliefs. Finally, it states that the state may not limit these rights except "in the interests of public safety, order, health or morals or for the protection of the fundamental rights and freedoms of others."

There are no restrictions of any kind placed on minority religions and the government does not regulate the majority religion. Catholic education is provided in public schools, but only on an optional basis and after school hours or during periods reserved for elective classes. The teachers are Catholic clergy whose salaries are paid by the government. In 1998, a government attempt to end all religious education in public schools was successfully opposed by a parental group. The government pays a monthly stipend to each of the country's seven parishes for the continuation of the historical work of maintaining vital records including of births and marriages despite the fact that the country also has a civil registration system. Also, according to the constitution, one of the two official Princes of Andorra is the Spanish Bishop of La Seu d'Urgell. The other Prince is the President of France. Both Princes are represented through a delegate, and the country, in practice, is ruled by an elected parliament.

Liechtenstein

Article 37 of Liechtenstein's constitution designates the Catholic Church as the state Church and guarantees religious freedom. Article 38 provides protection for the property rights of all religious institutions and states that "the administration of church property in the parishes shall be regulated by a specific law; the agreement of the church authorities shall be sought before the law is enacted." Article 16 states that religious instruction in public schools "shall be given by church authorities." In the past this meant that only confessional Catholic and Protestant courses were available. A 2003 agreement with the Catholic Church created a new system where students are given the option of confessional classes or non-confessional classes on Ethics and Culture. Before 2003, students were granted exemptions from religious education upon parental request. The government funds the state Church as well as other religious organizations from the general budget. Abortion is legal only in order to preserve the physical or mental health of the woman. It is not allowed in cases of rape, incest, fetal impairment, or for economic or social reasons.

Low Restrictions on Minorities

United Kingdom

The UK has no written constitution. The Church of England (Anglican) and the Church of Scotland (Presbyterian) are the official religions of the UK. The Monarch is the official head of the Church of England and must be a member of the Church, but this leadership is primarily symbolic. The Monarch officially appoints all officials of the Church of England on the advice of the Prime Minister and the Crown Appointments Commission, which includes church and lay representatives. The Church of Scotland appoints its own officials without government interference.

Other than a fund for repairing historical church buildings, the government does not fund the state churches. The government does fund several thousand "faith schools," which are mostly Anglican and Catholic schools with a religious character, but also include Jewish, Methodist, Sikh, Muslim, Greek Orthodox, and Seventh Day Adventist schools. Public schools are required to provide religious education, the exact content of which is determined locally. Parents can request that their children be exempted from this requirement. Schools also must provide a daily act of collective worship. In communities with large non-Christian populations this can include non-Christian worship.

While the UK laws provide for full religious freedom, there are limitations placed on some minority religions. For instance Scientology is not considered a religion for the purposes of England's Charity Law. Because of this Scientologists do not have tax-exempt status and Scientologist ministers cannot act as chaplains in government facilities, including prisons. While it is not enforced, it is technically against the law to engage in blasphemy against the Anglican Church and its doctrines.[14]

---

[14] "The Education System in England," http://perso.wanadoo.fr/gibaud/tetyc/backgd/ typesSchools.htm; "United Kingdom 'Constitution,'" at http://www.oefre.unibe.ch/law/icl/ uk00000_.html.

PREFERRED TREATMENT FOR SOME RELIGIONS OR SUPPORT FOR A PARTICULAR TRADITION

Nearly half of the Western democracies fit into this category. These countries have no official religion but support one or more religions more than they do other religions or otherwise endorse a specific religious tradition. This often takes the form of multitiered recognition systems for religions in which religions in each category are given different privileges and levels of support. Most but not all Western democracies in this category place some restrictions on minority religions.

No Restrictions on Minorities

Ireland

Ireland dropped Catholicism as the state's official religion in 1972 but Catholicism still remains influential. The preamble of Ireland's constitution includes significant Catholic and religious imagery, as do Articles 6 and 44 and the oaths of office in Articles 12, 31, and 34.

Article 44 guarantees religious freedom, freedom from discrimination based on religion, that the state will not endow any religion, the autonomy of religious institutions, and the protection of religious property. It also guarantees that state funding will not discriminate "between schools under the management of different religious denominations, nor be such as to affect prejudicially the right of any child to attend a school receiving public money without attending religious instruction at that school." Article 40 protects the right to form religious associations. Article 42 protects the rights of parents in the religious and moral upbringing of their children.

Religious education in public schools is permitted but not required. The Catholic Church runs the majority of schools in Ireland, which are funded by the government, as are schools belonging to other religious denominations. Parents may exempt their children from religious instruction in any of these schools.

While the constitution protects freedom of speech, the publication of blasphemous material is illegal. Abortion is illegal except to save the life of the mother.

Italy

Article 7 of Italy's constitution states that the "state and Catholic church are, each within their own reign, independent and sovereign" and that the relationship between the state and the Catholic Church "is regulated by the lateran pacts," which can be changed without a constitutional amendment. Article 8 guarantees the autonomy of all other religions, and states that the relationship between them and the state "is regulated by law, based on agreements with their representatives." Article 20 states that the "religious character or religious or confessional aims" of religious organizations "do not justify special limitations

or fiscal burdens regarding their establishment, legal capacity, or activities."
Article 117 states that the state has exclusive legislative power over "relations
between the republic and religious denominations." Article 3 protects against
discrimination on the basis of religion. Article 19 guarantees religious freedom.

The 1984 revision of the 1929 Concordant between Italy and the Catholic
Church gives the church certain privileges. The Church selects the government-
paid teachers who provide optional religion courses in public schools. The
other privileges granted to the Catholic Church can also be given to other
religions if they form an agreement called an *Intesa* with the government. This
agreement must be approved by the parliament. These privileges include:
automatic access by clergy to state hospitals, prisons, and military barracks;
civil registry of religious marriages; the facilitation of special religious practices
regarding funerals; exemptions from school attendance on religious holidays;
the right to open religious schools; and funding from a voluntary check-off
on taxpayer returns. The absence of an *Intesa* in no way restricts the free
practice of religion.

In 1998 the Ministry of Internal Affairs sent a report on cults to the lower
house of Parliament that listed 127 groups, none of which were accused of
illegal activities, but the report did include "numerous anti-cult stereotypes."
In 1996 an Italian court ruled that Scientology is not a religion because it does
not include a belief in God. In 1997 this decision was overruled because such
a definition of religion would also exclude some accepted religions such as
Buddhism. Abortion during the first 90 days of pregnancy requires a certificate
from a doctor, counseling, and a 7-day waiting period. Doctors may register
their refusal to do such a procedure and about 70 percent have done so. All
abortions must be done in a public hospital or government-approved facility.
Due to a lack of facilities, women seeking abortions must often wait 30 days.
Abortions after 90 days are legal only to save the life or physical or mental
health of the mother or if the fetus is deformed. Thus, despite liberal laws, in
practice abortion is restricted and illegal abortions are common.[15]

Luxembourg

Article 22 of Luxembourg's constitution provides that state actions with regard
to the internal workings of religious organizations are determined by a concordant between the organization and the state which must be approved by the
Chamber of Deputies. This includes appointing and dismissing religious ministers as well as other elements of religion–state relations. Article 119 states that
until such concordants are agreed upon, the previous laws and regulations
remain in force. Article 25 provides freedom of assembly except for "open-
air political, religious, or other meetings which are fully governed by laws and
police regulation." Article 106 states that "the salaries and pensions of ministers of religion shall be borne by the State and regulated by the law." Article 19

---

[15] Massimo (2001).

protects religious freedom. Article 20 guarantees the freedom not to take part in religious acts, ceremonies, or days of rest.

While there is no state religion, according to an 1801 concordant, some religions receive financial support from the state. Catholic, Protestant, and Jewish organizations receive this support, as do the Greek and Russian Orthodox Churches since 1998 and the Romanian Orthodox, Serbian Orthodox, and Anglican Churches since 2003. A Muslim petition to receive this support has been under consideration for several years.

All private schools, including religious ones, can receive state subsidies. The government also subsidizes a Catholic seminary. Religious education is provided in the public schools, primarily organized by the Catholic Church but taught by government-paid laypersons. Protestant instruction is available on request as is sometimes instruction in other religions. Students also have the option of taking an ethics course.

Advocacy groups claim that the government has an anti-sect policy. The government has published literature and taught in schools against the Unification Church. It is difficult for that church's members to get permits to speak publicly and there are claims of other isolated incidents of harassment.

New Zealand

New Zealand has no single constitution, but rather a series of formal documents that act as a constitution. Sections 13, 15, and 20 of New Zealand's Bill of Rights Act of 1993 guarantee religious freedom. Section 20 protects against discrimination on the basis of religion. The English Monarch is head of state and the Monarch's official title in New Zealand includes religious references.

The Education Act of 1964 permits non-mandatory religious education in state schools. The classes are generally held after school hours and including them in the curriculum is optional. The Private Schools Conditional Integration Act of 1975 included 303 private schools in the public school system, including over 250 Catholic schools. Some businesses are fined if they operate on Christmas Day, Good Friday, and Easter Sunday. However, recent legislation limits this practice. Abortion is available only to save the life, physical health, or mental health of the woman, and in cases of rape, incest, or fetal impairment. It is not allowed for economic reasons or on request. The law is strictly interpreted and only a few centers offer abortion services. This results in overburdened facilities and delays of up to four weeks.[16]

Portugal

Articles 13, 19, and 59 of Portugal's constitution protect against discrimination on the basis of religion. Article 35 prohibits the use of computerized data on religious beliefs. Article 41 protects religious freedom and declares official SRAS. Article 288 states that future constitutional revisions must respect SRAS.

---

[16] Website of the Governor-General of Aotearoa, New Zealand, http://www.gg.govt.nz/role/constofnz.htm.

Article 43 prohibits the state from planning "education and cultural development in accordance with any philosophical, aesthetic, political, ideological or religious precepts." The constitution also protects the separation between religion and other public institutions including political parties (Article 51) and trade unions (Article 55).

The 1940 concordant between the government and the Catholic Church, as amended in 1971, requires that the Catholic Church consult Portugal's government in the appointment of bishops. It also grants the church special privileges including full tax-exempt status, legal recognition for marriage, and chaplain visits to hospitals and prisons. The 2001 Religious Freedom Act grants these same privileges to any religion recognized in Portugal for 30 years or internationally for 60 years. Despite this law, the government has closer relations with the Catholic Church than with other religions. The commission that evaluates new religions for this status includes representatives from the Catholic Church. Government-funded chief chaplaincies in hospitals and the military go to Catholics. Also, the Papal Nuncio is always the dean of the diplomatic corps.

Public school classes on religion include courses on Catholicism by teachers who must be approved by the Catholic Church as well as a general survey course on world religions. If there is a sufficient number of students in a school, courses on another religion can be arranged. Abortion is available only to save the life, physical health, or mental health of the woman and in cases of rape, incest, or fetal impairment. It is not allowed for economic reasons or on request and must be performed in an officially approved location. Two physicians must certify these conditions and a 3-day waiting period is mandatory. Because few doctors in Portugal are willing to perform abortions, illegal abortions still occur.

Low Restrictions on Minorities

Austria

Article 10 of Austria's constitution includes "religious affairs" in the government's powers of legislation. This includes school–Church relations and religious instruction in schools (articles 14 and 14a). Articles 64, 72, and 101 allow "the addition of a religious assertion" to the oath of the president and members of the government and state governments. Articles 7 and 14 protect against discrimination based on religion. There is no explicit mention of a state religion or SRAS.

Austria has a three-tiered recognition system for religions. Religious societies recognized under an 1874 law can receive mandatory contributions collected by the government, teach religious courses in public schools, receive government subsidies for teachers in public and private schools, bring religious workers, including teachers, ministers, and missionaries, into the country, and engage in "quasi-public activities." For new groups to obtain this status they must exist in the country for at least 20 years, for 10 of which they must have the status of confessional communities, and have a membership equaling at least 0.2 percent of the country's population. The government also provides subsidies for private schools run by any of the 13 recognized societies. A 1998 law allows groups to register as religious confessional communities. Registration permits the groups to engage in legal and commercial activities, such as obtaining real estate, but grants none of the privileges given to religious societies. These groups must have at least 300 members and submit to the government information on the goals and doctrine of the group, the rights, and obligations of members, a list of officials, and financing. Groups may also apply for recognition under the Law of Associations under which corporations register. This grants them most of the same rights as religious confessional communities but they are not recognized specifically as religions.

Religious education is provided in public schools only in the religions of the 13 recognized religious societies. Students 14 years or older, and younger students at parental request can opt out of this education.

There is evidence of government suspicion toward some minority religions and a government policy to protect citizens from "dangerous religious cults and sects" that often places a considerable burden on members of new and small religions. Offices to monitor and provide information on "sects" exist at both the federal and provincial level to provide information to the government and citizens. Also, until 2002, the Ministry for Social Security and Generations distributed a brochure on non-recognized religious groups that depicted these groups in negative terms. The government has declared the Unification Church a "dangerous sect," denying it the right to incorporate, open a bank account, or own property. There has been some police harassment of members of the Church and children who attend public schools are "forced to listen to teachers denouncing their church as a dangerous cult." During the 1990s the government also refused to grant any official recognition to the Jehovah's Witnesses.[17]

Belgium

Article 24 of Belgium's constitution provides for religious education in public schools in one of the recognized religions or in "non-denominational moral teaching." It also states "all pupils of school age have the right to moral or religious education at the community's expense." Article 181 requires that the state contribute to the salaries and pensions of religious leaders. Articles 19 and 20 guarantee freedom of worship and the freedom not to practice any religion. Article 21 protects religious organizations from state interference in the appointment of ministers, communication between ministers and their superiors, and in "publishing their acts, except ... taking into consideration normal responsibilities in matters of press and publication."

[17] "Freedom of Religion and Belief and the New Austrian Law on the 'Legal Personality of Religious Belief Communities,'" Austrian Press and Information Website, http://www.austria. org/oldsite/press/49.html; "Religious Discrimination and Related Violations of Helsinki Commitments," International Helsinki Foundation for Human Rights, http://www.ihf-hr.org/ viewbinary/viewhtml.php?doc_id=3963.

The government provides subsidies to officially recognized religions including salaries, pensions, and lodging costs of ministers as well as for the construction and repair of religious buildings. These religions also have the right to provide government-paid religion teachers in schools. These religions include Roman Catholicism, Protestantism, Judaism, Anglicanism, Islam, and both Russian and Greek Orthodoxy. The government also provides these benefits to the Secular Humanists and the Central Council of Non-Religious Philosophical Communities of Belgium. Constitutional reforms in 2001 place this under the jurisdiction of regional governments.

For a religion to be recognized it must have a structure of hierarchy, a "sufficient" number of members, have existed in the country for "a long period of time," it "must offer a social value to the public," and abide by the laws of the state. The terms "sufficient," "a long period of time," and "social value" are not defined by the government. While, officially, Parliament recognizes religions, it follows the recommendations of the Justice Ministry. Religions without official status can worship freely and can gain tax-exempt status as nonprofit organizations.

Belgium places some restrictions on abortions including requiring written certification from the pregnant woman that she is determined to have an abortion, counseling at least six days prior to the procedure, that the physician must be convinced of her determination, and two physicians who certify the woman to be "in a state of distress." Also, after 12 weeks abortion is only permitted when the woman's health is endangered or in cases of fetal abnormality.

In 1995, a parliamentary commission was formed to combat the dangers that some sects may pose to society. A 1997 report listed 189 such sects including Seventh Day Adventists, Mormons, Quakers, Jehovah's Witnesses, Hasidic Judaism, several Pentecostal churches, four Roman Catholic organizations, and the Amish. The report differentiated between harmful and nonharmful sects but did not list which sects belonged to which category. In response to the report's recommendations, the government formed an "inter-ministerial cell" to monitor cults and tasked a federal prosecutor and magistrates to monitor cases involving sects. It also created a Center for Information and Advice on Harmful Sectarian Organizations, which provides information to the public on these sects as well as information on religious freedom in general. Some sects including the Assemblies of God and the Mormons have difficulty in obtaining visas to teach.

Republic of Cyprus (Greek)
While not declaring an official religion, the Republic of Cyprus, which is the portion of Cyprus controlled by the island's ethnic Greek community, incorporates religion into its constitution. It recognizes the Greek Orthodox Church of Cyprus and the Turkish Cypriot religious trust as autonomous bodies. Each is sovereign over its own affairs in which legislation can not interfere. The constitution also gives a lower level of recognition to the Armenian Orthodox, Roman Catholic, and Maronite Christian churches. All other religions must register as nonprofit organizations to open a bank account or engage in other financial activities.

While proselytizing is legal in Cyprus, the Orthodox Church monitors missionary activities and the police often investigate those who try to convert Orthodox Christians under laws that prohibit "physical or moral compulsion" in attempts at converting people, as well as through general civil order laws. The Church is Cyprus's largest landowner and, accordingly, has a significant impact on the economics of the island. The Greek Orthodox religion is taught in public schools but students can opt out of these courses.

Turkish Republic of Northern Cyprus
While not being recognized as a government by any state other than Turkey, the TRNC is the only autonomous governing body among Westen democracies with a Muslim majority. The TRNC constitution maintains strict SRAS. There is no state religion and the constitution guarantees religious freedom and that the government will not interfere in religious practice.

Nevertheless based on the 1960 Cypriot constitution prior to the time the TRNC split off from the Republic of Cyprus, the Muslim Wakf is the only religious organization that is tax exempt and receives government subsidies, including salaries for clergy. The TNRC flag includes a red crescent and star, both Islamic symbols.

Spain
Article 16 of Spain's constitution protects religious freedom and states that "no religion shall have a state character" but requires that "the public powers shall take into account the religious beliefs of Spanish society and maintain the appropriate relations of cooperation, with the Catholic Church and other denominations." Article 14 protects against discrimination on the basis of religion. Article 27 requires that the government assist parents in the "religious and moral formation" of their children.

The Catholic Church has a privileged status defined by four accords between the Spanish government and the Church. Spanish tax forms include an option to donate a percentage of one's taxes to the Catholic Church. While chaplains of all religions are allowed, the government funds only Catholic chaplains for the military, hospitals, and prisons. Muslim chaplains report that while being able to minister to Muslims in prisons they have not been allowed to hold services. Optional religion courses are offered in public schools supported by the Catholic Church and other religions. The government also supports private Catholic schools and gives the Catholic Church a number of tax benefits not given to other religions.

Non-Catholic religions, including Judaism, Muslims, and Protestants, have separate agreements with the Spanish government. Among other things, these agreements give official recognition to religious marriages, and tax-exempt status, as well as the right to religious education in public schools. Religions without official recognition, such as the Church of Scientology, are considered cultural associations. In order to gain those benefits that minority religions receive, they must register with the General Directorate of Religious Affairs of the Ministry of Justice.

Minority religions, including those with agreements with the government, report difficulties in gaining permits to build places of worship. While the government holds that the right to education supercedes dress codes, Muslim women have had difficulties with local schools over the wearing of headscarves.

Abortion is available only to save the life and physical or mental health of the woman and in cases of rape, incest, or fetal impairment. It is not allowed for economic reasons or on request and must be performed in an officially approved location.[18]

Sweden

While for most of its history, the Lutheran Church was the official state Church, the Swedish government and the Lutheran Church officially separated in 2000. Nevertheless, the government remains significantly involved in religious issues.

"The Instrument of Government" (IG), one of the four separate documents included in the Swedish constitution, protects freedom of worship and privacy with regard to religion (IG 2-1, 2-2). It states that "no restriction may be imposed solely on grounds of political, religious, cultural or other such opinions" (IG 2-2). Also, the state should help "ethnic, linguistic and religious minorities to preserve and develop a cultural and social life of their own" (IG 1-2). IG 2-20 gives similar protections to non-citizens. Finally, while some restrictions can be placed on freedoms "particular regard shall be paid to the importance of the widest possible freedom of expression and freedom of information in political, religious, professional, scientific and cultural matters" (IG 2-13).

As part of the process of separating church and state, Sweden passed a series of laws regulating religion–state relations in 1998 and 1999. The Church of Sweden was automatically registered. Other religions may register but there is no requirement to do so. The government collects mandatory fees for the Church of Sweden and other officially recognized religions but those who do not belong to any official religion are not required to pay the fees. These laws also provide for grants for a number of religious organizations and communities for general use, for repairing places of worship, and in some specific cases for seminaries.

Religious education is compulsory in the school curriculum. A 2001 law requires that circumcision of boys must be "performed only by a licensed doctor or, on boys under the age of two months, a person certified by the National Board of Health." While Jewish moels, who traditionally perform the circumcision, were certified to do the procedure, they are required to have a doctor or nurse present for anesthesia. The Jewish community has protested the law on the grounds that it restricts the free practice of the religion. The traditional Jewish and Muslim methods for slaughtering meat are illegal because they are considered inhumane, but importing kosher and Halal meat is allowed.

---

[18] Alejandro T. Gutierrez, "Religious Minorities in Spain: A New Model of Relationships?" *Center for Studies on New Religions*, http://www.cesnur.org/2002/slc/torres.htm; Susan Linnee, "Spain on Verge of Historic Accords with Major Religions," Associated Press, March 20, 1992; "Spain's Muslims and Jews Now Equal with Catholics," *Record*, December 26, 1992.

In 1998 Sweden appointed a commission to study "cults" and "sects." The commission concluded that the majority of members of new religious movements were not at risk and that existing laws provided adequate protection.[19]

Moderate to High Restrictions on Minorities

Germany

The preamble of Germany's constitution includes religious imagery. Article 3 protects against discrimination based on religion. Article 4 protects religious freedom. Article 33 protects against access to public office being restricted by religious affiliation. Article 7 establishes religion as "part of the ordinary curriculum in state schools, except for secular schools." The oath of office for the president, contained in Article 56, includes the phrase "so help me God," but the constitution allows for a nonreligious oath. Article 140 incorporates elements of the 1919 German constitution into the current one, including: religious freedom; that there is no state church; protections for the autonomy of religious organizations; granting religious organizations the power to use state organs to tax their members; and that "Sunday and the public holidays recognized by the state remain legally protected as days of rest from work and of spiritual edification."[20]

In effect, the German government treats different religions differently. Religions with "public law corporation status" can, among other things, have the state collect taxes from their members. In order to achieve this status, organizations must meet criteria of permanence, size, and, until a 2000 court decision, loyalty to the state. Other religions can register as nonprofit organizations. The state subsidizes the building and repair of some churches and synagogues because of past destruction and seizure by 1803 Napoleonic reforms and under the Nazi regime.

Public schools include religious instruction in cooperation with Protestant and Catholic organizations. Schools offer courses in Judaism if enough students request it. Some schools began offering courses in Islam in 2001 and in Buddhism in 2003. A nonreligious ethics course is available for those who do not wish religious instruction.

The German government closely monitors and often harasses Scientologists. Several state governments have published pamphlets about dangerous cults, including Scientologists. Firms bidding for government contracts must sign forms stating that their management and employees are not Scientologists. This wording was changed in 2001 to a promise that the "technology of L. Ron

---

[19] "The Riksdag at Work," Swedish Riksdag (Parliament) website, http://www.riksdagen.se/english/work/fundamental/introduction/introduction.ASP; Swedish Government's Public Administration website, http://www.sweden.gov.se/sb/d/3288/a/19564; Jonas Otterbeck, "The Legal Status of Islamic Minorities: The Case of Sweden," International and European Forum on Migration Research: 2003 Conference on the Legal Treatment of Muslim Minorities in Europe and the United States, http://www.fieri.it/convegni/giu2003/otterbeck.pdf; Tobin Fricke, "Immigration, Multiculturalism, Sweden," http://splorg.org/people/tobin/papers/multiculturalism.html.

[20] Axel Tschentscher, "The Basic Law: The Constitution of the Federal Republic of Germany," http://www.jurisprudentia.de/jurisprudentia.html.

Hubbard" will not be used in executing the contract. Government employment offices monitor companies that have suspected Scientologists working for them and warn prospective employees of these firms of this. Government officials have organized boycotts of movies starring John Travolta and Tom Cruise because they are Scientologists.

Many of Germany's major political parties, including the Social Democrats, the Christian Democratic Union, the Free Liberal Party, and the STAAT, have banned Scientologists from being party members. During the 1990s several regional governments asked the federal government to engage in a number of actions against Scientologists including criminal investigations; an investigation of whether membership in the Church should be regarded in the same way as drug addiction; the expansion of government "explanatory campaigns" on Scientology; and action to combat their economic influence. Government officials have published names of individual Scientologists and engaged in media campaigns against businesses run by them. Businesspeople have even advertised in newspapers that they are not Scientologists in order to avoid the social and economic repercussions of being associated with Scientology.

Germany's monitoring of sects is not limited to Scientologists. A July 2002 court ruling allows the government to characterize nontraditional religions as "sects," "youth religions," and "youth sects" and to provide accurate information about them to the public. However, the government may not use terms like "destructive," "pseudo-religion," or "manipulative." A German court allowed the government to refuse "public law corporation status" to the Jehovah's Witnesses until it investigated whether the group coerces its members in order to keep them from leaving the congregation and whether the groups' child-rearing practices violate human rights standards. The tax-exempt status of the Christliche Gemeinde Kolin was revoked in 1995. The founders of the Unification Church have been banned from the country and the Church has been denied tax-exempt status. A Muslim schoolteacher has been denied the right to teach while wearing her headscarf. In 2003 the Supreme Court overturned this decision because there was no explicit law against this practice, but by mid-2006 eight states had passed such a law. During the 1990s it was estimated that the German government spent as much as 100 million Deutschmarks on anti-sect activities, though it is likely that this estimation is inflated.[21]

Switzerland

The preamble of the Swiss constitution includes religious imagery. Article 8 protects against discrimination on the basis of religion. Article 15 protects religious freedom. Article 72 states that "the regulation of the relationship

---

[21] Boyle & Sheen (1997: 309–10); Mary Williams, "Germany Versus Scientology," *Los Angeles Times*, Feb. 6, 1997; World Wide Religious News, http://wwrn.org; Lord Duncan McNair, "Report of the Ad Hoc Committee to Investigate Discrimination Against Religious and Ethnic Minorities in Germany," October 1996.

between church and state" is decided by Switzerland's regional governments, which are known as cantons. This is because the Swiss government is basically a confederation that allows local governments to control all cultural aspects of government, including religion. Also, as part of the country's agreement between linguistically and religiously different groups, religion is one of the criteria for determining who holds a number of government positions.

Until a 2001 referendum, the Catholic Church needed government consent to form a new diocese in the country and was required to submit its choice of bishops for the approval of the government. The Unification Church has been denied the right to register as a religious organization and must register as an association. Abortion is legal only to save the life or the physical or mental health of a woman.

While there is no official religion in Switzerland, most of the 26 cantons financially support a form of Catholicism or Protestant Christianity and collect taxes on behalf of whatever church or churches they support. In some cantons this tax is mandatory, and in others it is not. Some cantons also collect taxes on behalf of Jewish institutions. Religious education is standard in Swiss schools, generally in the majority denomination of the canton, but classes in other religions are usually offered and students may opt out of the classes. Three of the country's 16 major parties, the Evangelical People's Party, the Christian Democratic Party, and the Christian Social Party, subscribe to religious philosophies.

While this matter is decided at the level of cantons, there is a trend toward discrimination against some religions. In general the government, supported by court rulings, considers Scientology a commercial enterprise and not a religion. This has resulted in some restrictions on proselytizing by Scientologists by some local governments on the grounds that they use "deceptive or dishonest methods," and restrictions on Scientologists being teachers in schools or operating private schools. Several local governments have also restricted the distribution of Scientologist literature.

Beginning in 2002, several Muslim clerics who advocate what the government considers radical views have been denied entry to Switzerland. A Muslim teacher who wrote an article in favor of stoning adulterers was fired from his job. In 2002 a court ruled that cantons can prohibit the wearing of headscarves by teachers in public schools. The government also bans ritual slaughter but permits the import of Halal and kosher meat. A July 1999 report on "sects" by the Business Review Commission of the National Assembly recommended that the government form a policy on sects. The government, in 2000, rejected the recommendation because it would infringe on religious freedoms.[22]

---

[22] Elizabeth Olson, "Swiss Vote on Church Laws Is Reawakening Old Ghosts," *New York Times*, June 10, 2001.

MODERATE SEPARATION

These countries maintain a moderate level of SRAS but still legislate several aspects of religion beyond support for religious education. Australia does not discriminate against religious minorities, but Canada engages in some isolated incidents of religious discrimination.

Australia

Section 116 of Australia's constitution bans laws that establish a religion, require religious observance, prohibit the free exercise of religion, or impose or require religious tests "as a qualification for any office or public trust under the Commonwealth."

With a few exceptions, Australia maintains full SRAS, protects religious freedom, and prohibits discrimination based on religion. While federal law allows abortion, most of Australia's states criminalize abortion except in order to preserve the health of the woman. Despite this, a series of court decisions over the past several decades have obfuscated these laws to the extent that many feel they are unenforceable. Upon parental request, public schools must provide religious education for students. Only the children of those parents who request the religious education receive it. The state of Victoria forbids the opening of entertainment establishments until 1 p.m. on Christmas Day and Good Friday. Before 2002 this prohibition required that cinemas must apply to show films on these days and that the films shown must not contain religious satire or violence.[23]

Canada

Canada has a series of historical documents and acts that make up its constitution. The Constitution Act of 1982 guarantees religious freedom and equal protection under the law for all citizens without regard to religion. However, the act also includes a "notwithstanding" clause, which allows the provincial governments to pass laws that conflict with many of the fundamental rights guaranteed in the act, including religious freedom. Both the 1867 Constitution and the 1982 Constitution Act protect the rights of denominational schools. In practice this means that some provinces fund religious schools. The preamble of the Constitution Act of 1982 also recognizes the supremacy of God. There is no section of the constitution that explicitly requires SRAS.

---

[23] Natasha Cica, "Abortion Law in Australia," Parliament of Australia, Parliamentary Library website, http://www.aph.gov.au/library/pubs/rp/1998-99/99rp01.htm; Matt de Bernardo, "Should Abortion Be Legalized in Queensland, Australia?" http://everest.fit.qut.edu.au/~n4393252/abortion.html; "Education Bill 2002," Australian Capital Territory Department of Education, Youth and Family Services, http://www.decs.act.gov.au/schools/pdf/education bill2002.pdf; "Theaters Act 1958," Parliament of Victoria, http://www.dms.dpc.vic.gov.au/l2d/T/ACT01227/2_1.html; "Theaters Repeal Act 2002," Parliament of Victoria, http://www.dms.dpc.vic.gov.au/sb/2002_Act/A01079.html.

In recent years there has been a trend in some of Canada's provinces toward removing the privileged status of some religions. Until the 1990s, the only public school system in Newfoundland was made up of Christian schools. Between 1995 and 1998 two referendums and a constitutional amendment abolished this system and replaced it with a secular public school system. Quebec continues to operate Protestant and Catholic school systems. Until May 2001, Ontario provided tax credits only for private Roman Catholic schools. At the time of this writing the province provides tax credits for all private school tuition. During the 2000–2001 school year, Saskatoon ended a policy of requiring students to either recite the Lord's prayer or remain silent. In September 1999, the Ontario Courts of Appeal issued an injunction preventing the custom of opening local council meetings in Ontario with the Lord's Prayer. Courts have also ruled that a law preventing Sunday shopping was unconstitutional because its purpose was to force observance of the Christian Sabbath. Nevertheless, many such "blue laws" remain on the books in Canada's provinces. Sikhs have been banned from wearing religious ceremonial daggers in public schools and universities. While court rulings have created a compromise, which allows for smaller than normal daggers to be worn, schools may still place restrictions on this practice. There have also been several incidents of judges requiring that Muslims remove head coverings in courts.[24]

NEAR FULL SEPARATION

These countries maintain close to no GIR. In the case of the USA none of the existing GIR affects the RAS codes. Neither of these countries restricts minority religious practices.

Netherlands

Article 23 of the Netherlands' 1983 constitution states that public education must pay "due respect to everyone's religion or belief" and guarantees that private schools have "the freedom to provide education according to religious or other belief." An "additional articles" section of the constitution provides for the continuation of funding and stipends for religious organizations and ministers. Article 1 protects against discrimination on the basis of religion. Article 6 protects religious freedom. Also, the parts of the 1972 constitution that still remain in force include oaths of office for the Regent and other government officials, all of which end with the phrase "so help me, God Almighty," though this phrase can be replace with "this I affirm."

The government funds all forms of private schools, including religious ones. It also funds religious health care facilities. A 2003 law gives employees the

[24] Wayland (1997); "Ruling Ends Lord's Prayer at Councils," *Ottawa Citizen*, CanWest Global Communications Corp. News: A3, September 26, 1999; "Human Rights Law in B.C.," *Canadian Human Rights Reporter,* http://www.cdn-hr-reporter.ca/religion.htm; "In Support of Religious Freedom in Quebec Schools," Petition Online, http://www.petitiononline.com/msikh/.

right to take off work on Sundays unless the nature of the work does not allow this, as is the case with health care workers.

United States of America

At the federal level, the USA is unique among all countries coded in the RAS dataset in that it has absolute-SRAS on all 62 variables included in the dataset. Article 6 of the US constitution states that "no religious test shall ever be required as a qualification to any office or public trust under the United States." The first amendment protects religious freedom and guarantees that the government will not establish any religion as the state religion.

In other ways, religion is not completely absent in US political culture. Its money includes the phrase "in God we trust," and its pledge of allegiance includes the phrase "under God." A recent federal court ruling stated that this violates the principle of SRAS but this ruling was overturned on technical grounds.

There are a number of religious issues that have repeatedly been brought to federal courts. One such issue is whether there can be organized prayers in state-funded schools. The US Department of Education released a comprehensive set of guidelines on prayer in public schools in 2001 based on a number of court decisions. These guidelines include the following provisions.[25] Students may pray in a nondisruptive manner when not engaged in school activities or instruction. In addition, students in informal settings, such as cafeterias and hallways, may pray and discuss their religious views with each other. However, the right to engage in voluntary prayer or religious discussion free from discrimination does not include the right to compel other students to participate, and school staff are required to ensure that students are not coerced to participate in religious activities. In addition, school officials may not mandate or organize prayer at graduation nor organize religious baccalaureate ceremonies.

Religious tenets may not be taught in public schools but religion can be taught as an academic or historical subject, and religious texts can be taught in the context of literature. Schools may teach about the cultural aspects of religious holidays and celebrate the secular aspects of religious holidays. School grounds may be used for religious events, on an equal level as any other event, but administrators and teachers may not encourage or solicit such activities.

While legal since the landmark 1973 *Roe vs. Wade* Supreme Court decision, abortion has been a controversial issue with many legislators at the state and federal level trying to limit it. Thus far, the federal courts have upheld the legality of abortion, though they have allowed some limitations to be imposed, including parental consent for minors, a 24-hour waiting period, as well as limitations on certain late-term abortion procedures.

The unique case of absolute-SRAS in the USA remains intact primarily due to enforcement of the first amendment of the US constitution by the US federal

---

[25] "President's Memorandum on Religious Expression in Schools," *New York Times*, July 13, 1995; "L.A. School Prayer Law Tossed by Court," *Los Angeles Times*, December 12, 2001.

courts. The US population is among the most religious of Western democracies and it is very likely that without the zealousness of federal courts, religious legislation would exist in the USA.

HOSTILITY

The hostility category includes states that are coded as "separationist," "inadvertent insensitivity," and "hostile" on the *official GIR* variable. These states have in common that they are all hostile to religion to varying degrees. These diverse categories of hostility are included in a single category because few states are coded in these categories.

France

France is unique in that it is the only Western democracy coded as hostile to religion. This is because in its zeal to maintain SRAS, the French government tends to take a slightly negative view of religion. Article 1 of the French constitution declares it is a secular state and ensures "the equality of all citizens before the law, without distinction of origin, race or religion." In addition, a 1905 law on SRAS prohibits discrimination on the basis of faith. There are also strict antidefamation laws against religiously or racially motivated attacks.

Religious organizations are not required to register. They can register either as religious associations or cultural associations. Only religious associations gain tax-exempt status. A 2001 law allows for the dissolution of religious groups under the following conditions: "endangering the life or the physical or psychological well-being of a person; placing minors at mortal risk; violation of another person's freedom, dignity, or identity; the illegal practice of medicine or pharmacology; false advertising; and fraud or falsification." Dissolved groups are prohibited from renting or owning property, publishing their teachings, and operating schools or seminaries. Attempting to revive a banned organization under a new name is illegal.

There are some historical exceptions to France's strict SRAS. Support is provided for religious buildings that predate the 1905 law. Parts of Alsace, Lorraine, and Moselle regions have historical-based exceptions to France's SRAS. Jewish, Lutheran Reformed Protestant, and Catholic individuals can have a portion of their taxes allocated to their religion. Local governments can support and build religious edifices. France also subsidizes private schools, including religious schools.

There exist some restrictions on religious activities. Foreign missionaries need to comply with strict visa requirements and must have a letter from a sponsoring organization. In 1996 a parliamentary commission listed 176 cults including some Baptist denominations, Jesuits, Jehovah's Witnesses, and Scientologists. In 1998 the government established the Inter-ministerial Monitoring Mission Against Sectarian Abuses to monitor "cults" and provide information on them to citizens and the government. The mandate of the mission includes educating people on the dangers of sects and methods for fighting against them.

There have also been some isolated incidents of government harassment of "cults." In 1989 the Church of Scientology was charged with fraud and the illegal practice of medicine. The charges were eventually dismissed. In 2001 some local authorities, citing their inclusion on the list of cults, would not rent the Jehovah's Witnesses space for public meetings. The decision was overturned by administrative tribunals. The tax authority in 2000 decided that the Jehovah's Witnesses were not a religious association but, rather, a cultural association and required payment of taxes. This includes a 60 percent tax on offerings by church members.

The issue of the wearing of religious symbols in public institutions has been a source of tension for some time. During the 1990s government workers could not wear Muslim headscarves, and headscarves were banned in some schools based on a law against proselytizing in schools. The Minister of Education strictly interpreted this law as prohibiting the wearing of the headscarves, which were considered too "aggressive." This ruling was not applied to other religions. A 2004 law explicitly bans headscarves and other "conspicuous" religious symbols and ornamentation in schools, including Jewish skull caps, and large Christian crosses. It might also apply to beards and bandanas considered religious in nature.[26]

SOME GENERAL OBSERVATIONS

Despite the considerable diversity in the relationships between religion and state in Western democracies, there are a number of trends worth noting. First, very few of them have anything close to absolute-SRAS. Over two-thirds of these governments can be placed into one of two clusters: six governments with active state religions and 13 governments who give preferential treatment to one or more religions.

Second, most of these states engage in relatively low levels of discrimination against minorities. This is to be expected since an aspect of liberal democracy is religious freedom and most of these countries have clauses in their constitutions (or equivalent) protecting religious freedom and against discrimination based on religion. Nevertheless, the majority of these states engage in some form of restrictions on minority religions. The most common form of discrimination is against religions considered "sects," especially Scientology, but some states also discriminate against other denominations that are new to their countries, many of which are considered more mainstream elsewhere. These include Seventh Day Adventists, Mormons, Quakers, Jehovah's Witnesses, Hasidic Judaism, and Pentecostalism. There are also restrictions on Muslims in several states, especially with regard to the wearing of headscarves by public officials, students, and teachers. This is consistent with the practice in several states of granting full recognized status to religions only when they have been present in the country for a specified

---

[26] Wayland (1997).

amount of time and the number of adherents reaches specified numerical requirements. This type of activity appears to have increased in recent years.

Third, several states have increased their level of SRAS or religious inclusiveness. Sweden has abandoned its official religion. Canada, Finland, Iceland, and Switzerland have made efforts to decrease the institutional entanglement between religion and state. Also, Luxembourg, Malta, and Portugal have increased the number of religions that receive state support. In terms of the RAS variable, between 1990 and 2002 there was a slight overall drop in GIR as measured by the *general GIR* variable in the RAS dataset from a mean level of 19.37 to 19.09. Thus, while it has decreased, the overall extent of GIR in Western democracies remains high.

While there is certainly likely to be change over time, it is unlikely that there will be any major changes in the overall extent of GIR among Western democracies. One illustration of this is a fourth trend: that, of the 18 states with no official religion, 14 of them have references to religion in their constitutions beyond the standard protections of religious freedom and against discrimination against religious minorities and a fifteenth, New Zealand, has no clause separating religion and state. Furthermore, that nearly all of the governments examined here include at least one of protections shows that they believe on some level that without these protections, infringement upon religions rights would be a likely occurrence. In fact, despite these protections, the courts of several Western democracies specifically prevented their governments from taking such actions. Also, as is discussed in more detail in Chapter 11, there have been relatively few shifts in state religion policy in Western democracies between 1990 and 2002. Thus there is stability in the region's countries' religion policies.

There are three factors that might help to explain these trends. Such an explanation is especially necessary in light of the fact that the populations of many of these states tend to be secular. The first is the historical role of religion in government. For nearly all of these states, at one time religion was an essential element of government with little real SRAS. Many of the remaining forms of GIR are historical remnants of this trend. Most of the recent examples of governments abolishing religious elements of their regime are cases where this type of historical remnant was eliminated.

The second factor is protection of culture. In this age of globalism and interdependency, cultures are often eroded by outside influences and migration. Many countries want to protect their cultural heritage, and religion is a part of that heritage. That every Western democracy other than the USA supports some form of religious education, most of them in public schools, fits well with this trend.

The final factor is fear of religion. The Treaty of Westphalia, which many argue was the beginning of the modern nation-state, established an international regime that intentionally removed religion from the international agenda precisely because the treaty ended a violent religious war, the Thirty Years War. It is arguable that this and many other historical events have given Europeans a healthy respect for the power of religion to disrupt politics. It is further arguable that for this reason many Western states become involved in religion in order to keep it under control. Such forms of regulation as state approval of religious appointments and the requirement of religions to register with the government fit into this pattern. The monitoring of new religions with which the state is unfamiliar also fits into this pattern.

There are two major exceptions to the general trends in this study. The USA stands out as the only country in the entire RAS dataset that maintains absolute-SRAS on all 62 variables measures in the RAS dataset. Yet, according to most surveys, its population is among the most religious in the West. The explanation for this phenomenon includes several elements. First, while the constitutions of most Western democracies promise religious freedom and many have SRAS clauses, only two constitutions other than that of the USA have a SRAS clause *and* do not contain additional clauses that are in some way supportive of religion. One of them is Portugal which, despite having official SRAS, gives the Catholic Church special privileges. The other is France, the second exception discussed here.

The second element of this explanation is the US court system. Despite constitutional protections for religious freedom, 17 Western states place restrictions on minority religions. In some cases, this is due to an official policy of multitiered statuses for religion, but in others it is simply restrictions on minority religions. What differentiates the USA from many of these states is the zeal of the US federal courts in protecting the rights of religious minorities. The descriptions provided in this chapter list a number of restrictions on religious liberty that US federal courts, based on current judicial policy, would never allow. Furthermore, some of these restrictions have been explicitly upheld by the court systems of other Western countries, despite constitutional protections.

The third reason is that, unlike most of the other states in this chapter, the USA post-dates the Treaty of Westphalia and was established in an age where the concept that religion and politics should not mix was beginning to gain acceptance. Furthermore, it was established by people from diverse backgrounds in a place with less history of religious conflict. Certainly, there were religious elements in the USA's pre-independence history and certainly many European governments have established new regimes, often multiple times, since the Treaty of Westphalia. However, it is arguable that the slate was cleaner for the USA. That Australia, Canada, and New Zealand, the other non-European Western democracies, have the lowest levels of GIR among Western democracies, other than the USA and the Netherlands, supports this argument.

France is also an exception because its government is slightly hostile to religion. This is arguably due to France's civic culture of secularism. That is, whereas the attitude in the USA is that religion is a good thing but it is simply not the business of government, in France there is a tendency to actively and perhaps militantly maintain secularism. In France, religion is seen as a potential threat to the state and civil order on a level more extreme than other European states. This explains France's extreme suspicion of religions that are not indigenous to the country. This manifests itself in the country's anti-sect policy and in the restrictions on wearing religious garb, especially Muslim garb, in schools.

Thus, the values of SRAS and religious freedom are values that, if left to the whims of the populace and legislators unbound by constitutional protections, likely would be eroded if not seriously undermined. That this is true of the very states which most strongly support civil liberties is a strong indicator that religion remains very relevant in the West in the new millennium.

In all, the analysis presented in this chapter indicates that in Western democracies religion is ubiquitous but manifests itself in diverse ways. Certainly the region has characteristics which differentiate it from other regions including a relatively low level of religious discrimination and particularly low levels of religious regulation. Yet, within these commonalities is a considerable amount of diversity ranging from the USA, the state with the lowest level of GIR in the RAS dataset, to Greece, which has a considerable amount of entanglement between government and religion.

6

The Former Soviet Bloc

During the communist era, the entire Soviet bloc was consistently antireligious. Since 1990 religion has returned with a vengeance including a considerable amount of state support for religion. Yet this pattern of support is different from that in Western democracies. While there are few, if any, instances of government support due to historical inertia, history has had a considerable impact on the current relationship between religion and state in the region.

The states in the region tend to have a paternalistic attitude toward religion in that they tend to feel a need to guide and protect their citizens with regard to religion. They accomplish this through regulating and controlling citizens' access to religion. Three interrelated manifestations of this phenomenon are particularly conspicuous. First, in all but one state religions must register. Second, the majority religion in these countries tends to be subjected to relatively heavy regulation. Third, religions seen as dangerous or nonindigenous to the state are often restricted. All of these trends are discussed here in more detail.

Despite these similarities, there is considerable diversity in the nature and extent of government involvement in religion (GIR) in the region. The information presented in Tables 6.1, 6.2, 6.3, and 6.4 makes it exceedingly clear that former Soviet bloc governments have become significantly involved in religious issues. Of the 27 governments examined here, only 1 has an official religion. However, only 2 are coded as accommodation, denoting a high level of separation of religion and state (SRAS), and another 3 as separatist, denoting a slight hostility toward religion.

While a majority of 22 of these governments support one or more religion, all but 1 of them also place limitations on at least some minority religions. Of the 16 categories of restrictions that can be placed on minority religions examined by the RAS project, all but 2 of them exist in at least one former Soviet bloc state. As is the case with Western states, the most common is the requirement for minority religions to register with the government, which exists in 23 states. There are 17 states that limit proselytizing or missionaries. There are 15 that place limits on building or repairing places of worship, which also included

TABLE 6.1. *Separation of Religion and State in the Former Soviet Bloc in 2002, Basic Information*

Country	Maj. religion	% Maj. rel.	# Min. groups with 5% of population	Official GIR	Official regulation	General GIR
Albania	Islam, Sunni	50.0	4	Accommodation	Practical limitations	7.69
Armenia	Orthodox	91.9	0	One official religion	Legal limitations	40.36
Azerbaijan	Islam, Shi'i	56.8	1	Separationist	Legal limitations	31.65
Belarus	Orthodox	70.0	3	Civil religion	Legal limitations	35.66
Bosnia-Herz.	Mixed	44.0	2	Cooperation	Practical limitations	16.33
Bulgaria	Orthodox	82.0	1	Civil religion	Legal limitations	36.72
Croatia	Catholic	88.5	1	Civil religion	Practical limitations	22.42
Czech Republic	Christian	40.0	2	Cooperation	Practical limitations	18.19
Estonia	Christian	29.2	3	Accommodation	No limitations	3.52
Georgia	Orthodox	75.0	2	Civil religion	Legal limitations	32.83
Hungary	Catholic	67.5	2	Cooperation	Legal limitations	22.79
Kazakhstan	Mixed	47.0	1	Cooperation	Legal limitations	31.75
Kyrgyzstan	Islam, Sunni	75.0	1	Separationist	Practical limitations	19.20
Latvia	Christian	22.8	3	Cooperation	Practical limitations	17.56
Lithuania	Catholic	85.0	2	Cooperation	Practical limitations	17.58
Macedonia	Orthodox	59.3	2	Civil religion	Legal limitations	27.17
Moldova	Orthodox	70.0	3	Civil religion	Legal limitations	32.34
Poland	Catholic	92.2	0	Civil religion	Practical limitations	22.21
Romania	Orthodox	77.0	3	Civil religion	Practical limitations	24.50
Russia	Orthodox	51.7	2	Civil religion	Legal limitations	30.48
Slovakia	Catholic	67.0	2	Cooperation	Practical limitations	19.88
Slovenia	Catholic	76.0	1	Cooperation	No limitations	11.96
Tajikistan	Islam, Sunni	80.4	2	Separationist	No limitations	11.57
Turkmenistan	Islam, Sunni	89.0	1	Civil religion	Legal limitations	38.91
Ukraine	Orthodox	61.5	2	Cooperation	Practical limitations	19.99
Uzbekistan	Islam, Sunni	76.2	1	Civil religion	Legal limitations	44.41
Yugoslavia	Orthodox	60.0	3	Cooperation	Practical limitations	16.75

TABLE 6.2. *Restrictions on Minority Religion in Former Soviet Bloc in 2002*

	Public obervance	Build or repair places of worship	Access to places of worship	Formal orgs.	Education	Arrest, detention, harassment	Materials	Publications	Personal status	Clergy	Conversions	Proselytizing	Registration	Other	Total
Albania										x					1
Armenia		x		x		x		x		x			x		6
Azerbaijan		x	x	x	x			x		x		x	x	x	9
Belarus		x	x	x	x	x		x		x	x	x	x		10
Bosnia-Herz.	x											x			2
Bulgaria	x	x	x	x	x	x		x				x	x	x	10
Croatia													x		1
Czech Rep.													x		1
Estonia													x		1
Georgia	x	x	x	x	x	x	x	x				x	x		10
Hungary													x		1
Kazakhstan		x	x	x		x		x				x	x		7
Kyrgyzstan												x	x		2
Latvia												x	x		2
Lithuania												x	x		2
Macedonia	x	x	x	x	x							x	x		7
Moldova		x	x	x		x						x	x		6
Poland				x				x					x		3
Romania	x	x	x	x					x			x	x		7
Russia	x			x				x				x	x	x	6
Slovakia	x	x	x						x				x		5
Slovenia		x											x		2
Tajikistan															0
Turkmenistan	x	x	x		x	x		x			x	x	x		9
Ukraine		x			x							x	x	x	5
Uzbekistan	x	x	x		x	x		x			x	x	x		9
Yugoslavia		x						x				x			3
TOTAL	9	15	11	11	8	8	1	11	2	4	3	17	23	4	127

The following categories of religious discrimination were not included in this table because none of these countries engage in these practices: forced observance; and forced conversions.

TABLE 6.3. *Government Regulation of the Majority Religion in the Former Soviet Bloc in 2002*

	Political parties	Arrest, detention, harassment	Orgs.	Public observance	Speech	Access to places of worship	Publications	Arrest nonleaders	Public display	Other	Total
Albania										x	1
Armenia	x										1
Azerbaijan	x	x	x				x	x		x	6
Belarus	x		x								2
Bosnia-Herz.											0
Bulgaria	x		x								2
Croatia			x								1
Czech Rep.										x	1
Estonia											0
Georgia											0
Hungary											0
Kazakhstan	x	x	x		x		x				5
Kyrgyzstan	x	x	x				x	x			5
Latvia					x						1
Lithuania											0
Macedonia										x	1
Moldova	x		x								2
Poland											0
Romania											0
Russia										x	1
Slovakia											0
Slovenia											0
Tajikistan	x	x		x		x				x	5
Turkmenistan	x	x			x		x			x	5
Ukraine	x									x	2
Uzbekistan	x	x	x		x	x	x	x	x		8
Yugoslavia											0
TOTAL	11	6	8	1	4	2	5	3	1	8	49

The following categories of religious restrictions were not included in this table because none of these countries engage in these practices: public gatherings.

TABLE 6.4. *Religious Legislation in the Former Soviet Bloc in 2002*

	Personal status	Conversions	Public dress	Blasphemy	Censorship	Optional education	Mandatory education	Fund education	Charity	Taxes	Fund clergy
Albania											
Armenia						x		x			
Azerbaijan											
Belarus											
Bosnia-Herz.							x	x			
Bulgaria						x		x			
Croatia	x					x		x			x
Czech Rep.								x	x		x
Estonia						x		x			
Georgia					x	x		x			
Hungary				x		x		x		x	
Kazakhstan											
Kyrgyzstan											
Latvia						x		x			
Lithuania						x		x			
Macedonia							x	x			
Moldova											
Poland						x		x			
Romania						x		x			x
Russia				x				x			
Slovakia						x		x			x
Slovenia						x		x			
Tajikistan											x
Turkmenistan											x
Ukraine								x			
Uzbekistan		x	x					x			x
Yugoslavia						x		x			
TOTAL	1	1	1	2	1	13	2	19	1	1	7

	Other funding	Approve clergy, speeches	Some clergy appointed	Gov. rel. dept.	Legislature or cabinet	Abortion	Flag	Identity cards	Registration	Sects	Other	Total
Albania				x					x			2
Armenia	x			x					x			5
Azerbaijan		x	x	x					x			3
Belarus	x			x					x	x		5
Bosnia-Herz.	x				x							4
Bulgaria	x		x	x					x	x		7
Croatia	x		x	x					x			8
Czech Rep.	x			x					x			6
Estonia				x					x			4
Georgia									x			4
Hungary	x								x	x		7
Kazakhstan	x								x			2
Kyrgyzstan				x					x			2
Latvia				x				x	x			5
Lithuania	x			x					x	x		6
Macedonia									x			3
Moldova	x			x					x		x	4
Poland				x		x			x			5
Romania	x			x					x			6
Russia	x			x					x	x		7
Slovakia				x					x	x		4
Slovenia				x					x			4
Tajikistan				x					x			3
Turkmenistan	x	x	x	x			x		x			7
Ukraine	x			x					x			4
Uzbekistan	x		x	x			x		x			9
Yugoslavia				x					x			4
TOTAL	15	2	5	21	1	1	2	1	26	6	1	130

The following categories of religious legislation were not included in this table because none of these countries engage in these practices: dietary laws; alcohol; inheritance; close businesses; blue laws; religious position for govt. official; govt. position for religious.

renting spaces in several of these states, and 11 that limit access to places of worship. There are 11 that place limits on religious organizations. Seven additional types of restrictions exist in 9 or fewer states.

Former Soviet bloc countries also significantly regulate their majority religions. Of the 11 forms of such regulation coded by the RAS project, all but 1 exist in at least 1 former Soviet bloc state. However, this type of GIR is less common than restrictions on minorities and 10 of the 27 states in the region do not regulate their majority religions. The most common form of regulation is to place limitations on religious political parties, and these exist in 11 of these states. Eight additional types of religious regulation exist in 8 or fewer states.

Religious legislation, while not quite as common as in Western democracies, is present in every state in the former Soviet bloc. Of the 33 types of religious legislation coded by the RAS dataset, at least 1 country legislates 26. The most common type of law is the requirement of religions to register, which exists in every state except Bosnia. The governments of 21 of these states have religious affairs departments. Religious education is funded by 19 of them, by 15 in public schools. There are 16 states that provide some other form of funding for religion. This includes collecting taxes, funding religious charities, funding clergy, and other forms of funding. Several other types of legislation exist in 6 or fewer states.

All of this serves to demonstrate that religion remains an important issue for most former Soviet bloc states. The next section of this chapter examines all of these trends through a brief examination of the role of religion in each of these states. This examination is facilitated by the taxonomy developed in Chapter 5 and further developed in this chapter. This taxonomy is presented in Table 6.5.

STATE-CONTROLLED RELIGIONS

This category represents states where the government tries to make the state religion an organ of the state in that the state government influences or controls the clergy and religious institutions but not the other way around. In these states religion does not really influence state policy but, rather, the state tries either to neutralize religion as an influence in the public sphere or to use it as an instrument of government.

Both of the former Soviet bloc states that fall into this category are Muslim republics that were formerly part of the Soviet Union. Both of them engage in high restrictions on minorities. This can be seen as part of these governments' campaigns to control religion. Most of the restrictions on religious minorities are on minorities that operate outside of the government-controlled context. These minority religions usually fit into the category of those the government considers unloyal, foreign, or a threat to the state.

Turkmenistan

Article 11 of Turkmenistan's constitution guarantees religious freedom and equality of different religions under the law. It also declares that religious

TABLE 6.5. *Taxonomy of Former Soviet Bloc States*

Separation of religion and state	Type of restrictions on minorities			
	None	Low (1–2)	Moderate (3–5)	High (6+)
Religious state	—	—	—	—
Active state religion	—	—	—	—
State-controlled religion	—	—	—	Turkmenistan Uzbekistan
Historical / cultural state religion	—	—	—	—
Preferred treatment for some religions or support for a particular tradition	—	Bosnia Croatia Czech Republic Hungary Latvia Lithuania	Poland	Armenia Belarus Bulgaria Georgia Kazakhstan Macedonia Moldova Romania Russia
General support	—	Slovenia	Slovakia	—
Moderate separation	—	Estonia Yugoslavia	Ukraine	—
Nearly full separation (2 or less on legislation)	—	Albania	—	—
Hostility	Tajikistan	Kygyzstan	—	Azerbaijan

organizations are separate from the state and the state educational system. Article 17 guarantees the equality of citizens regardless of their religious beliefs. Article 28 forbids political parties and other social associations that promote religious animosity as well as "forming militaristic associations or political parties based on national or religious traits." Article 8 extends the right of asylum to foreign citizens persecuted for their religious convictions. Turkmenistan's flag includes a white Islamic crescent on a green background.

In practice the government ignores many of these constitutional provisions. It closely monitors the majority religion, Sunni Islam. It approves the appointment of most senior clerics, requires them to report regularly to the Council on Religious Affairs, and pays the salaries of most clerics. In 1997 the government prohibited mosque-based imams from teaching Islam and closed all but a few madrassas. In 2001 it closed all university Islamic departments other than the one that is in a government-controlled school. In 2002 it limited the number of students in all Islamic educational programs. The government allows one mosque per city and funds them in large cities but otherwise limits the building of mosques through denial of building permits. The government severely restricts the number of people allowed to go on the Hajj to a fraction of the 4,600 quota set by Saudi Arabia. President Niyazov's spiritual guide, "Rukhnama," is required to be taught in schools and mosques. Refusal to do so can result in arrest.[1]

Religious organizations must register with the government. Until 2004 they needed 500 members in each locality in which they wanted to register. In practice only government-controlled Sunni Islam and a portion of the country's Russian Orthodox groups were able to register even though many other groups have enough members to do so. Unregistered groups may not conduct religious activities including gathering, proselytizing, and disseminating religious materials. Violations of these prohibitions are punished including the occasional razing of religious buildings, breaking up of religious meetings, and other forms of harassment. Foreign missionary activity is officially prohibited but unofficially occurs. The government confiscates Christian literature including non–Russian Orthodox bibles, claiming that they are not authentic Christian literature. Ethnic Turkmen who have converted to Christianity have been subject to governmental harassment. A 2003 law criminalized religious activities by unregistered religions. This was reversed by a 2004 presidential decree but these activities remain illegal and can result in fines. Unregistered organizations continue to be harassed by the government.

A 2004 law allowed for the registration of additional religious groups and lowered the minimum member requirement to five. Adventists were able to register, indicating that restrictions on minorities are lessening. The law also requires that religious organizations be headed by Turkmenistan citizens. Only

---

[1] President Niyazov served as head of state of Turkmenistan from 1985 until his death in December 2006. The information presented here on his influence on GIR in Turkmenistan is accurate for the 1990 to 2002 period covered by the RAS dataset.

adults can be members of a religious organization. Religious organizations must give 20 percent of their income to the government. Also, religious teachers require government approval.[2]

Uzbekistan

Article 18 of Uzbekistan's constitution guarantees the same rights and freedoms to all citizens regardless of their religion. Article 31 guarantees religious freedom. Article 57 forbids religious-based political parties and political parties and social associations that promote religious animosity. Article 61 declares that "religious organizations and associations are separate from the state and equal before the law" and that the state does not interfere with these organizations.

The 1998 Law on Freedom of Worship and Religious Organizations reiterates the protections for religion included in the constitution but also includes provisions that regulate and limit the practice of religion and its impact on public life. The law forbids the state from financing religious activities. Religion may not be used to encourage "anti-state and anti-constitutional propaganda, and to incite hostility, hatred, inter-ethnic discord, to undermine ethical norms and civil accord, to spread libelous, and destabilizing ideas, to create panic among the people and for other actions against the state, society . . . [or] encourage terrorism, drugs trade and organized crime." It bans religious education from the state school system. It provides for the registration of religious organizations, which must have at least 100 members over the age of 18 and be led by an Uzbek citizen who has "corresponding religious education." Noncitizen leaders of religious organizations require approval by the government's Committee for Religious Affairs. Religion can only be taught in government-licensed religious schools, not in private. Publishing or importing religious material also requires a license. Other than religious ministers, people may not appear in public in religious attire. Proselytizing is forbidden.

In practice the government supports a moderate version of Islam through the control and financing of the Spiritual Directorate for Muslims (Muftiate). The Muftiate controls the Islamic hierarchy, the content of Islamic publishing and imams' sermons. The government funds an Islamic university and citizens' participation in the Hajj. It controls all Islamic educational institutions in order

---

[2] Felix Corley, "Secret Police Close Down Mosque Refusing To Go Against Islam," *Human Rights Without Frontiers*, November 11, 2003, http://www.hrwf.net/html/turkmenistan_2003.html; Felix Corley, *Human Rights Without Frontiers*, April 7, 2004, http://www.hrwf.net/html/turkmenistan_2004.html; Felix Corley, "Turkmenistan Enacts Highly Repressive Law Against Religion," *Human Rights Without Frontiers*, April 12, 2003, http://www.hrwf.net/html/turkmenistan_2003.html; Felix Corley, "Unregistered Religious Activity Still Illegal," *Forum 18 News Service*, May 24, 2004, http://www.forum18.org; Felix Corley, "Religious Persecution's Latest Disguises," *Forum 18 News Service*, May 13, 2004; Felix Corley, "Religious Persecution Continues," *Forum 18 News Service*, May 10, 2004; John Kinahan, "Adventists Get State Registration, Baha'is May Be Next," *Forum 18 News Service*, June 3, 2004.

to assure that all future Islamic clergy is nonradical and loyal to the government. The Sunni Islam Muftiate also strictly controls the religious activities of Shi'i Muslims. This includes limiting the number of registered Shi'i mosques and an effective ban on Shi'i schools.

The government denies registration to any group it dislikes, including most radical Islamic sects. Non-Islamic groups are generally granted registration unless they attempt to convert Uzbek citizens or have too many ethnic Uzbek members. Some local governments, which take part in the registration process, have been known to delay or deny registration on technical grounds to some Christian churches. Members of nonregistered Christian groups are occasionally subject to arrest and harassment.

Religious activities by nonregistered groups are prohibited. This includes holding religious services, forming such a group, or persuading others to join such a group. These laws are enforced especially on Islamic groups that the government considers extremist and calls "Wahabbis." This includes the arrest and harassment of suspected extremists, especially after acts of violence by religious extremists. Thousands of suspected extremists are believed to be in prison. These prisoners are often denied the right to a Koran and to participate in religious activities, including praying and fasting on Ramadan. The government does not consider this religious repression but rather halting the activities of rebels. Anyone who displays an unusual amount of religious devotion, or has a beard, as well as any religious activity outside of registered mosques is considered suspicious. The Hizb ut-Tahrir, a political party that calls for the reestablishment of the Islamic Caliphate, is illegal. Several government agencies are allowed to censure religious publications and actively do so.[3]

PREFERRED TREATMENT FOR SOME RELIGIONS OR SUPPORT FOR A PARTICULAR TRADITION

About 59 percent of former Soviet bloc states fit into this category. These countries have no official religion but support some religions more than they do other religions or otherwise endorse a specific religious tradition. This often takes the form of multitiered recognition systems for religions in which religions in each category are given different levels of support and privileges. This differential treatment is often based on which religions are considered part of the traditional heritage of the country. All of these states place restrictions on minority religions.

---

[3] Igor Rotar, "State Control of Islamic Religious Education," *Forum 18 News Service*, May 11, 2004, http://www.forum18.org; Igor Rotar, "Tight Restrictions on Shia Muslim Minority," *Human Rights Without Frontiers*, April 27, 2004, http://www.hrwf.net; Igor Rotar, "Ex-KGB's 'Preventative Work' with Religious Minorities," *Human Rights Without Frontiers*, February 18, 2004.

Low Restrictions on Minorities

Bosnia

While the ethnic strife and warfare in Bosnia is well known, this assessment focuses on the religion policies of the governments that exist since the passing of Bosnia's constitution in 1995. The constitution's preamble accepts international agreements on "Rights of Persons Belonging to National or Ethnic, Religious and Linguistic Minorities." Article 1 guarantees that citizenship will not be denied on religious grounds. Article 2 protects religious freedom and protects against discrimination based on religion.

There are three governments in Bosnia, the federal government and two multiethnic constituent entities within the state: the Federation of Bosnia and Herzegovina (the Federation), which has a postwar Bosnian Muslim and Croat majority; and the Republika Srpska (RS), which has a postwar Bosnian Serb majority. The federal government has a joint presidency led by a Serb, a Muslim, and a Croat. Other positions in the federal cabinet are distributed based on an informal ethnic quota system. As ethnicity and religion are synonymous in Bosnia, this results in religious divisions and quotas at all levels of government.

While local governments do not directly restrict religious freedoms, they often create an atmosphere where restrictions can take place on the societal level. The majority ethnic group in a region tends to have religious freedom, but local minorities are sometimes harassed by members of the majority. The perpetrators are often not arrested or prosecuted. Most of these activities are not aimed specifically against religious freedom and take the form of more general harassment. Since 2000, this situation has been improving.

The RS provides funds to the Serbian Orthodox, Catholic, and Islamic religions, mostly to rebuild religious buildings, though permits for rebuilding places of worship belonging to religious groups that are a local minority are sometimes delayed or denied. During the late 1990s the RS repeatedly denied minorities the right to visit religious sites and graveyards in their previous areas of residence.

Religions are not required to register but most register as cultural or humanitarian organizations. Foreign missionaries must obtain visas but these visas are never refused. Deputies of the RS assembly can choose between taking a religious oath or a civil oath. While there is no nationwide education policy, most public schools offer religious education in the majority religion of the area. In the RS these classes are mandatory for Serbs but if there is a sufficient number of Muslims or Croats, schools in the RS usually organize classes in their religions. If offered, they are mandatory.[4]

---

[4] "Bosnia and Herzegovina – Christian Persecution in Bosnia and Herzegovina," http://www.persecution.org/humanrights/bosnia.html; "Protection, Promotion and Monitoring of Human Rights in Republika Srpska," Press release on activities within the project of the NED Grant No. 2002-074.0 Period: July 1 – September 30, 2002, Bijeljina, October, 2002, www.espero.org/documents/helsinki.htm.

Croatia

Articles 14 and 17 of Croatia's constitution protect against discrimination on the basis of religion, even in a state of emergency or direct threat to the state. Article 39 prohibits the incitement of religious hatred. Article 40 protects religious freedom. Article 41 provides for SRAS, guarantees equal treatment for all religious organizations and declares that "religious communities shall be free, in conformity with law, to publicly perform religious services, open schools, teaching establishments or other institutions, social and charitable institutions and to manage them, and shall in their activity enjoy the protection and assistance of the state." Article 47 allows for conscientious objection to military service based on religious beliefs.

Croatia has a multitiered status system for religions. The Roman Catholic Church has a special status based on a concordant with the Croatian government. The Serbian Orthodox Church and the Islamic community have a status that is slightly less privileged than the Catholic Church based on agreements signed in 2002. All of these religions receive funding from the government including support for salaries and pensions of priests. These agreements also recognize religious marriages and regulate chaplaincies and religious education in public schools. However, all religions are able to practice freely.

All public schools offer optional religion classes. If there is a sufficient number of minority students, classes in their religions are offered. Return of religious properties seized during the communist era remains an issue. While the only religion with a specific agreement on the topic is the Catholic Church, there does not seem to be any discrimination in the process for returning these properties.

In 2003 the government revised the criteria for registering a religion. A religious community needs 500 members and must be registered at least five years as an association to register as a religion.

Czech Republic

While the Czech constitution includes no mention of religion, other important documents do. Article 2 of the Charter on Fundamental Rights and Freedom states that the state "may not be bound either by an exclusive ideology or by a particular religious faith." Article 3 bans the denial of fundamental rights on the basis of religion. Article 15 guarantees religious freedom and the right to conscientious objection to military service. Article 16 protects the right of public worship, guarantees the autonomy of religious organizations, and allows the government to provide religious education in public schools.

In 2002 the government passed the Freedom of Religious Expression and the Status of Churches Act. It reiterates in detail the right to religious freedom. It guarantees the autonomy of religious organizations and prohibits the state from either promoting or restricting religion. The act also sets up a two-tiered registration system. A top-tier religious organization must have been registered as a lower tier religious organization for at least 10 years and have members equal to 0.1 percent of the population. Privileges given to top-tier organizations include teaching religion in public schools, providing chaplains to the military and prisons, state recognition of marriage ceremonies, and state funding. Lower tier organizations have a 300 member minimum, get limited tax exemptions and have a yearly reporting requirement. The law gives the government jurisdiction over opening places of worship and requires that religions use their funds for religious and not social purposes. It also allows the government to ban religions that act against the law or are a threat to the state.

Before this law, religious groups who registered automatically received top-tier status. Religious groups registered before 1991 do not need to meet the requirements of the law to keep top-tier status. Unregistered groups may worship freely but need to form a civilly recognized association in order to own property. In 1999 the government denied registration to the Unification Church.

The funding given to religious groups includes salaries for clergy and funding for schools and the maintenance of religious buildings. Some religious schools are fully funded by the state and act, in essence, as elite public schools, as admission is based solely on entrance exams. Religious education in these schools is optional.

The return of religious property seized during the communist and Nazi eras remains an issue but the government is making efforts to return property or provide compensation.[5]

Hungary

Article 60 of the Hungarian constitution declares SRAS and protects religious freedom. Article 65 provides the right to asylum for those suffering from religious persecution. Article 70 protects the human rights of all persons without regard to religion.

The 1990 Law on Freedom of Conscience and Religions as Well as Churches reiterates the principles of SRAS and religious freedom and makes it a crime for individuals to restrict religious freedom of others. It establishes a 100 member minimum for churches and associations to register. Registration is optional but grants a number of benefits. The law allows the government to fine someone who "causes a public scandal on premises designated for the purposes of the ceremonies of a registered church or insults the object of religious worship or an object used for conducting the ceremonies on or outside the premises designated for the purposes of ceremonies." The law allows the state to provide funding for church-run activities including "educational, teaching, social and health care, sports, children's and youth protection." It also allows churches to provide optional religious education in public schools after school hours. A separate law allows all registered religions to provide chaplains for the Hungarian military.

A 1990 concordant with the Catholic Church specifically gives it funds for religious education, institutions of higher learning, and ecclesiastical

---

[5] "The Church Autonomy in the Czech Republic – Ordinary of Ecclesiastical and Canon Law," Charles University, Faculty of Law, Prague.

schools. It allows citizens to donate 1 percent of their income taxes to the Church and guarantees that the Church will receive at least 0.5 percent of all income taxes collected. It provides funds for historical monuments, art, and libraries, and promises the return of church property seized during the communist era. Separate laws deal with the return of the properties of other religious groups and allow other religions as well as specified secular charitable institutions to receive similar income tax donations. In 2001 and 2002 the government completed agreements with 10 religions to support clergy in towns with populations of less than 5,000. Since 2003 donations to all registered religions are eligible for tax deduction. Previously this was true for only some religions.

Starting in 1999 the government's national security office provided an annual report on "religious movements that are dangerous to society." The 1999 report did not mention any religion by name but Scientologists complain that they were being observed. At the time of this writing, no legal action has been taken on the basis of these reports. The government tax authority has carried out wide-scale audits of some non-traditional churches including the Charismatic-Evangelical Faith Church and the Church of Scientology.

Overall, while Hungary maintains religious freedom, Hungary's traditional and larger religions tend to get preferential treatment by the government. Court decisions have acknowledged that the government can take into account the historical role of religious organizations in the country.[6]

Latvia

Article 99 of Latvia's constitution declares SRAS and guarantees religious freedom. However, Article 116 allows restrictions on religious freedom "in order to protect the rights of other people, the democratic structure of the State, and public safety, welfare and morals." Article 30 protects the privacy of religious belief.

The 1995 Law on Religious Organizations (as amended in 1997, 1998, and 2000) reiterates the principles of religious freedom and SRAS. It establishes the Board of Religious Affairs to handle relations between religions and the state. Optional religious education in public schools is allowed but can only be taught by the Evangelic Lutheran, Roman Catholic, Orthodox, Old Believers, Jewish, or Baptist religions. A congregation must have 10 adult members in order to register. New religious organizations must re-register yearly for 10 years before getting permanent approval. Only registered religious organizations can open religious schools, invite foreign clergy and missionaries into the country, own property, and engage in financial transactions. However registration is not necessary in order to practice one's religion. Religions denied

[6] Schanda (2002); Robert Traer, "Religious Freedom in Central and Eastern Europe," *Center for the Study of Ethics and Social Policy at the Graduate Theological Union*, http://www.geocities. com/r_traer/Culture/Europe/mission.nationalists.htm.

registration include the Latvian Free Orthodox Church, the Church of Christian Scientists, and the Rock of Salvation Church. Until 1998, the Jehovah's Witnesses were unable to register. Because the government does not recognize more than one religious association for each confession, splinter groups cannot register.

The government has a closer relationship with the six religions listed in the Law on Religious Organizations and is wary of other religions. In practice, visas for foreign religious workers can be difficult to obtain due to a cumbersome application process. While religion is not listed on state identity cards, ethnicity, which in some cases overlaps with religion, is listed. There is a negative attitude toward nontraditional religions in Latvia, but this has not yet caused significant discrimination against them beyond the level of negative stereotypes in the media.[7]

Lithuania

Article 25 of Lithuania's constitution bans instigating religious hatred or violence. Article 26 protects religious freedom. Article 27 states that "a person's convictions, professed religion or faith may justify neither the commission of a crime nor the violation of law." Article 29 bans discrimination or the granting of privileges based on religion. Article 40 requires state schools to be secular but to offer religious education at the request of the parents. Article 43 declares SRAS but also recognizes the "traditional Lithuanian churches and religious organizations, as well as other churches and religious organizations provided that they have a basis in society and their teaching and rituals do not contradict morality or the law." It also grants these organizations the freedom to act freely, provided they abide by the law, but also states that their specific status "shall be established by agreement or by law."

The Law on Religious Communities and Associations creates a multitiered recognition system, which gives traditional religions the highest status, followed by recognized religions, then registered religions. "State recognition denotes state backing of the spiritual, cultural and social heritage of religious associations." The country's traditional religions are the Roman Catholic, Greek Catholic, Evangelical Lutheran, Evangelical Reformed, Russian Orthodox, Old Believer, Jewish, Sunni Muslim, and Karaite faiths. All other religions must be registered for 25 years before they are recognized as religious associations. Religious communities may register if there are at least 15 members and religious associations need at least two communities to register. Both registered and recognized religions have the status of legal persons. Only traditional religious groups can teach religion in public schools and, as of 2001, can get funding for their private schools, but all recognized and registered groups can open private religious schools. The salaries of clergy are tax exempt.

---

[7] Nikandrs Gills, "New Religious Movements in Latvia in the Mirror of the Press," Center for the Study of New Religions, 1999, http://www.cesnur.org/testi/gills3.htm.

In this four-tiered system, traditional religions get all of the above rights, state funding, and special tax breaks. Recognized religions receive no regular funding but can get funding for specific projects. Both traditional and recognized religions get military exemptions and social benefits for their clergy and provide chaplains for the military. Registered groups get none of these rights but do have status as legal entities. They cannot buy land but can rent it. Nonregistered religions can worship freely but do not have the status of legal persons.

The Hasidic Chabad Lubavich community has been seeking unsuccessfully to be recognized as a traditional religion. Two groups have been denied registration, the Osho Ojas Meditation Center and the Lithuanian Pagans Community (Old Sorcerer). The government considers them nonreligious and suggested that they register as NGOs. In 2002, parliament suspended the registration of the Old Baltic Faith Community Romuva. While there are no restrictions on foreign missionaries, the government gives preference to missionaries from the country's traditional religions in gaining residency permits. Several groups considered by the government to be "sects" report particular difficulties in gaining permits. The return of religious property seized during the communist era is ongoing, but the Catholic Church has been the most successful at recovering its property.

The government established a commission in 2000 to investigate whether "sects" violate the law. Due to its recommendations the country's criminal code was altered to include "fines and imprisonment of up to three years for religious groups, communities, and centers that use psychological violence to persuade a person or his/her relatives to take illegal action or prevent him/her from pursuing legal action." There are media reports of the government monitoring the Jehovah's Witnesses. Also, in 2000 the Ministry of Justice warned the Collegiate Association for the Research of the Principle to discontinue proselytizing on behalf of the Unification Church because the activity was not described in their own statutes and thus violated the Law on Public Organizations.

Moderate Restrictions on Minorities

Poland

Article 25 of Poland's 1997 constitution gives all churches and religious organizations equal rights and guarantees their autonomy from the government. The relationship between the state and the Catholic Church, as well as other religions, is determined by an agreement. Article 35 gives minorities the right to establish institutions designed to protect their religious identity. Article 48 gives parents the right to raise their children based on their own convictions. Article 53 protects religious freedom and allows legally recognized religions to be taught in state schools. Article 85 allows for alternative service for conscientious objectors. Article 191 allows religious organizations to petition the constitutional court. Article 233 states that religious freedom may not be abridged even under emergency laws. The preamble makes two mentions of God and oaths of office for government officials can optionally include the phrase "so help me God."

Religious groups may register or form specific agreements with the state but do not need to do so in order to function freely. Registration requires 100 member signatures. Religion is taught in public schools, mostly in Catholicism, but courses in other registered religions are sometimes available upon request. The return of religious property seized during the Nazi and communist eras remains an issue, though the government is making efforts to resolve it.

Abortion is legal in the first 12 weeks of pregnancy in cases of rape, incest, fetal impairment, and to preserve the life, health, or mental health of the woman, and afterward if the pregnancy endangers the life or health of the woman. It is not available on demand or for economic or social reasons. If performed it must be by a specially qualified obstetrician or gynecologist.

There are other indications of the Catholic Church's privileged status. For instance, the Catholic Church has the right to re-license radio and television stations that operate on frequencies licensed to it. No other nongovernmental body may do this.

There are some restrictions on nontraditional minorities. The government has declared the Unification Church a dangerous sect, publishes anti–Unification Church literature, and teaches against it in the schools. The Unification Church is also prohibited from publishing, distributing literature, holding public meetings and speaking in public. Between 2001 and 2002 there was a department within the Ministry of Interior to monitor the activities of "new religious groups" and "cults." There are also reports that government officials as well as schoolteachers and administrators have been given anti-sect training by the Catholic Church, but the extent to which this has occurred is unclear.[8]

High Restrictions on Minorities

Armenia
Article 25 of Armenia's constitution protects religious freedom. However, according to Articles 45 and 55 this, along with other civil rights, can be limited when there is a threat to the constitutional order or in cases of martial law. Article 48 states that the rights in the constitution cannot be used to support religious hatred.

The Law on Freedom and Conscience, as amended in 1997, provides detailed protection for religious freedom, including freedom from religion. It requires a 300-member minimum for a religion to register and specifically recognizes the Armenian Apostolic Church. It protects the rights of religious

[8] "Government Rethinks Anti-sect Moves," *Human Rights Without Frontiers*, 2001, http://www.hrwf.net/html/poland2001.html.

associations but forbids proselytizing. However, no action is generally taken against missionaries. It forbids financing of religious organizations from abroad, though the government considers this unenforceable. It also forbids religious financing of political parties and associations.

The law contains a clause for SRAS and forbids state funding for religion except to preserve historical monuments, but also recognizes the "Armenian Apostolic Church as the national Church of the Armenian people." It also grants the Armenian Apostolic Church special rights, which the law calls "the monopoly of the Armenian Church." These include: to preach, proselytize, and disseminate their faith; "to re-create her historical traditions, structures, organization, dioceses, and communities"; to build or restore religious structures; "to contribute to the spiritual edification of the Armenian people and to carry out the same in the state educational institutes within the law"; to enhance moral standards; and to have permanent chaplains in hospitals, the military, prisons, and old-age homes. The law also promises that the government will protect Armenian Church activities outside Armenia.

Religious education in public schools is a monopoly of the Armenian Church, but is optional and only included if the principal requests it. Groups refused registration may not publish magazines or newspapers, broadcast programs on television or radio, rent meeting places, or officially sponsor the visas of visitors. The Jehovah's Witnesses have been refused registration because of their opposition to military service, and several groups with too few members to qualify have not sought registration. Until 1995, the Baptist Union of Armenia was denied registration and considered a dangerous sect. There are also reports of significant harassment of nontraditional religious communities by the public, including dismissal from work, physical attacks, and kidnappings, with the perpetrators consistently going unpunished. There are also reports of harassment by individual local officials and that since 2003 members of nontraditional religions are banned from serving on the police force. Customs officials also sometimes confiscate religious literature and correspondence by nontraditional religions.[9]

Belarus

Article 16 of Belarus's constitution declares all religions equal before the law and bans differential treatment of different religions. It also states that religious organizations may not engage in activities "against the sovereignty of the Republic of Belarus, its constitutional system and civic harmony, or [those that] involve a violation of civil rights and liberties." Article 31 protects religious

---

[9] Hendon & Kennedy (1995); September 13, 2002, Report of Special Rapporteurs to the Parliamentary Assembly of the Council of Europe on Armenia's Compliance with Council of Europe Human Rights Requirements; Felix Corley, "Secret Order Banishes Religious Minorities from Police," *Forum 18 News Service*, April 25, 2003, http://www.forum18.org; *ISKCON World Review* vol. 14, no. 1, May/June 1995.

freedom. Article 4 states that religious ideologies may not be made compulsory for citizens. Article 5 prohibits political parties and other public associations that promote religious hatred. Article 12 allows the state to grant asylum to those suffering from religious persecution.

The 2002 Law on Religious Freedom and Religious Organizations both reiterates the protections included in the constitution and limits them. Religious organizations may not participate in political activities. Registration is obligatory and the law requires all religious groups to re-register. Religious associations must have a 20-year presence in the country and include at least 10 religious communities. Religious communities must include at least 20 citizens over the age of 18, but there is no minimum presence requirement. "Republican religious association" status is given to those religions that operate in the majority of the country. The state reviews the religious principles of an organization before approving registration. The law includes a number of reasons for denying registration as well as for "liquidating" religious organizations. Only a Belarusian citizen can be the head of a religious organization. Religious literature can only be distributed on the premises of religious organizations. Technically, unregistered groups are not allowed to engage in basic religious activities including public worship. Many argue that this law is intended to establish the dominance of the Belarusian Orthodox Church and to deny Protestant denominations registration.

These registration requirements are cumbersome and the law effectively prohibits all religious activity by unregistered groups. The government tends to deny registration to groups it considers nontraditional, including Orthodox churches other than the Belarusian and Russian Orthodox churches, most Protestants, the Unification Church, Hare Krishna, and Scientologists. Only registered groups can open new churches and invite religious workers. Foreign religious workers may not engage in missionary activities outside of the institution that invited them. The government restricts the renting of property by nonregistered groups and requires all religious property to meet building codes that are specific to religious buildings. Local authorities often break up unauthorized religious meetings. Recently, local authorities have denied permits to registered organizations to purchase or rent property. The authorities often harass nonregistered communities, especially the Hindu and Pentecostal communities, including arresting and harassing community leaders. Vigilante attacks on members of minority religions tend to go unpunished. The state media often portrays nontraditional groups as destructive and fanatical.

In 2003, the government signed a concordant with the Belarusian Orthodox Church which establishes a special relationship between the Church and the state and recognizes the Church's "influence on the formulation of spiritual, cultural and national traditions of the Belarusian people." It also provides for cooperation in education, security, and culture as well as in combating "pseudo-religious structures that present a danger to individuals and society."

The return of religious property seized during Soviet rule remains an issue.[10]

Bulgaria

Article 13 of Bulgaria's constitution guarantees religious freedom and SRAS but also states that "Eastern Orthodox Christianity is considered the traditional religion in the Republic of Bulgaria." Article 37 restates the protection for religious freedom and notes that the state has an obligation to "assist the maintenance of tolerance and respect among the believers from different denominations, and among believers and non-believers." Articles 11 and 13 forbid political parties based on religion as well as the use of religious institutions and communities for political ends. Article 44 forbids religious incitement. Article 6 guarantees that all citizens are equal under the law regardless of their religion. Articles 37 and 58 state that religion cannot be the basis for breaking laws, for public disorder, or threatening the well-being of others or the state.

The government provides funds to the Eastern Orthodox Church and other religions considered traditional to Bulgaria, including Islam, Roman Catholicism, and Judaism. Optional religious education classes are taught in public schools, and classes are also available in some minority religions. The 2002 Confessions Act requires all religions, other than the Eastern Orthodox Church, to register but is unclear on the criteria for registration. The law also takes sides in an internal dispute over the leadership of the Eastern Orthodox Church, declaring one faction the official leadership and forbids any group that has broken off from a registered group from claiming that group's name or using its property. The government has also interfered in the appointment of the country's official Muslim Muftis.

The government restricts the practice of some minority religions. Even before the 2002 law, the registration process was "selective, slow and nontransparent." Members of registered religions can practice freely but those of unregistered religions are by law required to halt their activities, though this is enforced intermittently. All religions have been forced to periodically re-register and previously registered religions are often refused registration.

Religions must register at both the national and local levels. Many local governments refuse registration to nationally registered religions and sometimes restrict the building of places of worship by registered groups, especially

---

[10] Yuras Karmanau, "Belarus Adopts Religion Law Despite Criticism by Minority Faiths," Associated Press, June 27, 2002; Don Hill, "Belarus: New Religion Law May Be Restrictive, But It's Not All That Unusual," Radio Free Europe / Radio Liberty, http://www.rferl.org; "Persecuted Church News," Religious Liberty Commission of the World Evangelical Association, April 2003; W. Cole Durham, Jr., Melinda Porter, and Brian Gross, "Analysis of the 2002 Belarusian Draft Law, On the Introduction of Changes and Amendments to Law of the Republic of Belarus On Religious Freedom and Religious Organizations," BYU International Center for Law & Religion Studies, September 28, 2002; Michael Wines, "New Belarus Law Codifies Rising Religious Repression," *New York Times,* November 11, 2002; Geraldine Fagan, "Religious Freedom Survey, November 2003," *Forum 18 News Service,* http://www.forum18.org.

nontraditional groups like the Jehovah's Witnesses. Unregistered groups are subject to even higher levels of harassment by local authorities including bans on the distribution of religious literature, proselytizing in public, references to faith-healing, preaching to minors without parents' express permission, and holding prayer services at facilities not registered with the municipal authorities. However, recent pressure from the national government has limited some of these practices.

There are ample additional examples of restrictions on nontraditional religions. A 1996 law forbids the use of public buildings by "sects." Since 1993 "sects" have been denied the use of cultural centers. A 1999 law allows access to jails for clergy from traditional religions but does not allow access to clergy from nontraditional religions. Parents belonging to unregistered religions are often denied child custody on the basis of their religious beliefs.

Visa laws are often used to restrict entry of foreign missionaries into the country. There are also reports of harassment of missionaries by police and the confiscation of religious materials from missionaries entering the country as well as of foreign religious workers being expelled from the country due to their activities. The return of religious properties confiscated by the communist government remains an issue, but preference does not seem to be given to any particular religion on this issue. Bulgaria's media often presents negative stereotypes of religious minorities, including Christian "sects" and "nontraditional" Islam.[11]

Georgia

Article 9 of Georgia's constitution declares SRAS and freedom of religious belief but also "recognizes the special importance of the Georgian Orthodox Church in Georgian history." Articles 14 and 37 protect against discrimination based on religion. Article 19 protects religious freedom. In Article 71, the oath for the president includes reference to God.

The Georgian Orthodox Church has a tax-exempt status not given to other religious groups. Georgian schools teach history of religion courses in which the Georgian Orthodox Church has the unofficial right to approve the textbooks. The Church requires that these textbooks give absolute precedence to Orthodox Christianity. In 2002 the government signed a concordant with the Church reiterating its special place in Georgian history. The concordant also gave the church privileges not given to other religions, including authority over

[11] European Court of Human Rights webpage, "Hasan and Chuash vs. Bulgaria," http://www.echr.coe.int; "United States Policies in Support of Religious Freedom: Focus on Christians," U.S. State Department, July 22, 1997; World Religions and Cultures website, Bulgaria Report, http://wrc.lingnet.org/bulgaria.htm; International Helsinki Federation Report on Religious Freedom in Eastern Europe, 2000; HRWF International Secretariat, June 26, 2002, http://www.hrwf.net; "Report: Bulgaria"; "Minorities in Bulgaria, Muslim, 1999," Center for Documentation and Information on Minorities in Europe, www.greekhelsinki.gr.

all religious literature and construction, chaplaincies in the military and prisons, and compensation for damage to the Church during the Soviet era.

There is no process for registering religious organizations but they must register as charitable organizations in order to engage in basic activities including renting property and importing literature. Most religions practice freely but nontraditional religions are restricted by the practices of Orthodox extremists, and sometimes local officials, which the government fails to control or prosecute. This harassment is aimed particularly at missionaries of the Jehovah's Witnesses, Baptist, Evangelical, Pentecostal, and Hare Krishna faiths. Violent attacks have been common since 1999 and include the seizing of religious literature and the breaking up of religious meetings. Customs officials and police also sometimes seize religious literature belonging to nontraditional religions. In 2001 the supreme court upheld the government's revocation of the registration of the Jehovah's Witnesses. While the Georgian Orthodox Church has received most of the property seized during the Soviet era, many other religious groups, including Roman Catholic and Armenian Apostolic Churches, have not.[12]

Kazakhstan

Article 1 of Kazakhstan's constitution defines the state as secular. Articles 5 and 20 prohibit the incitement of religious enmity and hatred. Article 5 prohibits religious political parties and requires government approval for foreign religious entities. Article 14 prohibits discrimination based on religion. Article 19 protects the right of religious affiliation.

The 1992 Law on Freedom of Religion protects religious freedoms and declares the separation of religious associations from the state. It declares all religious associations equal under the law. It prohibits state financing of religious institutions and participation in political activities by religious institutions. It declares that the state educational system is secular but allows "disciplines involving the study of religion" to be included in the curriculum. It established the State Organ on Ties with Religious Associations, which registers religions and is responsible for government relations with religious organizations. Registration requires a minimum of 10 members. Unregistered religions are allowed to practice freely. However, Article 375 of the Administrative Code contradicts this law and allows the government to suspend the activities of unregistered religions and fine their leaders. The majority of cases brought under this law are dismissed by the courts.

A 2002 law on religion requires religious organizations to register and increases the minimum membership to 50. It bans "extremist religious associations" and authorizes local officials to suspend the activities of religious groups if one or more of their members commit criminal violations or if religious activities are conducted outside the place where they are registered.

---

[12] Human Rights Watch Statement: Freedom of Religion, September 12, 2002; "Amnesty International Report 2002: Georgia," http://web.amnesty.org/web/ar2002.nsf/eur/georgia!Open.

It requires that foreign religious organizations be affiliated with a national religious organization. It also requires that any Islamic organization receive the approval of the Muslim Spiritual Association in order to register but this was declared unconstitutional by the courts.

Registration by some nontraditional groups is sometimes delayed or denied on technical grounds. Local authorities often require religions to register locally. The Jehovah's Witnesses have had difficulty in registering with some local governments. Sometimes local authorities deny them permits to rent sites for religious meetings. Some local authorities claim, contrary to the law, that unregistered religions may not conduct religious activities. They have disrupted religious meetings by unregistered nontraditional religions held in private homes and confiscated religious literature. There have also been isolated attempts by local authorities to ban some nontraditional religions. Foreign missionaries complain of harassment by local officials. Registration of missionaries, while required, is considered a legal right but, in practice, many are required to find local sponsors. This harassment of nontraditional groups began to increase around 1998.

The government is concerned about the spread of religious extremism among Muslims and arrests and occasionally prosecutes members of the Hizb ut-Tahri – an extremist Islamic organization that advocates the establishment of an Islamic caliphate in Central Asia – for distributing literature. Arrests of religious extremists increased in 1999. In 1999 the government recalled all students studying in religious institutions outside Kazakhstan. The government has occasionally prosecuted foreign Arabic teachers for fomenting religious hostility and disseminating propaganda on the superiority of Muslims. It has also expelled unaccredited Muslim missionaries. The government has donated buildings or provided assistance for the building of new mosques, synagogues, and Russian Orthodox churches.[13]

Macedonia

Articles 9 and 54 of Macedonia's constitution guarantee equality and prohibit discrimination on the basis of religion. Article 110 states that the constitutional court protects this right. Article 19 guarantees religious freedom and states that religious groups "are free to establish schools and other social and charitable institutions, by ways of a procedure regulated by law." Article 20 states that political parties and other associations may not incite religious hatred or intolerance. Article 47 guarantees the protection of religious identity. The constitution was amended in 2001 to include mention of the Jewish community

---

[13] "Christians Fear Decade of Freedom Is Over," *Christianity Today*, March 11, 2002; Religious Discrimination and Related Violations of Helsinki Commitments, Kazakhstan, March 22, 1999, http://eurasia.org.ru/archive/2000/trib_en/03_26_Religious.htm; HRWF International Secretariat, September 8, 2000, http://www.hrwf.net; "Kazakhstan's Muslims Call for Harmony and Dialogue Amid Cries for Jihad," (PRWEB Newswire) February 13, 2003; "Muslims in Kazakhstan Arrested for Calling for Jihad Against Israel," Associated Press, April 16, 2002.

and the Methodist Church. Previously, only the Macedonian Orthodox Church was mentioned. No religion in Macedonia has official status or privileges.

The 1997 Law on Religious Communities and Religious Groups designates the Macedonian Orthodox Church, Islam, the Roman Catholic Church, Judaism, and the Methodist Church as religious communities. All other religions are designated as religious groups and have the same rights as religious communities. Religious rituals can only be performed at recognized religious facilities or with a permit in public places. The law limits religious education and the collection of contributions to facilities where religious rituals are performed. The headquarters of the organization must be in Macedonia. Foreign citizens can only perform religious activities and rituals with the permission of the government. Only Macedonian citizens can conduct education in religious schools, though foreign citizens can gain a temporary permit.

Based on this law it is technically illegal for unregistered religions to engage in religious activities. This has been a particular issue for the Serbian Orthodox Church because it is not recognized by the Macedonian Orthodox Church. While many of these regulations are not strictly enforced, the government acts if a complaint is filed. On occasion such complaints have been filed against Serbian Orthodox priests for engaging in religious rites and ceremonies, leading to fines and arrests. In at least one case the government razed an illegal church. The Unification Church has been forced to register as a secular organization. Members are allowed to meet in private dwellings but if too many members attend it is considered illegal and if a neighbor complains, the police break up the meeting. Visas have also been denied to missionaries from the church and some have been expelled from the country. Religious groups must register in order to build places of worship. Several registered Protestant groups were unable to obtain building permits for their churches. A number of mosques were destroyed or damaged during the violent conflict between the government and ethnic Albanians in 2000 and 2001. The issue of the return of religious property seized during the communist era is ongoing.

A 2003 law provides for optional religious education in public schools. The government also occasionally funds public religious structures.[14]

Moldova

Article 10 of Moldova's constitution guarantees all citizens the "right to preserve, develop and express" their religious identity. Article 16 protects against discrimination on the basis of religion. Article 31 declares SRAS, guarantees religious freedom, and forbids the incitement of religious hatred or enmity. Article 32 bans religious hatred. Article 35 ensures the freedom of religious

---

[14] Nicholas Wood, "Bishop's Struggle Reflects Wider Balkan Rift," *International Herald Tribune*, November 3, 2004; Branko Bjelajac, "Orthodox Monk and Bishop Fined, and Another Bishop Still Jailed", *Forum 18 News Service*, January 8, 2004, http://www.forum18.org; Branko Bjelajac, "Serbian Bishop Sentenced to Solitary Confinement," *Forum 18 News Service*, July 24, 2003.

education but also ensures a lay education. Article 72, which lists parliament's legislative powers, includes "the general status of religious worship."

The 1992 Law on Creeds allows the state to "maintain relations with the traditional Orthodox Church and other recognized creeds." It bans proselytizing (amended in 1999) and requires registration and government recognition for religious organizations to function including owning property and hiring employees. It bans religious political parties. It establishes the State Service for Creed Problems to oversee the state relationship with religious organizations. The preservation of historical religious buildings and art is subsidized by the state. It gives the state oversight on the economic and financial activities of religious organizations. Monks and single priests are exempt from taxes. Religious education in schools is optional. In 2000 this law was amended to make religious education mandatory for primary school students and optional for secondary school students.

While there is no official religion in Moldova, the Moldovan Orthodox Church gets preferential treatment. For example, the head of the Church and other high Church officials get diplomatic passports. Also, it has favored status in the return of religious properties seized during the communist era, though other religions have also received returned property.

Registration is denied to a number of groups including several Muslim groups, Mormons, Methodists, and some Baptist groups. Until 2002 a law denying registration to "schismatic movements" kept two Orthodox churches from registering. One of these churches was only registered after a court order. This law was only applied to Orthodox churches as multiple groups from several minority religions, including the Seventh Day Adventists, were able to register separately. Unregistered religions may not buy land or rent property in their names but often do so under the name of individuals. They are also forbidden from holding public assemblies such as revival meetings. Unregistered groups including Muslims and Evangelicals are often harassed by local authorities, who break up religious meetings. Since 1997 the Jehovah's Witnesses have been harassed based on a false document that claims to revoke their registration. Some local authorities have since revoked the registration of the Jehovah's Witnesses.

In 1999 a law allowing proselytizing came into effect but "abusive proselytizing," which is defined as "an attempt to influence an individual's religious faith through violence or abuse of authority," is still prohibited. A 2002 criminal code forbids "preaching religious beliefs or fulfillment of religious rituals, which cause harm to the health of citizens, or other harm to their persons or rights, or instigate citizens not to participate in public life or of the fulfillment of their obligations as citizens." This phrase was copied from a statute that was used in the Soviet era as a basis for anti-religious persecution.[15]

---

[15] Felix Corley, "Methodists Live Twilight Existence, Leader Claims," *Forum 18 News Service,* http://www.forum18.org; Felix Corley, "Police Move To Crush Baptist Street Libraries," *Forum 18 News Service,* April 29, 2003; "'Khrushchevite Smell' From New Criminal Code Article," HRWF International Secretariat, June 21, 2002.

Romania

Article 4 of Romania's constitution protects against discrimination on the basis of religion. Article 6 recognizes the right to protect and preserve minority religious identities. Article 7 declares that the state will preserve the development and expression of the religious identity of Romanians living abroad. Article 29 declares SRAS, protects religious freedom, and states that religions will receive support from the state including "the facilitation of religious assistance in the army, in hospitals, prisons, homes, and orphanages." Articles 29 and 30 prohibit the instigation of religious enmity or hatred. Article 32 guarantees the freedom of religious education. Article 44 states that religious weddings may only be celebrated after civil marriages. Article 72 includes "general statutory rules of religious cults" in parliament's legislative powers. The presidential oath of office in Article 82 ends with "so help me God."

A 1948 communist era decree that allows considerable government interference in religion is still technically the law that regulates government relations with religion. The State Secretariat for Religious Denominations claims that a large number of its provisions are effectively nullified by Romania's constitution and that the parts of the statute that interfere in religious practices are not enforced.

Romania has a three-tiered status system for religions. The highest tier is recognized religions. The 1948 law recognizes 14 religions. The government added the Greek Catholic Church in 1989. The process for recognition is heavily influenced by the Romanian Orthodox Church and bureaucratic obstacles exist for most religions trying to gain this status. Since 1989 only two religions have been added to the list; one of them, the Jehovah's Witnesses, was added only by court order and the government delayed the application of the order for several years. Recognized religions are allowed to "establish schools, teach religion in public schools, receive government funds to build churches, pay clergy salaries with state funds and subsidize clergy's housing expenses, broadcast religious programming on radio and television, apply for broadcasting licenses for denominational frequencies, and enjoy tax-exempt status." The second tier of religions are those registered as charitable foundations or religious associations. These groups have the status of a legal person and enjoy some tax exemptions.

The Romanian Orthodox Church exerts considerable influence as the majority religion of the country. It receives the most state funding, including most "off-budget" funds, and its leaders usually preside at state functions. The state has recently funded the building of a number of Orthodox churches.

Any recognized or registered religion can build a place of worship subject to the approval of a board, which includes members of the Romanian Orthodox Church but no official representatives of other religions. Even when building permits are granted, local governments often obstruct the building of minority religion houses of worship, especially in localities where the mayor is a Romanian Orthodox priest. Nontraditional religious groups often have difficulty gaining permits to use public halls for religious activities, usually due to objections by Orthodox priests. Local officials often interfere with religious meetings that have received permits.

A 2001 law requires that foreign religious workers represent a recognized religion. While a 1999 court ruling forbids the Ministry of Education from requiring Seventh Day Adventists to take exams on Saturdays, many local schools ignore this ruling. Despite legal protections, low-level government officials and Orthodox priests interfere with proselytizing. Only recognized religions can give religious assistance to prisoners and few military chaplains are not Orthodox priests. The government limits radio licenses for minority religions and restricts the number of hours they may broadcast. Census takers often refuse to note the religious affiliation of minorities on census forms, which is important as government funding for recognized religions is based on census results.

Religious education is optional in public schools and only the recognized religions may teach these classes. In practice, teachers from minority religions rarely gain accreditation because the inspectors who grant accreditation are usually Orthodox priests. There are reports of minority students being pressured into taking classes on the Orthodox religion.

The return of religious property seized during the communist era has, in general, been slow and difficult. This is especially so for the Greek Catholic Church which, under the communist regime, was forced to merge with the Romanian Orthodox Church. As a result the Orthodox Church claims many former Greek Catholic buildings.[16]

Russia

Articles 13 and 29 of Russia's constitution prohibit the incitement of religious hatred. Article 29 prohibits promoting ideas of racial superiority. Article 14 declares that the Russian Federation is a secular state, that religious institutions will be separate from the state, that all religions are equal before the law, and it prohibits a state-sponsored or mandatory religion. Article 19 protects equal rights regardless of religion and prohibits discrimination on religious grounds. Article 28 protects religious freedom including the right to disseminate one's religion. Article 59 allows for alternative military service for conscientious objectors.

The 1997 Law on Freedom of Conscience and Religions affirms and reiterates the rights guaranteed in the constitution but, in practice, allows for significant limitations on minority religions. It recognizes "the special role of Orthodoxy in the history of Russia" but also respects "Christianity, Islam, Buddhism, Judaism, and other religions, constituting an integral part of the historical heritage of the peoples of Russia." It declares that state education will be secular but allows, upon parental request, religious education outside of the general curriculum.

---

[16] Peter Finn, "A Matter of Orthodox Church and State: Building Program Alarms Romania's Ethnic Hungarians," *Washington Post*, February 11, 2000; "Romania: Protestant Radios Facing Closure," BBC, December 14, 1998.

This law required all previously registered religious organizations to re-register. Registration of local religious organizations requires at least 10 members and a 15-year presence in their region. A 1999 court decision exempted from this waiting period groups registered before the implementation of the law. National religious organizations must include at least three local ones. A 1999 revision of the law allows the government to liquidate groups that did not re-register after 1997. This has since happened to several groups.

Religious groups, which are defined as unregistered groups, do not have the status of legal persons and may not own property, open a bank account, proselytize, or engage in those practices reserved for registered organizations. Foreign religious organizations may obtain permission to send representatives to the country but may not "engage in cultural and other religious activity." Religious organizations may not participate in elections or political activities. Religious organizations have the exclusive right to invite foreign religious workers, publish their liturgical literature, and open educational institutions to train clergy. The law also contains numerous provisions that prohibit religious organizations from violating the law or national security. Groups that are in violation and those that are deemed a threat to society can be banned, which makes engaging in any religious activity illegal.

In practice the government does not always respect the protections for SRAS and religious freedom in its constitution. The government has entered into a number of agreements with the Russian Orthodox Church, giving it privileges on issues of public education, access to prisoners and hospitals, law enforcement, and customs. There is no religious education in state schools but in some regions the Russian Orthodox Church uses state school grounds for voluntary religious instruction after school hours. The texts for these courses contain "language against non-Orthodox, particularly Jews." The government of Tataristan, an Islamic region of Russia, has funded the building of about 1,000 mosques and several Islamic schools.

Russian law enforcement officials commonly speak of the need to control "sects" and "cults," which usually refers to Protestant groups. There are isolated incidences of local authorities detaining members of local religious minorities for expressing their religious views. While some Protestant clergy are given access to military bases, Muslim clergy are banned. In practice religions must register both locally and nationally. Local officials, influenced by the Russian Orthodox Church, often refuse to register religions, or create prohibitive bureaucratic obstacles to registration. Jehovah's Witnesses, Pentecostals, Scientologists, Buddhists, and Mormons have had particular difficulties in registering in some localities. Several local governments have also banned some nontraditional religions, which can result in orders to cease all religious activities. Some local governments have prevented nontraditional religious groups from renting large venues for religious events, have refused to grant title to properties purchased by them, and have prevented their occupation of rented properties. The provisions that protect against religious incitement are often not enforced, especially in cases of incitement against Jews.

Foreign religious workers have difficulty getting visas, are often harassed by customs officials, and sometimes are deported, even if they have valid visas. Roman Catholic priests, in particular, have been the targets of deportation.[17]

GENERAL SUPPORT

These countries support religion in general and, for the most part, no religion or group of religions in particular benefit from this support. Both of the former Soviet Bloc countries in this category place some restrictions on minority groups.

Slovakia

Article 1 of Slovakia's constitution declares that the government "is not linked to any ideology or religious belief." Article 12 guarantees basic rights and freedoms regardless of religion. Article 24 guarantees religious freedom and the internal autonomy of religious organizations. Article 25 protects the right of conscientious objection to military service.

Registration is not required but legally only registered religions can worship publicly. In practice members of unregistered religions can practice their religion freely but there are signs that this may be changing. In 2001, the Christian Fellowship, a group of Protestant congregations, was told that they would lose their registration as a civil association if they did not change their by-laws to exclude religious activity.

Registered religions get subsidies for clergy and religious education, which includes salaries of religion teachers in public schools. As the country's largest religion, the Catholic Church receives the majority of these funds. The government sometimes funds one-time projects such as the restoration of religious buildings and monuments. Registration is also necessary to build public places of worship, for clergy access to prisons, and to conduct legally valid weddings and funerals. There is a 20,000-member requirement to register unless a religion is already registered. Public schools give students the option of taking a class in religion or one in ethics. The return of religious property seized during the communist era is partial and ongoing.

The Institute of State-Church Relations monitors "cults" and "sects." Scientologists complain that the Slovak Information Service negatively portrays them and businesses owned by them. Also, the Slovak Intelligence Services monitors Scientologists and the Unification Church.[18]

---

[17] Geraldine Fagan, "Full Moscow Court Decision Slams Jews," *Forum 18 News Service*, May 25, 2004, http://www.forum18.org/.

[18] "Slovak Churches To Enter Schools," *Financial Times*, July 16, 2003; Felix Corley, "Why Can't Smaller Protestant Churches or Muslims Gain Legal Status?" *Human Rights Without Frontiers*, 2002, http://www.hrwf.net/; "Protestant Fellowship To Be Deregistered?" *Human Rights Without Frontiers*, 2001, http://www.hrwf.net/; "Slovak Intelligence Service's Report to Parliament Outlines Monitored Groups," *Financial Times*, May 16, 2004.

Slovenia

Article 7 of Slovenia's constitution declares SRAS and grants religious communities equal rights including the right to pursue their activities freely. Article 14 guarantees equal human rights irrespective of religion. Article 16 allows temporary suspension of human rights in extraordinary circumstances, but this suspension may not be on the basis of religion. Article 41 protects religious freedom. Article 63 declares unconstitutional the incitement of religious hatred or discrimination. Article 121 allows for conscientious objection to military service.

Religions must register with the Government's Office for Religious Communities to be recognized as legal entities, but this is not required in order to practice. While no requests for registration have been refused, between 2000 and 2003 several religious groups complained that their requests for registration received no response due to the influence of the office's director. Government pressure resulted in the end of these delays in 2003. In order to receive tax exemptions religious groups must register separately with the Interior Ministry. The municipal authorities in the country's capital, Ljubljana, refuse to allow the Muslim community to build a mosque.

The government contributes to social insurance in place of employers, if the individual in question works solely as clergy. It funds the maintenance of some cultural monuments owned by religious communities. Religious charitable programs compete for government funding on a basis equal to other charitable organizations. Religious education is only taught in schools supported by religious bodies. While religion is not taught in public schools, the government has introduced a course in religion and ethics. Private religious schools can receive up to 85 percent of their funding from the government in a manner comparable to the funding of public schools.[19]

MODERATE SEPARATION

These countries maintain a moderate level of separation of state but still legislate several aspects of religion. All of them engage in low or moderate levels of discrimination against minority religions.

Low Restrictions on Minorities

Estonia

Article 12 of Estonia's constitution prohibits the propagation of religious hatred or discrimination. Article 40 protects religious freedom and

---

[19] Felix Corley, "Hindus Registered, But Others Still Wait," *Human Rights Without Frontiers*, September 9, 2003, http://www.hrwf.net; "Religious Communities in Slovenia," *Republic of Slovenia Public Relations and Media Office*, http://www.uvi.si/eng/calendar/events/pope/information/religious-communities; "Why Can't Muslims Build Mosques?" *Human Rights Without Frontiers*, April 25, 2002.

declares that there is no state church. Article 124 provides for alternative service for conscientious objectors. The 1993 Churches and Congregations Act contains comprehensive protections for religious freedoms and against religious discrimination. It also provides for registration of religions with at least 12 adult members. Leaders of congregations must have no criminal record and be able to vote in municipal elections. The Employment Contract Act of 1992 makes it illegal to give preference to employees based on religion. The Estonian criminal code bans incitement of religious hatred or violence.

Optional Christian education is available in public schools as are optional comparative religion courses. The state has mostly completed the return of religious property seized during the communist era. A 2001 law that prevented registration of religions "whose permanent or temporary administrative or economic management is performed by a leader or institution situated outside Estonia" was repealed in 2002 after protests by religious organizations. Until 2002 the Estonian branch of the Russian Orthodox Church was unable to register due to objections by the Estonian Apostolic Orthodox Church.[20]

Yugoslavia (Serbia and Montenegro)

It is important to note that in February 2003 the Yugoslavian Federation was dissolved in favor of the state union of Serbia and Montenegro. Article 18 of the Yugoslavian Federation's constitution declares SRAS and the freedom and equality of all churches in performing religious rites. Articles 38, 42, and 50 ban publications and activities of political, trade-union, and other organizations as well as any action that foments religious intolerance and hatred. Article 50 bans any encouragement of religious inequality. Article 43 guarantees religious freedom. Article 137 provides for alternative service for conscientious objectors.

Article 13 of Serbia's constitution declares all citizens equal regardless of their religion. Article 41 declares SRAS, freedom of religion, allows religious communities to establish schools and charities, and allows the government to provide funds to religious communities. Articles 44 and 46 prohibit acts that foment religious intolerance and hatred.

The Montenegrin constitution recognizes the existence of the Serbian Orthodox Church, but not other faiths. Seventh Day Adventists and Jehovah's Witnesses are officially registered religions. However, their followers report that efforts to build and renovate church buildings have been impaired by persons they believe to be loyal to the local Serbian Orthodox Church.

Religious groups must register as a citizens' group to gain status as a legal person, but other groups need not register. Until 2003 religious groups were required to register with the Federal Ministry of Religious Affairs. This law and

[20] HRWF International Secretariat, April 19, 2002, http://www.hrwf.net.

the Ministry lapsed with the dissolution of the Yugoslavian Federation. The state union of Serbia and Montenegro has set up an office of religious affairs as part of its Ministry of Human and Minority Rights. As of 2002, in public schools religious education is required in one of seven of Serbia's "traditional religions" or alternatively in civic education. While there is no official religion, the state gives preference to the Orthodox Church including preferential access to state-run media.

In 2002 Jehovah's Witnesses complained of difficulties in getting visas and of limitations on importing religious literature. Their members, and, those of other groups, also complained of difficulties in gaining permits to build places of worship. With the disbanding of the Yugoslavian Federation in 2003 these problems seem to have abated.

The restrictions on Muslims in Kosovo during the 1990s and the subsequent war there, while motivated in part by religious nationalism, did not involve substantial restrictions on religious liberties. Rather, the activities of the government were designed mostly to restrict the political independence of the region.

Moderate Restrictions on Minorities

Ukraine

Article 11 of Ukraine's constitution states that "The State promotes ... the development of the ethnic, cultural, linguistic and religious identity of all indigenous peoples and national minorities of Ukraine." Article 4 grants equality regardless of religion. Article 34 protects religious freedom, declares SRAS, and separation of state schools from the Church. Article 34 allows alternative service for conscientious objectors. Article 37 bans political parties that promote religious hatred. The preamble mentions God.

The 1991 Freedom of Conscience and Religious Organizations Law, as amended in 1997, reiterates and elaborates the principles in the constitution. It prohibits religious organizations from taking part in the activities of political parties, supporting candidates for political office, and financially supporting political parties and election campaigns. The law requires religious organizations to register and requires a 10-member minimum for registration. Registration grants the organization the status of a legal person.

All religions must register at both the national and local offices of the State Committee for Religious Affairs. Occasionally, local governments in regions traditionally dominated by one religion discriminate against other religions in restitution of religious property and registration. This also includes a dispute between the Moscow and Kiev patriarchates of the Ukrainian Orthodox Church. Muslims have had difficulty registering with some local authorities and the Ministry of Education has not registered a single Islamic school. The law officially restricts the activities of non-native religious organizations (the native religions are Orthodox, Catholic, and Jewish). They may engage in religious activities only in the organizations that invited them into Ukraine and they must have government approval for their activities. This is rarely enforced in practice. Foreign religious workers require invitations from registered organizations in order to obtain a visa. Such visas are rarely denied.

There are reports that in the late 1990s some local officials impeded the activities of foreign religious workers but this seems to have abated. There are isolated reports of unregistered religious groups being harassed by local authorities.[21]

NEAR FULL SEPARATION

Countries in this category maintain close to no GIR. In the former Soviet bloc only Albania fits into this category. Albania engages in low levels of discrimination against religious minorities.

Albania

The preamble and Article 3 of Albania's constitution state that religious coexistence is among the bases for the state. Article 9 bans political parties and organizations that support racial hatred. Article 10 declares official SRAS, freedom of religion, the equality of religious communities, that religious communities are juridical persons, and that the relations between the state and religious communities are regulated by agreements between their representatives and the Council of Ministers and ratified by the Assembly. Article 18 protects against discrimination on the basis of religion. Articles 20 and 24 protect religious freedom. Article 134 gives religious communities the power to appeal issues to the constitutional court.

While no religions are required to register, they must register to have legal status as a judicial person, which allows them to own property and open bank accounts. While no religion has been denied registration, the State Committee on Cults, which was founded in 1999, maintains records of foreign religious organizations. Despite its name, the committee does not monitor "cults" in particular but, rather, acts as a ministry of religion including coordinating bilateral agreements between the state and religious communities. It also regulates religious schools, mostly to ensure that their curriculums are consistent with state guidelines. There is also a Religious Council of the State Secretariat, which operates under the authority of the Prime Minister, but it has no clear mandate.

Abortion was illegal in Albania until 1995 but in practice abortions began to become available in the early 1990s. While some property confiscated during the communist era has been returned to the various religious communities, a number of claims remain outstanding.

There is no religious education in public schools. There have been some isolated incidents of restricting the wearing of headscarves in public schools but appeals to a government office charged with protecting the civil rights of citizens generally overturn these restrictions.

---

[21] "Meetings of Unregistered Evangelical Baptists Prohibited," *Human Rights Without Frontiers*, December 22, 2003, http://www.hrwf.net.

While, for the most part, Albania does not directly restrict religious freedoms of minorities, there are some elements of its policy that have this result. Foreign religious organizations report difficulties in gaining visas to enter the country. This has created a shortage of clergy in some religions. The UN Commission for Human Rights reported that Orthodox priests have been pressured to conduct their liturgy in Albanian rather than in Greek. Also, "the Albanian Evangelical Alliance, an association of Protestant churches, has complained that they have encountered administrative obstacles to building churches and access to the media."[22]

HOSTILITY

These countries enforce SRAS and have a negative attitude toward religion. They attempt to control or strongly regulate the majority religion in order to neutralize its influence in society. While this is similar to the category of state-controlled religions, the key difference is that the government efforts at control tend more toward limiting the majority religion than supporting a particular version of it. All three states that fit into this category are former Soviet Islamic states. It is important to note that restrictions on all religions that also apply to minorities are not considered restrictions on minorities by the RAS project and are coded as restrictions on the majority religion or all religions.

No Restrictions on Minorities

Tajikistan

Article 8 of Tajikistan's constitution forbids the establishment of a state religion, forbids religious organizations from interfering in governmental affairs and bans organizations that advocate religious animosity. Article 26 guarantees religious freedom. A 1999 amendment allows the formation of religious political parties. A 1998 law forbidding religious institutions from providing support to political parties remains in force.

The Law on Religion and Religious Organizations, as amended in 1999, reiterates and expands upon these concepts. It provides for equality of all citizens regardless of their religion. Ministers of religious organizations may not be elected to legislative bodies. It forbids religious education in public schools but emphasizes that such education is a right during nonschool hours. Religious organizations must register and upon doing so gain the status of legal persons. Registration requires a 10-person minimum. The law also establishes the State Committee for Religious Affairs (SCRA). The Council of Islamic Scholars, which governs Islamic theology and education in Tajikistan, while officially independent, is in practice controlled by the SCRA.

While, for the most part, the government does not restrict religious activities, its policies reflect a "pervasive fear" of religious fundamentalism and tend to

---

[22] Gjuraj (2000).

actively keep religious organizations out of politics. The government has banned the activities of Hizb ut-Tahrir, an Islamic organization that advocates the nonviolent replacement of the government with an Islamic government. The government arrests and harasses members of the group, primarily due to their political agenda. Beginning in 2002 all mosques were required to register with the SCRA. About 700 were closed but most reopened as "teahouses" or similar public facilities where people are allowed to meet. The government also removed some imams it considered too political from mosques. The government is increasingly restricting visas for foreign Islamic missionaries who are perceived as extreme fundamentalists. In 1998 the government required that anyone participating in the Hajj must travel in government-approved transportation and in 2003 that they must travel by air. These rules are allegedly to assure a sufficient level of hygiene, and resulted in a drop in the number of people participating.

While, for the most part, local authorities do not interfere in the practice of religion, there are some exceptions. Local authorities on occasion have denied registration to non-Islamic religious organizations but the SCRA usually intervenes in order to assure registration. Some local authorities have broken up religious meetings by nonregistered Jehovah's Witnesses and Baptist groups. Other than this, nonregistered groups seem to be able to practice their religions freely. The Dushanbe city authorities plan to demolish the city's only synagogue in order to build a presidential palace on the site. The remaining Jewish community claims not to have sufficient resources to replace the building. The government of the Isfara district of northern Tajikistan does not allow women to appear in local identity photos wearing headcoverings, though headcoverings are allowed in passport photos.[23]

Low Restrictions on Minorities

Kyrgyzstan

Article 8 of Kyrgyzstan's constitution declares SRAS. It bans religious political parties, and bans religious organizations from engaging in political activities and religious interference "with the activity of state bodies." Article 15 prohibits discrimination on the basis of religion. Article 16 guarantees religious freedom. A 2003 amendment prohibits "propaganda or agitation that incites social, racial, international or religious hatred or antagonism."

A 1997 presidential decree requires all religions to register with the State Commission on Religious Affairs. Registration requires a minimum of 10

---

[23] "10 Muslim Clerics Banned from Preaching," *Human Rights Without Frontiers*, August 2, 2002, http://www.hrwf.net; Saodat Olimova, "Political Islam and the Conflict in Tajikistan," *Central Asia and the Caucasus*, http://www.ca-c.org/dataeng/11.olimova.shtml#up; Igor Rotar, "Dushanbe Jews Ordered to Vacate Synagogue by July," *Forum 18 News Service*, May 21, 2004, http://www.forum18.org; Igor Rotar, "Why Can't Women Wear the Hijab for Internal Identity Photos?" *Forum 18 News Service*, June 9, 2004.

members. While registration can in some cases take years, only the Russian Overseas Church has been refused registration. Unregistered religions are prohibited from engaging in activities. Missionary groups must also register but can usually operate freely. A number of missionaries have been deported for disseminating dogma "inconsistent with the traditional customs of Kyrgyz Muslims." Also, a 2004 government resolution instructs the National Security Service "to draw up measures to restrict and prevent the activities of missionaries who propagate religious fundamentalism and extremism and reactionary and Shiite ideas."

While religion is not taught in public schools, in response to concerns over the increasing influence of Wahabbism and "unconventional" religious sects, the government has asked the clergy to draw up plans for religious education in the schools. This program has not yet been implemented. The government has taken several other actions in response to a perceived threat by radical Muslims. A presidential decree allows the denial or revocation of the registration of religious organizations that threaten state security, social stability, interreligious or interethnic relations, or the morals and health of citizens. In 2003 eight mosques were closed based on this decree. In 2001 the criminal code was rewritten to include tougher sentences for "religious extremism." In 2002 Kyrgyzstan's Spiritual Directorate of Muslims announced plans to standardize Islamic educational literature as well as mosque construction and the activities of Islamic organizations. The government arrests and prosecutes anyone who is believed to be involved in Hizb ut-Tahrir, a militant Islamic organization. Those arrested are usually charged with the distribution of literature that incites ethnic, racial, or religious hatred.[24]

High Restrictions on Minorities

Azerbaijan

Article 18 of Azerbaijan's constitution declares SRAS, that all religions are equal, and that the state education system will be secular. Article 25 protects against discrimination based on religion. Article 47 protects freedom of speech but bans "propaganda inciting racial, ethnic or religious animosity or hostility." Article 48 protects religious freedom. Article 7 protects the privacy of religious convictions. Articles 85 and 86 prohibit ministers of religion from being members of parliament.

The 1992 Law on Religious Beliefs declares religious freedom and SRAS. It allows religious education in state schools. It requires that all Islamic communities be subordinate to the state-sponsored Caucasus Muslim Department. It requires that religious groups register with the government and imposes a 10-member minimum for registration.

Registration is often denied by the State Committee for Work with Religious Associations (SCWRA), which replaced the Department of Religious Affairs in

---

[24] Igor Rotar, "Will the Government or Won't the Government Target Ahmadis?" *Forum 18 News Service*, May 17, 2004, http://www.forum18.org.

June 2001. The SCWRA has sweeping powers over the publication, import, and distribution of religious literature, and the power to suspend the activities of religious groups that violate the law. Unregistered religions may not maintain a bank account or rent property. Unregistered groups are also more vulnerable to harassment by local officials – who often close down places of worship belonging to them – and, in practice, have difficulty operating. Much of this harassment is due to antipathy toward Muslims converting to other religions. Since 1991 religions were required by new laws to re-register three times. Each new process was more cumbersome and fewer religions successfully registered.

A 1996 law prohibits proselytizing by foreigners. The government publishes pamphlets against foreign missionaries and in official media outlets portrays nontraditional religions as spreading hatred. There is considerable anecdotal evidence that the government suspects all nonindigenous religious organizations, even those engaged in humanitarian work, of missionary activity. There are also reports of difficulties in importing religious literature.

The Law on Religion places all Muslims under the authority of the Spiritual Directorate of All-Caucasus Muslims. All other Muslim organizations are illegal. This Soviet-era organization, along with the SCWRA, appoints Muslim clerics to mosques, monitors their sermons, and is involved in the finances of mosques. The Azerbaijani government is particularly opposed to the spread of political Islam within its borders. Therefore, the government views the registration of new Muslim associations with extreme suspicion and hostility, claiming that these groups are seeking to seize power and are supported by foreign governments such as Iran. The government is also particularly suspicious of Wahabbi organizations, and has refused to register and has shut down schools run by Wahabbis. It also monitors Wahabbi mosques.

Beyond the limitations and harassment on nonregistered religions, there are significant additional restrictions on religious activities. Political parties cannot engage in religious activity. Local governments often monitor sermons. The SCWRA often denies the right to import and distribute religious literature, though there is some indication that this behavior is abating. Despite court orders to the contrary, officials often prevent women from wearing headcoverings for passport photos. Local governments often harass fundamentalist Muslims due to alleged links to terrorism. There are also reports of government harassment of Islamic communities that will not submit to the authority of the Caucasian Muslim Board.[25]

---

[25] Human Rights Center of Azerbaijan, "Report: Status of Civil and Political Rights in Azerbaijan in 2001," EurasiaNet.org; Felix Corley, "Traitor for Being Christian?" *Forum 18 News Service*, February 12, 2004, http://www.forum18.org; Felix Corley, "New Crackdown on Adventists," *Forum 18 News Service*, May 20, 2004; Felix Corley, "New Media Threats Against Protestants and JW's," *Forum 18 News Service*, February 3, 2004; Felix Corley, "Is Religious Censorship Getting Worse?" *Forum 18 News Service*, April 6, 2004; Felix Corley, "Half-free Imam To Challenge Suspended Jail Sentence," *Forum 18 News Service*, April 5, 2004; "Islamic Radicals Plan to Take Over Azerbaijan, Deputy Security Minister," Agence France Presse, May 3, 2001.

SOME GENERAL OBSERVATIONS

The descriptions presented here clearly show that there are few instances of real SRAS in the former Soviet bloc. Nearly all of these states either support religion, restrict it, or seek to control it. There are two trends that help to explain this resurgence of religion in this formerly militantly secular region of the world.

First, with the lifting of Soviet control, most of these states show a desire to reestablish and promote indigenous culture, including religion. Consequently, many of them try to protect their indigenous religions against encroachment from foreign and nontraditional religious influences. The majority of these states differentiate, either officially or unofficially, between those religions with a historical presence in their states and those without, often through a multi-tiered recognition system in which religions on the lowest rungs are sometimes effectively banned.

Another indication of this trend is that a limit on proselytizing, which is mostly placed on nonindigenous religions, is the second most common restriction on minority religions coded in the RAS data in the region. These limits can include outright bans or restrictions on visas or activities of foreign missionaries. They can also consist of less official patterns of harassment of missionary workers. In either case these activities represent a desire to protect "impressionable" citizens from foreign cultural influences.

A number of other laws also fit this pattern. These include minimum member and minimum time of presence in the state requirements for registration. When states allow religious education in schools, the dominant religion and sometimes other religions indigenous to the country are nearly always given preference. Many governments either officially or unofficially restrict religious literature.

The second trend in the former Soviet bloc is the fear of religion or the desire to control it. This trend likely has a number of sources. The states in this region inherited a paternalistic centralized style of government where all aspects of life, including religion, were controlled by the government. While most of these states have at least officially repudiated their communist past, it is likely that this attitude toward religion continues to influence many policy makers. Also, the fear of religion as a challenge to the regime in many cases is a real one. This is especially true in states where Muslim radicals actively try to undermine the state and replace it with an Islamic state. Religion's political power is also felt in a number of the Christian states. For instance, in Poland the Catholic Church was instrumental in the Solidarity movement of the 1980s that eventually led to the fall of the communist government and continues to influence Polish politics today. Armenia, Georgia, Romania, and Russia all give their Orthodox churches exclusive privileges in a number of crucial policy and cultural issues.

This trend of fearing and controlling religion manifests itself in a number of ways. Nearly every state in the region has some form of registration requirement. In some states, such as Belarus, Bulgaria, Kazakhstan, Moldova, and Uzbekistan the government restricts or forbids the operation of unregistered religions and avoids registering nonindigenous religions. In others, Estonia, Hungary, and Tajikistan, for example, this registration requirement is pro-forma, or failure to register does not limit religious freedom. Yet even in these cases, this government licensing of religion reflects a need to control or at least be aware of religious activities within the state. That, in many countries, part of the registration process includes submitting a detailed description of the religion's doctrine and institutions structures also reflects this need.

Nearly every one of these countries' constitutions contains a clause prohibiting religious animosity, incitement, or hatred. This reflects a fear of the volatile nature of religion and a desire to limit freedom of expression on the issue in order to avoid religious conflict. Similarly the two most common forms of restrictions that apply to all religions in a state are limitations on religious political parties and limitations on the participation in politics of religious organizations.

In some states government activities regarding religious education and literature also reflect this fear. In Uzbekistan religion can only be taught in religious schools, which must be licensed by the government. Uzbekistan also requires a license for publishing or importing any religious literature. In Latvia, only registered religions can open religious schools. In Macedonia religious education is limited to facilities where religious rituals are performed. In Azerbaijan the state has sweeping powers over the publication, import, and distribution of religious literature.

This fear of religion seems to be especially prevalent in the region's Muslim states. Two of them, Turkmenistan and Uzbekistan, have state-controlled versions of Islam and repress any form of Islam that is outside of the state-controlled institutions. Another three, Azerbaijan, Kyrgyzstan, and Tajikistan, have a tendency to repress or limit all manifestations of Islam. Kazakhstan officially maintains SRAS but, in practice, supports moderate Islam and to a lesser extent other indigenous religions including Russian Orthodoxy and Judaism. However, it has taken a number of measures to restrict what it considers Muslim radicals. Albania seems to be the only exception and does not significantly restrict or regulate Islam. Given the global context of the growth of radical Islam, these fears of an Islamic challenge to the state are not unrealistic. A comparison between policies of Muslim states in this region and in other world regions is provided in Chapter 11.

Another interesting trend is the tension on religious issues between national and local governments. In many states, much of the discrimination against religious minorities is carried out by local governments. Sometimes this occurs with the tacit approval of the national government and sometimes it occurs contrary to national policy. This likely reflects a tendency toward a grass roots bias against religious minorities. This pattern is particularly strong in Belarus, Azerbaijan, Bulgaria, Georgia, Kazakhstan, Romania, Russia, Tajikistan, Ukraine, and Uzbekistan.

As will be documented in more detail in Chapter 11, all of these trends increased in strength during the period covered by this study.

A final fact worth reporting is that all of these restrictions on religion and other forms of GIR occur despite clauses in most of these countries' constitutions declaring SRAS, religious freedom, and equality of all religions before the law. These types of clauses exist respectively in 20, 25, and 24 of these countries' constitutions and all of the former Soviet Bloc countries have at least two of these clauses. Many countries that lack one of these clauses in their constitutions have enacted them as laws. This shows that constitutional protections for religion are only relevant to the extent that a country's government has the political will to enforce them and a court system with the power and inclination to do the same.

7

Asia

Asia has a high level of diversity both in regard to religious identity and government religion policy. The region contains countries that strongly support a single religion, countries that repress all religion, and just about everything in between. However, one thing most of these states have in common is that their governments involve themselves significantly in religious issues. This is clear from the data presented in Tables 7.1, 7.2, 7.3, and 7.4. Of the 28 governments examined here, 9 have official religions and an additional 10 support religion. Five are hostile to religion and only 4 are coded as "accommodation," having separation of religion and state (SRAS).

All but 5 of these states place restrictions on minority religions, and all 16 types of restrictions coded by the RAS dataset are present in multiple Asian states. The most common form of restriction is limits on proselytizing, which are present in 18 of these states. In 14 states there are restrictions on building, maintaining, or repairing places of worship, and 14 restrict the printing, import, or distribution of religious literature. There are 11 states that arrest, detain, or harass religious minorities for practicing their religion. All of the other 12 types of restrictions not specifically mentioned here exist in at least 3 states in Asia.

Asian states also significantly regulate their majority religions. Of the 11 forms of regulation coded by the RAS project, nine exist in at least two Asian states. Of the 28 Asian states examined here, 17 engage in at least one of these practices. The most common forms of regulation in Asia are restrictions on religious organizations and restrictions on religious speech, both of which exist in 12 states.

Religious legislation is common in Asian states. Of the 33 categories coded by the RAS project, only 1 is not present in Asia. Other than Japan, which has only 1 of these types of legislation, all of the Asian countries included in this study legislate multiple categories of these laws with a regional average of nearly 8 per country. The most common form of legislation is restriction on abortion, which exists in 19 states. Seventeen countries fund religious education,

TABLE 7.1. *Separation of Religion and State in Asia in 2002, Basic Information*

Country	Maj. religion	% Maj. rel.	# Min. groups with 5% of population	Official GIR	Official regulation	General GIR
Afghanistan	Islam, Sunni	81.2	1	One official religion	Some illegal	49.17
Bangladesh	Islam, Sunni	83.0	1	One official religion	Practical limitations	32.69
Bhutan	Buddhist	75.0	1	One official religion	Legal limitations	40.83
Brunei	Islam	64.0	3	One official religion	Legal limitations	52.86
Burma	Buddhist	89.0	0	Civil religion	Legal limitations	46.43
Cambodia	Buddhist	93.0	1	One official religion	Practical limitations	29.58
China	Other	50.2	3	Inadvertent sensitivity	Some illegal	48.14
Fiji	Christian	43.0	3	Civil religion	No limitations	13.25
India	Hindu	77.5	1	Cooperation	Practical limitations	22.87
Indonesia	Islam, Sunni	65.0	2	Civil religion	No limitations	45.22
Japan	Other	49.4	1	Accommodation	Practical limitations	8.50
Laos	Buddhist	60.0	1	Inadvertent sensitivity	Legal limitations	37.18
Malaysia	Islam, Sunni	54.0	4	One official religion	Some illegal	57.52
Maldives	Islam, Sunni	99.2	0	One official religion	All illegal	65.13
Mongolia	Buddhist	62.0	2	Accommodation	No limitations	5.34
Nepal	Hindu	82.5	2	Civil religion	Legal limitations	29.44
North Korea	Other	71.2	2	Inadvertent sensitivity	Some illegal	40.78
Pakistan	Islam, Sunni	80.0	1	One official religion	Legal limitations	50.27
Papua New Guinea	Protestant	58.0	2	Civil religion	No limitations	15.75
Philippines	Catholic	83.0	2	Supportive	No limitations	7.13
Singapore	Mixed	31.0	4	Separationist	Some illegal	29.91
Solomon Islands	Protestant	78.0	1	Supportive	No limitations	6.50
South Korea	Mixed	48.0	1	Accommodation	No limitations	1.88
Sri Lanka	Buddhist	68.4	4	One official religion	Practical limitations	30.21
Taiwan	Other	68.0	2	Accommodation	No limitations	1.67
Thailand	Buddhist	88.5	1	Cooperation	Practical limitations	21.50
Vanuatu	Protestant	61.7	3	Cooperation	Practical limitations	16.54
Vietnam	Buddhist	50.0	4	Hostile	Some illegal	53.5

TABLE 7.2. *Restrictions on Minority Religion in Asia in 2002*

	Public observance	Build or repair places of worship	Access to places of worship	Forced observance	orgs.	Formal Education	Arrest, detention, harassment	Materials	Publications	Personal status	Clergy	Conversions	Forced conversions	Proselytizing	Registration	Other	Total
Afghanistan	x	x							x			x		x			5
Bangladesh														x		x	2
Bhutan	x	x			x				x					x			5
Brunei	x	x	x			x	x		x		x	x		x		x	10
Burma	x	x	x		x	x	x		x		x	x	x	x	x		12
Cambodia		x											x				2
China	x	x	x		x	x	x	x	x	x	x	x	x	x	x		14
Fiji																	0
India					x				x					x			3
Indonesia		x			x		x		x			x		x		x	7
Japan										x						x	2
Laos	x	x			x		x	x	x			x	x	x			9
Malaysia		x		x	x		x		x					x	x		7
Maldives	x	x	x			x	x	x	x		x	x		x	x		11
Mongolia									x					x	x	x	4
Nepal	x	x					x					x		x			5
North Korea		x												x			2
Pakistan	x	x	x				x	x	x	x	x			x		x	10
P. N. Guinea																	0
Philippines																	0
Singapore					x									x	x		3
Solomon Isl.																	0
South Korea																	0
Sri Lanka							x				x						2
Taiwan															x		1
Thailand									x					x		x	3
Vanuatu					x												1
Vietnam	x	x	x	x	x	x	x		x			x		x	x		11
TOTAL	10	14	6	2	10	5	11	4	14	3	6	9	4	18	8	7	131

TABLE 7.3. *Government Regulation of the Majority Religion in Asia in 2002*

	Political parties	Arrest, detention, harassment	Orgs.	Public observance	Speech	Access to places of worship	Publications	Arrest nonleaders	Other	Total
Afghanistan										0
Bangladesh					x					1
Bhutan										0
Brunei			x		x					2
Burma	x	x	x		x					4
Cambodia										0
China			x	x	x	x	x		x	6
Fiji										0
India	x		x						x	3
Indonesia			x		x				x	3
Japan	x									1
Laos		x	x		x			x		4
Malaysia	x		x		x	x		x	x	6
Maldives		x			x				x	3
Mongolia			x						x	2
Nepal	x									1
North Korea		x	x	x	x	x		x	x	7
Pakistan		x	x		x			x	x	5
Papua New Guinea										0
Philippines										0
Singapore	x		x		x					3
Solomon Islands										0
South Korea										0
Sri Lanka										0
Taiwan										0
Thailand									x	1
Vanuatu										0
Vietnam		x	x	x	x			x	x	6
TOTAL	6	6	12	3	12	3	1	5	10	58

The following categories of religious restrictions were not included in this table because none of these countries engage in these practices: public gatherings; public display.

15 of them in public schools. Sixteen fund religion through 1 or more of the 4 categories of noneducational funding. Sixteen countries have official government branches that deal with religion, and 16 require religions to register with the state.

In all, GIR is the norm in Asia, and the few states that keep this involvement to a minimum, including Japan, Mongolia, South Korea, and Taiwan, are the exceptions rather than the rule. Furthermore, GIR in Asia has increased slightly between 1990 and 2002. On average, religious legislation, restrictions on minority religions, and government regulation of the majority religion all increased during this period. However, beyond these commonalities there is a wide diversity of relationships between religion and state in Asia.

At first glance there is no specific pattern in this diversity but upon closer examination a pattern emerges based on two factors: the religious identity of the majority in the state, and whether the government is communist. These two factors alone produce a reasonable ability to predict the general pattern of government involvement in religion (GIR) for specific states, though there are certainly exceptions. Consequently, in this chapter the order of country presentations is based not on the taxonomy developed in Chapters 5 and 6, but on these two variables. Accordingly, Table 7.5 shows not only where each state falls in this taxonomy, it also shows the majority religion of each state and whether the state is communist.

COMMUNIST STATES

This category includes all communist states because the communist distrust of religion outweighs the specific religious tradition in its influence on state behavior toward religion. All four communist Asian states follow a combination of overt hostility to all religion and the requirement that all religious expression in the state occur in state-controlled formats. Three of these states are included in the taxonomy as hostile and one as a state-controlled religion. This is based on my judgment of whether general hostility or the effort to control religion is the dominant policy in a state. All these countries engage in moderate to high restrictions on religious minorities.

State-controlled Religion

Laos

Article 9 of Laos' constitution states that "the state respects and protects all lawful activities of the Buddhists and of other religious followers, mobilizes and encourages the Buddhist monks and novices as well as the priests of other religions to participate in the activities which are beneficial to the country and people. All acts of creating division of religions and classes of people are prohibited." Article 30 protects religious freedom.

In practice the national government and some local governments restrict religious freedom as part of a larger policy to oversee all religion in order to

TABLE 7.4. *Religious Legislation in Asia in 2002*

	Dietary laws	Alcohol	Personal status	Inheritance	Conversions	Marriages	Public dress	Blasphemy	Censorship	Close businesses	Optional education	Mandatory educ.	Fund education	Fund religious charity	Taxes	Fund clergy
Afghanistan	x	x		x	x	x	x	x		x		x	x			
Bangladesh			x	x				x	x		x		x			
Bhutan											x		x			x
Brunei	x	x	x	x	x	x	x	x				x	x			
Burma					x		x	x	x			x	x	x		x
Cambodia													x			x
China																
Fiji																
India			x			x		x				x	x			
Indonesia			x	x		x		x	x			x	x			
Japan																
Laos																
Malaysia	x		x	x	x		x	x	x			x	x	x	x	
Maldives		x	x	x	x	x		x	x			x	x			x
Mongolia																
Nepal					x											
North Korea													x			
Pakistan		x	x					x	x		x		x		x	
P. N. Guinea											x		x			
Philippines									x							
Singapore			x						x							
Solomon Isl.											x		x			
South Korea																
Sri Lanka			x									x	x			
Taiwan								x								
Thailand											x	x	x	x		x
Vanuatu													x			
Vietnam																
TOTAL	3	4	9	6	6	5	4	10	7	1	6	9	17	3	2	5

	Other religious funding	Approve clergy & speeches	Some clergy appointed	Gov. rel. dept.	Religious position for gov. official	Gov. position for rel. official	Religious requirements	Relig. courts	Legislature/ cabinet	Abortion	Flag	Identity cards	Registration	Sects	Women	Other	Total
Afghanistan				x				x		x	x				x	x	16
Bangladesh			x	x						x					x		10
Bhutan	x								x	x							10
Brunei				x		x	x	x		x		x	x		x		19
Burma	x	x	x	x	x					x		x	x		x	x	14
Cambodia	x			x							x		x	x			6
China	x			x									x	x			4
Fiji	x									x							2
India										x							7
Indonesia				x			x	x		x		x			x	x	14
Japan													x				1
Laos		x	x							x						x	5
Malaysia	x	x		x				x		x		x	x			x	19
Maldives		x		x			x	x		x	x	x		x			17
Mongolia	x												x				2
Nepal					x					x							3
North Korea	x		x														3
Pakistan	x			x			x	x		x	x	x	x		x	x	16
P. N. Guinea										x						x	6
Philippines				x				x		x			x				5
Singapore				x				x		x			x			x	5
Solomon Isl.													x	x			4
South Korea	x			x						x							3
Sri Lanka				x						x			x				7
Taiwan	x												x				2
Thailand	x			x			x					x	x				9
Vanuatu	x									x		x	x				5
Vietnam		x	x	x								x	x				5
TOTAL	13	5	5	16	2	1	5	8	1	19	4	9	16	4	6	8	219

The following categories of religious legislation were not included in this table because none of the Asian states engage in these practices: blue laws.

TABLE 7.5. *Taxonomy of Asia*

Separation of religion and state	Type of restrictions on minorities			
	None	Low (1–2)	Moderate (3–5)	High (6+)
Religious state	—	—	Afghanistan	Brunei Maldives
Active state religion	—	**Bangladesh**	*Bhutan*	**Malaysia Pakistan**
State-controlled religion	—	—	—	*Burma* LAOS
Historical / cultural state religion	—	*Cambodia Sri Lanka*	—	—
Preferred treatment for some religions or support for a particular tradition	<u>Fiji</u> P. N. Guinea	Vanuatu	India Nepal *Thailand*	Indonesia
General support	<u>Philippines Solomon Isl.</u>	—	—	—
Moderate separation	South Korea	—	*Mongolia*	—
Nearly full separation (2 or less on legislation)	—	Japan Taiwan	—	—
Hostility	—	—	NORTH KOREA* Singapore	CHINA *VIETNAM*

* North Korea does not single out religious minorities for persecution but severely persecutes all religions.
Bold = Muslim state
Italics = Buddhist state
<u>Underline = Christian state</u>
ALL CAPITALS = Communist state

make sure that it contributes to good citizenship. This is reflected in a 2002 decree by the prime minister, which allows legitimate religious activities as long as they conform to the country's laws and regulations. The government uses the constitutional provision against creating religious divisions to restrict and control religion. Religious activities by members of any religion, such as attending or holding unauthorized religious services, often result in arrest if government officials feel this somehow violates social order.

The government especially monitors the majority religion. This includes government support, oversight, and often control of its institutions, religious training, and clergy. The government approves all clergy appointments. Buddhist monks are required to read the works of Marx and Lenin and attend political meetings. Until 2002 religious affiliation was listed on state identity cards. Government approval is required for conversion. Abortion is illegal except in order to save the life of the mother, which requires special approval from the Health Ministry.

Within this government-controlled context, most in Laos can practice their religions freely. However, there are some restrictions on minority religions. The government discourages activities by Animists that it considers outdated or unhealthy. This includes the killing of infants with birth defects and the keeping of the bodies of the deceased in their relatives' homes. Foreigners may not proselytize and those caught distributing religious literature are subject to expulsion. While not illegal, in practice proselytizing by Laotian citizens is also prohibited. Printing and importing non-Buddhist religious texts is restricted and distributing such texts outside of one's congregation is illegal.

The majority of discriminatory activity by local governments is against Protestant groups. Local governments have closed or destroyed churches, denied construction permits to new ones, and restricted religious meetings in private homes. Some have also restricted the public celebration of Christian holidays forcing Christians to travel to other villages to celebrate holidays such as Christmas. Some local governments have forced Protestants to attend political training on Sundays and have interpreted the Christian concept of obedience to God as disloyalty to the government. Since 1998 there have been reports of authorities forcing Christians to renounce their faith on pain of arrest, expulsion from their village, and denial of educational opportunities for their children. Since 2002 such incidents have been less frequent but continue to occur. Since 1998 arrests of Christians have increased.

Hostility

China

Article 35 of China's constitution guarantees all citizens the right to vote regardless of their religion. Article 36 protects religious freedom and "normal religious activities" but "no one may make use of religion to engage in activities that disrupt public order, impair the health of citizens or interfere with the educational system of the state." Article 36 also requires that religious organizations be free from foreign domination.

A 1982 document outlines the attitude of the Chinese government toward religion. The document describes religion as a complex historical phenomenon that will eventually disappear in the modern socialist period but that will take a long time to do so. A combination of freedom of religious belief and promotion of atheism, rather than coercion, will better address religion by making it a private matter and eventually irrelevant. However, communist party members must be atheist. Criminal and counter-revolutionaries "hiding behind the facade of religion" will be prosecuted. Religious professionals are to be educated in patriotism and all religions must have a cadre of fervent patriots. The document also establishes religious patriotic associations for the country's major religions. All places of worship are under the administrative control of the Bureau of Religious Affairs but run by the individual religions.

China's policy is to control religion, limit it to registered activities and places of worship, and prevent it from becoming a separate source of authority or basis for organizing or opposition. All religious venues must register. Currently five are officially recognized: Catholicism, Protestantism, Buddhism, Islam, and Taoism. All of them are closely supervised by a government-controlled religious patriotic association. Religious groups that wish to register are usually required to associate with one of these associations. The Catholic Patriotic Association has not been allowed to recognize Papal authority.

China allows aliens to participate in religious ceremonies in registered places of worship. They may preach only at the invitation of a registered religious body, the Department of Religious Affairs, or a provincial government. Other than for personal use and approved cultural and academic exchange, the importation of religious articles is prohibited. Chinese citizens need government approval to study religion abroad. Other missionary activities are generally prohibited. In practice the government does not interfere with the religious activities of foreigners where they do not involve Chinese citizens.

The government has banned all "cults," including the Falun Gong and the Zhong Gong movements. In 1995 it published a list of additional banned "cults." Over 100,000 members of the Falun Gong have been detained or placed in reeducation camps. Religious expression, the building of mosques, and religious teaching is limited in some Muslim areas, generally those where there have been ethnic uprisings. In other regions the government permits religious expression, and even subsidizes the building of mosques and participation in the Hajj. The government supports the rebuilding and repair of religious buildings destroyed or damaged during China's cultural revolution but it destroys unregistered houses of worship. This policy is combined with pressure on unregistered places of worship to register. House churches tend to be tolerated until they grow too big. Unregistered groups that preach doctrine that is different from the approved doctrine for their religion or that have charismatic leaders tend to face higher levels of harassment including the arrest of leaders and other members. The extent to which these practices occur varies from local government to local government.

Due to restrictions between 1955 and 1985 there is a shortage of trained clerics. In theory the government allows the training of clerics in China and students can go abroad for training. In practice this is limited by bureaucratic obstacles. Religious literature, such as bibles and the Koran, can be bought at official places of worship, but there is a chronic shortage due to limited press runs at government printing houses.

The government considers Buddhism in Tibet to be a particular challenge to the state and closely regulates Tibet's religious institutions, especially when there is any suspicion of influence by the Dalai Lama. Religious activities are generally allowed unless they are perceived as vehicles for political dissent. The government limits the number of monks in monasteries and oversees their daily operation. All monks and nuns undergo patriotic education. A number of them have been detained for actions against state security. The government has also attempted to seize control of the process for recognizing reincarnated lamas, though those lamas living outside of Tibet rarely recognize the government's selections. Sometimes, as is the case with the Panchen Lama, second in importance to the Dalai Lama, the government and lamas have recognized different individuals as the true reincarnation.

North Korea

Article 66 of North Korea's constitution allows all citizens to be elected to office regardless of religion. Article 68 states that "citizens have freedom of religious beliefs. This right is granted by approving the construction of religious buildings and the holding of religious ceremonies." It also states that "no one may use religion as a pretext for drawing in foreign forces or for harming the State and social order."

The government promotes a personality cult of the country's leader, Kim Jong-Il, combined with "self-reliance" as the country's spiritual ideology. After decades of repression, the government formed several state-sponsored religious organizations in the 1980s. All organized religion outside of the auspices of these organizations is discouraged. The government has opened several schools and seminaries for training Protestant and Buddhist clergy but critics claim that these were opened mostly to attract foreign aid. The government selects church officials and reportedly churches often remain closed until foreign visitors arrive. Many churches and temples have been taken over by the government for secular use but some are maintained by the government as cultural treasures.

Proselytizing is banned. Those violating this law are arrested and subject to harsh penalties. The government fears that religious groups outside its government-controlled format have political goals and generally considers them subversives, especially if they have connections to foreign religious organizations. Nearly any public expression of religion outside the state-controlled format is grounds for arrest. Members of underground churches are often arrested, beaten, tortured, and killed for their beliefs. It is illegal to carry bibles in public or distribute religious literature.

Those who participate in state-controlled religious organizations are given a lower official status than those who don't, resulting in fewer privileges and opportunities, including in the areas of employment and education. The government has made an effort to root out indigenous beliefs, which has resulted in the disappearance of practices of shamanism and fortune-telling.

Many Koreans flee to China but the North Korean government, with the help of China, often tracks them down. According to one report, during interrogations they are asked if they have had any connection with South Korean missionaries, have read the Bible, or have attended church. Those answering yes are imprisoned and sentenced to death.[1]

---

[1] Janet Chismar, "Against All Odds, Faith Flourishes Quietly in North Korea," *Human Rights Without Frontiers*, March 14, 2003, http://www.hrwf.net; "Christians Under Dark Reign of Kim Jong Il," February 25, 2004, http://persecution.org; Doug Struck, "Keeping the Faith, Underground; North Korea's Secret Christians Get Support from the South," *Washington Post*, April 10, 2001, p. A01.

Vietnam

Article 54 of Vietnam's constitution grants the right to vote to all citizens 18 and older regardless of religion. Article 70 declares religious freedom and that all religions are equal before the law, but beliefs and religion may not be misused in order to "contravene the law and State policies." Article 70 also states that "the places of worship of all faiths and religions are protected by the law." Article 112 includes the implementation of policies on religion in its list of state duties.

People may worship freely if they are members of a recognized religion. Non-recognized religions are restricted by some local governments. Religions must register. The government uses registration to control religious organizations, as it does with all social organizations. The Government officially recognizes Buddhist, Cao Dai, Hoa Hao, Muslim, Protestant, and Roman Catholic religious organizations, but not all religious groups of these denominations choose to operate under the auspices of the officially recognized organizations. Recognized organizations must consult with the government on issues of administration and leader selection as well as the training, appointment, and transfer of all clergy. They also need government permission for any activities outside of the regular religious calendar, for religious training, meetings, conventions, and building or renovating their buildings.

All Buddhist monks must work under the government-approved organization. The government limits the number of monks that receive training. Several nonrecognized religious groups, including the Unified Buddhist Church of Vietnam, are considered illegal. Their leaders are often arrested and harassed. All public assemblies, including religious ones, are restricted. A 1999 law prohibits religious activities in prisons and visits to prisons by religious workers. Religious affiliation is included on state identity cards. All religious publishing must be done by the government religious publishing house. According to some sources, bibles are printed illegally because the authorities withhold authorization for Christians to print them for use in churches. The government bans several of the Cao Dai Church's ceremonies because they are considered superstitious. Proselytizing by foreigners is prohibited and proselytizing outside of designated places of worship is discouraged.

The restrictions on nonregistered religions vary from place to place and are sometimes enforced unevenly. Some regions prohibit Christmas celebrations. Efforts to force Protestants to return to traditional Animist faiths are common. In some cases Christian students are banned from schools and Christians are sometimes driven from their villages by local officials. Government regulations requiring approval for the building or renovation of places of worship are used to close or demolish unregistered places of worship. Religious meetings and unauthorized religious groups are often broken up. Charges of "attempting to undermine national unity" by promoting "division between religious believers and non-believers" and abusing religious freedom are used to imprison members of nonregistered religions. Leaders of house churches, especially among ethnic minorities, as well as other religious leaders are often harassed and detained. Beatings are not uncommon and in some cases people are beaten to death. Despite all of this, religious activity, especially among Protestants, is growing in Vietnam.[2]

MUSLIM STATES

This category of states is defined solely by whether the majority of those living in the state are Muslims. Except Indonesia, all of these states have official religions. The difference between religious states and active state religions is based on my judgment of whether religion controls the state or the state government or, while actively supporting Islam, the state maintains a level of independence from it. Other than Bangladesh, these states place moderate to high levels of restrictions on religious minorities.

Religious States

Afghanistan

This description focuses primarily on the post-Taliban regime beginning on December 22, 2001, when the Afghan Interim Administration took office. While high levels of GIR existed under the Taliban regime, both the pre- and post-Taliban regimes also engaged in high levels of GIR. The major difference between the regimes is the extent of that GIR and the extent of the zealousness in the enforcement of religious laws. The pre-Taliban, Taliban, and post-Taliban regimes engaged respectively in 6, 9, and 5 types of religious discrimination, as well as legislating 18, 22, and 16 of the types of religious laws, as measured by the RAS project.

Article 1 of Afghanistan's 2004 constitution declares it an Islamic republic. Article 2 declares Islam the official state religion and protects religious freedom "within the limits of the provisions of law." Article 3 bans laws contrary to Islam. Article 17 requires the state to develop religious education and improve "the conditions of mosques, madrassas and religious centers." Article 35 bans political parties with programs and charters contrary to Islam but also bans parties based on an Islamic school of thought. Article 45 states that "the state shall devise and implement a unified educational curriculum based on ... Islam, national culture, and in accordance with academic principles." Article 54 includes "elimination of traditions contrary to the principles of the sacred religion of Islam" in the definition of the psychological well-being of a family. Articles 66 and 80 prohibit the president and ministers from acting based on linguistic, ethnic, religious, political, and regional considerations. Article 118 states that education in Islamic jurisprudence qualifies a person to serve on the Supreme Court. Article 149 states that "The provisions of adherence to the fundamentals of the sacred religion of Islam

---

[2] Philip Shenon, "Vietnam To Try Dissident Buddhist Monk Despite U.S. Protest," *New York Times*, August 18, 1995, p. A-7; Philip Shenon, "4 Buddhist Monks in Vietnam Get Prison Terms," *New York Times*, November 17, 1993, p. A-11; Philip Shenon, "Vietnam Said To Arrest 2 Protesting Buddhist Monks," *New York Times*, January 9, 1995, p. A-3; Bob Harvey, "A Hymnal Costs 71 Cents – and Years in Jail," *Ottawa Citizen*, April 30, 2000, p. A-6; "Vietnam Imprisons an Outspoken Priest," *New York Times*, October 21, 2001, p. A-6.

and the regime of the Islamic Republic cannot be amended." The constitution also contains numerous symbolic references to religion.

The country's civil penal code only covers "less serious" crimes, and "more serious" crimes fall under Islamic law. This includes blasphemy and converting away from Islam, both of which are punishable by death. However, the current government takes a more lenient approach to implementing punishments. For example, the hands of thieves in post-Taliban Afghanistan are rarely cut off. A 2002 press law includes an injunction against anything that could insult Islam or other religions. Religious education is part of the curriculum in Afghanistan's schools. The past curriculum of preaching Jihad is being replaced by textbooks that focus on general Islamic terms and principles.

Religious groups are not required to register. Afghanistan's Shi'i Muslim minority is allowed to practice their religion freely in public. Proselytizing is not explicitly illegal but is considered contrary to the principles of Islam. Members of minority religions including Hindus and Sikhs, report that they are freer to practice their religion than they were under the Taliban regime, though it is too soon to judge the full extent of their freedom. There is some tension on this issue between the national government and local governments. For instance, despite a promise by Afghanistan's Religious Affairs Ministry that Hindus and Sikhs may resume their practice of cremating the dead, many local governments prevent this practice.

Women's rights have also improved. A 2002 presidential decree allowed women to choose whether or not to wear the country's traditional full body and face covering, though most women still do so due to choice or community pressure. Female singers are not allowed on public television or radio. There are no other religious restrictions placed by the national government on the media, but there are reports of local restrictions. While schools have been opened for women, there are reports that in some places married women are banned from attending schools to prevent them from talking about married life with unmarried female students.[3]

Brunei

Brunei is governed by its 1959 constitution as amended in 1984 when it gained full independence from the United Kingdom. The constitution[4] establishes the Sultan as head of state and head of the national religion, the "Shafeite sect of Islam." Both the Sultan and the prime minister must be members of the official religion. The Sultan is advised by five councils including the Religious Council. "Religious freedom is safeguarded by the constitution."

It is illegal to insult another person's religion, damage or defile places of worship or sacred objects, or to cause a disturbance to an assembly engaged in religious worship or to a funeral with the intent of insulting anyone's

---

[3] Shahabuddin Tarakhel, "Funeral Woes for Hindus," *Human Rights Without Frontiers*, November 10, 2003, http://www.hrwf.net; "Wives Face School Ban," *Human Rights Without Frontiers*, November 10, 2003, http://www.hrwf.net; Burt Herman, "Afghanistan Weighs Use of Islamic Law," *Human Rights Without Frontiers*, October 31, 2003.

[4] I was unable to obtain an English translation of Brunei's constitution so the following description of its contents may be incomplete.

religion. The state's obscenity law contains an exception for religious publications. State identity cards include the bearer's religion.

Brunei's government promotes adherence to Islamic laws and values. Alcohol is illegal and Halal practices for the slaughter of meat are enforced. Islam is a required subject in schools for all students, including in private schools and Christian missions. No other religion is taught. Other religions may only be taught by parents in their homes. The only school in the country that is free of these restrictions is the Bandar Seri Begawan International School, which citizens and permanent residents cannot attend. Islamic garb is encouraged but not required, except as part of school uniforms. Abortion is illegal except to save the life of the woman.

Islamic law influences family law in Brunei and there is an Islamic court system for matters of personal status and other matters of Islamic law. There is a separate court system for other matters of law and for non-Muslims. The Muslim family laws are described in more detail in Chapter 8. Marriages may be refused registration if the registrar thinks the marriage is in violation of the laws of the couple's religion or in cases where the couple belong to different religions. The 1999 Married Woman Act, which provides for the rights of married women, only applies to non-Muslims.

All religious organizations not specifically mentioned in the constitution must register or face charges of unlawful assembly. Zoning laws are sometimes used to deny registration by non-Muslim organizations. Permits to build, repair, or expand non-Muslim places of worship are often denied. All minority religions need permission for processions or ceremonies outside of their designated places of worship. The country's only Chinese temple must get permission for each of its seasonal religious ceremonies held on temple grounds. State agents monitor religious services at Christian churches. Proselytizing is banned and those caught proselytizing are arrested. Conversion away from Islam is allowed only with the permission of the Ministry of Religious Affairs. Foreign non-Muslim clergy are often denied entry and the government restricts the importation of religious publications including the Bible. Christians are occasionally arrested for "cult activities" when the government feels that these activities undermine the Islamic character of the country. In 1998 the government temporarily confiscated gold and other precious Christian and Buddhist icons claiming that their open display violated the law.

The government bans what it considers radical Muslim groups and subjects those it thinks have been influenced by them to mandatory education.[5]

---

[5] "The Constitution of Brunei," Brunei Government Website, http://www.brunei.gov.bn/ government/contitut.htm; Laws of Brunei website, http://www.agc.gov.bn/LoB_list.htm; Islamic Family Law Website, Emory Law School, http://www.law.emory.edu/IFL/legal/brunei.htm; Jeff Taylor, "Seven Christians in Brunei Detained for 'Cult' Activities," *Human Rights Without Frontiers*, February 13, 2001; Jeff Taylor, "Five Christians Released in Brunei," *Human Rights Without Frontiers*, March 1, 2001; Jeff Taylor "Brunei Christians Suffer for Government 'Cult' Fears," *Human Rights Without Frontiers*, April 24, 2001; "Forced Conversions and Arrests," *Human Rights Without Frontiers*, April 6, 2001, http://www.hrwf.net.

Maldives

Article 1 of the Maldives' constitution states that the country "shall be a sovereign, independent, democratic republic based on the principles of Islam." Article 7 establishes Islam as the state religion. The various oaths of office for all of the country's officials include the phrase "I ... swear in the name of Almighty Allah that I will obey the religion of Islam." Article 25 guarantees freedom of conscience "unless prohibited by law in the interest of protecting the sovereignty of the Maldives, of maintaining public order and of protecting the basic tenets of Islam." Articles 34 and 47 require the president to be a Sunni Muslim who has never been convicted of a serious Islamic crime. Article 38 declares the president "the supreme authority to propagate the tenets of Islam in the Maldives." Article 57 requires that the attorney-general never was convicted of a serious Islamic crime. Articles 66, 107, 113, and 119 do the same for a member of the people's assembly. Articles 107, 113, and 119 require that a number of other government officials be Muslims. Articles 84 and 104 state that no member of the People's Majlis (Assembly) and the Special People's Assembly "shall be held liable in respect of any thought expressed or anything said without contradicting the basic tenets of Islam." Article 134 requires that a citizen be a Muslim in order to have the right to vote. Articles 16, 23, 43, and 156 make it clear that Sharia law is the law of the land.

The practice of any religion other than Islam in the Maldives is illegal, but foreigners may practice their religion in private. Sharia law is the supreme law of the land but civil law is usually applied in criminal cases. This includes the standard Islamic laws with regard to family law and women. The government sets theological standards for those who preach at mosques and monitors their speeches. Statements contrary to Islam are banned. In 2002 the government began arresting Islamic militants who distributed antigovernment literature for breaking the basic tenets of Islam. Islamic instruction is a mandatory part of school curriculums. Abortion is only allowed to save the life or physical health of the woman and only with the consent of the spouse.

Non-Muslim proselytizing or public worship and conversion away from Islam are prohibited. Groups who are suspected of proselytizing are generally arrested and expelled. There are no non-Muslim places of worship and the importation of icons or religious statues is prohibited. However, the import of religious literature for personal use is allowed.

Despite all this, the Maldives is lenient in the application of Islamic law compared to other Islamic states. Women are not required to cover themselves. Also, the more severe of Islamic punishments, such as cutting off a thief's hands, are rarely if ever applied. The government promotes literacy programs for women as well as programs to make women aware of their legal rights.[6]

---

[6] "Islamic Justice," http://www.ourmaldives.com/indexhello.php.

Active State Religions

Bangladesh

Article 2A of Bangladesh's constitution declares Islam the state religion but also states that "other religions may be practiced in peace and harmony." Article 8 includes "absolute trust and faith in the Almighty Allah" in the "fundamental principles of state policy" and "the basis of all actions." The preamble also makes reference to Allah. Article 24 requires the state to "endeavor to consolidate, preserve and strengthen fraternal relations among Muslim countries based on Islamic solidarity." Article 28 bans discrimination on the basis of religion. Article 29 does the same for public employment except in religious institutions. Article 41 protects the rights of religious freedom, of religious communities to establish and maintain religious institutions, and not to attend religious classes in any educational institution. Article 121 bans allocating electors for parliamentary elections on the basis of religion.

Family laws in Bangladesh are determined by the religious laws of one's faith but there are no limitations on interfaith marriages. This results in the usual disadvantages for Muslim women in divorce and inheritance. The government provides financial support for mosques as well as for Hindu and Christian religious buildings. Religion is taught in government schools. Minorities have the right to classes in their own religion. In practice these classes are often unavailable or taught by members of another religion. In 2001 the High Court declared illegal all *fatwas* (expert religious decisions or opinions on Islamic law) in order to prevent local leaders from enacting and enforcing extrajudicial punishments. Bangladesh's penal code prohibits the deliberate slander of religious feelings. Other than to save the life of the woman, abortion is illegal.

There is no legal right to proselytize but it is not illegal. Nevertheless many local governments restrict the actions of missionaries and state security sometimes monitors them. The government often does not renew the visas of foreign missionaries who are seen as trying to convert Muslims. Muslims who convert to another faith are often ostracized socially or beaten. Many choose to practice their new faiths in secret. Since the early 1990s religious minorities have been the targets of attacks by religious extremists and, since the late 1990s, of communal violence. Other than a few reports involving local officials there appears to be no government complicity in these acts but the government has been accused of not properly protecting religious minorities. This rise in religious extremism can be traced to the fact that many people in Bangladesh receive their education in the country's 64,000 madrassas.[7]

---

[7] Sarah Page, "Death of Evangelist Highlights Growing Tension in Bangladesh," *Human Rights Without Frontiers*, May 23, 2003, http://www.hrwf.net.

Malaysia

Article 3 of Malaysia's constitution declares it an Islamic federation but "other religions may be practiced in peace and harmony." It also declares that each state's "Ruler" is that state's head of Islam and makes provisions for appointing heads of Islam in states with no "Rulers." Article 8 prohibits discrimination on the basis of religion, unless the constitution says otherwise. One such exception is that a public religious office should be held by a member of the appropriate religion. Article 11 protects religious freedom, bans religious taxes, and grants religious groups the right to run their own affairs, including maintaining religious institutions and owning property. It also allows the government to restrict proselytizing to Muslims in the Federal Territories of Kuala Lumpur and Lubuan. Article 12 prohibits religious discrimination in access to public schools and government funding for education. It also allows all religious groups to establish religious schools, allows the government to fund Islamic schools, and states that no one can be required to take part in religious education or ceremonies. Several parts of the constitution discuss the Yang di-Pertuan Agong, who is officially deputy head of state but in practice is the head of Islam in Malaysia. This office has only religious authority. Its holder cannot hold any other government position and receives no compensation. Article 38 sets up a Council of Rulers to oversee Malaysia's religious affairs and has veto power over some laws involving religion. Article 42 gives the religious heads of some states the power to pardon those convicted in religious courts. Article 76 forbids the parliament to make laws on any aspect of Islamic law or custom. Article 97 states that if the government raises any religious revenues only the state can authorize the spending of them. Article 150 states that the government's emergency powers do not allow it to override the constitution's protections of religious rights. The definition of the term Malay in Article 160 includes the profession of Islam. Article 161E requires the approval of religious officials to amend the constitution to change the state religion.

It is government policy to "infuse Islamic values" into its citizens and to enforce the official version of Sunni Islam. Muslims are required to follow Islamic law in family, property, and religious matters. Since 2000 several state governments have passed laws enforcing traditional Muslim dress for women in general or, in some cases, only for civil servants. Some state governments have legislated Islamic dietary and cultural laws. These include bans on restaurants during the Fast of Ramadan, on public dancing and music, on unisex hair salons, and on unisex checkout lines in stores. The national government also restricts Karaoke bars and arcades. Alcohol advertisements in the media are illegal. In 2002 the government began requiring all Muslim civil servants to take classes in Islam. Religion is included on state identity cards. Public speech and literature that insults Islam is restricted.

The government funds religious institutions but recently withdrew support from 260 Islamic schools that were teaching their students to oppose the government. Islamic education is compulsory for Muslims in public schools. It is illegal for ethnic Malays to congregate in Christian houses of worship. Abortion is legal only to preserve the life or physical or mental health of the woman and requires authorization by a medical professional.

Shi'i Muslims are sometimes restricted and monitored. Under the law, members of "deviant sects" of Islam, including the Shi'i, can be detained by the government. In 1995, the government banned the Al-Arqam Islamic movement for deviationist teachings and arrested some of its members. In most cases, rather than banning a group the government "councils" its members to join the "right path," but arrests are common. Since September 11, 2001, this has included closer monitoring and more frequent arrests of Islamic militants, though this trend predates 9/11 and is in response to growing violence in Malaysia by Islamic militants. The government monitors sermons at mosques, bans imams who support the opposition, and actively replaces mosque leaders with ones who support the state.

Worship by religious minorities is not restricted but other restrictions exist. Religious organizations must register. The government can close unregistered institutions. In 2001 the government refused to register the Falun Gong, but it has not interfered with public worship by the group. Permits to build places of worship face bureaucratic obstacles and are often delayed or denied. Muslims who convert to other religions require approval from the country's Islamic courts, which, in practice, makes such conversions nearly impossible. Proselytizing to Muslims is illegal but proselytizing to non-Muslims is allowed. The distribution of bibles and other Christian literature in the Malay language is, in practice, forbidden.[8]

Pakistan

The preamble of Pakistan's constitution includes numerous references to Islam and protects the religious freedom of religious minorities. Article 1 officially

---

[8] Umm Mutma'inna, "Malaysia Detains 16 Indonesian Muslims for 'Deviant Religious Teachings,'" *Human Rights Without Frontiers*, March 6, 2002, http://www.hrwf.net; Simon Cameron-Moore, "Malaysian Muslim Sect Rebels Face Gallows or Life," *Human Rights Without Frontiers*, December 27, 2001; "Malaysia To Clamp Down on Islamic Militants: Mahathir," *Human Rights Without Frontiers*, November 10, 2001; "Malaysia Vows To Stop Students from Joining Cults," *Human Rights Without Frontiers*, July 10, 2000; Lewa Pardomuan, "Malaysia Pledges Tough Action Against Cults," *Human Rights Without Frontiers*, July 8, 2000; "Malaysia: Getting Serious About Fun: Recent Edicts by Kelantan's Ruling Party Draw Fire," *Asiaweek*, November 10, 1995, p. 37; Ian Stewart, "Alliance Strains May Unite Malaysian Foes," *Australian*, February 14, 1996; Seth Mydans, "Blame Men, Not Allah, Feminists Say," *New York Times*, October 10, 1996, p. A-4; Ian Stewart, "Karaoke Curfew to Aid Marital Harmony," *South China Morning Post*, September 20, 1996, p. 21; Abdul Razak, Ahmad, "DPM: Video Game Arcades Get until December To Close Shop," *New Straits Times*, October 5, 2000, p. 1; "Guidelines on Alcohol Adverts Welcomed," *New Straits Times*, May 30, 1995, p. 2.

names the country the Islamic Republic of Pakistan. Article 2 declares Islam the official religion. Article 19 subjects the freedom of the press to Islam. Article 20 protects religious freedom and the right to establish and maintain religious institutions, "subject to law, public order and morality." Article 21 bans the requirement for people to pay a religion tax or support any religion other than their own. Article 22 prohibits educational institutions from requiring students to take religious education or participate in religious ceremonies in any religion other than their own. It also guarantees the right to religious education and bans religious discrimination in educational institutions that receive state funding. Articles 26 and 27 prohibit various types of discrimination on the basis of religion. Article 31 makes observation of Islam and Islamic education mandatory for Muslims. Article 37 bans alcohol except for medicinal purposes and religious ceremonies of non-Muslims. Article 40 requires the state to support and strengthen relations with Islamic countries. Articles 42 and 61 require that the president be a Muslim, have knowledge of Islamic law and practices, and not be someone who violates Islamic law. Article 62 has similar requirements for members of the national assembly but allows for non-Muslim members who are of good moral reputation. Article 51 reserves seats in the national assembly for non-Muslims (amended in 2002). Article 196 requires that provincial legislatures reserve seats for non-Muslims (amended in 2002). Articles 203A to 203J establish a Sharia court, which has the power to judge any of Pakistan's laws or government actions to be against Islam and to review court cases for adherence to Islamic law. Articles 227 to 231 require all laws to be consistent with Islam and provide for a government-supported Islamic Ideology Council to advise on whether laws are consistent with Islam. It also exempts non-Muslims from Islamic personal laws. Article 260 contains the definition of Muslim and non-Muslim. Bahais and Ahmadis are specifically defined as non-Muslims. The constitution was indefinitely suspended after the 1999 military coup in Pakistan, but most of its provisions with regard to religion effectively remain in force.

Sunni Muslims pay a 2.5 percent religious tax. Some provincial governments support mosques and, in some cases, Hindu temples. Bureaucracy and corruption make it difficult to obtain permission to buy land and build houses of worship, even for Muslims. Islam is a required subject in all schools. Non-Muslims are exempted but no alternative religious education is provided. Blasphemy laws are regularly enforced. In practice those accused are usually convicted in the religious courts, in part due to death threats sent to judges when they do not convict the accused. Foreign books are censored for anti-Islam content but religious literature of minority religions is not substantially restricted. The government restricts some religious icons such as those of the Trinity and Jesus. Stirring up religious hatred of any kind is illegal under an anti-terrorist law. Religion is included on passports and Muslims must take a religious oath to obtain one. Marriage is performed only under religious auspices. The penal code, which applies to all citizens, includes elements of Sharia law including the criminalization of all extramarital sex.

Abortion is allowed only to save the life or the physical or mental health of the woman.

In 2001 the government began banning extremist Islamic organizations and arresting their members, especially those that use violence against the government or minorities. The sentences are severe, and can be death. In addition the government has arrested several religious leaders, barred certain political groups from organizing rallies, and prohibited the use of loudspeakers in mosques to convey political sentiments. In 2002, the government declared a ban on mosque construction without prior government permission and demanded the registration of all existing mosques with the authorities. The government also began requiring all madrassas to register and prohibited them from accepting foreign aid. Foreign students in these madrassas are now required to obtain "no objection" certificates from the government in order to attend. Registered schools are also required to teach modern subjects along with Islam.

The government does not officially ban Ahmadis but the practice of the Ahmadi branch of Islam is severely restricted. They are not considered Muslims by the government. It is illegal for Ahmadis to call themselves Muslims, insult the faith of other Muslims, preach their faith, proselytize, or accept converts. The government has destroyed several Ahmadi mosques. Religious oaths for Muslims are used to prevent Ahmadis from voting, attending school, and obtaining passports. The government reportedly monitors Ahmadi institutions. Ahmadis are targets for accusations under blasphemy laws. This occurs to a lesser extent to other religious minorities. Since 1985 Ahmadis have been banned from holding any conferences or gatherings.

In 2002 the government eliminated the spaces in the federal and provincial legislatures reserved for minorities. Minorities now vote like any other citizens. Proselytizing by non-Ahmadis is legal as long as missionaries openly acknowledge they are not Muslims and do not preach against Islam. Foreign missionaries require special visas. Non-Muslims are at a disadvantage in all court proceedings as their testimony is given less weight. Some Sikh holy sites seized by the government at independence remain under government control.[9]

---

[9] "Religious Extremists Arrested," *Human Rights Without Frontiers*, January 15, 2002, http://www.hrwf.net; "Pakistani Court Sentences Three Militants To Death," *Human Rights Without Frontiers*, April 7, 2004, http://www.hrwf.net; "Pakistan Moves To Contain Religious Extremism," *Human Rights Without Frontiers*, December 15, 2001; "Human Rights Grave Concern About the Condition of Minorities in Pakistan," *Pakistan Newswire*, December 9, 2002; Nadeem Yaqub, "Minorities Tell of Religious Persecution," *Human Rights Without Frontiers*, January 20, 2004; Norimitsu Onishi, "A Nation Challenged: Politics; Pakistan Tries to Split Army from Mullahs," *New York Times*, November 9, 2001, p. B-1; Erik Ekholm, "The India-Pakistan Tension: Islamabad; Pakistan Pledges To Bar Any Groups Linked to Terror," *New York Times*, January 13, 2002, p. A-1.

Preferred Treatment for Some Religions or Support for a Particular Tradition

Indonesia

Article 29 of Indonesia's constitution states that "the State shall be based upon the belief in the One and Only God" but also protects religious freedom. Article 9 states that the oath of office for the president and vice president includes the word God, phrased appropriately for the individual's religion. The preamble includes several symbolic references to religion.

A significant minority of Indonesians want the country to become an Islamic state. Matters of family law are determined by one's religion, making interfaith marriages difficult to obtain. Adoptive parents must be of the same religion as the child. Religious instruction is required in all schools in the student's faith. National identity cards include the bearer's religion. Religious groups must obtain permits for public events including concerts. Such permits are usually granted. Religious speech is allowed as long as it is delivered to members of the same religion and not intended to proselytize. Other than to save the life of the woman, abortion is illegal. The consent of the woman's husband or family is also required. The Aceh province was given special autonomy to implement Sharia law, but only if it does not contradict national law and each element of Sharia law must be incorporated into the legal code separately.

The government officially bans some messianic Islamic groups but allows them to operate in practice. The government closely monitors Islamic sects that it considers to deviate from orthodox tenets, and on occasion dissolves such groups.

The Ministry of Religion recognizes Islam, Catholicism, Protestantism, Hinduism, and Buddhism. Practicing most other religions is legal; these groups can register only as social organizations. Atheism is illegal. Until 2000 the Bahai and Confucian faiths were illegal as were the Jehovah's Witnesses until 2001. Members of unregistered faiths must place another religion on their identity cards. They also have difficulty registering marriages and births. Places in the army's officer corps are proportional to the country's ethnoreligious population, but only for recognized religions. All government employees take an oath that includes belief in one supreme God. Permits to build places of worship are required from the Ministry of Religious Affairs and a local council. They are difficult to obtain for recognized minority religions and nearly impossible for others. All proselytizing, dissemination of religious materials to members of other faiths, and attempts to convert others to one's faith are banned. This includes Muslims. However, conversion itself is legal. Foreign religious groups need government permission to provide aid to religious groups in Indonesia. This law is enforced sporadically and disproportionably upon minority religions. Foreign religious workers report difficulty in obtaining visas and their term of residence in the country is limited by law.

Indonesia experiences considerable interreligious violence. While the government generally takes preventative measures and punishes the perpetrators, local officials are sometimes complicit in the violence. This violence includes incidents where Muslims have forced Christians to convert to Islam as well as violence by Christians against Muslims.

BUDDHIST STATES

Buddhist states, other than those that are communist, tend to support religion, but not to the same extent as Muslim states. Other than Burma, states engage in low to moderate levels of restrictions on religious minorities.

Active State Religions

Bhutan

Bhutan has no constitution. In 2001 the King appointed a committee to draft one, and several drafts exist, but they have not been adopted.[10] Buddhism and Hinduism are the only recognized religions and the Drukpa Kagyupa school of Mahayana Buddhism is the country's official religion.

Matters of family law are guided by one's religion, in practice either Buddhism or Hinduism. The Monastic Body, a body of 3,500 monks, determines all major religious issues as well as some matters of state. This body, a number of Buddhist temples, monasteries, and shrines, as well as a third of the country's Buddhist monks receive financial support from the government. 10 of 150 seats in the national assembly and 2 of 11 seats of the Royal Advisory Council are reserved for Buddhist monks of the Drukpa discipline. Religious classes by the Drukpa Kagyupa and Ningmapa Buddhist denominations are allowed in schools, but classes in other religions are not. In public places all citizens are required to wear traditional Buddhist dress, though this is enforced sporadically.

The law provides for religious freedom but this right is limited in practice. Proselytizing is illegal. Bhutanese NGOs claim that conversion is illegal, that no religious materials are permitted to enter the country other than Buddhist texts, and that Buddhist prayer is compulsory in all government schools. The government denies these claims. Permits are necessary to build a religious building. Hindu temples are often denied permits. Advocacy groups claim that the government has made Christianity illegal. The government counters that people may practice any religion privately in their homes but attempts to convert others to different faiths are strictly forbidden. This includes public preaching. Recently, local governments have been harassing Christian services held in private homes and otherwise harass those participating in the services. There are also reports that since 2000 public Christian worship has been banned.

The government is protective of the local interpretation of Buddhism. For example, it is Bhutan's policy that if a Tibetan lama reincarnates in Bhutan

[10] Copies of these draft constitutions are available at http://www.constitution.bt/html/constitution/constitution.htm.

"those coming to recognize the reincarnation should report the matter to the Government and be accompanied by [government] representatives." Furthermore, if the reincarnation were found to be genuine "he would be permitted to stay at the place of his birth, but he would neither be permitted to introduce any new religious system nor to set up any new monastery or monk body."[11]

State-controlled Religion

Burma

Burma's 1974 constitution has been suspended since 1988. Since 1962 the country, also known as Myanmar, has been ruled by a military regime.

There is no official state religion but since 1962 the government associates itself with Theravada Buddhism. All religions must register. Buddhist education is optional. Buddhist prayers are mandatory in public schools but non-Buddhist students are allowed to leave the room during prayers in some schools. The government provides utilities to registered religions at reduced rates and funds state universities to train Buddhist monks. Other than to save the life of the woman, abortion is illegal.

Since 1990 only the nine officially recognized Buddhist monastic orders have been allowed to operate, and they are subject to the authority of the State Monk Coordination Committee. The state has imposed a code of conduct upon monks and can try them for "activities inconsistent with and detrimental to Buddhism." The government monitors meetings of Buddhist organizations, along with meetings of all other types of organization. Buddhist clergy may not call for democracy or oppose government policy. The government has arrested large numbers of monks and the army often searches them and their temples. Several prominent monks have been imprisoned for refusing to attend religious ceremonies organized by the authorities.

Government authorities oppose the spread of Christianity and often ban public meetings by Christian groups. Soldiers have beaten Christian clergy who refuse to sign documents promising not to preach to non-Christians and, since 2001, have been reported as disrupting Christian services. The government often denies permission for the building or repair of churches and mosques. On occasion, in the context of fighting rebels, government forces have been known to arrest Christian clergy, destroy places of worship, and prohibit religious services. All publications, religious and secular, are subject to censorship. In practice, importing religious literature, including the Bible and the Koran, is difficult as is gaining permits to print them in Burma. Religion is sometimes included on citizen identity cards. The government severely restricts visas for foreign clergy. Permanent foreign religious missions have not been permitted since the 1960s. Many of these restrictions can be attributed to the

---

[11] "Bhutanese House Churches Raided after Easter Services," *Human Rights Without Frontiers*, April 23, 2004; "Bhutan Denies Vatican Report of Christian Persecution," *Human Rights Without Frontiers*, April 28, 2001, http://www.hrwf.net.

government's authoritarian nature and a high concentration of religious minorities among ethnic minorities that the government has been fighting for decades.

These forms of repression are especially strong against the Chin Christian minority. Since 1990 the government has supported the forced conversion of Chins to Buddhism as part of a campaign to "Burmanize" them. There are reports of similar activities toward the Naga minority. The government has destroyed mosques in the Arakan State and reportedly forced Muslims there to donate money to Buddhist buildings. Since 2001 there has been systematic communal violence against Muslims in Burma, with the tacit permission of authorities.[12]

Historical or Cultural State Religion

Cambodia

Article 31 of Cambodia's constitution guarantees equality regardless of religion. Article 43 declares Buddhism the state religion but guarantees religious freedom provided that it "does not affect other religious beliefs or violate public order and security." Article 68 states that "the State shall disseminate and develop the Pali schools and the Buddhist Institutes." There are several symbolic mentions of religion in the constitution.

The government provides training for Buddhist monks and modest funds for an institute that researches Khmer culture and Buddhist traditions. All religions, including Buddhism, require permits in order to build places of worship and conduct religious activities. These permits are generally granted but there are occasional reports of delays in granting them to minority religions. Much of the country's primary school system is run by Buddhist institutions.

The government generally does not restrict minority religions unless the government suspects them of engaging in illegal political activities. In 2003 the Ministry on Cults and Religions published a directive banning proselytizing.

Sri Lanka

Article 1 of Sri Lanka's constitution recognizes the "multi-religious character" of its society. However, Article 7 gives Buddhism "the foremost place and, accordingly, it shall be the duty of the State to protect and foster the Buddha Sasunu giving adequate protection to all religions and guaranteeing to every person the rights and freedoms granted by ... Article 15," which protects religious freedom. Article 11 prohibits discrimination on the basis of religion or caste. A similar provision exists in Article 245 with regard to the Interim Council for the Northern and Eastern Region. Article 16 allows restrictions on the freedom of speech in order to protect religious harmony. Articles 17, 18, and 19 do the same for freedom of peaceful assembly and association as well as

---

[12] CIA World Factbook, http://www.cia.gov/cia/publications/factbook/geos/bm.html.

the right to enjoy and promote culture and use of language. Article 27 states that emergency laws do not allow discrimination on the basis of religion. Article 57 includes "the creation of the necessary environment to enable adherents of all religions to make a living reality of their religious principles" in the principles that guide the state in making laws.

The government has separate ministries for Buddhist, Muslim, Hindu, and Christian affairs. Religion classes are mandatory in the public school system. Classes are offered in Buddhism, Islam, Hinduism, and Christianity. Issues of family law are regulated by the religious law of the individual in question. Abortion is legal only to save the life of the woman.

The government limits the number of Christian clergy allowed to enter and tends to grant visas only to those who are members of registered religions. Some Christian clergy face opposition to proselytizing at the local level but there is no evidence of complicity by the national government. In 2003 an order of nuns running a hospital was refused registration because its medical services to the poor were considered proselytism. An evangelical group was similarly refused registration because the group coupled religious education with charitable deeds. The ongoing civil war in Sri Lanka, primarily between the majority Buddhists and the Hindu Tamils, has affected the lives of members of all religions in Sri Lanka but, while including some religious motivations, is primarily motivated by nationalist issues. Recently there has also been a rash of anti-Christian violence by Buddhists in response to the efforts of some Christian groups to convert the poor.[13]

Preferred Treatment for Some Religions or Support for a Particular Tradition

Thailand

Article 5 of Thailand's 1997 constitution grants equal protection regardless of religion. Article 9 states that "the King is a Buddhist and Upholder of Religions." Article 30 prohibits discrimination on the basis of religion. Article 38 grants religious freedom as long as this does not contradict a citizen's civic duty, public order, or good morals. Article 66 states that "every person shall have a duty to uphold the Nation, religions, the King and the democratic regime of government." Article 73 states that "the State shall patronize and protect Buddhism and other religions, promote good understanding and harmony among followers of all religions as well as encourage the application of religious principles to create virtue and develop the quality of life." Article 106 prohibits any "Buddhist priest, novice, monk or clergy" from voting.

In effect the country's religion is Theravada Buddhism, but the constitution explicitly does not make it the official religion in order not to offend religious

---

[13] Joshua Newton, "Violence Against Christians Escalates in Sri Lanka," *Human Rights Without Frontiers*, January 22, 2004, http://www.hrwf.net; Sarah Page, "Buddhist Mobs Attack Five Churches in Sri Lanka," *Human Rights Without Frontiers*, August 5, 2003.

minorities. The Religious Affairs Department recognizes a new religion if it has a unique theology, is not politically active, a national census shows that it has 5000 members in the country, and it is accepted into an officially recognized ecclesiastical group. Registration brings tax benefits, access to state subsidies, and preferences in visa and land allocation. No religions have registered since 1984 but nonregistered groups can practice freely. State funding for religion includes funding for education, including in public schools, daily allowances for senior clergy, health care for clergy, and funds for the upkeep and renovation of holy places. The government grants a small amount of funds for Christian social welfare programs. Religious education is mandatory in public schools and is generally offered in Buddhism and Islam. It is illegal to insult Buddhism. National identity cards optionally include religion. Abortion is legal to save the life or physical and mental health of the woman, as well as in cases of rape or incest, but not in cases of fetal impairment, for economic reasons, or upon request.

Recently the government has limited the activities of the Falun Gong. Some members have been denied visas to enter the country and public Falun Gong events are discouraged. In one case a Falun Gong member's house was raided and the member was expelled. In general, foreign missionary groups proselytize freely, but the government has a policy of giving preference to proselytizing by its citizens. There is a quota on visas for foreign missionaries but those entering the country on other types of visas are not restricted. While officially Muslim civil servants are not allowed to wear head coverings, in practice their supervisors generally allow them to do so. Religious minorities have complained that the government disseminated school textbooks containing religious information, but only on Buddhism.

Moderate Separation

Mongolia
Article 9 of Mongolia's constitution states that "the State shall respect the Church and the Church shall honor the State. State institutions may not engage in religious activities and the Church may not pursue political activities. The relationship between the State and the Church is regulated by law." Article 14 protects against discrimination on the basis of religion. Article 16 guarantees religious freedom. Article 19 states that the government's emergency powers do not allow it to violate religious freedom.

A 1993 law contains the following provisions on religion. "The State will respect the predominant position of the Buddhist religion in Mongolia." "The organized propagation of religion from outside" and religious education in state schools are forbidden. Religious groups must register with the government. The government can limit the number of places of worship and clergy.

Despite this, the government, with a few exceptions, maintains a substantial level of SRAS. It has contributed to the restoration of some Buddhist sites considered of historical or cultural importance. Religious registration is sometimes difficult, mainly due to the corruption of some local officials. The government has the right to limit the number of places of worship and clergy but generally does not do so. Proselytizing is not illegal but it is restricted by a 1993 law against "the use of incentives, pressure, or deceptive methods to introduce religion."

HINDU STATES

The two Asian Hindu states in this study have similar approaches to religion. Both support Hinduism but do not make it the country's official religion. Both make efforts to avoid religious tensions, most likely in order to avoid tensions between the different Hindu castes. Both also engage in moderate levels of restrictions on minority religions.

India

Article 15 of India's constitution prohibits discrimination on the basis of religion. Article 16 prohibits religious discrimination in public employment, except when the office is in connection with a particular religion. Articles 23, 29, 30, and 325 prohibit religious discrimination with regard to other specific state activities. Articles 25 and 26 guarantee religious freedom subject to morality and order. Article 25 allows the government to "throw open Hindu religious institutions of a public character to all classes and sections of Hindus" as well as non-Hindu minorities. Article 25 allows Sikhs to wear kirpans, their ceremonial daggers. Article 27 prohibits religious taxes. Article 28 bans religious education in institutions "wholly maintained out of State funds," but otherwise religious education is allowed. Article 30 gives religious minorities the right to establish schools. Article 51A includes in the duties of a citizen "to promote harmony and the spirit of common brotherhood amongst all the people of India transcending religious, linguistic and regional or sectional diversities." Article 290A requires the State of Tamil Nadu to pay a specified sum into a fund for the preservation of Hindu temples and shrines. Article 371 states that no law regarding the religious or social practices of the Nagas and Mizos will apply to their regions without their consent. The oaths of the president, vice president and governors in Articles 60, 69, and 159 contain optional references to God.

Marriage, divorce, adoption, and inheritance laws are determined by one's religion. Muslim laws discriminate against women. Religious affiliation is included on birth certificates. Most Hindus attend government schools or Christian schools. Some Muslim schools receive government aid. The government may ban a religion for terrorism, sedition, provoking intercommunal friction, or violations of restrictions on funding from abroad. The government has banned some Muslim groups for suspicion of complicity in acts of terrorism. Preaching against other religions in public is considered a violation of national security. Foreigners on tourist visas may not preach without government permission. It is illegal to encourage communal hatred on religious grounds, to undermine the harmony between religious groups, to deface a place of worship or any sacred object for purposes of offending religious feelings or religion in general, to obstruct or interfere in religious ceremonies, or to use sounds and gestures to insult religious feelings. The Religious Institution (Prevention of Misuse) Act bans using any religious site for political aims or for protecting anyone accused or convicted of a crime. Religious sites hold the same status as they did at independence in order to avoid conflict between religious groups over ownership. Abortion is not available on request in India but is allowed to save the life, health, or mental health of the woman, in cases of rape, incest, or fetal impairment, for economic and social reasons, and in cases when contraception failed.

While the national government generally respects the rights outlined in India's constitution, local governments sometimes restrict them. Some local governments require foreign clergy to register. This particularly restricts Christian missionary groups. The state of Uttar Pradesh requires a permit to build new houses of worship and restricts new mosques it considers fundamentalist. Several states ban conversion, and some of these bans include bans on "forcing" or "alluring" someone to convert. Other states require some form of government approval to convert. In some regions there are accusations of selective application of the law in order to disadvantage religious minorities. This includes allocation of land and heightened scrutiny of foreign contributions. There has also been a considerable amount of interreligious communal violence. Often local officials and police are complicit in the violence, do not take measures to stop it, or fail to prosecute Hindu offenders. Following particularly bad riots in 1992 the national government banned several Hindu and Muslim organizations.

The BJP, one of India's political parties, when in power pursued a policy of making India a Hindu state. This included a campaign to reconvert Indian citizens believed to have been "forcibly" converted away from Hinduism. The campaign, however, has also included efforts to "reconvert" citizens who have been Christian or Muslim for generations. This campaign was carried out mostly at the local level and, other than the passing of the anti-conversion laws, was carried out by nongovernmental groups. Also, while religious education is not allowed in public schools, recently the curriculum began to include efforts to teach and reinforce Hindu culture.

Nepal

Article 2 of Nepal's constitution states that the Nepalese nationality is irrespective of religion. Article 4 declares that the country is a Hindu constitutional monarchy. Article 11 prohibits discrimination on the basis of religion or caste. Article 19 guarantees religious freedom "provided that no person shall be entitled to convert another person from one religion to another." It also allows each religious denomination to maintain their independence and manage their religious places and affairs. Articles 25 and 26 include maintaining harmony amongst religions among the government's goals. Article 27 requires that Nepal's King be a Hindu. Article 74 separates the funds of religious endowments from the general budget of the state. Article 112 bans religious political parties. Article 113 forbids political parties that link membership to religion or promote religious divisions in the country.

Abortion is only allowed to save the life of the woman, but in practice it is sometimes allowed to save the physical or mental health of the woman, as well as in cases of rape, incest, or fetal impairment. The publication of material that may cause animosity between people of different castes or religions is illegal. Proselytizing is banned, but religious organizations that do not proselytize operate freely. Those who violate this law are arrested. The government sometimes restricts the public celebration of Buddhist holidays but allows them to take place privately. Since 2002 the government has required Muslim madrassas to register and supply information on their funding sources. The police occasionally harass members of minority religions and there are occasional incidents of Hindu extremist violence against minorities.[14]

CHRISTIAN STATES

Asia's Christian states tend to support religion but do not have official religions. All of them also place few restrictions on religious minorities.

Preferred Treatment for Some Religions or Support for a Particular Tradition

Fiji

Article 5 of Fiji's 1997 constitution states that "although religion and the State are separate, the people of the Fiji Islands acknowledge that worship and reverence of God are the source of good government and leadership." Articles 6 and 35 guarantee religious freedom, including the freedom to observe, worship, practice, and teach. This right can only be limited to protect the rights of other people, public safety, order, morality, or health. Article 35 also guarantees that people will not be required to take religious education or oaths. Article 39 guarantees the right to build and maintain places of religious education. Articles 23 and 26 give those who are arrested the right to see a religious counselor. The preamble includes several symbolic references to religion. All of the oaths found in the constitution contain the word God but also allow for secular alternatives.

The government respects the religious rights outlined in the constitution. Between 1989 and 1995 organized sports, movies, and night clubs were prohibited on Sundays. Abortions are legal to preserve the pregnant woman's life, or her physical or mental health, and must be performed by a licensed practitioner in a hospital. Also, a physician must authorize the abortion, stating that the procedure is essential in preserving the physical and/or mental health of the woman. Physicians are instructed to take "into account the social

---

[14] Alex Buchen, "Mob Destroys Church in Nepal After Vandal Desecrates Hindu Temple," *Human Rights Without Frontiers*, September 7, 1999, http://www.hrwf.net.

circumstances of the patient" when authorizing abortions. Abortions are not available in the case of rape, incest, fetal impairment, or upon request.[15]

Papua New Guinea

Article 32 of Papua New Guinea's 1975 constitution protects general freedom and ends with the phrase "this section is not intended to reflect on the extra-legal existence, nature or effect of social, civic, family or religious obligations, or other obligations of an extra-legal nature, or to prevent such obligations being given effect to by law." Article 45 protects religious freedom. Article 55 gives all citizens equal rights regardless of their religion. Article 233 states that emergency laws may not alter religious freedom. The oath of allegiance in Article 7 includes the phrase "so help me God" but also contains a secular alternative. The preamble includes several symbolic references to religion.

The Department of Family and Church Affairs officially has a role in policy making but generally reiterates the government's policy of maintaining respect for church autonomy. Most of the country's schools as well as much of its public health system were built and run by churches, which receive government funding. In those public schools not run by the churches, one hour a week is set aside for religious education taught by church officials of the religion of the parents' choice. It is possible to opt out of this education. The Customs Recognition Act allows the country's courts to take local customs, including religious ones, into account in their rulings. In order to obtain titles or properties, churches must register as corporate bodies. Abortion is only legal in order to save the life or the physical or mental health of the woman.

Vanuatu

Article 5 of Vanuatu's constitution prohibits discrimination on the basis of religious or traditional beliefs. It also protects the freedom of conscience and worship. The preamble includes religious imagery.

Due to concerns over missionary activity by new religions, in 1995 the government began requiring religions to register. While some religions have voluntarily registered, this law is not enforced. Oaths of office are generally taken on the Bible. The government provides funds for the construction of Christian churches and Christian-operated schools. Public schools provide Christian education but students may opt out. Abortion is legal only to save the life or physical or mental health of the woman.

General Support

Philippines

Article 2, Section 6, of the Philippines' constitution states that "the separation of Church and State shall be inviolable." Article 3, Section 5, provides for

[15] "Fiji Parliament Votes to Repeal Sunday Observance Law," Radio Australia External Service, in: *The British Broadcasting Corporation Summary of World Broadcasts*, September 21, 1995, Part 3, Asia-Pacific.

religious freedom and prohibits both establishing a religion and religious tests for the exercise of civil or political rights. Article 2, Section 12, protects "the life of the unborn from conception." Article 6, Section 5, reserves seats in the legislature for minorities, but excludes religion as a basis for selecting these minorities. Article 6, Section 28, exempts religious institutions, organizations, and property from taxation. Article 6, Section 29, prohibits the government from funding religious organizations and clergy, except clergy "assigned to the armed forces, or to any penal institution, or government orphanage or leprosarium." Article 9, Section C1, prohibits religious denominations or sects from registering as political parties. Article 14, Section 3, allows optional religious education in public schools if the teachers are provided at no cost to the government. Article 14, Section 4, states that all educational institutions other than religious ones must be owned by Philippine citizens "or corporations or associations at least sixty per centum of the capital of which is owned by such citizens." Article 15, Section 3, protects a couple's right "to found a family in accordance with their religious convictions and the demands of responsible parenthood." The preamble includes religious imagery. The oath for the president and vice president optionally includes the phrase "so help me God."

Religions must register, which includes the submission of the group's articles of faith and by-laws. A religion may also register as a general nonprofit organization. The law requires that the religious rights of students in schools be protected. Thus, religious garb is permitted. Abortion is legal only to save the life of the woman and requires authorization by a panel of professionals. Divorce in the Philippines is not possible and those wishing one must obtain it in another country. This is considered an element of the influence on society of the Catholic Church, which takes an active role in civil society and often seeks to influence policy issues.

The Office on Muslim Affairs, which is part of the president's office, fosters and coordinates Islamic practices. In 1990 the government established the Autonomous Region in Muslim Mindanao (ARMM) to settle a violent Muslim rebellion in that region. In 1996 the autonomy was strengthened as part of a peace agreement and in 2001 a plebiscite expanded the ARMM to some adjacent regions. The government recognizes Islamic law as one of the bases for family law, but this applies only to Muslims. There is a system of Islamic courts to deal with these issues. Despite these efforts at peace, radical Muslim groups continue to engage in violence against Christians.[16]

Solomon Islands
Article 11 of the Solomon Islands' constitution protects religious freedom, the right to establish and to maintain places of worship, religious education, and

---

[16] "Ex-senator Backs Church Fight Against Poll Fraud," *South China Morning Post*, June 12, 1996; Uli Schmetzer, "President's Ploy Elbowed Out by Prelate Power," *Hobart Mercury*, September 23, 1997; "Arroyo Upsets Church with Death Penalty Plan," *Bangkok Post*, October 29, 2001.

the freedom from religious education. It also guarantees that no one has to take a religious oath against their will or an oath against their religious beliefs. This article does not limit the rights of the government to pass laws in "the interests of defense, public safety, public order, public morality … public health or … protecting the rights and freedoms of other persons," as well as the right of the government to set the curriculum in schools. The preamble includes religious imagery.

All religious groups must register. There are no reports of registration being refused. The government does not generally subsidize religion but much of its school and health care systems are run by churches. Health care institutions receive government funding as do the schools if their curriculums meet government standards. The public school system includes religious instruction in Christianity, the specifics of which are agreed upon by the country's various churches. Upon request students can be excused from these courses. Abortion is only legal to save the life of the woman.

OTHER RELIGIOUS TRADITIONS

All four of the states in this category happen to be among the most economically developed Asian states. They are those states that do not fit into any of the above categories and tend to be secular. Three of them have considerable SRAS and the fourth, Singapore, is slightly hostile to religion.

Moderate to Full Separation

Japan

Article 20 of Japan's constitution guarantees religious freedom, including freedom from religion. It states that "no religious organization shall receive any privileges from the State, nor exercise any political authority," and that "the State and its organs shall refrain from religious education or any other religious activity." Article 80 forbids the use of state money to support religion.

Some Buddhist and Shinto temples receive government support. Religious organizations may register as a religious corporation in order to gain tax and other benefits. Registration has never been refused. Requirements for registration are a minimum of three years of operation, having one's own religious facilities, and letting members initiate and terminate membership at will. The 1951 Religious Corporations Act allows the government to dissolve a religious corporation if it "substantially deviates from religious activities" or "poses a threat to the public."

After the Aum Shinrikyo terrorist attacks in 1995 the government amended the law of religious organizations to allow increased oversight of religious organizations and require increased disclosure of their financial assets. The group lost its religious status in 1995 and remains under government surveillance. A 1999 law against mass murder increased the legal scope of measures that can be taken against the group. Members of new religions are often kidnapped at the behest of family members in order to de-program them. The police are lax in preventing this.[17]

South Korea

Article 11 of South Korea's constitution guarantees equality under the law regardless of religion. Article 20 declares SRAS and protects religious freedom. In 1987 the government passed the Temple Preservation Act to protect historical Buddhist sites. The government funds the upkeep of these sites. As of 1999, foreign missionaries are no longer required to register with the government. Religious instruction is not permitted in public schools. Abortion is available on request, but married women need the consent of their spouses.

Taiwan

Article 7 of Taiwan's constitution guarantees equality before the law regardless of religion. Article 13 guarantees religious freedom. Religious organizations need not register and can operate as the personal property of their leaders but registration brings tax-exempt status. Concern over abuse of this tax exemption has led to the refusal of registration for some new religions when their doctrine was unclear, but this does not influence the right to practice. Religious instruction is prohibited in public schools and schools with Ministry of Education accreditation. However, high schools may provide courses in religious studies as an academic topic.

Hostility

Singapore

Articles 12 and 16 of Singapore's constitution prohibit discrimination on the basis of religion except for employment in religious institutions. Article 16 also states that all religious groups have the right to establish educational institutions and that in educational institutions "no person shall be required to receive instruction in or to take part in any ceremony or act of worship of a religion other than his own." Article 15 protects religious freedom, bans mandatory religious taxes, and allows all religious groups to manage their own affairs, maintain institutions, and own property. However, it "does not authorize any act contrary to any general law relating to public order, public health or morality." Article 76 gives the Presidential Council for Minority Rights the power to "consider and report on such matters affecting persons of any racial or religious community in Singapore." Article 150 states that the country's emergency power laws do not allow it to violate religious freedom. Article 152 states that "it shall be the responsibility of the Government constantly to care for the interests of the racial and religious minorities in Singapore ... [and to] safeguard, support, foster and promote their ... religious ... interests." Article 153 requires the legislature to

---

[17] Hau Boon Lai, "Japan's Cult Menace," *Straits Times*, January 2, 2000, pp. 30–1; "Japanese Cult Loses Status; Assets Exposed," *Baltimore Sun*, October 31, 1995.

"make provision for regulating Muslim religious affairs and for constituting a Council to advise the President in matters relating to the Muslim religion."

The constitution also makes several references to the 1990 Maintenance of Religious Harmony Act. This act sets up a Council of Religious Harmony to advise the government on religious matters. It also allows the minister responsible for religious affairs to place a restraining order on any clergy member or person of authority in a religious institution if they engage in any of the following acts: causing animosity between religious groups; using religion to promote a political party or cause; "subversive activities under the guise of propagating or practicing any religious belief"; or "exciting disaffection" against the government. The restraining order can restrict freedom of speech, the freedom to publish and distribute religious literature, and can prohibit one from "holding office in an editorial board or a committee of a publication of any religious group." The restrictions on freedom of speech can be placed on anyone inciting religious animosity. There is no judicial review of the actions taken under this law. The president is required to confirm all restraining orders within 30 days or they are cancelled.

There is no religious instruction in public schools. Traditional headcoverings for Muslim females are banned from public schools. In 2000 the government gave all madrassas eight years to bring their curriculums into accordance with national standards or face closure. Islamic law for marriages is the national law for Muslims. In general the government prohibits the discussion of sensitive racial and religious issues and monitors public speech to enforce this. Any unauthorized public mixing of religion and politics usually results in government action.

All religions are required to register. The Jehovah's Witnesses (1972) and the Unification Church (1982) have had their registration revoked. While it is not illegal to believe in these religions, public meetings are illegal. The ban on the Jehovah's Witnesses is because its members refuse to serve in the military and to take public oaths. In the past Jehovah's Witnesses have been banned from schools for refusing to sing the national anthem or to participate in the flag ceremony. The Jehovah's Witnesses are not allowed to publish and distribute religious literature. While proselytizing is legal for groups that have not been banned, the government discourages activities that are likely to incite religious sensitivities.[18]

SOME GENERAL OBSERVATIONS

This survey shows that most Asian states either support or try to significantly restrict or control religion. As shown in Chapter 11, this trend became stronger between 1990 and 2002.

---

[18] Singapore Expels Four Falun Gong Members for Vigil," *Human Rights Without Frontiers*, April 27, 2001, http://www.hrwf.net.

It can be said that a state's majority religious tradition is a central issue in Asia for a number of reasons. First, Asian states with different religious identities behave differently toward religion. Muslim states tend to be the most strongly supportive of state religions and, on average, place the most restrictions on religious minorities. With the exception of those states that are communist or have military governments, Buddhist states tend to support Buddhism but less intensely than Muslim states support Islam. Hindu states support Hinduism but do not declare it to be an official religion. Christian states tend to support Christianity or religion in general and tend to be tolerant of minorities. Communist and authoritarian states tend to try to control and restrict religion. The states with the most SRAS tend to be those that do not fit into any of the above categories and have a less distinct religious identity. Chapter 11 provides a discussion of how this compares with the impact of religious tradition on GIR in other world regions.

Second, many of these states have religiously diverse populations with a history of tension and conflict between the various denominations. Consequently some laws and policies that technically restrict religion based on the RAS codings are intended to prevent religious conflict. This pattern is particularly prominent in India, Indonesia, Laos, Nepal, Pakistan, Singapore, Sri Lanka, and Vietnam. This includes limitations on preaching or proselytizing to members of other religions, trying to convert member of other religions, and incitement against any religion. Yet this can still legitimately be called GIR since the state must intervene in religious affairs in order to preserve the peace.

Third, several Asian countries attempt to protect the dominant religion of the state. This occurs in the religious states but it also occurs in others. In India, Laos, and Vietnam this has taken the extreme form of governments taking measures to get members of their local religions who converted to Christianity to convert back. Similar efforts occurred at the societal level in Bangladesh and Indonesia. Also, a number of states place restrictions on converting in the first place. This protection of religious identity also explains why the most common form of restriction on religious minorities in Asia is restrictions on proselytizing.

Fourth, local and regional governments in many states restrict religious minorities or legislate the state's dominant religion to a greater extent than does the central government. This occurs in particular in Afghanistan, Bangladesh, Bhutan, India, Indonesia, Laos, Malaysia, and Vietnam. This tension between local and national governments is probably because local governments are more likely to be influenced by grassroots sentiments. The national governments are more likely to focus on the larger picture and to desire to maintain calm throughout the country. They are also more likely to be influenced by international trends and pressures to resolve conflicts and minimize discrimination.

As is the case with the former Soviet bloc, most Asian countries have clauses in their constitutions protecting against discrimination on the basis of religion as well as religious freedom. Also, as in the former Soviet bloc, the reality often differs from the precepts set out in the constitution. It is the international regime that dictates that states must nominally provide for basic freedoms including religious freedom. As demonstrated here, some Asian states uphold these principles, but the majority do not.

8

The Middle East and North Africa

The Middle East and North Africa (MENA) region scores higher on the RAS measures than any other world region. Despite a number of commonalities, there is considerable diversity in the nature of government involvement in religion (GIR) in the region. For the purposes of this study the MENA includes the Arab states of what is commonly known as the Middle East, as well as Israel, Turkey, and the Arab states of North Africa.

Islam is particularly influential in the region. For example, in nearly all of the region's states, including Israel and Lebanon, Islamic Sharia law guides family law for Muslims. Eighteen of the 20 states in this region are ruled by Muslims. Israel is governed by Jews but it has a substantial Muslim population and Muslims are elected to its parliament. Lebanon is governed jointly by Christians and Muslims.

As presented in Tables 8.1, 8.2, 8.3, and 8.4, separation of religion and state (SRAS) is practically nonexistent in the MENA. Overall, MENA states have the highest average scores on all of the RAS variables and, as documented in Chapter 11, these numbers have increased since 1990. All but three of the region's governments have an official religion. Two are coded as civil religion, meaning that while there is no official state religion, the government behaves as if there is one. The final state, Lebanon, supports several religions precisely because of its consociational agreement, which divides all aspects of politics along religious lines. Similarly, all of these states place limitations on at least some minority religions or give preferential treatment to the majority religion. This includes six of these states that make at least one minority religion illegal and one, Saudi Arabia, that officially declares all minority religions illegal.

All of the MENA states engage in at least two of the specific restrictions on minority religions monitored by the RAS project. The most common is restrictions on proselytizing, which exist in all MENA states except Lebanon and Libya. In many cases it is a crime that can carry the death penalty, though this is rarely imposed. Fourteen states place restrictions on conversion away from the majority religion, a crime that also carries a death penalty in some of these

TABLE 8.1. *Separation of Religion and State in the Middle East in 2002, Basic Information*

Country	Maj. religion	% Maj. religion	# Min. groups with 5% of population	Official GIR	Official regulation	General GIR
Algeria	Islam, Sunni	99.0	0	One official religion	Legal limitations	53.35
Bahrain	Islam, Sunni*	29.0	1	One official religion	Practical limitations	39.89
Egypt	Islam, Sunni	94.0	1	One official religion	Some illegal	62.92
Iran	Islam, Shi'i	89.0	1	One official religion	Some illegal	66.59
Iraq	Islam, Shi'i	63.0	1	One official religion	Legal limitations	53.66
Israel	Jewish	80.1	1	One official religion	Practical limitations	36.84
Jordan	Islam, Sunni	92.0	1	One official religion	Some illegal	60.51
Kuwait	Islam, Sunni	45.0	3	One official religion	Legal limitations	46.82
Lebanon	Islam	34.0	4	Cooperation	Practical limitations	22.17
Libya	Islam, Sunni	97.5	0	One official religion	Legal limitations	48.13
Morocco	Islam, Sunni	99.0	0	One official religion	Legal limitations	51.86
Oman	Islam, Sunni	87.4	1	One official religion	Legal limitations	46.23
Qatar	Islam, Sunni	95.0	0	One official religion	Legal limitations	52.90
Saudi Arabia	Islam, Sunni	93.0	0	One official religion	All illegal	77.56
Syria	Islam, Sunni	74.0	2	Civil religion	Some illegal	43.69
Tunisia	Islam, Sunni	98.0	0	One official religion	Legal limitations	53.73
Turkey	Islam, Sunni	80.0	1	Civil religion	Some illegal	47.21
UAE	Islam, Sunni	80.0	1	One official religion	Legal limitations	54.70
Western Sahara	Islam, Sunni	100.0	0	One official religion	Legal limitations	49.36
Yemen	Islam	99.0	0	One official religion	Legal limitations	48.41

* Bahrain's rulers are Sunni Muslims but the majority of the country's population is Shi'i Muslim.

TABLE 8.2. *Restrictions on Minority Religion in the Middle East in 2002*

	Public observance	Build or repair places of worship	Access to places of worship	Forced observance	orgs.	Formal Education	Arrest, detention, harassment	Materials	Publications	Personal status	Clergy	Conversions	Proselytizing	Registration	Other	Total
Algeria	x					x			x				x		x	5
Bahrain							x						x			2
Egypt	x	x	x			x	x	x				x	x		x	9
Iran	x	x	x	x	x	x	x	x	x	x		x	x		x	13
Iraq	x	x	x			x	x	x	x	x		x	x		x	11
Israel			x							x			x			3
Jordan		x		x						x	x	x	x	x		7
Kuwait		x	x			x		x	x		x		x	x		8
Lebanon										x				x		2
Libya	x	x					x		x			x	x			6
Morocco		x					x		x			x	x			5
Oman	x	x	x		x		x	x	x			x	x	x		10
Qatar		x							x				x			3
Saudi Arabia	x	x	x	x	x	x	x	x	x	x	x	x	x		x	14
Syria					x		x						x			3
Tunisia		x			x		x				x	x	x			6
Turkey		x		x	x	x	x		x		x	x	x			9
UAE	x	x			x			x	x			x	x	x		8
Western Sahara		x					x		x			x	x			5
Yemen	x	x							x			x			x	5
TOTAL	9	14	7	4	7	7	10	8	12	6	5	14	18	7	6	134

The following categories of religious restrictions were not included in this table because none of these countries engage in these practices: forced conversions.

TABLE 8.3. *Government Regulation of the Majority Religion in the Middle East in 2002*

	Political parties	Arrest, detention, harassment	Orgs.	Speech	Access to places of worship	Publications	Arrest nonleaders	Public gatherings	Public display	Other	Total
Algeria	x	x		x		x					4
Bahrain	x			x	x						3
Egypt	x	x		x					x	x	5
Iran	x			x							2
Iraq	x			x							2
Israel	x		x								2
Jordan		x		x						x	3
Kuwait	x										1
Lebanon											0
Libya	x	x		x						x	4
Morocco	x	x	x	x	x		x				6
Oman				x							1
Qatar				x							1
Saudi Arabia	x		x	x					x		4
Syria	x	x	x	x	x		x				6
Tunisia	x	x	x		x	x					5
Turkey	x	x	x					x	x	x	5
UAE			x	x		x					3
Western Sahara	x	x	x	x	x		x				6
Yemen	x	x		x						x	4
TOTAL	15	10	8	15	5	3	3	1	3	5	68

The following categories of religious restrictions were not included in this table because none of these countries engage in these practices: public observance.

TABLE 8.4. *Religious Legislation in the Middle East in 2002*

	Dietary laws	Alcohol	Personal status	Inheritance	Conversions	Marriages	Public dress	Blasphemy	Censorship	Close businesses	Blue laws	Optional education	Mandatory education	Fund education	Fund religious charity	Taxes	Fund clergy
Algeria	x	x	x	x	x	x		x	x				x	x			x
Bahrain	x		x	x		x	x	x	x						x		x
Egypt	x	x	x	x	x	x	x	x	x				x	x			x
Iran	x	x	x	x	x	x	x	x	x				x	x			x
Iraq	x	x	x	x	x	x	x	x									
Israel			x			x		x		x	x	x		x			x
Jordan	x	x	x	x	x	x	x	x	x	x	x		x	x			x
Kuwait	x	x	x	x	x			x						x			
Lebanon			x	x		x		x	x								
Libya	x	x	x	x	x	x	x	x	x								x
Morocco	x	x	x	x	x	x	x	x	x				x	x	x		x
Oman	x	x	x	x	x	x	x	x	x				x	x			x
Qatar	x	x	x	x	x	x	x	x	x	x			x	x			x
Saudi Arabia	x	x	x	x	x	x	x	x	x	x	x		x	x		x	x
Syria			x	x		x		x	x				x	x			
Tunisia	x		x	x	x	x	x	x	x				x	x			
Turkey							x	x	x			x	x	x			
UAE	x		x	x	x	x	x	x	x	x	x		x	x			x
Western Sahara	x		x	x	x	x	x	x	x				x	x			x
Yemen	x	x	x	x	x	x	x	x	x				x	x		x	x
TOTAL	16	12	19	18	15	18	15	20	17	5	4	2	14	16	2	2	14

	Other religious funding	Approve clergy & speeches	Some clergy appointed	Gov. rel. dept.	Religious position for gov. official	Gov. position for religious official	Religious requirements	Relig. courts	Legislature/ cabinet	Abortion	Flag	Identity cards	Registration	Sects	Women	Other	Total
Algeria	x	x	x	x			x			x	x				x		19
Bahrain	x	x	x	x			x	x					x				16
Egypt	x	x	x	x			x	x		x			x		x		22
Iran	x	x	x	x	x		x	x	x	x	x	x			x		23
Iraq				x		x	x	x	x	x	x	x					17
Israel	x		x	x				x		x	x					x	15
Jordan	x	x	x	x				x	x	x	x	x	x		x	x	25
Kuwait				x						x			x		x		14
Lebanon							x	x	x	x		x	x		x		12
Libya	x	x		x						x					x		15
Morocco		x			x					x						x	16
Oman	x	x		x				x		x					x		19
Qatar	x	x		x			x	x		x			x		x		21
Saudi Arabia	x	x	x	x		x	x	x		x	x	x			x	x	27
Syria	x	x	x				x	x		x		x	x		x	x	15
Tunisia	x	x	x	x			x	x			x		x				19
Turkey	x			x							x	x	x	x			13
UAE	x	x	x	x				x		x			x		x		22
Western Sahara					x					x							12
Yemen	x			x			x	x							x		16
TOTAL	15	13	12	16	3	2	11	14	4	16	8	7	10	1	13	5	359

states. Fourteen states place restrictions on building or repairing places of worship, and 12 place restrictions on minority religious publications. Half of them arrest or harass members of the minority religion due to their religious affiliation or practices. All of the other types of restrictions on minority religions, except forced conversions, exist in between 5 and 9 of the states in the MENA. Iran, Iraq, Saudi Arabia, Qatar and Oman all engage in at least 10 of these types of restrictions.

All of the MENA states except Lebanon in some way regulate the majority religion. The most common forms of regulation are restrictions on religious political parties and restrictions on public religious speech, both of which exist in 15 MENA states. The latter type of restriction usually takes the form of monitoring the religious and political content of speeches by imams made in mosques. Ten of these states arrest or harass religious leaders. In most cases this harassment is directed toward those considered radical or militant, and in some cases it is directed against anyone who opposes the state's official version of Islam. All of the other forms of regulation of the majority religion monitored by the RAS project exist in at least one MENA state, except restrictions on the public observance of religion.

Every type of religious legislation tracked by the RAS project exists in the MENA. Of the 33 types of religious legislation, 21 of them exist in at least half of the MENA states. The states with the lowest number of types of legislation are Lebanon and the Western Sahara, both of which have 12 of these categories of legislation.

Since almost all of the MENA states have official state religions, in this chapter the "religious state" and "active state religion" categories are divided into more detailed categories. The "religious state" category is divided into states where even members of the minority religion are obligated by the religious laws of the majority religion, and states where these laws, for the most part, only apply to those who belong to the majority religion. The "active state religion" category is similarly divided into states where the tendency is for the government to control the religion, and states where the tendency is to support the religion. To be clear, all states in the "active state religion" category tend to both support and control the official religion. This taxonomy is based on a judgment of which of these two trends is dominant. The latter of these two categories is different from the "state-controlled religion" in that the term state-controlled religion refers to a situation where the state completely controls the religion and the religion does not really influence the state. In countries with active state religions, religious institutions and clergy still influence the state even as the state tries to control them. The categorization of MENA states into this taxonomy is presented in Table 8.5.

A GENERAL NOTE ON SHARIA CODE

Before beginning the country by country description of the MENA it is important to briefly discuss Sharia (Islamic) law. All Sharia law is based on the Koran,

TABLE 8.5. *Taxonomy of The Middle East*

Separation of religion and state	Type of restrictions on minorities			
	None	Low (1–2)	Moderate (3–5)	High (6+)
Religious state: religion mandatory for all				Saudi Arabia
Religious state: religion mandatory for members of religion		*Bahrain*	*Oman*	*Iran* *Kuwait* *Qatar* *UAE*
State-controlled religion		**Libya**		
Active state religion: control over support			Algeria	**Egypt** Iraq **Morocco** **Tunisia** **Western Sahara**
Active state religion: support over control		Israel	Yemen	Jordan
Historical / cultural state religion				
Preferred treatment for some religions or support for a particular tradition		Lebanon	Syria	Turkey

Italics = Gulf State
Bold = North African State

and the Sunna, which are sayings and stories attributed to the prophet Mohammed. It is not monolithic and is open to many interpretations but there are some general aspects of Sharia law that are implemented similarly in many MENA states. The two major areas of Sharia law that are encoded into the civil law of many MENA states are family law and law regarding the status of women.

MENA interpretations of family law generally contain the following types of provisions. All personal status is defined by Sharia. While men can divorce their wives without cause, it is difficult and sometimes impossible for women to get a divorce without their husband's consent. Muslim women are often not allowed to marry non-Muslim men, but Muslim men may marry non-Muslim women. When this occurs, the non-Muslim women are rarely given custody of their children in cases of divorce. Such children are considered Muslims and it is often illegal to raise them as members of another religion. Sharia law allows men to have up to four wives. Women are also at a disadvantage in inheritance, tending to get smaller shares of their parents' estates than do their brothers. In some cases, when all of the direct heirs are women, the closest male relative is given a large portion of the inheritance. If a woman is not a Muslim she often has no right of inheritance from her husband.

Women often have the official status of minors throughout their lives. They need the permission of their father or closest male relative in order to marry. In many countries they also need permission to leave the country or obtain passports. In some cases, they may not leave their homes unless accompanied by a male relative. In court their testimony is considered half of that of a male. Sharia requires women to dress modestly. The manner of interpretation and extent of enforcement of this law varies from state to state. In some cases it is not enforced while in others women are required to wear loose-fitting full body coverings with holes only for their eyes.

Sharia law also contains some standard rules that tend to be applied in the region including: restrictions on alcohol and pork; ritual slaughter of meat (Halal); restrictions on proselytizing to Muslims; restrictions on conversion away from Islam; and blasphemy laws. The extent to which these laws are applied and enforced varies from state to state.

Finally, while many Middle Eastern constitutions guarantee freedom of religion or belief, they usually include qualifiers, such as "in accordance with local traditions and beliefs," or "subject to public policy and morals." These qualifiers often mean that people have freedom of belief as long as it does not contradict Islam and Sharia law as applied in the state in question. On the strict end, countries like Saudi Arabia officially ban all religions other than Islam, though they tolerate some unofficially. Others tolerate some, though those religions have an unofficial status, but ban or severely restrict religious groups, like the Bahai and Druze, who are considered by many Muslims to be apostates. Others officially tolerate only religions Islam considers "peoples of the book." These are monotheistic religions that predate Islam and are considered earlier but corrupted divine revelations. According to most interpretations of Islam, these religions, which include Christianity and Judaism, are officially tolerated, but their followers are considered second-class citizens and certain restrictions can be placed upon them, including special taxes and restrictions on building, maintaining, and repairing places of worship. Sometimes other religions, such as Zoroastrianism, are also considered peoples of the book. Some countries are more tolerant of non–peoples of the book but still make it clear that Islam is the dominant religion.

RELIGIOUS STATE: RELIGION MANDATORY FOR ALL

This category represents those states where the religion arguably controls the state as much or more than the state controls the religion and the state religion is, by law, mandatory for all those who live in the state. Saudi Arabia is the only state that fits into this category. It scores the highest of any state in the MENA on restrictions on minority religion and religious legislation. Based on the RAS measures, Saudi Arabia is closer to being a full theocracy than any other state in the world.

Saudi Arabia

Twenty-three of the 83 articles in Saudi Arabia's 1992 constitution reference religion. Article 1 declares Islam its official religion. Article 3 declares that the country's flag will include the phrase "there is but one God and Mohammed is His Prophet." Article 5 declares that the King is inaugurated "in accordance with the principles of the Holy Koran and the Tradition of the Venerable Prophet." Article 6 uses the same phrase to describe citizens' allegiance to the King. Article 7 declares that the government "derives power from the Holy Koran and the Prophet's tradition." Article 8 declares the Sharia the basis for law in Saudi Arabia. Articles 9, 10, 11, and 13 link family and education to Islam. Article 17 declares that the country's economic laws are in accordance with Sharia. Article 38 declares that the country's criminal law is Sharia law. Articles 46 and 48 declare that there is an independent judiciary to apply Sharia law. Article 21 institutes a religious alms tax. Article 23 states that the state protects Islam and implements Sharia. Article 24 requires the state to build and protect holy places and fund the Hajj. Articles 25, 26, 29, 33, and 34 link world peace, human rights, science, culture, and the armed forces to Islam. Article 45 declares that the government appoints the country's senior clerics and controls their ability to make *fatwas* (religious pronouncements). Article 55 states that the King implements Sharia law and carries out the nation's policy in accordance with Islam. Article 57 declares that other government officials are also responsible for implementing the Sharia.

All citizens must be Muslims and the public practice of all other religions is strictly prohibited. Any noncitizen caught publicly practicing another religion is arrested and deported, sometimes after being whipped. All Muslims must adhere to the state-sponsored version of Islam. A religious police force enforces this. State law is Sharia law as interpreted by the Wahabbi tradition. The strictest possible interpretation is usually applied, resulting in severe restrictions on women. The country's Shi'i population is allowed to use its traditions to guide family law, inheritance, and personal status. Conversion away from Islam is illegal and punishable by death. The government finances most mosques in the country and pays the salaries of all of the mosques' imams. Since the 2003 terrorist attacks in Saudi Arabia, the government has fired numerous imams for "immoderate preaching" and sent over 1000 for retraining. Foreign imams are generally not allowed to preach or lead prayers. Classes in the government version of Islam are mandatory in public schools, including for Shi'i Muslims. Non-Muslims attending private schools are not required to study Islam. Private religious schools are illegal. "Sorcery," "black magic," and "witchcraft" are illegal and people suspected of engaging in these practices are arrested. Blasphemy and insulting Islam is illegal and can be punished by death. The media is censored for conformity with religious standards. The government prohibits Western music and the study of evolution, Freud, Marx, and Western philosophy. Abortion is legal only to save the life, physical or mental health of the woman and must be approved by a panel of physicians.

People are routinely arrested for holding religious services in their homes. Proselytizing by non-Muslims and the distribution of non-Muslim religious literature is illegal. Customs officials often seize non-Muslim religious material meant for personal use. Non-citizens must carry an identity card that shows whether or not they are Muslims. The public display of non-Muslim religious symbols, including the Red Cross, is illegal. Saudi Arabia is the only country in the Middle East where, officially, even those religions designated as "peoples of the book" are illegal. Public celebration of all non-Muslim holidays is illegal. Foreign non-Muslims must publicly observe Muslims holidays including the fast of Ramadan. The Bahai religion is specifically illegal.

The government regularly restricts public religious gatherings by Shi'i and the public celebration of Shi'i religious holidays and ceremonies. It bans a number of Shi'i books, but this is enforced sporadically. The Shi'i rarely get permission to build private mosques and refuse to build government-sponsored ones because they fear the government will restrict the inclusion of Shi'i motifs into the architecture. Shi'i religious leaders are often arrested and detained. Shi'i students are sometimes coerced by teachers to convert to Wahabbism. The Shi'i are prohibited from engaging in their form of ritual slaughter of meat.[1]

RELIGIOUS STATE: RELIGION MANDATORY FOR MEMBERS
OF RELIGION

In these states, the state religion is only mandatory for members of the state's official religion and at least some religious minorities are allowed to practice

[1] "Saudis Sentence Man To Death for Insulting Religion," *Human Rights Without Frontiers*, February 3, 2003, http://www.hrwf.net.

their religion, though this right may be restricted. These states tend to control the religious institutions of the majority religion but, at the same time, are deeply influenced by the religion to the extent that any perceived deviation from it by the government and its leaders as well as by citizens of the majority religion would be considered illegitimate.

Interestingly, the broader category of religious states – all of the states in this category and Saudi Arabia, where religion is mandatory for all – are Gulf states and, other than Iraq, all of the Gulf states are religious states.

Low to Moderate Restrictions on Minorities

Bahrain

Article 1 of Bahrain's 2002 constitution declares it "a fully sovereign, independent Islamic Arab State." Article 2 declares Islam the state religion and that Sharia is a principal source for legislation. Article 5 states that the family derives its strength from religion and guarantees inheritance as a right governed by Islamic law. It also guarantees the equality of women as reconciled with their family duties and without breaching Islamic law. Article 6 states that "the State safeguards the Arab and Islamic heritage ... [and] strives to strengthen the bonds between the Islamic countries." Article 7 places education, including religious education, under the government's purview. Article 9 creates a right to property "in accordance with the principles of Islamic justice." Article 17 bans discrimination based on religion. Article 22 guarantees freedom of religion and public worship "in accordance with the customs observed in the country." Articles 23 and 27 guarantee freedom of expression and association provided that the principles of Islam are not infringed. Article 33 declares that the King should be "the loyal protector of the religion" and includes an oath that begins "I swear by Almighty God." Article 78 contains a similar oath for other members of the government. Article 89 gives members of the government the freedom to express their opinions "unless the opinion expressed is prejudicial to the fundamentals of the religion." The preamble includes religious imagery.

The government monitors and funds all Islamic institutions including mosques, community centers, and charitable foundations, mostly in order to prevent political activity in these institutions. In the past the government has closed mosques for allowing protests near their grounds and arrested religious leaders for giving political sermons. Access to internet sites that are considered anti-government or anti-Islamic is restricted. The High Council for Islamic Affairs reviews and approves the appointments of all Sunni and Shi'i Muslim clerics and oversees all citizens studying religion abroad. The legal system combines Sunni and Shi'i Islamic law with tribal law. Family laws are guided by Sunni and Shi'i Islamic law, depending on the religion of the person in question. Shi'i women who are sole heirs can receive an entire inheritance, but Sunni women only receive a portion of it, with the rest being distributed among male relatives. Jews and Christians may use their own laws of inheritance. Abortion is available on request subject to approval by a panel of physicians.

All religions must register with the Ministry of Islamic affairs and other ministries when relevant. For example, opening a school requires registering with the Ministry of Education. Registration is usually granted and unregistered minority religions are generally allowed to practice their faith privately. Proselytizing is discouraged and anti-Islamic writings are illegal. Until 2001 many Shi'i leaders were jailed for violations of national security but were pardoned and released by the King in that year. The government has also in the past restricted activities in Shi'i religious institutions in response to antigovernment violence. Conversion from Islam to other religions is not illegal but tends to bring social sanctions.[2]

Oman

Oman has no constitution. A basic law serves the same purpose. Article 1 of this law declares Oman an Islamic state. Article 2 declares Islam the state religion and that Sharia is the basis for legislation. Article 5 requires that the Sultan be a male adult Muslim who is the son of Omani Muslim parents. Article 10 includes the Sharia as one of the political principles of the state. Article 11 declares that inheritance law is governed by Sharia. Article 17 prohibits discrimination on the basis of religion. Article 28 guarantees "the freedom to practice religious rites in accordance with recognized customs ... provided that it does not disrupt public order or conflict with accepted standards of behavior." The oaths of office for the Sultan and ministers in Articles 7 and 50 begin with the phrase "I swear by Almighty God."

All schools must provide instruction in Islam except for those servicing foreigners. All sermons must be within guidelines set by the government and imams are expected to avoid political topics. The government monitors sermons for compliance. Sharia law determines the status of women. A 1994 law places restrictions on public gatherings, all of which need government approval. Hindus and Zoroastrians have occasionally been unable to get approval for the public celebration of religious festivals. Abortions are legal only to save the life of the woman. Alcohol is forbidden to citizens but is available to tourists.

All non-Muslim religious organizations must register. The criteria for registration are unclear. Some organizations are unable to register but may operate if they are sponsored by a legal organization. The government provides lands for places of worship including Protestant and Catholic churches as well as a Hindu temple. Proselytizing to Muslims is illegal as is conversion away from Islam. Printing non-Muslim religious material is illegal but such material may be imported.[3]

          ·rs in Several Mosques Banned After Violence in Bahrain," *Deutsche Presse Agentur*,
          19, 1996.
               Consular Information Sheet," June 19, 2001, http://travel.state.gov/oman.html.

High Restrictions on Minorities

Iran

The constitution of the Islamic Republic of Iran makes numerous references to religion. This summary is not exhaustive but, rather, emphasizes some of the highlights. Many rights and powers outlined in the constitution are considered subject to Islam. For example, freedom of speech and the press are granted but cannot be used contrary to Islam. Verses from the Koran are quoted throughout the document.

Article 1 establishes Iran as an Islamic republic. Article 2 includes among the state's fundamental principles "the One God ... His exclusive sovereignty and right to legislate, and the necessity of submission to His commands." Article 4 states that "all civil, penal, financial, economic, administrative, cultural, military, political, and other laws and regulations must be based on Islamic criteria." Articles 2, 5, and 57 give the leadership of the country to a religious leader and the clergy. Article 12 declares Twelver Shi'i Islam the state religion but recognizes other branches of Islam. Article 13 recognizes Zoroastrianism, Judaism, and Christianity as the only legal minority religions. Article 14 guarantees these minorities treatment in conformity with "ethical norms and the principles of Islamic justice and equity, and to respect their human rights" as long as they "refrain from engaging in conspiracy or activity against Islam and the Islamic Republic of Iran." Article 61 requires that the courts conform to Islam. Article 64 grants a small number of seats in the government's legislative body to religious minorities. Article 72 prohibits laws contrary to Islam. Articles 91 through 99 establish an Islamic Guardian Council, which supervises elections and reviews laws for conformity with Islam. Article 115 requires that the president believe in Islam. Article 144 requires that "the Army of the Islamic Republic of Iran must be an Islamic Army." Article 167 states that all judicial rulings must be based upon "authoritative Islamic sources and authentic fatwa." All oaths of office in the constitution make reference to Islam but members of religious minorities are allowed to take alternative oaths appropriate to their religion.

Family law is based on a relatively strict interpretation of Islamic law with regard to gender segregation and female modesty. Women need permission of a male relative to marry and only female physicians may treat women. A vigilante force enforces public morals. The government breaks up private gatherings of unmarried men and women or where alcohol is served. Adultery is punishable by stoning and flogging. All candidates for public office must be approved by the Guardian Council. The government monitors Shi'i clergy for conformity with government interpretations of Islam and for opposition to the government. It arrests those whose views deviate including those with more lenient interpretations of Islamic law or who question the country's rulers. Abortion is illegal except to save the life of the woman.

Recognized religious minorities do not need to register but are monitored closely by the government. Non-Muslim owners of grocery shops must indicate their religious affiliation on the front of their shops. Conversion away from Islam is punishable by death. Proselytizing is illegal. This is enforced strictly and sometimes violently. Evangelical churches are often shut down and members of those allowed to remain open must carry membership cards. Iranian guards posted outside check the identity of worshipers. Membership in these congregations requires government approval and services are allowed only on Sundays. The printing and distribution of bibles is severely restricted. Native Christian populations, including the Assyrians and Armenians, worship without interference but are still subject to the general restrictions on religious minorities. Most religious minorities have difficulty attending university because admission requires passing a test in Islamic ideology. Private schools for minority religions are allowed but the director must be a Muslim and all non-Persian language texts need government approval. Sunni Muslims have been unable to build a mosque in Tehran. Many of their clergy have been killed, allegedly by government agents. Jews are allowed to practice their religion but Jewish schools are restricted in distributing Hebrew texts. Also they are often forced to remain open on Saturdays, the Jewish Sabbath. Jews are subject to arrest and severe anti-Semitism by both the authorities and the populace, often on charges of spying for Israel. Zoroastrian "Towers of Silence," on which the corpses of Zoroastrians are laid for vultures to consume are illegal.

The Bahai are subject to particular restrictions because they are considered apostates. They may not practice or teach their religion and can be arrested and even put to death for doing so. Nor may they maintain links with other Bahai abroad. Bahai communal property, including holy places, places of worship, and cemeteries were seized after the 1979 revolution and have not been returned. The Bahai are not allowed to bury their dead in accordance with their religious traditions or perform mourning rituals. Until 2000 Bahai marriages were not recognized by the government. This effectively prevented members from marrying and anyone who did could be arrested for having marital relations out of wedlock. Children of these marriages are considered illegitimate and cannot inherit from their parents. Members also suffer from severe economic, political, educational, and social discrimination.[4]

Kuwait

Article 2 of Kuwait's constitution declares Islam the state religion and Sharia the main source of legislation. Article 9 states that the family "is founded on religion, morality, and patriotism." Article 12 states that "the State safeguards the heritage of Islam." Article 18 declares that inheritance is governed by Sharia law. Article 29 guarantees equality regardless of religion. Article 35 protects

[4] Boyle & Sheen (1997); "Iran Parliament Demands Lifting of Death Sentence Against Reformist Sch~'   Human Rights Without Frontiers, October 11, 2002; "Iranian Cleric Jailed for Seven Liberal Views on Veil," Human Rights Without Frontiers, March 14, 2003; "No ʿ Press for Religious Minorities," Human Rights Without Frontiers, July 2, 2001, hrwf.net.

religious freedom "in accordance with established customs, provided that it does not conflict with public policy or morals." Article 4 states that the royal heir must be "a legitimate son of Muslim parents." The preamble and oaths of office for the Amir and members of the legislature in Articles 60 and 91 include religious imagery.

Islamic instruction for Muslims is mandatory in all schools. Married women require their husband's permission to obtain a passport and all minors need their father's permission. Sharia law governs the country including in matters of personal status, inheritance, and restrictions on women. Journalists who defame Islam can be sent to jail. Converting away from Islam is illegal and non-Muslims may not become citizens. Abortion is legal only to save the life, physical health, or mental health of the woman or in cases of fetal impairment, and must be approved by an official committee. Alcohol and pork products are prohibited.

Non-Muslim religions must register. This process is unclear, complicated, and involves a number of government ministries. The government registers only Christian denominations. They may worship freely and are provided with police protection. However, their ability to build new facilities or expand existing ones is severely limited. Members of other Christian denominations and of religions not recognized in the Koran, such as Hindus and Buddhists, are allowed to worship in private homes. A Sikh temple was ordered closed by the government in 2002 but was allowed to reopen in 2003. Proselytizing to Muslims is illegal. Organized education in a religion other than Islam is illegal but in practice it is allowed in private homes. Publishing facilities for non-Islamic religious litera-ture are illegal but some churches are allowed to print religious materials solely for their congregations. Only one company is allowed to import Christian materials for the use of recognized congregations. On occasion, customs officials confiscate religious materials brought by individuals for personal use. Formal training facilities for non-Islamic clergy are illegal but some informal training exists. Shi'i Muslims are allowed to worship freely but the government is slow to grant permits to build or repair Shi'i mosques. Due to lack of educational facilities Shi'i clerics must seek training outside of the country.[5]

Qatar

Article 1 of Qatar's 2003 constitution declares Islam the state religion and Sharia the main source of legislation. Article 9 states that "the Heir Apparent shall be a Muslim and from a Qatari Muslim mother." Article 21 declares religion a pillar of the family. Article 35 prohibits discrimination on the basis of religion. Article 51 states that inheritance is governed by Sharia law. The oaths of office for a number of government officials including the Emir, Heir Apparent, prime minister, and Advisory Council in Articles 10, 74, 92, and 119 include religious imagery.

[5] "Kuwait – Consular Information Sheet," May 7, 2001, http://travel.state.gov/kuwait.html.

The government controls the construction of mosques, adult Islamic education, and the education of converts. The Emir personally funds the Hajj for those who cannot afford it. Converting away from Islam is a capital offense but no one has been executed for this since 1971. Islamic education is mandatory in public schools. Sharia courts have jurisdiction over matters of family law and can adjudicate civil cases if both litigants agree. Alcohol is illegal, but is available to tourists in some hotels. The public consumption of food and drink during the Ramadan fast is forbidden. The government irregularly censors pornography and material considered hostile to Islam. The government occasionally arrests those who speak publicly against its religion policy. Abortion is legal to save the life, physical or mental health of the woman or in cases of fetal impairment. It must be approved by a board of physicians.

The government officially recognizes some Christian denominations but building new non-Muslim places of worship requires government permission. In 2000, for the first time ever, the government authorized the building of three Christian churches to accommodate foreign residents. Large services and events require advance approval. Non-Christian minority religions have less freedom but are not harassed as long as they worship privately. Proselytizing by non-Muslims and the importing, publishing, and distributing of non-Muslim religious literature is illegal. In practice, non-Muslims may import religious literature for personal use. On occasion Christians are deported from Qatar without explanation, though it is likely due to their religious activities. Shi'i Muslims may practice freely except that they may not organize some public celebrations and rites such as self-flagellation.[6]

United Arab Emirates

The UAE is a federation of seven separate emirates each with its own laws. The federal constitution declares Islam the official religion but guarantees religious freedom in accordance with established customs.[7] Sharia law is the principle source of legislation. The government funds most Sunni mosques and hires all imams. It also issues guidelines for sermons in all mosques and monitors them for political content. In practice the government supports a moderate version of Islam. The government pardons prisoners who convert to Islam. Islamic education is mandatory in all public schools and private schools for Muslims. There is a dual court system with some criminal offences tried in Sharia courts and some in civil courts. Family and inheritance law for Muslims is under the jurisdiction of Sharia courts, which results in the usual restrictions on women. Alcohol is illegal but non-Muslims may buy it in specially licensed shops and

6 "... aw," http://www.qatarlaw.com/English/infoq16.htm; "Qatar Frees Religion Scholar," ... Press, April 8, 2001; "Filipino Pastor To Be Deported," *Human Rights Without* ... pril 28, 2003; Barbara G. Baker, "Indian Christian Family Deported by Qatar," ... *Without Frontiers*, January 30, 2003, http://www.hrwf.net.
... obtain an English-language translation of the UAE constitution so the description ... may be incomplete.

hotels. Heresy is punishable by death, and blasphemy by imprisonment or expulsion. Public desecration of Ramadan may result in flogging, imprisonment, or expulsion. Abortion is legal only in order to save the life of the woman. Sexual relations out of wedlock are illegal. Women who are not citizens who give birth out of wedlock are deported and in some emirates the mother is forced to marry the father of the child.

Noncitizens may be non-Muslims. The government grants de-facto recognition to some religions by granting them lands for churches. The majority, but not all, of such facilities are Christian. For example, Abu Dhabi has donated land for a Bahai cemetery. There are also Sikh and Hindu temples but no Buddhist temples. Denominations without temples either use the facilities of other denominations or private homes without government interference. Shi'i Muslims may construct their own mosques and worship freely but do not receive funds from the government. Their mosques are subject to the same guidelines and monitoring as are Sunni mosques. Hindus require a permit for each individual funeral rite as these rites involve cremation. Proselytizing and distributing non-Muslim literature are illegal. Violators are arrested and deported. However, importing religious literature for the use of non-Muslims is permitted.[8]

STATE-CONTROLLED RELIGIONS

These states have an official religion but completely control its institutions. The religion, or at least its institutions and clergy, does not significantly participate in setting state policy.

Libya

Article 2 of Libya's constitution declares Islam the state religion and protects religious freedom "in accordance with established customs." Article 3 states that "the family, based on religion, morality, and patriotism, is the foundation of society." Article 3 also states that the state's socialism is inspired by, among other things, its Islamic heritage. Article 8 states that inheritance is governed by Sharia law.

The state supports and controls a moderate version of Islam called the Islamic Call Society (ICS). All Islamic groups whose teachings differ from those of ICS are banned. Most Islamic institutions are under government control and private mosques adhere to ICS. Members of "illegal" versions of Islam are arrested and imprisoned, especially if they mix religion with politics. Beginning in the late 1980s the government actively suppresses Islamic fundamentalism. Reportedly men have shaved their beards in order to avoid harassment. Alcohol

---

[8] "New Crackdown on Alcohol in UAE," ArabicNews.com, October 10, 1997; Ahmed Mardini, "Gulf Religion: Self Proclaimed Messiah To Die For Heresy," *Inter-Press Service*, September 13, 1995; "Blasphemy Drama," *Press Association Limited*, May 2, 1993; "Quick Snack Lands Teenager In UAE Jail During Ramadan," *Agence France Presse*, February 13, 1995.

is banned. Abortion is legal only to save the life of the woman and requires the approval of a specialist in gynaecology and obstetrics.

Other religions may worship freely but some Christian denominations have had trouble gaining permits to build churches. These and members of other faiths, such as the Bahai, Buddhists, and Hindus, worship in private homes. Those denominations that can build churches are limited to one per city. The majority of non-Muslims in Libya are foreigners.

ACTIVE STATE RELIGIONS: CONTROL OVER SUPPORT

These states actively support a religion but the religion maintains a level of independence from the government and it is clear that the government rules the state and not the religion. Most of these states in some ways control religion, with this tendency toward control being stronger than the tendency toward support.

Moderate Restrictions on Minorities

Algeria

Article 2 of Algeria's constitution declares Islam the state's religion. Article 178 prohibits changing this clause. Article 9 prohibits government "practices that are contrary to the Islamic ethics." Article 42 bans religious political parties. Article 73 requires that the president be a Muslim. Articles 171 and 172 establish a High Islamic Council. The presidential oath in Article 76 and the preamble include religious imagery.

Non-Muslim religious groups require official recognition in order to conduct religious activities. Only the Protestant, Roman Catholic, and Seventh Day Adventist Churches have this recognition. Several other Christian denominations practice in private without government interference. Proselytizing is illegal but missionary groups may engage in humanitarian practices. Importing non-Islamic religious literature requires the approval of several government ministries, but individuals may bring them into the country for personal use.

The government appoints the imams of all mosques and maintains the right to review all of their sermons. It provides some financial support for the imams' salaries. The use of mosques for public meetings outside of prayer times is prohibited. The study of Islam is required in public schools and closely regulated by the Ministries of Education and Religious Affairs. Many of these restrictions are likely motivated by the violent fundamentalist rebellion that has been occurring in Algeria since the early 1990s. Women are subject to many of the standard restrictions placed upon them by Sharia law with regard to family law and inheritance.

Abortion is legal only to save the life, or physical or mental health of the woman. The Algerian flag includes religious symbols. Alcohol is prohibited but is available in the more expensive hotels.[9]

[9] Algeria: Social Profile, World Travel Guide, http://www.travel-guide.com/data/dza/dza460.asp.

High Restrictions on Minorities

Egypt

Article 2 of Egypt's constitution declares Islam the state religion and Islamic jurisprudence the principal source of legislation. Article 9 states that "the family is the basis of the society founded on religion, morality and patriotism." Article 11 grants women equality "without violation of the rules of Islamic jurisprudence." Article 12 contains a list of principles by which the state must abide, including religious education. Article 19 makes religion a "principal subject" of general education courses. Article 40 bans discrimination on the basis of religion. Article 46 guarantees religious freedom. The preamble and oath of office for the president and people's assembly in Articles 79 and 90 include religious imagery.

All mosques require licenses and the government appoints and pays the salaries of their prayer leaders. The government recently began to bring under its control unofficial mosques located in residential buildings. Religious political parties are illegal. The Muslim Brotherhood, a fundamentalist Islamic organization, is banned. Several people each year, mostly homosexuals, are tried for engaging in behavior deviant from Islamic law. Others are tried for blasphemy or having "unorthodox" Islamic beliefs. On occasion, the courts force Muslim men considered apostates to divorce their wives. The government censors and confiscates publications for being anti-Islamic. Family law for marriage, divorce, alimony, child custody, and burial is based on one's religion. Only Islam, Christianity, and Judaism are recognized for these purposes. Inheritance law for all citizens is based on Islamic law. Public and private schools provide religious education in the religion of the student. Religion is included on identity documents. Abortion is illegal except to save the life of the woman, but is sometimes allowed in cases of serious health risks. Alcohol, while illegal, is available.

The government arrests and detains suspected members of Islamic opposition movements that have engaged in violent attacks on the government as well as the country's Coptic Christian minority. This government activity seems to be motivated by political and not religious concerns. Despite this, the government tends to not adequately investigate incidents of violence against the Copts, and those who are arrested tend to be acquitted or given light sentences. Local police are sometimes complicit in this violence. In some cases Copts who reported such violence were themselves arrested. There are also reports of the kidnapping of Copt girls who are then forced to convert to Islam.

Failure to register by religious minorities can result in prosecution. Jewish and Christian groups are generally recognized and allowed to worship freely. However, anti-Semitism is common in the government-controlled media. Minority religions require a presidential decree and a permit in order to build or repair a place of worship. In practice they are often difficult to obtain. Proselytizing is not illegal but those who do so are often harassed by the police and tried for insulting Islam or, if they are foreigners, detained and deported. While it is not illegal to convert away from Islam, the government does not recognize such conversions. This lack of recognition has caused some converts who altered their religion on their identity documents to be tried for falsifica-tion of documents. The police often harass these converts and the government considers their children to be Muslims. Christians are reportedly segregated from Muslims in some public schools and forced to memorize passages from the Koran as part of their Arabic studies. However, a small number of seats in the legislature are reserved for Copts.

Egypt's penal code prohibits inciting youth "to depart from religious values and loyalty to the fatherland," and denying the three "heavenly" religions: Islam, Christianity, and Judaism. Accordingly, religions not recognized by Islam, such as Hinduism and Buddhism, are illegal. In 1960 the Bahai religion was specifically banned and their community properties were confiscated.[10]

Iraq

The era covered by the RAS project predates the US invasion of Iraq so this description primarily reflects that era. Article 4 of Iraq's 1990 constitution declares Islam the state religion. Article 19 bans discrimination on the basis of religion. Article 25 guarantees religious freedom "in accordance with the rules of the constitution and laws and in compliance with morals and public order." Articles 39 and 59 include the oaths for the president, vice president, and ministers, all of which begin with "I swear by God Almighty."

The Hussein-era Iraqi Government restricted the religious freedom of all faiths. It regulated and monitored all political and religious activity. It banned new political parties with an ethnic or religious nature. The Iraqi Ministry of Endowments and Religious Affairs exercised strict control over all places of worship including the appointment of clergy, approval of the building or repair-ing of places of worship, and the publication of religious literature. Iraq had no Sharia courts but civil courts used Sharia law for issues of personal status in-cluding marriage and divorce. In 1995 Iraq introduced Sharia punishment for certain types of criminal offenses. Despite a 1994 law banning the sale of alcohol in Iraqi hotels, bars, clubs, and restaurants, alcohol was readily avail-able to tourists at international hotels and the airport "duty-free." Abortion was legal only to save the life of the woman and required approval from two physicians and the written consent of the woman's husband.

The government banned all of the following among Shi'i: communal Friday prayer; broadcasts on government radio or television; publishing books; funeral rituals except private funeral processions, which required government

---

[10] "Egyptian Travel: Tips and Information," http://www.osirisweb.com/egypt/travel.html; "Egypt Detains Men Suspected of Unorthodox Beliefs," *Human Rights Without Frontiers*, October 2, 2001, http://www.hrwf.net; "Briefs; Islamic Militants Lose a Round in a Cairo Court," *Reuters*, December 19, 1996; "Ninety-six of Hundred Acquitted in Egypt Case," *Human Rights Without Frontiers*, February 5, 2001; Barbara Baker, "Egyptian Police Protect Coptic Girl's Kidnappers," *Human Rights Without Frontiers*, October 27, 2003; "Four Christians Arrested in Egypt," *Human Rights Without Frontiers*, March 31, 2004; Barbara G. Baker, "Egypt Cracks Down Against Converts to Christianity," *Human Rights Without Frontiers*, October 29, 2003.

approval; and processions and public meetings in honor of holy days. The government also restricted the activities of Shi'i mosque libraries. Government security agencies routinely desecrated Shi'i mosques and holy sites. They were known to use Shi'i mosques and religious property for secular purposes, including as interrogation centers. Authorities also arrested tens of thousands of Shi'i over the years, and actively interfered with Shi'i religious education and religious rites. Security agents were stationed at major Shi'i mosques and routinely harassed and arbitrarily arrested worshipers.

The government harshly discriminated against non-Muslims. For example, the 1990 Iraqi constitution did not provide for a (Christian) Assyrian or Chaldean identity, despite the fact that each group speaks its own, and distinct, language. Also, conversion away from Islam was illegal.

It is difficult at the time of this writing to determine the specifics of the religion policy of the post–Saddam Hussein era government, but it is clear that Islam will remain prominent. The October 15, 2005, draft of Iraq's constitution clearly favors Islam. Article 2 declares Islam the state religion and a fundamental source of legislation. It also "guarantees the Islamic identity of the majority," and bans laws that contradict "the established provisions of Islam."

However, there are numerous protections for religious freedom. Article 2 guarantees religious freedom. Article 35 protects against "intellectual, political and religious coercion." Article 39 protects the use of one's own religious beliefs with regard to personal status. Article 10 protects "holy shrines and religious places in Iraq," including "the free practice of rituals in them." Article 14 bans discrimination on the basis of religion. Article 41 protects religious rights, management of religious endowments and institutions, and freedom of worship, and guarantees the protection of places of worship. Article 13 states that "a law shall regulate the decorations, official holidays, religious and national occasions and the Hijri and Gregorian calendar." Article 29 states that "the family is the foundation of society; the State preserves its entity and its religious, moral and patriotic values." Article 89 states that "experts in Islamic jurisprudence" will be included on the supreme court. The oath of office for the Council of Representatives in Article 48 includes references to God.[11]

Morocco and the Western Sahara
Morocco retains administrative control over the Western Sahara so the country's status with regard to SRAS is similar to that of Morocco.

Article 6 of Morocco's constitution declares Islam the official religion but also guarantees freedom of worship. The preamble declares Morocco an Islamic state. Article 39 limits parliamentary immunity in cases of acts that are injurious to Islam, the monarchial system, or the King. Article 106 states that the parts of the constitution regarding religion may not be revised. The constitution also includes several symbolic references to religion.

---

[11] Boyle & Sheen (1997); Paul Lewis, "Reporter's Notebook; Dollars Can Still Get You Scotch and Waterford Crystal in Baghdad," *New York Times*, May 7, 1991, p. 10.

The government monitors mosques, koranic schools, and Islamic organizations for adherence to approved doctrine and to prevent political activity. The government occasionally shuts mosques after Friday services to prevent their use for political activity, and strictly controls the construction of new mosques. In 2002 the government banned the Justice and Charity Organization, a radical Islamic group. Before that, the government harassed its members, using methods including arrests and the closing of organization newspapers. The government funds Islamic education in public schools and religious education in Jewish public schools. It also funds literacy programs through mosques. Family law and inheritance for Muslims is determined by Sharia law and for Jews by Jewish law. This results in the usual restrictions on Muslim women. The government appoints imams in mosques and gives them general guidance in their sermons. Abortion is only legal in order to save the life or physical or mental health of the woman and only during the first six weeks of the pregnancy.

With some exceptions minority religions are allowed to practice freely. Judaism and Christianity receive the highest levels of tolerance. Officially it is illegal for members of religions other than Islam to assemble publicly, but this is not enforced strictly and there are several churches in the country. Most non-Muslims congregate in private homes for religious services. Officially, Bahais may not meet or participate in communal activities, but this rule is rarely enforced. Attempting to convert a Muslim is illegal, but so is attempting to stop anyone from exercising their religious beliefs or attending religious services. Converting away from Islam is not illegal, but it is strongly discouraged and, in the past, such converts have been arrested. Proselytizing to non-Muslims is allowed. Christian citizens, especially those engaged in missionary activities are occasionally questioned by the authorities. Arabic-language bibles are sometimes confiscated by authorities, but can also be bought in bookstores.

Tunisia

Article 1 of Tunisia's constitution declares Islam the official religion. Articles 38 and 40 require the head of state to be a Muslim. Article 5 guarantees freedom of conscience and "protects the free exercise of beliefs, with reservation that they do not disturb the public order." The oath of office for the president, in Article 42, begins "I swear by God Almighty." The constitution contains additional religious imagery.

The government funds and controls all mosques and pays the salaries of prayer leaders. Mosques are closed other than at prayer times and for other recognized ceremonies such as weddings. Political parties based on religion are illegal. Militant Islamic organizations are monitored and their leaders and members are often arrested. The government revokes the identity cards of thousands of Islamists, effectively barring them from employment. The government also questions those who are seen regularly at mosques.

Sharia law is applied in cases of inheritance, but there are legal ways to avoid this. Family law is subject to Sharia law but a combination of a liberal application of Sharia and civil codes that protect women mitigate the negative effect this would otherwise have on women. Islamic education is mandatory in all public schools. All publications, including religious ones, are censored by the government. Women working in government offices are not allowed to wear traditional headcoverings. Men are discouraged from growing beards because this is considered a sign of militant Islam. Abortion is legal during the first trimester.

All Christian and Jewish organizations that existed before independence in 1956 are legal. However, the government does not allow new churches to be built. The government partially subsidizes Tunisia's Jewish community. The Bahai are considered a heretical Islamic faith and may only practice their religion in private. Bahai leaders are sometimes called in for questioning. Proselytizing, especially by foreigners, is illegal. The distribution of Arabic-language non-Muslim religious texts is illegal and other non-Muslim religious texts may only be distributed by recognized organizations.[12]

ACTIVE STATE RELIGION: SUPPORT OVER CONTROL

This category is identical to the above category, except that the government's tendency to support the state religion is stronger than the tendency to control it.

Low Restrictions on Minorities

Israel

It is important to note that this description focuses on GIR in Israel. It does not address other aspects of human rights issues, or the Israeli-Palestinian conflict, unless they are directly connected to government policy and behavior toward the practice of religion. This description focuses on the state of Israel and does not address the behavior of the Palestinian Authority.

Israel has no constitution. A series of basic laws act as a constitution. Several of them refer to Israel as a Jewish state and parties running for the Knesset – Israel's parliamentary body – may not deny "the existence of the State of Israel as the state of the Jewish people." Israel's declaration of independence describes it as a Jewish state but provides for equality regardless of religion. These laws establish a religious court and prevent judges of religious courts and "rabbis and ministers of other religions while holding office for a remuneration" from being members of the Knesset. They also prohibit desecration of holy sites and guarantee access to those sites. Any Jew who wishes to return to Israel gains automatic citizenship. Until a 2002 supreme court ruling, this did not apply to those who converted to Judaism under non-Orthodox auspices.

---

[12] David Lamb, "Tunisia Remains Island of Calm in Midst of Extremism," *Los Angeles Times*, September 3, 1995, p. 34; "Women Under Islamic Law," *Atlanta Journal and Constitution*, June 28, 1992, p. 2; Chris Hedges, "Tunisia Cracks Down Harder on Islamic Militants," *New York Times*, January 20, 1992, p. 3.

Aspects of Jewish law are enforced upon the country's population based on a "status-quo" agreement where the situation that existed at Israel's founding remains in force. A number of restrictions are enforced on the Jewish Sabbath and religious holidays. Most businesses must close, most buses and the national airline do not operate, and the streets in some ultra-Orthodox Jewish neighborhoods are closed to vehicles. Recognized religions have religious tribunals responsible for matters of personal status. Marriage, but not divorce, is possible only through one of these religious tribunals, making religious intermarriage effectively impossible. Many who are not considered by the Rabbinical Courts to be Jewish can only get married in foreign states. Such marriages are recognized as valid by the Interior Ministry. Under Jewish law, a husband must consent to a religious divorce. Jewish women who have obtained only secular divorces cannot remarry in the country. During the period covered by the RAS study, the religious and secular courts had concurrent jurisdiction over divorce, alimony, and child custody. Inheritance is under the jurisdiction of the secular courts, unless all parties agree for it to be moved to the religious courts. A 2006 supreme court ruling removed issues of alimony, child custody, and inheritance from the religious courts. Most cemeteries in the country are controlled by religious authorities. Israel's Chief Rabbinate maintains exclusive authority to determine whether food can be called kosher. However, other organizations may certify food as abiding by a stricter standard than that of the Rabbinate. Many of the recognized religions receive government funding for their operation. The government funds both religious and secular schools, including religious schools for Muslims. However, among the religious schools, Jewish Orthodox schools receive the most funding. Many secular Jewish schools also include religious education in the curriculum.

A law allows for the establishment of Jewish religious councils in communities. Those councils are funded by national and municipal funds. Only the Druze receive similar funding. Until 2002, the government included nationality, including "Jew," on identity cards. Religious organizations may apply to the government for funds to build or maintain holy sites. In 2004 parts of the formerly independent Religious Ministry became departments of the Justice and Interior Ministries. Israel's two Chief Rabbis (of European and Middle Eastern descent) are elected to a 10-year position by rabbinical elders and political leaders. Abortion in Israel is legal to save the life, physical health, or mental health of the woman, as well as in cases of rape, incest, or fetal impairment. It is not allowed for economic or social reasons and is not available on request. All abortions must be approved by a committee of two physicians and a social worker appointed by the Health Ministry or the hospital where the abortion takes place.

The law provides for freedom of worship, which in practice is generally respected, with some exceptions. Proselytizing is not illegal but it is illegal to offer or receive material benefits for conversion. This law is rarely enforced. Based on an agreement with the government, Mormons do not proselytize. The government limits those Muslims making the Hajj to those over 35 and only one trip per person in order to meet quotas set by Saudi Arabia. Zoning laws for the building of places of worship are enforced selectively. While illegally built synagogues are often left alone, illegally built mosques are more often closed by the government. In 2002 the government also halted the construction of a mosque near a church in Nazareth because of the interreligious friction it was causing. The government limits the number of Muslims who may pray on the Temple Mount due to past violent incidents there. The government has banned two extremist Jewish political parties on the grounds that they are racist. Incitement against religion is illegal in Israel, though this tends to be enforced against Jews who incite against Islam more often than against incitement against Judaism.[13]

Moderate Restrictions on Minorities

Yemen

Article 1 of Yemen's constitution describes it as an Islamic nation. Article 2 declares Islam the state religion. Article 3 declares Islamic Sharia the source of all legislation. Article 7 includes "Islamic social justice" among the bases for the economy. Article 21 requires the state to collect a religious tax. Article 23 guarantees the right of inheritance "in accordance with Islamic tenets." Article 26 describes religion as one of the pillars of the family. Article 31 grants women "rights and duties, which are guaranteed and assigned by Sharia and stipulated by law." Article 46 states that "no crime or punishment shall be undertaken without a provision in the Sharia or the law." Article 51 states that "places of worship . . . have a sanctity which may not be violated through surveillance or search except in the cases stipulated by the law." Article 53 requires the state to provide young people with religious education. Article 59 states that "defending religion and the homeland is a sacred duty." Articles 63 and 106 require that candidates for the presidency and House of Representatives be people who fulfill their Islamic duties. The oath for the president in Article 159 includes religious imagery.

The government monitors mosques for political activity. For similar reasons, in 2002 the government began implementing a 1992 law to consolidate the curriculums of publicly funded schools, including Islamic schools. Public schools provide instruction in Islam. Family and inheritance law is based on Sharia law, resulting in the usual restrictions on women. However, women recently received the rights to vote, run for office, and demand a divorce. Since 9/11 the government has detained numerous members of Islamic groups and students from religious schools, closed down illegal fundamentalist schools, and deported a number of foreign students. Abortion is legal only to save the

---

[13] Elazar (1986); Karin Laub, "Israel Halts Mosque Construction," *Human Rights Without Frontiers*, January 9, 2002, http://www.hrwf.net; Joel Greenberg, "Non-Orthodox Gain Support from Ruling in Israeli Court," *New York Times*, February 21, 2002; Clyde Haberman, "Israel Votes Ban on Jewish Groups Linked to Kahane," *New York Times*, March 14, 1994.

life of the woman. Causing religious strife, especially in publications, is illegal. Alcohol is banned but is sometimes available in hotels.

Proselytizing to Muslims and conversion away from Islam are illegal. Non-Muslims are occasionally harassed by police for possession of religious litera-ture, though the possession of such literature is not illegal. The police also sometimes open and censor the mail of non-Muslim clergy. Government per-mission is needed to build new places of worship. There are no non-Muslim places of worship in the former North Yemen. Services of denominations with no official facilities are regularly held in private homes without harassment.[14]

High Restrictions on Minorities

Jordan

Article 2 of Jordan's 1952 constitution declares Islam the official religion. Article 6 prohibits discrimination on the basis of religion. Article 14 guarantees religious freedom "in accordance with the customs observed in the Kingdom, unless such is inconsistent with public order or morality." Articles 99, 104, 105, 106, 108, 109, and 100 create religious courts for Muslims and other religious communi-ties. Article 105 gives Sharia courts jurisdiction over personal status, cases con-cerning blood money, and Islamic charitable trusts. Article 107 allows the government to regulate Islamic charitable trusts. Oaths of office for the prime minister, ministers, and senators, in Articles 43 and 80, include religious imagery.

The Ministry of Religious Affairs and Trusts manages all Islamic institutions including mosques and training centers for clergy. It appoints these organiza-tions' clergy and staff, and monitors their public speeches. Religion is mandatory in school curriculums. Christians can receive education in Christianity. Bahai are exempt. Some seats in the Parliament and Senate are reserved for Christians. It is illegal to use houses of worship for political activities. People are prosecuted for blasphemy, usually when it occurs in publications. Matters of personal status are under the jurisdiction of the religious courts of one's religion. This includes the usual restrictions on Muslim women, but a 2001 law allows women to sue for divorce in Sharia court. In criminal courts a woman's testimony is equal to that of a man but in Sharia courts it takes two women to equal one man's testimony. Only recognized religions have such tribunals and members of other religions must get the sanction of an official tribunal in order to marry. During the Fast of Ramadan restaurants are closed during daylight hours and all public eating is discouraged, with the exception of eating facilities for tourists. Abortion is legal only to save the life, physical health, or mental health of the woman.

Only Christian and Jewish groups are recognized by the government. Christian groups need government approval before they can own land and perform

[14] Riphenburg (1999); "Yemen: Social Profile," WorldTravelGuide.Net, http://www.worldtravel-guide.net/data/yem/yem460.asp; "Freedom in the World: Yemen: Six Americans Among More than 100 Religious Students Scheduled for Deportation," Associated Press, February 7, 2002; "Yemen Editor Charged with Causing Religious Strife," Reuters, May 15, 2000.

marriages or other sacraments. In order to be recognized, a Church must include some citizens. The Druze, Bahai, and several Christian denominations, while not illegal, are not recognized. They cannot have their faiths included in state identity cards but may practice freely. The Bahai may not register schools or places of worship. Public proselytizing and encouraging conversion away from Islam are illegal as is conversion away from Islam. On occasion the government prohibits the public celebration of Christian holidays when such celebrations are considered too ostentatious.[15]

PREFERRED TREATMENT FOR SOME RELIGIONS OR SUPPORT FOR A PARTICULAR TRADITION

Low Restrictions on Minorities

Lebanon

This report focuses on the post–civil war era in Lebanon based on the 1989 Taif Accord.

Article 9 of Lebanon's constitution guarantees religious freedom including observation of personal status laws, provided it does not interfere with public order. Article 10 states that education may not "interfere with the dignity of any of the religions or creeds" and guarantees religious communities the right to their own schools. Article 19 grants the heads of religious communities the right to consult the Constitutional Council on a number of religious matters. Article 22 requires that all religious communities be represented in the Senate of the Parliament. Article 24 requires that until a nonconfessional basis for elections is achieved, the Chamber of Deputies have equal representation of Christians and Muslims and proportional representation among the confessional groups within each religious community. Article 95 states that grade one posts in the bureaucracy should be distributed equally between Christians and Muslims. The preamble declares the abolition of confessionalism a national goal.

Lebanon is severely split along sectarian lines. This sectarianism affects everything from economics to marriage, and even influences the composition of the government. While there is no official religion, all aspects of government are based on religious representation. Religion is included on identity cards. Unofficially, the president is a Maronite Christian, the prime minister a Sunni Muslim, and the speaker of the Parliament a Shi'i Muslim. State recognition is necessary for religions to engage in a number of practices including the application of personal status laws. While nonrecognized religions can practice freely, the confessional nature of the political system limits their political rights unless they participate under the umbrella of a recognized religion. People may change their religion if the head of the religion they wish to join approves. Because personal status laws are based on religion, members of nonrecognized

---

[15] Haddad (1998); Barbara G. Baker, "Jordanian Government Cancels Christian Celebration," *Human Rights Without Frontiers*, May 2, 2000, http://www.hrwf.net.

religions cannot marry, divorce, or inherit, but civil marriages from outside the country are recognized.

It is illegal to blaspheme God publicly. Religious personal status laws result in the usual limitations on female Muslims. Abortion is illegal, except to save the woman's life. Two physicians other than the one performing the abortion must approve the procedure.[16]

Moderate Restrictions on Minorities

Syria

Article 3 of Syria's constitution declares that the president must be a Muslim and that "Islamic jurisprudence is a main source of legislation." Article 35 protects religious freedom and the right to hold religious rites, "provided they do not disturb the public order." The constitutional oath contained in Article 7 begins "I swear by God the Almighty."

All religious groups must register. All religious meetings, other than for worship, require government approval, but this is also true of nonreligious meetings. The government does not generally interfere with religious groups if they avoid politics, but it actively encourages moderate Islam by appointing moderate Muslims to leadership positions. The government actively monitors militant Muslim groups, mostly because they are perceived as a political threat. The government also monitors all religious services for political content. Laws of personal status and inheritance are guided by one's religion, resulting in the usual restrictions on Muslim women. Religious education is required in all public schools and is available in Islam and Christianity. In the past there was a separate public school for Jews but it closed due to the decreasing size of Syria's Jewish community. Abortion is legal only to save the life of the woman.

For the most part, religious minorities can practice freely. Proselytizing is not illegal but it is discouraged. Missionaries are allowed to function as long as they do so discretely. Jehovah's Witnesses are officially banned, but are allowed to practice in private.[17]

High Restrictions on Minorities

Turkey

Article 10 of Turkey's constitution bans discrimination on the basis of religion. Article 15 states that even under emergency laws "no one may be compelled to reveal his or her religion, conscience, thought or opinion." Article 24 protects religious freedom including freedom of worship. It also places religious education under state supervision, makes religious education in schools mandatory, bans the exploitation or use of religion "for the purpose of personal or political

---

[16] Ofiesh (1999).

[17] "Jehovah's Witnesses Arrested and Released," *Human Rights Without Frontiers*, October 10, 2001, http://www.hrwf.net.

influence," and bans the basing of "the fundamental, social, economic, political, and legal order of the state on religious tenets." Article 136 establishes the Department of Religious Affairs, which will exercise its authority based on "the principles of secularism." The preamble bans interference "by sacred religious feelings in state affairs and politics."

Despite the provisions of the constitution, Islam is the country's de-facto religion. The government in practice recognizes this, but also significantly regulates Islam. Based on a 1997 law, the government regulates the country's mosques and must authorize the construction of all new mosques. It appoints local and provincial imams who are civil servants. Religious services outside of designated locations are illegal. The government opposes militant Islam and has banned several religious parties that it considers too radical. Civil servants and teachers considered too religious have been fired, denied promotion, or otherwise harassed. However, the current government is run by the moderate, Islam-affiliated Justice and Development Party. Mystical Sufi Islam orders have been banned since the 1920s, but some continue to operate. Only the government Ministry of Religious Affairs may provide religious training, and does so in public schools. Religious minorities recognized by the 1923 Lausanne Treaty are exempted but all others must attend. Illegal Koran courses are sometimes raided by the government. Traditional Muslim female headcoverings are banned in universities and the civil service. Religion is listed on national identity cards. Unrecognized religions are not listed. Those who wish to change their official identity away from Islam tend to be harassed. Turkey's penal code forbids debasing any religion, disrupting religious services, or defacing houses of worship or religious monuments.

Minority religions are regulated by a separate government entity and register as foundations. Until 2002 these foundations were not allowed to acquire new property. Now they may do so, but only after a burdensome application process. The government confiscates unused minority religious properties. Non-recognized religions must worship in private homes but these meetings are sometimes broken up by the police. Occasionally services for these religions are held in embassies. Proselytizing is not illegal, but those who do so are often harassed and arrested by the police. A 2001 government memo encouraged local governments to use existing laws to regulate "Protestants, Baha'is, Jehovah's Witnesses, [and] believers in Christ," and resulted in additional harassment of these groups. This includes the closing of several churches and a Christian radio station.

All of this is part of a two-pronged religion policy: the government supports secularism, and all Islam in the country is to conform to the official Hanafi school of Islam.[18]

---

[18] "UN Report on the Elimination of All Forms of Religious Intolerance – Situation in Turkey, 2000"; "Closure of Two Kingdom Halls," *Human Rights Without Frontiers*, November 11, 2003, http://www.hrwf.net; Barbara G. Baker, "Turkish Police Close Iskenderun Protestant Church," *Human Rights Without Frontiers*, July 9, 2002; "Turkish Radio Station Suspended for Propagating Christianity," *Human Rights Without Frontiers*, March 26, 2002.

SOME GENERAL OBSERVATIONS

The most prominent trend in the MENA is that it scores higher than any other region on all of the RAS variables. There are a number of additional trends that are prevalent in the region. First, there is a strong distinction between the public and private expression of religion. For most of the states in the MENA, religion is an overtly public issue. People are expected to conform to, or at least not openly oppose, the state religion. Consequently, there is a high number of religious laws, and significant restrictions on the public practice of religion by religious minorities. However, in many such states, practicing minority religions in private is tolerated. In some cases this is true even of religions that are officially illegal.

Second, other than in Israel and Lebanon, Islam often takes precedence over other issues. The majority of the constitutions of the MENA promise religious freedom but state that this freedom is subordinate to Islam, local customs, public order, or some similar qualification, which effectively allows significant restrictions on religious freedom. In most of these states there is not full freedom even for Muslims as the states tend to support one version of Islam or restrict some interpretations of Islam that they consider undesirable. In some cases, this appears to be mostly in order to prevent opposition groups from using religion as a tool to oppose the government, but in others this involves enforcing a state-supported version of Islam to the exclusion of all other versions.

Third, while the summaries here do not directly address the issue, the MENA is one of the most autocratic regions of the world. Even if the MENA states were to become more democratic, it is likely that they would be democracies for Muslims with non-Muslims remaining second-class citizens. As the region is also the most Islamic and has the lowest level of SRAS, this begs the question of whether these factors are related. The analysis provided in Chapter 11 addresses this issue.

Finally, despite the striking similarities in GIR in the MENA, it is important to emphasize that there is still considerable diversity. No two states have exactly the same policy with regard to religion and there are some regional differences among these states. The MENA can be divided into three distinct geographical groups that correlate highly with state policy toward religion. First, the Gulf states, with the exception of Iraq, are nearly synonymous with religious states in the MENA. In North Africa the government is more powerful than the religion and the state seeks to control the religion. Finally, all of the other states in the MENA have more liberal policies toward religion, at least in comparison to the Gulf and North African states.

9

Sub-Saharan Africa

Sub-Saharan Africa is perhaps the world's most diverse region with regard to government involvement in religion (GIR). While some countries have nearly full separation of religion and state (SRAS) as measured by the RAS variables, others are among those with the least. However, no state in this region has absolute-SRAS and states with low levels of GIR are in the minority.

This diversity is reflected in Tables 9.1, 9.2, 9.3, and 9.4. A clear majority of the 46 sub-Saharan African governments in the study do not substantially support religion based on the official separation measure. Unlike other world regions where a majority of the states support religion, 25 (54.3 percent) in this region are coded as accommodation, and another 2 as separationist. The official regulation variable shows that a large minority of 20 (43.5 percent) states give no preference to any religion and do not place significant limits on religion. There are 21 states that place practical or legal limitations on some religions or give some religions benefits not given to others. Five states make at least one religion illegal. In most of these countries this refers to witchcraft.

Sub-Saharan African states also exhibit a high level of tolerance for minority religions. Nineteen of them, 41.3 percent, do not engage in any of the types of restrictions on minority religions that are monitored by the RAS project. This is the best record of any region in the world, though Western democracies come close at 40.7 percent. An additional 14 engage in low levels of restrictions (no more than 2 types). Of the 16 types of restrictions on minorities measured by the RAS project, 15 exist in sub-Saharan Africa, but none of them exist in more than one-third of the states. The most common forms of restrictions are registration requirements (15 states), arrest, detention, or harassment of people for practicing their religion (13 states), and limits on proselytizing (12 states). Nine states restrict building or repairing places of worship. The other 11 types of restrictions exist in between 1 and 6 states.

All but one of the types of government regulation of the majority religion monitored by the RAS project exist in sub-Saharan Africa. Eighteen states restrict religious political parties and 11 arrest or harass religious leaders. The

TABLE 9.1. *Separation of Religion and State in Africa in 2002, Basic Information*

Country	Majority religion	% Majority religion	# Min. groups with 5% of population	Official GIR	Official regulation	General GIR
Angola	Christian	47.0	2	Accommodation	No limitations	1.67
Benin	Animist	61.0	2	Accommodation	No limitations	1.25
Botswana	Other	50.0	2	Accommodation	Practical limitations	7.71
Burkina Faso	Islam, Sunni	50.0	2	Accommodation	No limitations	1.88
Burundi	Catholic	60.0	3	Accommodation	No limitations	1.88
Cameroon	Mixed	40.0	2	Accommodation	Some illegal	17.27
Cape Verde	Catholic	90.0	1	Civil religion	No limitations	16.28
Central African Republic	Christian	35.0	4	Accommodation	Some illegal	18.73
Chad	Islam	51.0	3	Cooperation	Some illegal	26.71
Comoros	Islam, Sunni	98.0	0	One official religion	Legal limitations	43.13
Congo Brazzaville	Christian	40.0	2	Accommodation	No limitations	0.63
Djibouti	Islam, Sunni	93.0	1	One official religion	Practical limitations	34.79
Equatorial Guinea	Christian	93.0	1	Civil religion	Practical limitations	26.79
Eritrea	Christian	46.0	1	Separationist	Legal limitations	28.39
Ethiopia	Mixed	45.0	2	Cooperation	Practical limitations	21.05
Gabon	Christian	60.0	1	Accommodation	Legal limitations	13.54
Gambia	Islam	87.2	1	Accommodation	No limitations	1.88
Ghana	Christian	48.5	3	Accommodation	No limitations	4.32
Guinea	Islam, Sunni	75.0	1	Civil religion	Practical limitations	21.36
Guinea-Bissau	Mixed	48.0	2	Accommodation	Legal limitations	11.25
Ivory Coast	Mixed	38.6	4	Cooperation	Practical limitations	19.99
Kenya	Christian	35.0	4	Cooperation	Legal limitations	26.90

Lesotho	Christian	37.5	3	Accommodation	No limitations	0.63
Liberia	Mixed	41.7	4	Accommodation	No limitations	3.69
Madagascar	Animist	50.0	3	Cooperation	Practical limitations	19.19
Malawi	Protestant	55.0	2	Accommodation	No limitations	3.75
Mali	Islam, Sunni	82.0	1	Accommodation	Legal limitations	17.42
Mauritania	Islam, Sunni	99.2	0	One official religion	Legal limitations	43.96
Mauritius	Mixed	49.5	3	Cooperation	No limitations	10.50
Mozambique	Animist	50.4	4	Accommodation	No limitations	4.30
Namibia	Protestant	60.0	3	Accommodation	No limitations	0.63
Niger	Islam	84.4	1	Separationist	Practical limitations	19.45
Nigeria	Islam, Sunni	50.0	2	Cooperation	Practical limitations	23.74
Rwanda	Catholic	55.0	2	Accommodation	Practical limitations	9.77
Senegal	Islam	90.5	1	Accommodation	No limitations	3.73
Sierra Leone	Islam	55.0	4	Cooperation	No limitations	12.32
Somalia	Islam, Sunni	98.9	1	One official religion	Legal limitations	38.75
South Africa	Christian	37.0	3	Accommodation	No limitations	2.50
Sudan	Islam, Sunni	70.0	2	One official religion	Legal limitations	54.91
Swaziland	Christian	40.0	4	Accommodation	No limitations	3.31
Tanzania	Christian	31.8	4	Cooperation	No limitations	18.70
Togo	Animist	50.5	3	Cooperation	Practical limitations	16.48
Uganda	Christian	35.0	3	Accommodation	Some illegal	19.75
Zaire	Catholic	50.0	3	Accommodation	No limitations	2.92
Zambia	Christian	30.4	3	One official religion	Practical limitations	29.94
Zimbabwe	Christian	40.3	3	Accommodation	Some illegal	18.3

TABLE 9.2. *Restrictions on Minority Religion in Africa in 2002*

	Public observance	Build or repair places of worship	Access to places of worship	Forced observance	Formal orgs.	Education in schools	Arrest, detention, harassment	Materials	Publications	Personal status	Conversions	Forced conversions	Proselytizing	Registration	Other	Total
Angola															x	1
Benin																0
Botswana														x		1
Burkina Faso																0
Burundi																0
Cameroon							x									1
Cape Verde																0
Cent. African Republic	x						x							x		3
Chad	x						x									2
Comoros		x	x	x			x	x	x	x		x	x		x	10
Congo Braz.																0
Djibouti													x	x		2
Eq. Guinea																0
Eritrea		x					x		x				x	x		5
Ethiopia		x					x						x			3
Gabon		x											x	x		3
Gambia					x											0
Ghana																0
Guinea						x							x	x		3
Guinea-Biss.																0
Ivory Coast							x									1
Kenya	x		x	x			x			x				x		7
Lesotho																0
Liberia																0
Madagascar							x						x	x		3

Country	1	2	3	4	5	6	7	8	9	10	11	12	Total
Malawi													0
Mali			x								x		2
Mauritania			x			x		x		x			4
Mauritius													0
Mozambique													0
Namibia		x											1
Niger								x		x	x		3
Nigeria								x		x	x		4
Rwanda			x		x						x	x	4
Senegal													0
Sierra Leone													0
Somalia								x		x			2
South Africa													0
Sudan	x	x	x	x	x	x		x	x	x	x	x	13
Swaziland	x										x		2
Tanzania	x			x									2
Togo											x		1
Uganda		x			x						x		4
Zaire											x		1
Zambia													0
Zimbabwe	x												1
TOTAL	6	5	4	2	13	4	2	3	2	12	15	3	85

The following categories of religious restrictions were not included in this table because none of these countries engage in these practices: education; clergy.

TABLE 9.3. *Government Regulation of the Majority Religion in Africa in 2002*

	Political parties	Arrest, detention, harassment	Orgs.	Public observance	Speech	Access to places of worship	Publications	Public gatherings	Public display	Other	Total
Angola											0
Benin											0
Botswana											0
Burkina Faso											0
Burundi											0
Cameroon		x									1
Cape Verde	x									x	2
Cent. Afr. Rep.										x	1
Chad		x			x						2
Comoros											0
Congo Braz.											0
Djibouti											0
Eq. Guinea	x	x		x	x			x		x	6
Eritrea	x		x	x	x	x				x	6
Ethiopia						x			x	x	3
Gabon											0
Gambia											0
Ghana	x										1
Guinea			x								1
Guinea-Biss.											0
Ivory Coast	x	x			x						3
Kenya	x	x									2
Lesotho											0
Liberia	x	x									2
Madagascar	x									x	2
Malawi											0

											Total
Mali	x				x						2
Mauritania											0
Mauritius											0
Mozambique	x		x								2
Namibia											0
Niger	x	x	x								3
Nigeria	x	x					x			x	4
Rwanda								x			1
Senegal			x								1
Sierra Leone	x										1
Somalia											0
South Africa											0
Sudan	x	x	x								3
Swaziland		x									1
Tanzania	x		x		x						3
Togo	x										1
Uganda	x										1
Zaire											0
Zambia	x										1
Zimbabwe		x									1
TOTAL	18	11	7	2	6	2	1	2	1	7	57

The following categories of religious restrictions were not included in this table because none of these countries engage in these practices: arrest of nonleaders.

TABLE 9.4a. *Religious Legislation in Africa in 2002, Part 1*

	Dietary laws	Alcohol	Personal status	Inheritance	Conversions	Marriages	Public dress	Blasphemy	Censorship	Close businesses	Optional education	Mandatory education	Fund education	Fund religious charity	Fund clergy	Other religious funding
Angola																
Benin																
Botswana													x			
Burkina Faso																
Burundi																
Cameroon																
Cape Verde																
Cent. African Rep.																
Chad																
Comoros		x					x									
Congo Brazzaville												x	x			
Djibouti			x		x							x	x		x	
Equatorial Guinea						x						x	x			
Eritrea																
Ethiopia							x	x		x						x
Gabon																
Gambia											x		x			
Ghana											x		x		x	x
Guinea																
Guinea-Bissau																
Ivory Coast																
Kenya											x		x			x
Lesotho				x							x					
Liberia										x						
Madagascar											x		x			
Malawi												x	x			
Mali			x	x								x	x			x

	1															
Mauritania	x	x	x	x	x		x	x			x		x		x	x
Mauritius		x	x	x									x		x	x
Mozambique																
Namibia																x
Niger			x	x												x
Nigeria		x	x	x			x	x			x	x	x			
Rwanda								x			x	x	x			
Senegal								x			x	x	x			
Sierra Leone								x			x	x	x			
Somalia			x	x	x		x	x	x		x	x	x			
South Africa									x			x	x	x		
Sudan		x	x	x	x	x	x	x	x		x	x	x			
Swaziland					x	x							x			
Tanzania			x	x	x		x	x	x		x	x	x			
Togo																
Uganda																
Zaire											x	x	x		x	
Zambia											x	x	x		x	
Zimbabwe												x	x	x		
TOTAL	1	4	8	8	4	2	5	6	3	3	13	5	20	2	4	8

TABLE 9.4b. *Religious Legislation in Africa in 2002, Part 2*

	Approve clergy & speeches	Some clergy appointed	Gov. rel. dept.	Religious position for gov. official	Gov. pos. for rel. official	Religious requirements	Relig. courts	Legislature/ cabinet	Abortion	Flag	Identity cards	Registration	Sects	Women	Other	Total
Angola									x			x				2
Benin									x			x				2
Botswana									x			x				3
Burkina Faso			x						x			x				3
Burundi									x			x			x	3
Cameroon									x			x				2
Cape Verde												x			x	2
Cent. African Rep.												x			x	3
Chad									x			x				2
Comoros					x				x	x						7
Congo Brazzaville									x							1
Djibouti		x	x	x	x	x	x		x			x				13
Equatorial Guinea			x	x	x				x			x				5
Eritrea			x						x			x				3
Ethiopia									x			x			x	7
Gabon									x			x		x		3
Gambia									x							3
Ghana									x							4
Guinea						x			x			x				4
Guinea-Bissau									x			x				2
Ivory Coast									x			x				5
Kenya							x		x			x				6
Lesotho									x							1

																Total
Liberia																3
Madagascar								x	x			x			x	5
Malawi			x		x			x	x			x				6
Mali	x								x			x				15
Mauritania						x			x					x		4
Mauritius						x			x							3
Mozambique			x						x			x				1
Namibia									x							5
Niger									x			x				11
Nigeria							x		x			x			x	4
Rwanda									x			x			x	5
Senegal									x			x				4
Sierra Leone			x				x		x							10
Somalia			x				x		x						x	4
South Africa			x													15
Sudan							x		x			x		x	x	3
Swaziland									x			x				9
Tanzania									x	x	x	x				2
Togo												x	x			3
Uganda									x			x			x	4
Zaire									x			x				5
Zambia			x						x			x				2
Zimbabwe									x							2
TOTAL	1	1	9	1	2	3	7	2	43	2	1	35	1	3	8	215

The following categories of religious legislation were not included in this table because no African states engage in these practices: blue laws; taxes.

other nine types of regulation exist in 1 to 7 of these states, and 27 (58.7 percent), engage in at least 1 of these practices.

Religious legislation is common in sub-Saharan Africa. The average country in the region legislates 4.67 of the 33 types of legislation monitored by the RAS project and all countries legislate at least one. This average is lower than that of any region except Latin America. Yet the region has several countries with 10 or more of these types of legislation, all of them with large Muslim populations. Also, all but two of these types of legislation exist in at least one of these states. The most common type is restrictions on abortion, which exist in 43 states, followed by the requirement for religions to register, which exists in 35 states. Another 29 types of legislation exist in a minority of states.

The categorization of African states into the taxonomy used here is presented in Table 9.5.

ACTIVE STATE RELIGIONS

This category includes six sub-Saharan African states. In all but one of them Islam is the official religion.

No to Low Restrictions on Minorities

Djibouti

Djibouti's constitution declares Islam the state religion but also protects religious freedom.[1] The president is required to take a religious inauguration oath. Islamic family law is applied for all Muslims and is under the jurisdiction of a special set of Islamic law judges.[2] Members of other religions are allowed to practice freely, with a few exceptions, and can marry through civil marriage. While not illegal, proselytizing is discouraged. All religions must register. The government refuses to register the Bahais. In the past, Bahais were occasionally detained and harassed by the police, but since 2002 this practice appears to have stopped. The government subsidizes Catholic schools. Abortion is legal to save the life of the woman or for "therapeutic" purposes.

Somalia

Since the collapse of its government and the beginning of a civil war in 1991, Somalia has no active constitution. There is a nominal Transnational National Government, but Somalia is in practice ruled by local warlords. Despite this, the country is essentially an Islamic state. Various national charters, which are not in force, make Islam the country's official religion and some local governments, such as "the Republic of Somaliland" and "Puntland," have made Islam their official religion. Most local courts rely on a mixture of tribal and Sharia law. This results

---

[1] I was unable to obtain an English-language copy of Djibouti's constitution so this description may be incomplete.
[2] For a discussion of Muslim (Sharia) law see Chapter 8.

TABLE 9.5. *Taxonomy of Africa*

Separation of religion and state	Type of restrictions on minorities			
	None	Low (1–2)	Moderate (3–5)	High (6+)
Religious state				
Active state religion	*Zambia*	**Djibouti**	Mauritania	**Comoros**
		Somalia		**Sudan**
State-controlled religion				
Historical / cultural state religion				
Preferred treatment for some religions or support for a particular tradition	*Cape Verde*	**Chad**	*Ethiopia*	*Kenya*
	Equatorial Guinea	*Ivory Coast*	**Guinea**	
	Mauritius	*Tanzania*	*Madagascar*	
		Togo	**Nigeria**	
General support				
Moderate separation	**Burkina Faso**	Botswana	*Central African Republic*	
	Burundi	**Mali**	*Gabon*	
	Gambia	*Swaziland*	*Rwanda*	
	Ghana	*Zaire*	*Uganda*	
	Liberia			
	Malawi			
	Mozambique			
	Senegal			
	Sierra Leone			
	South Africa			
Nearly full separation (2 or less on legislation)	Benin	*Angola*		
	Congo Brazzaville	Cameroon		
	Guinea-Bissau	*Zimbabwe*		
	Lesotho			
	Namibia			
Hostility		**Niger**	*Eritrea*	

Italics = Christian
Bold = Muslim

in the usual restrictions on women in family law and inheritance. In 2006 these courts were becoming the basis for a new government, but were overthrown by outside forces. Most localities prohibit proselytizing by non-Muslims. Non-Muslims who attempt to practice their religion publicly are harassed. According to the penal code in force before the civil war in Somalia, abortion is illegal except to save the life of the woman. Due to the lack of a central government it is difficult to determine the current status of abortion in Somalia. A number of militant Islamic groups try violently to enforce Islam on the populace.

Zambia

The preamble of Zambia's constitution, as amended in 1996 declares the country "a Christian nation" but upholds freedom of "conscience or religion." Article 19 includes detailed protection for religious freedom and prohibits mandatory religious education or ceremonies in places of education, except in one's own religion, as well as oaths contrary to one's religion. These rights can be limited "in the interests of defense, public safety, public order, public morality or public health; or for the purpose of protecting the rights and freedoms of other persons." Articles 11 and 23 prohibit discrimination on the basis of religion. In 1993 the courts ruled that Article 21 of the constitution prohibits religious political parties.

All religious groups must register but there are no reports of registration being refused. Unregistered groups are not allowed to operate. The public school curriculum includes optional education in Christianity. Abortion is legal in order to save the life, physical health, or mental health of the woman, in cases of fetal impairment, and for economic and social reasons, with the approval of a panel of physicians. It is not available on request or in cases of rape and incest.

Moderate to High Restrictions on Minorities

Comoros

Comoros' 2001 constitution protects religious freedom. It replaced the 1996 constitution, which was suspended in 1999 and prohibited discrimination based on religion.[3] The 1996 constitution also required that all laws be in conformity with Islam. Since 1999 the mechanism for enforcing this has changed from a formal council that advised the president to a more informal consulting process. The interim constitution, which was in force between 1999 and 2001, did not specifically provide for religious freedom. The 2001 constitution declares Islam the country's official religion. The government discourages, but does not prohibit, the practice of other religions. Islam is taught in all public schools. Bans on alcohol and immodest dress are enforced sporadically. Alcohol can be imported and sold with a government permit. Abortions are only legal is cases of "serious medical reasons." While this includes saving the

---

[3] I was unable to obtain English-language copies of Comoros' constitutions so this description may be incomplete.

life and physical health of the mother it is unclear whether it includes reasons of mental health.

Through all of these governments Christians have been prohibited from proselytizing, and local governments often restrict their right to practice. Many churches are open only to citizens, forcing foreign Christians to worship in private. Some local authorities ban Christians from local events and ban Christian burials. Occasionally the police arrest Christians for anti-Islamic activities and try to force them to convert. Muslim citizens found in possession of Christian literature are arrested.

Mauritania

Article 1 of Mauritania's 1991 constitution declares the country an Islamic republic. Article 4 declares Islam the official religion of the state and its citizens. Article 23 requires that the president be a Muslim. Article 94 creates a High Islamic Council that consults with the president. The preamble includes religious imagery. Unlike the previous constitution, this one does not grant religious freedom.

All schools include Islamic education, which is technically mandatory but in practice optional. After a coup attempt by Islamic radicals in 2003 the government passed a law against using mosques for any kind of political activity and closed Saudi-funded Islamic schools. The government provides a small stipend for the imam of the Central Mosque in its capital but does not otherwise fund clergy without official government positions. Mauritania's court system conforms to Sharia law, which has been the law of the land since 1983. The resulting restrictions on women are moderate compared to most Middle Eastern Islamic states. The application of the Sharia laws against apostasy and conversion away from Islam are unclear. According to the US State Department these aspects of Sharia law have not been codified into civil law or enforced. However, according to an Italian government report, the law provides for capital punishment for the crime of apostasy and Muslims who refuse to pray. Abortion is permitted only in order to save the life of the woman.

While all citizens must be Muslims, non-Muslim residents and those considered Christians from birth can practice their religions freely. Proselytizing is not illegal but the government bans it through the use of a law that "bans the publication of any material that is against Islam or contradicts or otherwise threatens Islam." This law also restricts the distribution of non-Islamic religious literature. Possession of such literature in private homes is not illegal.[4]

Sudan

Sudan has been experiencing one of the world's most violent and protracted civil wars since 1983 between the Muslim-dominated government in the north of the country and the primarily Christian and Animist population in the south.

---

[4] "Presidential Elections Set for November Despite Coup Attempt," *Africa News,* June 13, 2003.

The current round of violence began when the government decided to impose Sharia law on the entire country, violating a 1972 agreement not to do so. This summary focuses on GIR and does not otherwise mention this conflict unless directly relevant to that issue.

Article 1 of Sudan's 1998 constitution declares Sudan "a country of racial and cultural harmony and religious tolerance." It declares Islam the religion of the majority of the population but recognizes Christianity and traditional religions. Article 6 requires the state to "guard against religious parties [and] political sectarianism." Articles 12 and 13 require the state to encourage religious values among society and youth. Article 16 prohibits the consumption of alcohol by Muslims. Article 17 requires that the government's foreign policy respect all peoples' religious freedoms. Article 18 states that public officials should worship God as well as preserve and be guided by religion. Article 21 prohibits discrimination on the basis of religion. Article 24 protects religious freedom. Article 27 guarantees that minorities may preserve their own religion and raise their children in that religion. Article 65 includes Sharia among the sources of legislation. Article 132 states that even in a state of emergency the government may not discriminate on the basis of religion. Article 139 includes religious freedom and Sharia as a source of law among the principles of the constitution that may not be suspended. The preamble, Article 4, and the oaths of office in Articles 40, 48, and 71 include religious imagery.

The constitutional protections for religious freedom are largely ignored. Sharia law is imposed on the entire country including religious minorities. Sharia law is used for family law and inheritance for Muslims, resulting in the usual restrictions on women. The Islamic dress code for women and a ban on alcohol are enforced sporadically. Courses in Islam are required in public schools in the north. In the south, Christian courses are officially available, but the government often does not provide teachers for these courses. A 1992 law Islamized all education. Many Catholic missionary schools were closed and non-Muslim educators were dismissed at all levels, from primary schools to universities. The media was also Islamized in 1992, and all Christian radio broadcasts were suspended. It is illegal to insult Islam and journalists are arrested for doing so.

A 1996 law requires gender segregation in public places and events. It also requires modest dress by women in public places. This includes a ban on form-fitting clothes on female athletes, as well as a ban on playing cards in public. A 2000 law makes it illegal for women to hold jobs where they deal with the public, but this law is not enforced. Abortion is legal only to save the life of the woman.

All religious groups must register in order to gather legally. The government often denies registration to Christian groups, especially evangelical groups. It also restricts permits to build churches and has denied permission for building any new Roman Catholic churches. In 1997 the government began sporadically razing churches and Christian schools, primarily those in displacement camps for refugees of the country's ongoing conflict. The government also regularly harasses Roman Catholic priests. This is part of a dispute over the Catholic Church's refusal to re-register under a 1994 registration law because it claims that its previous registration is still valid.

The government regularly detains people based on their religious belief. Conversion away from Islam is punishable by death under a 1991 law. The government does not recognize Christian holidays. Christians are often forced by their employers to work on Sundays and Christian holidays. Christian students are often required to take exams on these days. Prisoners and people in government-controlled camps for the internally displaced are sometimes pressured to convert to Islam. Children in such camps are required to study the Koran. Christians who participate in the compulsory national service are indoctrinated in Islam. Children of unknown parentage are considered Muslims and may not be adopted by non-Muslims. Given the violence of the civil war in Sudan, this undoubtedly results in many children of Christian parents being raised as Muslims. There are also reports of abductions of non-Muslim children, sometimes as slaves, who are then forcibly converted to Islam, and the reports of the use of food distribution to compel people to convert to Islam.

Reports regarding proselytizing are mixed. According to the US State Department, proselytizing is not illegal but it is discouraged by the government. Restrictions on proselytizing are higher on groups relatively new to the country, such as evangelical Christians. Other sources report that proselytizing by non-Muslims is illegal and foreign missionaries are regularly denied visas and otherwise harassed. Christian literature, such as bibles, may only be sold in churches, and Christian films may only be shown in churches.

The government does restrict one Islamic group, Taqfir al-Hijra, because it commits terrorist acts against other Muslims. The government also monitors other antigovernment Islamic groups.[5]

PREFERRED TREATMENT FOR SOME RELIGIONS OR SUPPORT FOR A PARTICULAR TRADITION

No Restrictions on Minorities

Cape Verde
Articles 1 and 22 of Cape Verde's 1992 constitution recognize the equality of all citizens regardless of their religion. Article 27 protects religious freedom. Article 35 prohibits extraditing aliens for religious reasons. Article 42 prohibits computerized registration of individuals that includes information on religion. Article 44 protects the right to both religious and civil marriage. Article 45

---

[5] Chris Hedges, "Sudan Presses Its Campaign to Impose Islamic Law on Non-Muslims," *New York Times*, June 1, 1992; "Sudanese English-Language Daily Closed, Editor Jailed," *Agence France Presse*, May 11, 2003; "Sudan's Capital Bans Mixing of Sexes in Public," *New York Times*, October 27, 1996; James C. McKinley Jr., "Sudan Christians Take War's Culture Clash North," *New York Times*, April 5, 1998.

protects the freedom to "express and to disseminate" ideas regardless of their religious content. Article 47 allows the right of broadcasting to be given to religious institutions and guarantees them the right of reply. Article 48 declares SRAS and includes detailed protections for religious freedom. It also protects "cult places, insignias and religious rites," and prohibits "their imitation or ridicule." Article 49 recognizes the right to educate one's children in one's religion but prohibits the state from programming education and culture along religious directives and declares that "public education shall not be religious." Articles 61 and 125 prohibit trade unions and political parties from being associated with a religion. Article 297 states that states of emergency do not allow the state to restrict religious freedom.

Despite these strict provisions of SRAS, the Catholic Church enjoys a somewhat privileged status in Cape Verde. For example, the government gives it free air time on national television stations. Religions must register but those that do not practice freely. There are no reported cases of violation of religious freedom.

Equatorial Guinea

Article 9 of Equatorial Guinea's 1996 constitution bans political parties based on religion. Article 13 guarantees freedom of religion and worship. Article 15 bans acts of partiality or discrimination based on religion. Article 23 allows religious education in public schools and guarantees the right to religious schools as long as they are "oriented toward the official pedagogical plan." The preamble includes religious imagery.

A 1992 law gives official preference to the Catholic Church and the Reform Church of Equatorial Guinea. This is especially true of the Catholic Church. Most government ceremonies include a Roman Catholic mass. Religious groups must register to function legally. There are no reports of registration being refused. Officially, religious activities outside places of worship require government approval, but this does not appear to significantly restrict such activities. Religious education is required in public schools. It is usually but not always exclusively available in Catholicism. The government monitors the speech and activities of all religious groups for antigovernment sentiment and harasses those it deems critical of the government. Abortion is legal only in order to save the life, physical health, or mental health of the woman.

Mauritius

Article 11 of Mauritius' constitution includes detailed guarantees for religious freedom. It guarantees the right to religious instruction and bans mandatory religious education, mandatory participation in religious ceremonies, and being forced to take oaths contrary to one's religion. These rights can be limited "in the interests of defense, public safety, public order, public morality, public health, or for the purpose of protecting the rights and freedoms of other persons." Article 14 includes the right to establish religious schools. Article 3 prohibits discrimination on the basis of creed. Several of the oaths in the constitution include optional references to God. The first schedule of the constitution includes the Hindu and Muslim communities as officially recognized communities.

Religious groups present in the country before independence have automatic recognition and receive lump-sum payments from the government. These religions are the Catholic Church, the Church of England, Presbyterians, Seventh Day Adventists, Hindus, and Muslims. The government pays the salaries of Muslim teachers and imams. Other religions must register and do not receive financing. There are no reported cases of refusal of registration. The government does not restrict the activities of missionaries but it limits the number of foreign missionaries allowed to enter the country and their stay is usually limited to five years. Abortion is legal only in order to save the life of the woman and must be approved by the Solicitor General. However, according to a pro-life advocacy group, this is not strictly enforced.[6]

Low Restrictions on Minorities

Chad
Chad's constitution declares SRAS, protects religious freedom, and prohibits legislation that differentiates between religions.[7] However, the government supports religious activities. For instance it funds the Hajj pilgrimage for some government officials.

Religious instruction in public schools is prohibited but private religious education is allowed. All religious groups must register. No groups are refused registration and there does not seem to be any penalty for failure to register. However, Christian groups claim that Muslim groups are given preference in obtaining permits for public celebrations and get more unofficial funding from the government. Abortion is illegal unless the life of the woman is at risk.

In 1998 the government banned the Faid al-Djaria, a Sufi Islamic religious group from Nigeria and Senegal, due to pressure from local Islamic leaders who consider their practices un-Islamic. This ban was reiterated in 2001 following an increase in activity by the group in 2000, resulting in a number of arrests. In 1998 the government began restricting fundamentalist Muslim leaders who are believed to be promoting conflict. These restrictions include arrests and restrictions on public speech.

The country experiences periodic ethnic turmoil between northerners, who are mostly Muslims, and Christian tribal farmers in the south.

Ivory Coast (Cote d'Ivoire)
The Ivory Coast's 2000 constitution protects religious freedom, as did the previous constitution.[8] It also forbids religious political parties and discrimination

---

[6] *Life Coalition International*, http://www.lifecoalition.com/mauritius1.html.

[7] I was unable to obtain a copy of Chad's constitution so this description may be incomplete.

[8] I was unable to obtain copies of the Ivory Coast's constitutions so this description may be incomplete.

on the basis of religion. In 2003 the government created a ministry of religion. While there is no state religion, the government favors Christianity. The government subsidizes Christian schools, especially Catholic ones, but not Muslim schools, despite the country's significant Muslim population. It also has funded pilgrimages to Rome by Catholics. The government funds the construction of both Christian and Islamic places of worship. All religious groups must register. Those that do not register are not penalized, but registration brings benefits including gifts from the government and subsidies for schools. Religious education by established Islamic, Catholic, and Protestant groups is allowed in public schools. A 1996 decree limits this education to Catholic and Protestant teachings, but the decree is not enforced. The government monitors all religious groups for political activity. Abortion is legal only to save the life of the woman.

Following a September 2002 coup attempt the government began cracking down on those believed to be sympathizers with the rebellion, most of whom are Muslims. This has resulted in the arrest, harassment, and killing of Muslim leaders, and searches of several mosques. While religious identity seems to be a factor in these activities, religious practices do not. These activities have resulted in retaliation against Christian clergy by the rebels.[9]

Tanzania

Tanzania's constitution guarantees religious freedom subject to maintaining public order.[10] There is no official state religion, though an official Mufti (Muslim leader) is elected periodically. Discrimination on the basis of religion is prohibited but accusations that this occurs are common, especially in the civil service. All religions must register. There are no reports of registration being refused. Islamic law is used for family law for Muslims. A lack of Muslim judges in the courts results in Christian judges applying Islamic law. Religion classes are allowed in national schools but are not part of the national curriculum. They are usually taught on an ad-hoc basis, and need the school administration's approval. Religious organizations may not participate in politics and politicians may not use language intended to incite religious hatred or to get a religious group to vote in a particular way. A law banning the publication and distribution of inflammatory materials is sometimes used to ban religious-based criticisms of the government by Muslims. Religious identity is not included on identity cards and passports but is included on police reports, school registration forms, and applications for medical care. Abortion is legal only to save the life, physical health, or mental health of the woman.

Since 1998 tensions between the government and the Muslim minority have been increasing, resulting in growing numbers of demonstrations against the government and arrests and harassment of Muslims. This includes arrests of religious leaders and the closure of mass religious ceremonies not approved by

[9] Elizabeth Kendal, "Priest Stabbed to Death in Gohitafla," *Human Rights Without Frontiers*, June 11, 2004, http://www.hrwf.net.
[10] I was unable to obtain a copy of Tanzania's constitution so this description may be incomplete.

the government. This harassment seems to be directed more at perceived political opposition than religious activities.

Togo

Togo's constitution guarantees religious freedom and prohibits political parties that are religious or identify with a particular religion.[11] There is no state religion. Roman Catholicism, Protestantism, and Islam have automatic recognition from the government. Other religions must register. Groups may practice freely from the time they apply. Registration is rarely refused as long as the group does not breach public order. In 2000 the government formed a commission to investigate groups "whose mode of worship harms the welfare of society." Abortion is legal only to save the life of the woman. In practice it can be performed with the permission of the woman's family up to the third month of pregnancy.

Moderate to High Restrictions on Minorities

Ethiopia

The preamble of Ethiopia's constitution includes the objective of living without religious discrimination. Article 3 declares that the national flag must reflect Ethiopia's religious communities. Article 11 declares SRAS, that there is no state religion, and that the state and religion may not interfere in each other's affairs. Article 21 gives prisoners the right to meet with religious counselors. Articles 25 and 38 prohibit discrimination on the basis of religion including in voting. Article 27 provides detailed protection for religious freedom including the right to religious education. However this right can be limited in order to "protect public safety, peace, health, education, public morality or the fundamental rights and freedoms of others, and to ensure the independence of the state from religion." Article 34 gives adults the right to marry and divorce regardless of their religion, allows the government to recognize religious marriage ceremonies, and allows the government to use religious laws to adjudicate matters of family law. Article 78 allows the government to establish religious courts. Article 90 states that public education shall be free from religious influence.

All religious groups must register yearly but there is no apparent penalty for not registering. The government grants lands to all religions for places of worship, schools, cemeteries, and hospitals, but all schools and hospitals are subject to government closure at any time. Minority religious groups complain of discrimination in this land allocation. In 2003 the government began banning political parties based on religion. Defamation against religious leaders is considered a crime. Religious education is not permitted in any schools, even private ones, but Sunday schools are allowed. Many public schools ban the

[11] I was unable to obtain an English-language copy of Togo's constitution so this description may be incomplete.

wearing of traditional Muslim headcoverings for women. Abortion is legal only in order to save the life, physical health, or mental health of the woman.

There is considerable tension between Ethiopia's Muslim and Christian communities. It has resulted in violent intercommunal riots and the destruction of religious property, mostly churches. There is also occasional violence between Protestants and members of the Orthodox Church, usually with the latter attacking the former. After one such incident in 2002 two Pentecostal elders were arrested and held without charges for ten months.[12]

Guinea

Guinea's constitution protects religious freedom and refrains from either recognizing Islam as the state religion or declaring SRAS.[13] The government sponsors the National Islamic League (NIL), which is responsible for Islam in the country. The NIL actively reenforces the Islamic character of the country, including appointing imams and distributing sermons to mosques. It also pressures government ministers to convert to Islam. Between 2000 and 2002 the government funded the renovation of Conakry's grand mosque. In 2000, the government began requiring government ministers to take an oath on the Koran. The NIL has spoken against Shi'i Muslim radicalism but has not substantially restricted their religious practices other than obstructing the opening of a foreign-funded Shi'i school. By law, all Christian churches must join the Association of Churches and Missions but those that do not seem to be able to practice freely. The registration process is slow, taking an average of two years. The government requires missionary groups to make a declaration of their aims and activities but otherwise does not restrict proselytizing with the exception of some isolated reports of harassment of Jehovah's Witnesses. Abortion is allowed only to save the life, physical health, or mental health of the woman and needs the approval of two physicians, including a court-appointed physician.

Kenya

Article 66 of Kenya's constitution provides for a minimum of four Islamic judges, who have jurisdiction over "questions of Muslim law relating to personal status, marriage, divorce or inheritance in proceedings in which all the parties profess the Muslim religion." Article 78 protects religious freedom and the right to religious education. It also bans requiring anyone to take religious education or participate in a religious ceremony of a religion other than their own as well as any oath contrary to their religion. These protections can be limited "in the interests of defense, public safety, public order, public morality

---

[12] Barbara Baker, "Ethiopian Evangelical Killed by Orthodox Church Mob," *Human Rights Without Frontiers*, August 5, 2002; "Magistrate Releases Two Jailed Protestants," *Human Rights Without Frontiers*, March 7, 2003, http://www.hrwf.net.

[13] I was unable to obtain a copy of Guinea's constitution so this description may be incomplete.

or public health; or for the purpose of protecting the rights and freedoms of other persons."

All religious groups must register. Some religious groups accuse the government of revoking their tax-exempt status based on suspicions that they supported the opposition, and some religious groups have difficulty registering. While religious political parties are not specifically illegal, in 1992 the government denied registration to the Islamic Party of Kenya because it violated the secular nature of the state. In largely Christian areas, public schools have mandatory prayer sessions but students may stay silent. There are also Islamic schools that receive government support. Christian classes are given in public schools. Abortion is legal only in order to save the life, physical health, or mental health of the woman.

Practicing witchcraft is banned but people are usually only prosecuted in conjunction with another crime, such as murder. Occasionally, witchcraft practitioners are arrested on charges such as causing mysterious illnesses. The government occasionally arrests and harasses members of religious institutions it believes are associated with rebel activities. Beginning in 2002, there are reports that Seventh Day Adventists have been penalized for refusing to participate in school activities and tests held on Saturdays. In 2002 the head of a traditionalist religion was jailed for preaching against Christianity. Recently the government has begun arresting and harassing a doomsday cult called the Tent of Living God. This seems to be part of a larger policy of cracking down on cults. After the bombings of US embassies in Africa in 1998, the government banned six Islamic organizations. There is a history of tension and occasional violence between Muslims and Christians in Kenya and there are reports of local governments temporarily shutting down places of worship in order to end or prevent this violence.[14]

Madagascar

Article 1 of Madagascar's constitution declares it a secular state and bans discrimination based on religion. Article 10 guarantees religious freedom subject to public order. Article 14 bans political parties that preach religious segregation. Article 28 bans "injury" in employment based on religion. Article 77 states that one-third of the seats in the Senate "shall consist of members representing economic, social, cultural, and religious groups." The preamble includes religious imagery.

Christian organizations take an active part in political life, including education, supporting candidates, election monitoring, and a national AIDS campaign. From 2001 to 2002, the government detained and harassed some politically involved Church leaders. This practice seems to have stopped by

---

[14] "Spiritual Leader of Religious Sect Arrested," *Human Rights Without Frontiers*, May 1, 2002, http://www.hrwf.net; "Police Arrest Seven Doomsday Cult Members," *East African Standard*, March 22, 2002; "State and Church Urged to Wage Battle on Cults," *World Religion News Service*, January 9, 2002; "This Is Religious Tolerance" *Nation*, May 22, 2002.

2003. While the government strongly recommends the registration of religious organizations, it is not mandatory and groups that do not register can practice freely. The Unification Church was denied registration in 1998. Abortion is legal only to save the life of the woman and must be approved by a court-appointed physician.

Nigeria

Article 10 of Nigeria's 1999 constitution prohibits national and state governments from adopting a state religion. Article 15 prohibits discrimination on the basis of religion and makes integration a duty of the state. This includes promoting religious intermarriage and cross-religious associations. Article 17 requires that there be "adequate facilities for ... religious and cultural life." Article 23 includes religion among the national ethics. Article 38 protects religious freedom including the freedom to change one's belief. It also prohibits mandatory religious instruction or attendance of religious ceremonies in a religion other than one's own in schools, but protects the right to religious education. Article 42 prohibits laws and their application that differentiate according to religion. Article 222 requires that all political parties be open to everyone regardless of their religion and that the name and logo of political parties be free from religious connotations. Article 237 requires that some of the judges on the Court of Appeal be "learned in Islamic personal law." The constitution also discusses Sharia courts in Articles 6, 84, 185, 240, 244, 247, 260 through 264, 275 through 279, 289, 292, and 318. These courts have jurisdiction over family law and inheritance for Muslims as well as civil cases between Muslims who wish to use them. The constitution discusses a Sharia Court of Appeals, though the federal government has yet to establish this court. The preamble and oaths of office include religious imagery.

Since Nigeria's 1999 return to civilian rule, religion has been becoming an increasingly volatile issue, though this was also true before 1999. Nigeria's federal government generally respects religious freedom but many state governments do not. Nigeria's northern states tend to have Muslim majorities and favor Islam and the southern states tend to have Christian majorities and favor Christianity. Since 2000, there has been considerable Muslim-Christian violence.

Starting in 2000, some Muslim-majority states adopted aspects of Sharia criminal law resulting in a few death penalties for such crimes as adultery. Due in part to the national government's intervention, no death penalties have been implemented. Before 2000, Sharia courts were limited mostly to family law, resulting in the usual restrictions on women. Some northern states have applied other aspects of Sharia law, including the segregation of schools, health care facilities, and public transportation by gender, restrictions on alcohol, mandatory Islamic dress codes in schools, and bans on insulting Islam. All these laws are based on a constitutional provision that permits the use of customary religious law by courts. Reportedly, this resurgence of Sharia law is at least in part fueled by inefficiencies and corruption in the secular court system. The

Sharia courts are perceived as fairer and less corrupt. Many northern states allow unofficial vigilante groups to use violence to enforce Sharia law, including on non-Muslims. After religious violence in 2000 many northern states have banned outdoor mass proselytizing. Some northern state governments have sporadically enforced bans on proselytizing.

The national government bans religious advertisements and religious organizations on primary school campuses. Religious education in one's own religion is mandatory in public schools but courses in Christianity are often unavailable in northern states as are courses in Islam in southern states. Since 1998 the government has required permits for open air gatherings, including religious ones. Those believed likely to lead to violence are refused permits. In 2003 this caused a ban on public Easter celebrations, which was widely ignored. Proselytizing is not illegal but it is discouraged by the federal government because it leads to religious tensions. The government also creates bureaucratic delays in permitting some foreign missionaries to enter the country. Many Nigerian states fund religious causes including places of worship and pilgrimages. Beginning in 2000 construction of all new mosques and churches require approval by the Corporate Affairs Commission. This law is intended to regulate the proliferation of new buildings in the absence of zoning laws. Many groups ignore this law and some of these places of worship are shut down. There are accusations of selective enforcement of this law, especially in the north. Mobs regularly attack and destroy churches in the north. Religious organizations must register with the government. Nigeria has two sets of abortion laws, one for the northern states and one for the southern states. All states allow abortions to save the life of the woman. Southern states also allow it in order to save the woman's physical or mental health.[15]

MODERATE SEPARATION

No Restrictions on Minorities

Burkina Faso
Burkina Faso's constitution guarantees religious freedom.[16] The government actively protects this right and all religions can practice freely. While registration is required, failure to do so has no penalty other than the lack of the status of a legal person. Religious groups can be restricted if they harm public order or

[15] "Nigerian State Introduces Full Islamic Law," *ZENIT*, November 26, 2000; "Journalists to be Flogged for Offensive Religious Stories," *Panafrican News Agency*, November 9, 2000; "13th Nigerian State Adopts Islamic Law," *ZENIT*, December 18, 2001; Stephan Faris, "Religion and Justice in Nigeria," *Human Rights Without Frontiers*, March 19, 2002, http://www.hrwf.net; Emman Usman Shehu, "Nigerian State Government Implements New Anti-Christian Measures," CNSNews.com, January 1, 2002; Obed Minchakpu, "Christians Defy Ban on Easter Celebrations," *Compass*, April 22, 2002.
[16] I was unable to obtain a copy of Burkina Faso's constitution so this description may be incomplete.

commit slander but this has never occurred. There is no religious education in public schools and the government does not fund private religious schools. Private schools, including religious ones, are required to have a curriculum that meets state standards, and teachers of nonreligious topics must have the necessary qualifications. Abortion is legal to save the life, physical health, or mental health of the woman, and in cases of rape, incest, or fetal impairment. It is not available on request or for economic or social reasons.

Burundi

Burundi has been experiencing a violent civil war between Hutus and Tutsis, both of whom are mostly Catholic. This report does not address this conflict unless directly relevant to issues of religion and state.

Burundi's 2001 Transnational Constitutional Act protects religious freedom, does not establish an official religion, and bans discrimination on the basis of religion.[17] Religious groups must register and maintain a headquarters within Burundi. The heads of major religious groups are given diplomatic status. During the ongoing civil war, clergy have occasionally been targeted by rebels. On one occasion in 2001 the government arrested a religious leader who made claims of divinity after a conflict broke out with a rival religious leader. Abortion is legal only in order to save the life, physical health, or mental health of the woman.

Gambia

Gambia's constitution protects religious freedom.[18] The government proclaims its laity. Optional religious education in Christianity and Islam is available in public schools. In 2003 the government announced a policy limiting men to two wives. Some Muslims consider this a violation of religious freedom. In 2003 some schools refused to allow female students to wear veils because it violated school dress codes. The government intervened to end this practice. Abortion is legal only in order to save the life, physical health, or mental health of the woman.

There are some indications that the government's tradition of SRAS is changing. It has participated in the formation of a Supreme Muslim Council and is involved in its day to day affairs. Mosques are being built in public institutions, including the State House. The government has also created a Religious Affairs Ministry.[19]

Ghana

Article 12 of Ghana's 1992 constitution guarantees fundamental human rights regardless of religion. Articles 17 and 35 ban discrimination on the basis of religion. Articles 21 and 26 guarantee religious freedom. Article 28 states that

---

[17] I was unable to obtain a copy of this act so the description provided here may be incomplete.

[18] I was unable to obtain a copy of Gambia's constitution so this description may be incomplete.

[19] "Gambians Freeze on Polygamy," BBC News, July 22, 2003; D. A. Jawo, "An Increase of Religious Intolerance – A Dangerous Trend," *Banjul Independent*, May 26, 2003.

"no child shall be deprived ... of medical treatment, education or any other social or economic benefit by reason only of religious or other beliefs." Article 30 provides a similar protection for adults. Article 55 bans religious political parties and religious symbols for political parties. Article 56 states that "Parliament shall have no power to enact a law to establish or authorize the establishment of a body or movement with the right or power to impose on the people of Ghana a common program or a set of objectives of a religious or political" nature. According to Article 166 the national media council will include representatives from Christian and Muslim religious groups. According to Articles 206 and 209 the national and regional prisons councils will include "a representative of such religious bodies as the President may, in consultation with the Council of State, appoint." The preamble and oaths of office include religious imagery.

Religions may register yearly but this is not necessary in order to practice one's religion. Until 2000 schools commonly required all students to attend Christian devotional services. After complaints by Muslims, the government directed that these services should not be mandatory. Classes in Christianity are offered in schools and were mandatory until 2000. There have been a number of clashes between religious groups. While in the past the government has been lax in punishing the participants, this is changing. Abortion is legal in order to preserve the life, mental health, or physical health of the woman, as well as in cases of rape, incest, or fetal impairment.

Liberia

Article 14 of Liberia's constitution protects religious freedom except when protecting "public safety, order, health, or morals or the fundamental rights and freedoms of others." It also declares SRAS, requires equal treatment for all religions, and bans religious tests for political offices and the exercise of civil rights. Article 11 grants all fundamental rights regardless of creed. Article 18 protects the right to employment regardless of religion. Article 78 includes religious groups in the definition of "associations." Article 79 requires all political parties to be open to every citizen regardless of religion and that "the name, objective, emblem or motto of the association or of the independent candidate and his organization is free from any religious connotations." The preamble includes religious imagery.

Official functions usually open with Christian, and occasionally Muslim, prayers. All religious groups must register. There are no reported cases of registration being refused. Businesses must close on Sundays. The government only began enforcing this law in 2002. Leaders of religious denominations may not hold public office. Abortion is legal to save the life, physical health, or mental health of the woman, as well as in cases of rape, incest, or fetal impairment.

The country has a long history of ethnic violence and conflict between Christian and Muslim ethnic groups. This has periodically led to attacks on clergy and places of worship.

Malawi

Article 13 of Malawi's constitution includes the elimination of religious intolerance in its list of national policies. Article 20 bans discrimination on the basis of religion. Articles 33 and 44 protect religious freedom. Article 42 gives detainees and prisoners the right to a religious counselor. Article 68 reserves one-third of the seats in the country's Senate for social groups, including religious ones. The oath for the president in Article 81 includes religious imagery.

Religions, like all other organizations, must register. There are no reports of refusal of registration. Schools include "Bible Knowledge" in the curriculum. Abortion is permitted only to save the life of the woman.

Mozambique

Article 9 of Mozambique's constitution declares it a secular state. It also makes religious instruction a subject of law and "recognizes and values the activities of religious denominations which promote a climate of social understanding and tolerance and strengthen national unity." Article 66 gives all citizens equal rights regardless of religion. Article 69 bans "situations of privilege or discrimination" based on religion. Article 78 protects religious freedom and states that "religious denominations shall have the right to pursue their religious aims freely and to own and acquire assets for the purpose of achieving these aims."

According to a 1989 law, all religious groups and missionary organizations must register. This includes divulging sources of funding and providing a list of 500 members. No groups were refused registration and groups that have not registered are not restricted. Religious political parties are illegal and religious institutions may not engage in political propaganda. Religion classes in public schools are forbidden. Abortions are legal only in order to save the life, physical health, or mental health of the woman, or in cases of contraceptive failure.

Senegal

Senegal's 2001 constitution declares the country a secular state and guarantees religious freedom as long as public order is maintained.[20] The previous constitution did the same. The government often grants money on an ad-hoc basis to religious institutions for the building and maintenance of places of worship, as well as for special events. It funds participation in the Hajj as well as similar Christian pilgrimages. It funds religious schools if they meet national education standards. Although they are a minority, Christian schools receive the largest share of these funds. In 2002 the government introduced optional religious education into the public schools, which is available in Christianity and Islam. In order to have legal status religious groups must register. Registration is rarely refused and religious groups that do not register can practice freely. The government monitors foreign NGOs, including religious ones, for political activity. Those engaging in unacceptable political activity can be expelled. Otherwise

---

[20] I was unable to obtain an English-language copy of Senegal's constitution so this description may be incomplete.

they are allowed to operate freely. Family law is based on a combination of Sharia and customary law resulting in the usual restrictions on women. Abortion is legal only to save the life of the woman.

There are isolated incidents of violence against the country's Christian minority, usually involving Muslims attacking churches, occasionally with the support of local officials. The central government actively opposes this behavior.[21]

Sierra Leone

Article 6 of Sierra Leone's 1991 constitution requires the state to "promote national integration and unity and discourage discrimination on the grounds of . . . religion." Article 8 requires that work conditions include adequate facilities for religious life. Article 13 requires that every citizen respect the religion of others. Article 24 guarantees the following rights: religious freedom; to change one's religion; to not be required in a place of education to take classes or participate in a religious ceremony in any religion other than one's own; religious education; and not to be required to take an oath contrary to one's religion. These rights can only be limited "in the interest of defense, public safety, public order, public morality or public health; or for the purpose of protecting the rights and freedoms of other persons." Article 35 bans political parties that are religiously exclusive in their leadership or membership, parties that pursue religious goals, and parties that use symbols that are particular to a certain religion. Several oaths contained in the second schedule include optional references to God.

Optional religious education in public schools is permitted and available in Islam and Christianity. Local courts apply tribal and customary law, including Sharia law, to family issues. Abortion is legal only to save the life, physical health, or mental health of the woman. Until a 1999 peace accord, Muslim revolutionary groups on occasion attacked Christians and Muslims engaging in acts such as drinking alcohol or eating in public during the fast of Ramadan.

South Africa

Article 6 of South Africa's constitution requires the government to promote all languages used in the country, including Hebrew and those languages used for religious purposes. Article 9 prohibits discrimination on the basis of religion. Article 15 guarantees religious freedom. It also allows religious ceremonies in state institutions on an equitable basis and allows legislation recognizing religious laws with regard to family law issues. Article 16 excludes advocacy of religious hatred from the freedom of expression. Article 31 allows persons belonging to religious communities to practice their religion and to form, join, and maintain religious associations. Article 35 guarantees detainees access to

---

[21] "Muslim Mob Storms Church and Forces Closure in Senegal," *Human Rights Without Frontiers*, June 20, 2002; "Tensions Abate Following Attacks on Church in Senegal," *Human Rights Without Frontiers*, September 22, 2003, http://www.hrwf.net.

a religious counselor. Article 37 bans discrimination solely on the basis of religion in states of emergency. Articles 181, 185, and 186 establish the Commission for the Promotion and Protection of the Rights of Cultural, Religious and Linguistic Communities. The preamble includes religious imagery.

Optional religious education is allowed in public schools but many public schools do not include it in their curriculum.

Low Restrictions on Minorities

Botswana

Article 11 of Botswana's constitution includes detailed protections for freedom of religion and conscience.[22] It allows for the suspension of religious freedom for purposes of national defense, security, public health, civil order, and public morality. There is no state religion. However, the constitution allows for places of religious instruction at the community's expense but prohibits forced religious instruction, forced participation in religious ceremonies, and forcing someone to take an oath contrary to their religion. All religions must register. For the most part, registration has been refused only to those religions that are believed to have submitted false information or signatures. In 1984 the Unification Church was denied registration. Abortion is legal to save the life, physical health, or mental health of the woman, as well as in cases of rape, incest, or fetal impairment.

Mali

Article 2 of Mali's 1992 constitution prohibits discrimination based on religion. Article 4 guarantees religious freedom. Article 12 gives the right of asylum to anyone persecuted for their religious beliefs. Article 17 declares that public education is nonreligious. Article 25 declares that the motto of Mali is "One People – One Purpose – One Faith." It also declares Mali a secular state, as does the preamble. Article 28 requires political parties to respect this principle. Article 118 states that the "secularity of the State ... may not be made the object of revision." The oath for the president in Article 37 begins "I swear before God."

In 2002 the government established a High Council of Islam to coordinate preaching in mosques. Family and inheritance law are based on a mixture of Islam and local customs. The government can prohibit publications that defame a religion but there are no reports of this law being invoked. All religions except for traditional religions must register, as must any public association. There are conflicting reports on the application of this law. According to one source it is rarely enforced, and according to another the Bahai have been refused registration. However, all sources agree that, for the most part, Mali

---

[22] I was unable to obtain a copy of Botswana's constitution but a summary of its articles is available at the Botswana Centre for Human Rights webpage, at http://www.ditshwanelo.org.bw/index/Other/Botswana%20Constitution.htm.

is generally tolerant of non-Islamic religions. Abortion in Mali is legal only to save the life of the woman.

Swaziland

Swaziland's constitution was suspended in 1973. In 2006 the new constitution came into force and included protections for religious freedom. While earlier drafts included a declaration that Christianity was the country's official religion, this clause was dropped in the final draft. Even before the constitution came into force, the government generally supported religious freedom. Swaziland is a monarchy and the current ruler, King Mswati III, believes that God supports him and his absolute rule. He also believes that the Bible is against democracy and human rights and that women should not wear pants. In 2000 miniskirts, and the women who wear them, were blamed as the cause of AIDS and banned from schools.

The government does not favor any particular religion, but Christian broadcasts are the only religious broadcasts allowed on government stations. New religious groups must register and meet requirements of financial stability or, for traditional religions, an established place of worship. Nonregistered groups can worship freely. Building places of worship requires government approval in urban areas and permission from tribal chiefs in rural areas. The government sometimes delays building permits to non-Christian groups. Beginning in 1997 there are occasional reports of the government breaking up religious meetings deemed to have political goals that oppose those of the regime. The government does not otherwise interfere with worship activities. Some local chiefs have banned nighttime vigils claiming that they allow for immoral activity. Abortion is legal only in order to save the life of the woman.[23]

Zaire (Democratic Republic of Congo)

The Democratic Republic of Congo has been experiencing a violent civil war since 1994. This summary does not address this civil war unless some aspect of it is directly relevant to issues of religion and state, nor does it address the activities of the rebel groups, though these groups are known to have poor respect for religious rights and, in particular, to attack the Catholic Church. There are also reports of government soldiers ransacking places of worship, contrary to government policy.

The Democratic Republic of Congo has no constitution in effect. The previous one protected religious freedom and prohibited discrimination based on religion. The government tends to respect religious freedom as long as religious

[23] "Heavenbound Via Mswati," *Africa Analysis*, May 2, 2003; Bill Ferguson, "Swazi King: Blessed Are the Skirt-Wearers," *Macon Telegraph*, June 7, 2003; Jenny Lyn Bader, "Ideas & Trends; The Miniskirt as a National Security Threat," *New York Times*, September 10, 2000; "Police Raided Catholic Bishop's House in Swaziland," *Associated Press Worldstream*, October 20, 1997; Tom Holloway, "Swaziland; Swazi Prince Bans Night Church Vigils," *Africa News*, December 5, 1996.

groups do not undermine public order. Religious organizations must register in the same manner as other nonprofit organizations. Registration is rarely refused or suspended. The government suspended the registration of the Jehovah's Witnesses in 1990. This suspension was later reversed by the courts. A separatist religious group was banned and its members arrested between 2002 and 2003, but this seems to be based solely on their political beliefs. Unregistered indigenous groups can practice freely but foreign groups must register with the government. A 1971 law allows the government to disband religious groups, but other than the incidents just mentioned, the government has not done so. The majority of primary and secondary education is run by missionary schools. Abortion is legal only in order to save the life of the woman.

Moderate Restrictions on Minorities

Central African Republic
The Central African Republic's constitution was suspended on March 15, 2003, after a seizure of power. It protected religious freedom, and prohibited intolerance and fundamentalism.[24] This provision was generally understood to be targeted at Muslims but, for the most part, the now deposed government allowed most religions to practice freely. The country's new government has not substantially changed its policy on religion as of the time of this writing.

There is no state religion. Except for traditional indigenous religious groups, all religions must register. The Interior Ministry keeps track of those groups that have not registered but other than this there seems to be no penalty for not registering. Religions that are considered politically subversive are refused registration or banned. The Unification Church has been banned since the mid-1980s and the government closed a church in 2001 that was operated by a political opponent of the president. It was reopened after the 2003 seizure of power by that opponent, General Bozize. There is no religious education in public schools. The practice of witchcraft is illegal but people are usually prosecuted for witchcraft only in conjunction with serious crimes, such as murder. The government grants free radio time to the country's larger religions but requires payment for air time from smaller religions. Abortion is illegal but is generally allowed in order to save the life of the woman.

Gabon
Gabon's 1991 constitution protects religious freedom provided that "public order is maintained."[25] It also guarantees the right to form religious associations that can administer their affairs independently as long as they don't violate national sovereignty or public order.

---

[24] I was unable to obtain an English-language copy of the Central African Republic's constitution so this description may be incomplete.

[25] I was unable to obtain an English-language copy of Gabon's constitution so this description may be incomplete.

Acts of racial, ethnic, or religious discrimination are illegal. The government registers religions but such registration is not required. The government does not register traditional religious groups. A 1970 decree bans the Jehovah's Witnesses because they "do not protect adequately individuals who might dissent from the group's views," but this decree is not enforced. The government also claims to allow the Jehovah's Witnesses to proselytize, but this claim is uncorroborated. The government has also refused to register several other groups. Religious primary and secondary schools must register with the Ministry of Education and must comply with the same standards as public schools. The government gives free transmission time to the Catholic Church, some Protestant denominations, and Islamic mosques. Abortion is legal only if there is no other way to save the life of the woman, and requires the approval of two physicians, including one appointed by the courts.

Rwanda

While Rwanda has experienced a considerable level of violence since the beginning of the 1990s, which included genocidal episodes in which hundreds of thousands were killed, this summary refers to this violence only when relevant to the issue of SRAS. Since both sides of this conflict, the Hutus and Tutsis, are predominantly Catholic, religion is not a major element of it. However, members of the clergy have participated in the conflict, including some accused of participating in genocide. Similarly clergy and places of worship have been targets of attack. Interestingly many Rwandans are converting to Islam because the Muslims were among the few who protected people during the periods of genocide.

Article 16 of Rwanda's 1991 constitution prohibits discrimination on the basis of religion. Article 18 guarantees religious freedom. Oaths included in Articles 41, 56, and 60 and the preamble include religious imagery. Article 1 of Rwanda's 2003 constitution declares it a secular state. Article 11 prohibits discrimination on the basis of religion. Article 33 guarantees religious freedom "in accordance with conditions determined by law." Article 137 states that a state of emergency does not undermine this right. Article 54 bans political parties based on religious divisions. Oaths included in Articles 61 and 104 include religious imagery.

Since 2001 all religious organizations must register. Registration is rarely denied but the registration of two groups was revoked for activities deemed to be too political. Public schools include optional religion education. In some cases missionary schools act as public schools. In the past the government banned all outdoor nighttime religious meetings because insurgents used these meetings to organize. As of 2003 such meetings are allowed if the group provides advance notification. Otherwise all religious meetings must be in established places of worship. Interfering in a religious service or with a minister in the exercise of his profession is illegal. Jehovah's Witnesses have been arrested for refusing to take part in nighttime security patrols and expelled from schools for refusing to attend on Saturdays. Protestant groups, especially those of denominations relatively new to the country, are sporadically arrested and harassed by local police. Abortion is legal only to save the life, physical health, or mental health of the woman.[26]

Uganda

Article 3 of Uganda's 1995 constitution states that "every effort shall be made to integrate all the peoples of Uganda while at the same time recognizing the existence of their ethnic, religious, ideological, political and cultural diversity." It also states that "everything shall be done to promote a culture of co-opera-tion, understanding, appreciation, tolerance and respect for each other's cus-toms, traditions and beliefs." Article 8 states that "religious bodies ... shall be free to found and operate educational institutions if they comply with the general educational policy of the country and maintain national standards." The preamble includes religious imagery.

All religious organizations must register. The World Last Message Warning Church was denied registration following its suspected involvement in the kill-ings of over 1000 citizens in 2000. There are no reports of registration being refused to any other organization. Permits are required to construct religious facilities. There are no reports of such permits being denied. A 2002 law bans political parties whose membership is based exclusively on religion. Especially since 2000, local governments often harass groups considered cults. This includes bans on nighttime services, closure of unregistered facilities, and the use of building codes to close facilities. This seems to be a direct consequence of the killings in 2000. In the wake of this, the government also disbanded several cults. Between 1996 and 2000 there were reports of police harassment of Muslims, but this activity seems to have stopped. Abortion is legal only to save the life, physical health, or mental health of the woman.[27]

NEAR FULL SEPARATION

No Restrictions on Minorities

Benin

Benin's constitution describes Benin as a secular state and guarantees religious freedom.[28] Religious education is prohibited in public schools. Religious groups must register. There are no reports of registration being refused. The government actively protects religious freedom. For example, when villagers prevented people from traveling through their village to attend Christian

---

[26] "Rwanda Turns to Islam After Genocide," Associated Press, November 7, 2002; "Islam Blooms in Genocide's Wake," *Chicago Tribune*, August 2002.

[27] Maurice Okore, "Cult Leaders Convicted," *Human Rights Without Frontiers*, July 25, 2002; Jean-Francois Mayer, "A Report on the Events of Kanungu," *Human Rights Without Frontiers*, June 5, 2002, http://www.hrwf.net.

[28] I was unable to obtain an English-language copy of Benin's constitution so this description may be incomplete.

services, the Constitutional Court declared this action unconstitutional. The government has been known to restrict the activities of religious groups that threaten public security and safety. For example, in 1993 it temporarily banned the activities of a Christian group accused of destroying Voodoo temples. Abortion is legal only to save the life of the woman, and requires the approval of a court-approved physician.

Congo Brazzaville (Republic of Congo)

The Republic of Congo's 2002 constitution provides for religious freedom and forbids discrimination on the basis of religion.[29] The previous constitution, which was suspended in 1992, and the Fundamental Charter of the Republic, which was in effect between the two constitutions, also provided for religious freedom. The Charter declared SRAS and prohibited the use of religion for political purposes. Between 1995 and 1999 the government nationalized all religious schools not run by Catholics. During the country's civil war, clergy and religious buildings were occasionally the targets of rebels.

There is no state religion. All organizations, including religious ones, must register, as must nonreligious organizations. Some local unrest was caused by the "Ninja" group, which practices a mixture of Christianity, ancestor worship, and indigenous religions, but the government signed a peace accord with this group in 2003. Abortion is illegal but in general it is allowed to save the life of the woman.

Guinea-Bissau

Guinea-Bissau's constitution recognizes freedom of religion.[30] Despite a violent change of government and transition to democracy, the 1984 constitution remains in effect. The government requires that all religious groups be licensed. There are no reports of any applications for these licenses being refused. Officially abortions are illegal except to save the life of the woman, but this Portuguese-era law is rarely enforced and in practice abortions in the first three months of pregnancy are allowed.

Lesotho

Articles 4, 16, and 26 of Lesotho's constitution guarantee several rights regardless of one's religion. Article 13 guarantees religious freedom. Article 23 guarantees the right to religious education. It also bans mandatory religious education, mandatory participation in religious ceremonies, and forcing people to take oaths that are contrary to their religions. These rights can be limited "in the interests of defense, public safety, public order, public morality or public health; or for the purpose of protecting the rights and freedoms of other

---

[29] I was unable to obtain a copy of the 2002 constitution so this description may be incomplete.
[30] I was unable to obtain a copy of Guinea-Bissau's constitution so this description may be incomplete.

persons." Article 18 bans discrimination on the basis of religion. Several oaths in the constitution mention God.

With a few exceptions the government maintains SRAS. The Catholic Church owns and operates about 75 percent of the elementary and secondary schools in the country. Abortion in Lesotho is legal only to save the life of the woman.

Namibia

Article 1 of Namibia's constitution declares the state secular. Article 10 prohibits discrimination on the basis of religion. The preamble guarantees the right to "life, liberty and the pursuit of happiness" regardless of religion. Article 14 guarantees the right to marry, divorce, and found a family regardless of religion. Article 19 guarantees the right to "enjoy, practice, profess, maintain and promote any ... religion subject to the terms of [the] Constitution and further subject to the condition that the rights protected by this article do not impinge upon the rights of others or the national interest." Article 21 guarantees religious freedom. Article 97 allows the state to grant asylum to those persecuted for their religion. The oath for the president in Article 30 includes religious imagery.

The government actively protects religious freedom. Abortion is legal only to save the life, physical health, or mental health of the woman, and in cases of rape, incest, and fetal impairment.

Low Restrictions on Minorities

Angola

Article 8 of Angola's constitution declares both SRAS and that Angola shall be a secular state. Article 159 requires all amendments to the constitution to comply with these provisions. Article 8 also states that "religions shall be respected and the State shall protect churches and places and objects of worship, provided they abide by the laws of the State." Article 18 declares all citizens equal regardless of their religion. Article 52 states that the declaration of a state of emergency can not abridge religious freedom. A 2004 law defines religious rights in more detail and reinforces the principles described in the constitution.

Beginning in 2002, all religions must register and those that do not have been shut down. A colonial-era law bans all non-Christian religions. It is not enforced but the Justice Minister has warned that it would be enforced against "any radical religious groups advocating terrorism or public disturbances." A 1995 law bans "cult demonstrations" outside expressly approved locations. It appears to be aimed at Evangelical Protestant churches but is generally not enforced. Abortion is illegal. In practice it is allowed to save the life of the woman.[31]

---

[31] "Parliament Passes Law on Freedom of Conscience, Worship, Religion," *Human Rights Without Frontiers*, May 31, 2004, http://www.hrwf.net.

Cameroon

The preamble of Cameroon's constitution declares "that the human person, without distinction as to race, religion, sex or belief, possesses inalienable and sacred rights." It prohibits "harassment" on the grounds of religion and guarantees religious freedom. It declares the state secular as well as the "neutrality and independence of the State in respect of all religions."

All religions must register. Registration is rarely refused and there seem to be no sanctions against groups that fail to register. The government occasionally arrests and harasses clergy and worshipers, usually claiming that the worshipers somehow violated the law. It is unclear whether this is a pretext. Since 2001 this harassment seems to be especially targeted against Muslims. Witchcraft is illegal but people are generally prosecuted for witchcraft only in conjunction with another crime. In 2002 the government banned a traditional religious sect after the sect's members beat to death a 6-year-old girl in an attempt to extract the Devil from her "possessed" body. There are reports that Muslims, who control Cameroon's northern provinces, have attempted to force non-Muslims to pay religious taxes. Abortion is legal to save the life, physical health, or mental health of the woman, as well as in cases of rape or incest.

Zimbabwe

Article 19 of Zimbabwe's constitution includes detailed protections for religious freedom. It also forbids mandatory religious education or ceremonies in places of education in a religion other than one's own, as well as requiring one to take an oath contrary to one's religion. These rights can be limited "in the interests of defense, public safety, public order, public morality, public health, [or] for the purpose of protecting the rights and freedoms of other persons." Articles 19 and 20 grant the right to religious instruction and establish religious schools. This is not dependent on whether religious schools receive public funds. The oaths of office in Schedule 1 of the constitution optionally include the phrase "so help me God."

Religion classes are not allowed in public schools. Religious organizations run many of Zimbabwe's schools and hospitals, because the government is unable to provide these services. A law criminalizes both witchcraft and accusing someone of witchcraft. This law is considered restrictive of some indigenous religious practices. The government has arrested and harassed clergy members who publicly criticized the government-sanctioned violence surrounding the 2000 and 2002 elections. The government restricts foreign missionaries. Abortion is legal to save the life or physical health of the woman, but not her mental health. It is also allowed in cases of rape, incest, or fetal impairment.[32]

---

[32] "Church Leaders Arrested in Zimbabwe," *Human Rights Without Frontiers*, February 21, 2002, http://www.hrwf.net.

HOSTILITY

Eritrea

Article 14 of Eritrea's 1997 constitution prohibits discrimination on the basis of religion. Article 19 protects religious freedom.

A 1995 law prohibits political activity by religious groups. As the government owns all land, groups wanting to build religious facilities need government approval. Religious groups must register, and, since 2002, may not engage in religious activities until registered. Groups without significant historical ties to the country are generally refused registration. The government recognizes only four religions: Orthodox Christians, Muslims, Catholics, and the Evangelical Church of Eritrea. Muslims and Catholics must pay a tax for the return of properties seized by the previous regime. This tax is not enforced for Orthodox places of worship. A 1998 law nationalized all religiously run places of education but this law has yet to be implemented. Abortion is legal only in order to save the life, physical health, or mental health of the woman.

The government harasses many small Protestant churches and the Jehovah's Witnesses. It began closing all nonregistered places of worship in 2001 and in 2002 began stopping religious meetings of more than three to five people in private homes. Members of nonrecognized religions are regularly harassed, arrested, and sometimes tortured. The level of harassment has been steadily increasing. In 2004 possessing a bible was grounds for arrest, and entire families, including children, were arrested for holding religious services in their homes. There are also reports of police forcing people to sign agreements to give up their evangelical beliefs and return to the Orthodox Church and of forced conscription of Protestant youths.

Jehovah's Witnesses are among the most severely harassed. In part this is due to their conscientious objection to military service. The government restricts what it considers fundamentalist Islam by banning preaching by foreign preachers and monitoring closely all Muslim missionary groups.[33]

Niger

Niger's 1999 constitution describes the state as nonconfessional and guarantees "the right of the free development of each individual in their spiritual, cultural, and religious dimensions."[34] It also bans political parties based on religion. Religious freedom is respected, as indicated by the fact that Niger is one of

---

[33] "Eritrean Government Confiscates Full Gospel Church," *Human Rights Without Frontiers*, October 30, 2003; "Silent Vigil in London for 375 Evangelicals and Pentecostals in Prison," *Human Rights Without Frontiers*, May 11, 2004; "Christian Families Jailed for Praying Together," *Human Rights Without Frontiers*, April 2, 2004; "Eritrean Commanders Intensify Harsh Measures" *Human Rights Without Frontiers*, August 27, 2003; "Eritrea Arrests, Conscripts More Protestant Christians," *Human Rights Without Frontiers*, May 5, 2003, http://www.hrwf.net.

[34] I was unable to obtain an English-language copy of Niger's constitution so this description may be incomplete.

the few Muslim states that allows Muslims to convert to another religion. All religions must register and building places of worship requires government approval. There are no reports of the government refusing either. Foreign missionaries must work for groups registered with the government. The government does not favor any religion.

Violence and harassment by Muslims, usually members of fundamentalist organizations, against Christians and other minorities occasionally occurs. The government attempts to arrest and punish the perpetrators. After riots in 2000 the government banned six militant Islamic organizations, and an additional two in 2001. The latter two continued to call for Jihad and the imposition of Sharia law. In response the government arrested these organizations' leaders in 2002, charging them with incitement to revolt, but these leaders were released in 2003.[35]

SOME GENERAL OBSERVATIONS

Sub-Saharan Africa is one of the world's most diverse regions with regard to GIR. In some ways it is the most secular, with 26 of 46 countries maintaining at least moderate SRAS. This includes 8 states that score lower than 2 on the *general GIR* measure. Yet 6 states have active state religions.

Much of the diversity in the region can be explained by religious identity. All but one of the sub-Saharan African states with official religions are Muslim states. Yet, even among these Muslim states there is diversity. The region includes some of the world's most secular Muslim states. Of the 10 Muslim states that score below 20 on the *general GIR* score, 6 are in sub-Saharan Africa, including the 3 that score the lowest. In fact, these 3 states, Burkina Faso, Gambia, and Senegal, are representative of a uniquely sub-Saharan Africa form of tolerant Islam, where many practice Islam but do so privately and allow complete freedom and equality to other religions. With the possible exception of Albania, every other country in the world with a Muslim majority is not neutral with regard to Islam in the public sphere. Most support Islam, implementing some aspects of Sharia law as state law. All but one restrict the practice of minority religions. However, some take the opposite approach and repress Islam. The one non-sub-Saharan African Muslim state that does not restrict the practice of minority religions, Tajikistan, fits into this category.

All of this illuminates a larger and more important pattern. It appears that in the twenty-first century, states with Muslim majorities, for the most part, seem unable to remain neutral with regard to religion. While the findings of the RAS project show this to be true of all religious traditions, the analyses in Chapters 4 and 11 show that this is particularly true of Islam.

A second regional trend is the significant level of missionary activity in sub-Saharan Africa by both Christian and Muslim groups. Militant Islamic groups

---

[35] "Police in Niger Arrested 17 Moslem in Niger," Agence France Presse, September 18, 1996.

are active in African countries. This is occurring on several fronts. First, they are attempting to get states with Muslim populations to be more Islamic, including pushing for the implementation of Sharia law. In some countries, like Nigeria, this policy is implemented through local and regional governments despite opposition from national governments. Second, these groups are actively seeking to get individual Muslims to be more religious both in countries where Muslims are the majority and in countries where they are in the minority. The recruitment methods vary, but the most common is through welfare and foreign-supported Islamic schools. Third, some Muslim minorities, such as those in the Ivory Coast and Tanzania, are actively rebelling against their states. While these rebellions are not always religiously motivated, the potential for Muslim extremists to exploit these conflicts is significant. Fourth, there is increasing support for international Muslim terror groups. Given all of this, the uniquely tolerant brand of Islam that exists in several sub-Saharan African states is in danger.

Western Christian groups, particularly the Catholic Church and North American Protestant movements, are also active in sub-Saharan Africa. These groups seem to focus on individuals and the private sphere rather than the public sphere. Like the Muslim missionaries, they also accomplish their goals through education and welfare. In most cases, this recruitment is at the expense of traditional religions and previously existing Christian groups. In some countries, Eritrea for example, this causes considerable government hostility. All of this missionary activity by both Christians and Muslims is probably the reason that restrictions on proselytizing are among the most common restrictions on religious minorities in the region.

One of the reasons that Muslim and Christian groups have been successful is that many sub-Saharan African states are weak states that do not have the resources to fully control all of their territory and provide basic services. Many of them rely on religious groups to provide education and in some cases other services, such as welfare and medical services. Christian groups, especially the Catholic Church, seem to have the most developed networks, but the Muslim groups are not far behind. This weakness of central governments also provides a potential explanation for the low levels of GIR in many of the region's states; it is possible that governments do not interfere in religion because they have a limited ability to do so.

This relative weakness often allows local governments to set GIR policies that are at odds with those of the national government. In countries like Nigeria, local governments have used their discretion to legislate many aspects of the religion of the local populace into law, despite opposition by the national government. In such states as Benin, Senegal, Swaziland, and Uganda, local officials at the town, tribal, or village level harass members of minority religions. There are also many states, for example Burundi, Congo Brazzaville, the Ivory Coast, Rwanda, and Zaire, with rebel-controlled areas where the rebels attack clergy and places of worship.

In all, sub-Saharan Africa is a region in flux. This is true both politically and religiously. Regimes change more often in Africa than in any other region in the world and it has a high percentage of the world's active rebel movements and violent conflicts. This instability has contributed to the success of religious groups in influencing civil society and local governments. Whether this will lead to more dramatic changes at the national and regional levels remains to be seen, but it seems unlikely that all of this activity will not significantly influence a number of states in the region. Given all of this, religion is very much in play in sub-Saharan Africa.

10

Latin America

Latin America is relatively religiously homogeneous. The majority population in most states is Catholic, and most non-Catholics are Christian. The information presented in Tables 10.1, 10.2, 10.3, and 10.4, shows that nearly all Catholic states give preferential treatment to the Catholic Church. Four states, all Catholic states, have official religions, and an additional 12, also all Catholic, are coded as civil religion – which is defined by the RAS project as a case where one religion is clearly given preferential treatment compared to others, but this religion is not declared the official religion. Among the Catholic majority states, only Brazil, Ecuador, Mexico, and Uruguay do not give the Catholic Church preferential treatment. The pattern of non-Catholic majority states is nearly the opposite. Only Jamaica, among the 7 such states, gives preferential treatment to both Protestant and Catholic churches. Suriname supports all religions more or less equally. The other 5 are either neutral or hostile to religion.

Other than those having to do with conversion, all of the types of restrictions on minorities coded by the RAS project are present in Latin America, but none are common enough to be present in a majority of Latin American states. The most common forms of restrictions are registration requirements and limits on proselytizing, mostly through restrictions on visas for foreign religious workers. Thus, overall, Latin America is comparatively tolerant of its religious minorities.

Other than in Cuba and Guyana, there is very little regulation of the majority religion by Latin American states. Religious legislation is not uncommon in Latin America, but it is relatively homogeneous. The majority of all religious laws in Latin America fall into 1 of 5 categories that account for 105 of the 119 religious laws coded for the region by the RAS project. First, nearly all Latin American states restrict abortion. Second, 18 states fund religious education. Third, 15 provide some other form of funding for religion. Fourth, most have some form of registration requirement for religious organizations. Fifth, 11 have government departments that deal with religion.

Overall, based on the general GIR indicator, Latin American states have lower government involvement in religion (GIR) than any region except Africa. However, if one excludes non-Catholic states, the mean level of this variable

TABLE 10.1. *Separation of Religion and State in Latin America in 2002, Basic Information*

Country	Majority religion	% Majority religion	# Min. groups with 5 % of population	Official GIR	Official regulation	General GIR
Argentina	Catholic	91.0	1	One official religion	Practical limitations	30.00
Bahamas	Protestant	76.0	1	Accommodation	No limitations	1.88
Barbados	Protestant	65.0	2	Accommodation	No limitations	3.52
Belize	Catholic	76.0	3	Civil religion	Practical limitations	20.13
Bolivia	Catholic	85.0	1	One official religion	Practical limitations	33.71
Brazil	Catholic	75.0	1	Accommodation	No limitations	2.29
Chile	Catholic	77.0	2	Civil religion	Practical limitations	20.33
Colombia	Catholic	95.0	0	Civil religion	Practical limitations	19.92
Costa Rica	Catholic	76.3	2	One official religion	Practical limitations	31.61
Cuba	Mixed	39.0	2	Inadvertent insensitivity	Legal limitations	46.52
Dominican Rep.	Catholic	90.0	0	One official religion	Practical limitations	28.54
Ecuador	Catholic	94.1	0	Accommodation	No limitations	1.84
El Salvador	Catholic	77.5	1	Civil religion	Practical limitations	22.36
Guatemala	Catholic	65.0	1	Civil religion	No limitations	16.96
Guyana	Christian	32.0	4	Accommodation	No limitations	1.67
Haiti	Catholic	80.0	1	Civil religion	Practical limitations	21.98
Honduras	Catholic	86.1	1	Civil religion	Practical limitations	21.11
Jamaica	Protestant	56.0	2	Cooperation	Practical limitations	16.33
Mexico	Catholic	91.0	1	Separationist	No limitations	15.21
Nicaragua	Catholic	80.0	1	Civil religion	Practical limitations	19.50
Panama	Catholic	84.0	1	Civil religion	Practical limitations	22.36
Paraguay	Catholic	92.0	1	Civil religion	Practical limitations	20.96
Peru	Catholic	90.0	1	Civil religion	Practical limitations	22.00
Suriname	Mixed	27.4	3	Supportive	No limitations	6.50
Trinidad & Tobago	Mixed	30.7	4	Accommodation	No limitations	4.79
Uruguay	Catholic	74.2	1	Separationist	No limitations	8.54
Venezuela	Catholic	94.1	0	Civil religion	Practical limitations	22.21

TABLE 10.2. *Restrictions on Minority Religion in Latin America in 2002*

	Public observance	Build or repair places of worship	Access to places of worship	Forced observance	Formal orgs.	Education	Arrest, detention, harassment	Materials	Publications	Personal status	Clergy	Proselytizing	Registration	Other	Total
Argentina													x		1
Bahamas															0
Barbados	x				x										2
Belize															0
Bolivia							x		x		x		x		4
Brazil												x			1
Chile											x		x		2
Colombia													x		1
Costa Rica			x												1
Cuba	x	x	x		x	x	x	x	x		x	x	x		11
Dominican Rep.													x		1
Ecuador															0
El Salvador												x	x	x	3
Guatemala							x						x	x	3
Guyana				x											1
Haiti															0
Honduras												x			1
Jamaica							x			x					3
Mexico															0
Nicaragua															0
Panama												x			1
Paraguay													x		1
Peru															0
Suriname															0
Trinidad & Tobago												x			1
Uruguay															0
Venezuela	x											x			2
TOTAL	3	1	2	1	2	1	4	1	2	1	3	7	9	2	39

The following categories of religious restrictions were not included in this table because none of these countries engage in these practices: forced conversions; conversions.

TABLE 10.3. *Government Regulation of the Majority Religion in Latin America in 2002*

	Political parties	Arrest, detention, harassment	Orgs.	Public observance	Speech	Access to places of worship	Publications	Arrest nonleaders	Public gatherings	Other	Total
Argentina											0
Bahamas											0
Barbados										x	1
Belize											0
Bolivia										x	1
Brazil											0
Chile											0
Colombia											0
Costa Rica					x					x	2
Cuba	x	x	x	x	x	x	x	x	x	x	10
Dominican Rep.											0
Ecuador											0
El Salvador										x	1
Guatemala	x									x	2
Guyana											0
Haiti										x	1
Honduras										x	1
Jamaica											0
Mexico	x		x	x	x				x	x	6
Nicaragua											0
Panama										x	1
Paraguay											0
Peru											0
Suriname											0
Trinidad & Tob.											0
Uruguay											0
Venezuela											0
TOTAL	3	1	2	2	3	1	1	1	2	10	26

The following categories of government regulation were not included in this table because none of these countries engage in these practices: public display.

TABLE 10.4. *Religious Legislation in Latin America in 2002*

	Personal status	Blasphemy	Close businesses	Optional educ.	Mandatory education	Fund educ.	Fund rel. charity	Fund clergy	Other rel. funding	Some clergy appointed	Gov. rel. dept.	Legislature/ cabinet	Abortion	Registration	Sects	Other	Total
Argentina				x		x			x		x		x	x			6
Bahamas				x		x			x				x	x			6
Barbados												x	x				2
Belize				x		x						x	x			x	5
Bolivia				x		x		x	x		x		x	x		x	8
Brazil				x		x							x				3
Chile				x		x							x		x		4
Colombia				x		x							x	x			4
Costa Rica	x			x		x		x	x				x	x			7
Cuba											x			x			2
Domin. Rep.						x			x		x		x	x			5
Ecuador					x												1
El Salvador											x		x	x			3
Guatemala				x		x							x	x			4
Guyana													x			x	2
Haiti				x		x		x		x	x		x	x			7
Honduras													x	x		x	3
Jamaica													x	x			4
Mexico											x		x	x			3
Nicaragua						x			x				x	x			4
Panama				x		x					x		x	x			5
Paraguay									x		x		x	x		x	5
Peru				x		x	x	x		x	x		x	x		x	8
Suriname			x	x		x	x				x		x				4
Trin. & Tob.		x		x		x			x		x		x	x			7
Uruguay											x		x	x			3
Venezuela						x		x			x		x	x			7
TOTAL	1	1	1	15	1	18	2	5	8	2	11	2	25	20	1	6	119

The following categories of religious legislation were not included in this table because none of these countries engage in these practices: dietary laws; alcohol; inheritance; conversions; marriages; public dress; censorship; blue laws; taxes; approve clergy & speeches; religious position for government official; government position for religious official; religious requirements; religious courts; flag; identity cards; sects; women.

TABLE 10.5. *Taxonomy of Latin America*

Separation of religion and state	Type of restrictions on minorities			
	None	Low (1–2)	Moderate (3–5)	High (6+)
Religious state				
Active state religion				
State-controlled religion				
Historical / cultural state religion		Costa Rica		
		Argentina Dominican Republic	Bolivia	
Preferred treatment for some religions or support for a particular tradition	Belize Haiti Nicaragua Peru	Chile Colombia Honduras *Jamaica* Panama Paraguay Venezuela	El Salvador Guatemala	
General support				
Moderate separation	*Bahamas*	Brazil *Trinidad & Tobago*		
Nearly full separation (2 or less on legislation)	*Barbados* Ecuador	Guyana		
	Suriname			
Hostility	Mexico Uruguay			*Cuba*

Italics = non-Catholic

rises from 17.88 to 19.35, which is about the same as the average score for Western democracies. The non-Catholic states score 12.74, which is lower than the score for any of the other world regions. This demonstrates a clear difference in the relationship between religion and state in Latin American Catholic and non-Catholic majority states.

The categorization of Latin American states into the taxonomy used here is presented in Table 10.5.

ACTIVE STATE RELIGIONS

Costa Rica

Article 75 of Costa Rica's 1997 constitution declares the Roman Catholic and Apostolic religion the state's official religion and requires that the state contribute to its maintenance, but protects freedom of worship for other religions "that are not opposed to universal morality or good customs." Article 28 bans the use of religion in political propaganda. Article 74 states that the enumeration of civil rights in the constitution "does not exclude others that may be derived from the Christian principle of social justice or established by law." Article 131 requires that the president be a layperson. The oath for public officials in Article 194 contains two mentions of God.

Government funding for the Catholic Church includes salaries for clergy, funds for buildings, tax exemptions, and occasional land donations for Catholic churches. Religious groups register in the same manner as lay groups in order to have the status of a legal entity. Any group engaged in fund-raising must register. Religious education is optional in public schools. The religion teachers must be certified by the Catholic Church, which does not certify teachers in other religions. Catholic marriage ceremonies are automatically recognized by the state. The Catholic Church is often invited to participate in state policy issues such as labor negotiations. Abortion is legal in order to save the life and health of the woman. While the law is not specific on the topic, this is usually interpreted to include her mental health.

With a few exceptions, Costa Rica promotes religious freedom. Advocacy groups report that the Unification Church has been declared a dangerous sect and there are reports of local governments closing non-Catholic churches due to complaints over noise and traffic.[1]

HISTORICAL OR CULTURAL STATE RELIGIONS

Low Restrictions on Minorities

Argentina

Section 2 of Argentina's constitution states that "the Federal Government supports the Roman Catholic Apostolic religion." Article 14 guarantees the right

---

[1] Boyle & Sheen (1997).

to profess a religion. Article 20 grants foreigners the right to practice their religions. Article 19 states that "the private actions of men which in no way offend public order or morality, nor injure a third party, are only reserved to God and are exempted from the authority of judges." Article 93 states that the oaths for president and vice president should respect their religious beliefs. The preamble includes religious imagery. A 1994 amendment removed the requirement (formerly in Article 76) that the president and vice president be Catholic.

The government provides the Catholic Church with a variety of subsidies worth several million dollars. Relations between the government and all religions are regulated through the Secretariat of Worship in the Ministry of Foreign Affairs, International Trade, and Worship. All religious organizations must register with the Secretariat in order to carry out public worship. Private worship does not require registration. Public education is secular but students may request religious education, which is sometimes given in public schools. Abortion is legal to save the life or health of the woman, though it is unclear whether this includes mental health. The law is also unclear on whether abortion is legal in cases of rape.

While the government generally respects religious freedom, there are reports that non-Catholic churches sometimes encounter significant bureaucratic obstacles to obtaining permission for religious activities. It is unclear whether these obstacles are discriminatory or due to bureaucratic inefficiency. Foreign missionaries must register with the government but are otherwise allowed to act freely. The Secretary for Religious Affairs maintains that "non-Catholic creeds have other status, not inferior, but different." A 1988 law makes discrimination on the basis of religion illegal.

Dominican Republic

The Dominican Republic's 1996 constitution provides for religious freedom "subject to respect for public order and good customs."[2] Religious discrimination is illegal. The government has a concordant with the Vatican that gives the Catholic religion special privileges, including funds for rehabilitating church facilities and a waiver on customs and duties. It is unclear whether this concordant makes Catholicism the official religion of the country. All other religions must register with the government and may request the same customs and duty waiver granted to the Catholic Church. The only religious marriages given civil recognition are those performed by the Catholic Church. The police force encourages its officers to attend mass, but this is not required and the only chaplains for the military are Catholic ones. According to a 2000 law the Bible must be read in public schools, but this law is not enforced. Abortion is illegal but the general principles of criminal legislation allow abortions in cases of necessity.[3]

---

[2] I was unable to obtain an English-language version of the Dominican Republic's constitution so this description may be incomplete.

[3] "Library of Congress Country Studies: The Dominican Republic," http://countrystudies.us.

Moderate Restrictions on Minorities

Bolivia

Article 3 of Bolivia's constitution "recognizes and upholds the Roman Catholic Apostolic Religion." Article 3 also guarantees religious freedom and declares that Bolivia's relationship with the Catholic Church is governed by a concordant.[4] The government provides limited funds to the Church, including stipends to about 300 priests. Optional Catholic religious education is available in public schools.

A 2000 presidential decree requires groups, including religious ones, to consult civil authorities before holding large public gatherings, in order to address concerns including traffic. The previous rule required government permission for such meetings. The decree also requires the signature of a public notary on the fund-raising reports of religious groups in order to prevent money laundering. Clergy are not allowed to hold the offices of president or vice-president and may not run for national representative unless they resign their religious position 60 days before the election.

While the government generally respects religious freedom, there are some exceptions and preferential treatment is given to the Catholic Church. The government requires non-Catholic religious groups to register. Registration is rarely denied but the registration process is expensive and time consuming causing some groups to abandon attempts to register. However, there are no apparent restrictions on worship by nonregistered groups. In the 1980s the Hare Krishnas were denied registration as a religious group but continue to operate as an educational group. Advocacy groups claim that there have been limitations on the distribution of literature by the Unification Church and minor harassment of its officials by government officials. There are similar reports of harassment of members of Evangelical faiths. In 1994 the army began banning non-Catholic clergy from military bases.

Abortion is permitted only to save the life, physical health, or mental health of the woman, or in cases of rape and incest.

PREFERRED TREATMENT FOR SOME RELIGIONS OR SUPPORT FOR A PARTICULAR TRADITION

As noted, this category is the most common in Latin America and includes 13 countries, nearly half the countries in the region. Nine of these countries engage in some restrictions on minority religions.

---

[4] I was unable to obtain an English-language copy of Bolivia's constitution so this description may be incomplete. The text of Article 3 of the constitution is available at "Handbook on Religious Liberty Around the World," http://religiousfreedom.lib.virginia.edu/rihand/.

No Restrictions on Minorities

Belize

Article 11 of Belize's constitution includes detailed guarantees for religious freedom. Article 11 also guarantees that no one in prison, serving in the military, or attending a place of education will be required to "receive religious instruction or to take part in or attend any religious ceremony or observance if that instruction, ceremony or observance relates to a religion other than his own." It guarantees religious institutions the right to educate without interference regardless of whether they receive financial support from the government. It prohibits requiring anyone to take an oath contrary to their religious beliefs. It also states that these protections cannot be contrary to "defense, public safety, public order, public morality or public health; or for the purpose of protecting the rights and freedoms of other persons" as well as "for the purpose of regulating educational institutions in the interest of the persons who receive or may receive instruction in them." Article 3 protects freedom of conscience regardless of creed. According to a 2002 amendment one of the country's senators is appointed by the governor general on the advice of the Belize Council of Churches and the Evangelical Association of Churches. The preamble includes religious imagery. The "Oath of Allegiance and Office" optionally ends with the phrase "so help me God."

Foreign religious workers can work and proselytize freely but they must obtain a religious worker's permit. The country's education system includes religion in the curriculum and attendance at religious ceremonies. Most educational institutions are church-affiliated. However, students can opt out of religion classes. Abortion is permitted to save the life, physical health, or mental health of the woman, as well as in cases of fetal impairment. It is also permitted for economic and social reasons. It is not available upon request, or in cases of rape or incest.

Belize's civic culture is strongly influenced by Roman Catholicism and politicians generally avoid taking positions that overtly contradict Catholic positions.[5]

Haiti

Article 30 of Haiti's 1987 constitution guarantees religious freedom "provided the exercise of that right does not disturb law and order." It also protects against being forced to join a religious organization and receiving religious education contrary to one's convictions, and states that "the law establishes the conditions for recognition and practice of religions and faiths." Article 55 gives the right to aliens to own property necessary for religious purposes. The oaths of office for the president and members of the High Court of Justice, in Articles 135 and 187, include mentions of God.

---

[5] US Library of Congress Country Studies: Belize, http://countrystudies.us.

While the 1987 constitution ended the Catholic Church's role as the country's official religion, the Catholic Church remains important. According to an 1860 concordant that is still in effect, the country's Catholic bishops are paid by the state and nominated by the president of the republic. A number of official and semi-official government events are held in Catholic churches. Religions must register with the Bureau of Religious Affairs. There are no reports of registration being refused and groups that do not register are allowed to practice freely. It is illegal for religious schools to require that students receive religious education, though providing such education to willing students is legal. This is significant because about 85 percent of schools in Haiti are private and many of these private schools are religious schools. Officially abortion is allowed only to save the life of the woman. In practice it is allowed to preserve the physical health of the mother as well as in cases of rape, incest, and fetal impairment.

Nicaragua

Nicaragua's constitution guarantees religious freedom and prohibits discrimination on the basis of religion.[6] There is no official religion, but the Catholic Church has a distinct prominence in the country. Government officials routinely meet with senior Church officials and the Church is sometimes given important tasks, such as distributing relief goods after a national disaster. In the past the government funded purely religious church activities. Registration is necessary to have legal status, but many nonregistered groups operate freely. Mandatory special visas for foreign religious workers are rarely refused but those obtaining them often encounter bureaucratic delays. Religion is not taught in the public schools, but the government funds many private Catholic schools. Abortion is legal to save the life of the woman. The law also allows "therapeutic" abortions but does not define "therapeutic."

Peru

Article 2 of Peru's constitution bans discrimination on the basis of religion and guarantees religious freedom "as it does not cause moral offense or public disorder." Article 2 includes the right to keep one's religious convictions secret. Article 14 states that "religious education is imparted with respect for liberty of conscience." Article 37 bans the extradition of people being persecuted on the basis of religion. Article 50 states that "within an independent and autonomous regime, the State recognizes the Catholic Church as an important element in the historical, cultural and moral formation of Peru, and renders its collaboration." It also states that "the State respects other religious denominations and may establish mechanisms of collaboration with them as well." The preamble includes religious imagery.

---

[6] I was unable to obtain an English-language version of Nicaragua's constitution so this description may be incomplete.

The Catholic Church has a preferred status in Peru based on a 1980 concordant that gives it a legal status independent from the state. In contrast, other religions must register as associations in order to operate legally. Non-Peruvian Catholic clergy are granted automatic visas to enter the country while other clergy must apply for religious visas. Catholic clergy are exempt from income taxes and some get income subsidies from the government. The government also gives direct subsidies to each diocese in the country. By law all public and private school curriculums must include religious education, which is generally available only in Catholicism. The teachers of these courses must be approved by the local bishop. Parents must specifically request that their children be exempted from this education. There have been instances where such requests were denied. Non-Catholics may organize, at their own expense, religious classes in other religions. Some schools have been exempted from this law. Marriages performed by the Catholic Church are given legal recognition in some circumstances.

The church also exerts considerable political influence. For example, the head of the Catholic Church in Peru, Cardinal Cipriani, was instrumental in the resignation of former Prime Minister Beatrice Merino. Abortion is legal only to save the life, physical health, or mental health of the woman.

During the country's internal conflict, between 1980 and 1995, Marxist terrorist groups targeted members of Evangelist and Mormon churches.[7]

Low Restrictions on Minorities Religions

Chile

Article 19 of Chile's 1980 constitution provides for religious freedom. Article 6 allows religious communities to erect and maintain places of worship, protects the rights of religious institutions, and grants them tax-exempt status. The preamble includes religious imagery.

The 1999 Law of Worship expands upon these rights including detailed protection for religious freedom and a ban on discrimination on the basis of religion. This law officially gives non-Catholic religions the same status as the Catholic Church but this is not always followed in practice. The law provides for the registration of religious organizations and states that the government may not deny registration, but in practice registration is often cumbersome. The law allows non-Catholic chaplains equal access to hospitals and prisons but an absence of implementation laws allows local officials to arbitrarily restrict access.

The military has tried to block efforts to appoint non-Catholic chaplains and sometimes requires recruits to attend Catholic events. Public events often include a Catholic mass. Schools are required to offer optional religious education, which, in practice, is nearly exclusively Catholic. In 1995 the government

---

[7] García-Montúfar, Solis, & Isaacson (2004).

passed a law forbidding disturbances on the streets. Some interpret this law as targeted against Evangelical groups engaging in street witnessing. There exists a parliamentary commission on cults, which investigates what it considers cults, including the Jehovah's Witnesses. I found no evidence of activity by this body other than hearing testimony and writing reports during 2001.

Abortion is illegal, though some argue that it may be legal in order to save the life of the woman based on the principle of self-defense. In practice, illegal abortion is common.[8]

Colombia

Article 13 of Colombia's constitution prohibits discrimination on the basis of religion. Article 18 guarantees freedom of conscience. Article 19 provides for the religious freedom and the equality of all religions and churches before the law. Article 42 grants civil status to religious marriages and annulments. Article 67 prohibits mandatory religious instruction in public schools. The preamble and the oath for the president in Article 192 include religious imagery.

The 1994 Law of Worship elaborates on these rights and freedoms. It provides for SRAS and includes detailed protections for freedom of religion, and autonomy and rights of religious institutions. The penal code bans restrictions on the free exercise of worship.

There are numerous laws regulating non-Catholic religious entities. Religious organizations may register as either legal entities or religious ones. Foreign missionaries require special two-year visas and must be sponsored by a registered religion. Non-Catholic religions must be granted accession to a 1997 agreement in order to send chaplains to public places like hospitals and prisons and for civil recognition of religious marriages. Optional religious education is available in public schools in Catholicism and religions that have acceded to the 1997 agreement. The Catholic Church provides all education in rural areas with no public schools. Abortion is illegal but the general principles of criminal legislation allow abortions in order to save the life of the woman.

Religious leaders have been the targets of kidnappings, killings, and extortion by armed rebel groups though this seems to be politically motivated.

Honduras

Honduras' constitution protects religious freedom "provided that they do not violate law and public policy" and grants the president the power to give "judicial personality" to religious organizations.[9] This status is necessary for certain privileges, including tax exemptions, but not to practice one's religion freely. The Ministry of Government and Justice handles these applications, which are rarely refused. Foreign missionaries are required to obtain entry

---

[8] Elizabeth H. Brooke, "Latin America May Outpace U.S. in Abortions," *New York Times*, April 12, 1994, p. 5.

[9] I was unable to obtain an English-language version of Honduras' constitution so this description may be incomplete.

permits and visas, but these are rarely refused. Legally people can be deported for witchcraft, but this law is rarely, if ever, invoked. However, missionaries of religions that claim to use witchcraft or satanic rituals are denied visas. The government has declared the Unification Church a dangerous sect and does not allow entry of its missionaries. In 1997 the government expelled over 100 Unification Church members.

While there is no official religion, the Catholic Church has close relations with the government. The armed forces have an official saint. The government often consults the Church on policy issues like education and foreign debt. Also, the government sometimes appoints Catholic clergy to head government commissions on official issues. However, clergy are forbidden from otherwise engaging in politics and using religion for political ends. A 2001 law requires ten minutes of bible reading at the beginning of every school day, but the law has yet to be implemented. All abortions are illegal but, in practice, are allowed to save the woman's life.

Jamaica

Article 21 of Jamaica's constitution includes detailed guarantees for religious freedom, and states that students cannot be forced to take religion classes or participate in religious ceremonies in a religion other than their own, and no one can be forced to take an oath contrary to that person's religious beliefs. Article 21 also protects the autonomy of religious organizations. These rights can be limited "in the interests of defense, public safety, public order, public morality or public health; or for the purpose of protecting the rights and freedoms of other persons." Article 13 guarantees freedom of conscience, regardless of creed. Article 24 bans discrimination based on creed. The oaths contained in the first schedule all end with the phrase "so help me God."

There is religious education in public schools through junior secondary school, provided by Catholic and Protestant churches. Church properties must register with the government but there is no mandatory registration of religions. Recognition by parliament grants certain rights to religious organizations, including tax breaks and the ability for clergy to visit prisoners. Rastifarians claim that the police discriminate against them, but this discrimination is likely due to their ritual marijuana use. Abortion is legal in order to save the life, physical health, or mental health of the woman, and requires the spouse's consent. In cases of mental health, fetal impairment, rape, and incest, the approval of two specialists is required.

Panama

Article 34 of Panama's constitution[10] recognizes Roman Catholicism as "the religion of the majority of Panamanians," but does not designate it as the official religion. Article 34 also guarantees religious freedom, as long as people

---

[10] I was unable to obtain an English-language version of Panama's constitution so this description may be incomplete.

respect "Christian morality and public order." The constitution gives religions with "juridical capacity" the freedom to manage their own affairs. In practice this status is rarely refused by the government. Article 101 states that Catholicism should be taught in public schools, but these classes are optional. Religious leaders may not hold public office except for positions dealing with scientific research, education, and social assistance. Senior officials in religious hierarchies must be native Panamanians.

The Catholic Archbishop has the privilege of immunity, which is usually given only to government officials. Most foreign religious workers need to register with the government every 15 months in a bureaucratically intensive process that includes an AIDS test and a police certificate of good conduct, but this registration is rarely refused except to members of the Unification Church. Foreign Catholic workers use a streamlined process that must be repeated once every five years. Abortion is legal in order to preserve the life or physical health of the woman, as well as in cases of rape or incest.

Paraguay

Article 24 of Paraguay's constitution protects religious freedom, declares that the state is secular, and declares that "relations between the State and the Catholic Church are based on independence, cooperation, and autonomy." Article 24 also guarantees the independence of other religions. However, Article 82 recognizes "the role played by the Catholic Church in the historical and cultural formation of the Republic." Article 37 recognizes the right of conscientious objection. Article 63 protects the rights of "Indian peoples," including their religious rights. Article 74 guarantees the right to religious education. Article 88 protects workers from discrimination on the basis of religion. Articles 197 and 235 forbid ministers and clergy from serving in the government's legislative body or as president or vice-president. The preamble includes the phrase "pleading to God."

All religions are required to register with the government, but many small churches have not done so and operate freely. The Catholic chaplaincy in the military is so large, that the Catholic Church appoints a bishop to oversee the program. The Catholic Church often performs mass at government functions. The government funds Catholic activities and tends to give preference to Catholic clergy over other clergy. Abortion is legal only in order to save the life of the woman.

Venezuela

Article 65 of Venezuela's constitution guarantees religious freedom, "provided it is not contrary to the public order or to good customs." The constitution also does not allow religion to justify breaking the law or violating the rights of others, and subjects religions to "supreme inspection of the national Executive, in conformity with the law."[11] A 1964 concordant with the Catholic Church

---

[11] I was unable to obtain an English-language version of Venezuela's constitution so this description may be incomplete.

gives it preferential treatment. Several religious groups receive government funding. The majority is given to the Catholic Church because the funds given to religions other than the Catholic Church are limited by law. This funding includes money for Catholic schools, salaries, and Catholic charities. All members of the military chaplain corps are Catholic. Non-Catholic groups must register in order to have official status. Abortion is legal only in order to save the life of the woman. In 1997 the government began to restrict "new religious movements." This included revoking the registration of the Unification Church.[12]

Moderate Restrictions on Minorities

El Salvador

Article 25 of El Salvador's constitution provides for religious freedom. Article 26 specifically recognizes the Catholic Church, giving it legal status. The constitution also prohibits discrimination on the basis of religion and requires the president and a number of other government officials to be laypersons.[13] Registration is not required but is necessary to gain legal status. Foreign religious workers who wish to proselytize or actively promote a religion must obtain a special visa. Those with standard visitor visas may not proselytize. According to a 1996 law, the government oversees the finances of religious organizations but the Catholic Church is exempted from this requirement. Abortion is illegal in El Salvador but it is a matter of dispute whether necessity to save the life of the woman can justify an abortion. Until 1997 abortions to save the life of the woman were explicitly legal.

Guatemala

Guatemala's constitution protects religious freedom. While there is no state religion, the constitution explicitly recognizes the legal status of the Catholic Church. The constitution allows, but does not require, religious education in public schools.[14] The government sometimes provides funds to schools established by religious organizations. Minority religions are required to register as legal entities in order to rent or own property. Registration requires 25 members and the organization must submit its by-laws. While registration is rarely refused, the process can take several years. Due to a lack of political will to enforce existing laws, Guatemala's indigenous peoples do not have full access to their traditional ceremonial sites, which are often controlled by the ministry of culture. Indigenous peoples wanting to perform rituals are often charged the

---

[12] Kenneth D. MacHarg, "Venezuela Restricts Unification Church," *Christianity Today*, November 17, 1997.
[13] I was unable to obtain an English-language version of El Salvador's constitution so this description may be incomplete.
[14] I was unable to obtain an English-language version of Guatemala's constitution so this description may be incomplete.

same entrance fees as are tourists visiting the sites. Clergy are often targeted for violence due to their involvement in political and human rights activism. Abortion is legal only to save the life of the woman.

GENERAL SUPPORT

Suriname
Article 8 of Suriname's constitution bans discrimination on the basis of religion. Article 18 guarantees religious freedom. Article 28 guarantees several workers' rights independent of religion. The oaths of office for several public offices, in Articles 65, 93, 114, and 125, contain the optional phrase "so help me God Almighty." Religious instruction is available in some public schools on a voluntary basis. Also, some parts of the public school system are operated by religious organizations. Abortion is legal only in order to save the life of the woman.

MODERATE SEPARATION

All of the countries in this category engage in either no restrictions on minority religions or low levels of restrictions.

The Bahamas
Article 22 of the Bahamas' constitution includes detailed guarantees for religious freedom. It also guarantees that places of education cannot require anyone to "receive religious instruction or to take part in or attend any religious ceremony or observance of that instruction, [where that] ceremony or observance relates to a religion other than his own." It guarantees religious institutions the right to educate without interference, regardless of whether they receive financial support from the government. It prohibits requiring anyone to take an oath contrary to their religious beliefs. Finally, it states that these protections cannot be contrary to "defense, public safety, public order, public morality or public health; or for the purpose of protecting the rights and freedoms of other persons." The government may also take actions "reasonably justifiable in a democratic society." The preamble contains religious imagery.

There is no registration requirement for religions, but they must incorporate legally in order to acquire lands. Religion is taught as an academic topic in all schools and is included in standardized achievement exams. This education focuses on Christianity, but also includes other religions. The right to opt out of these classes is respected, but rarely exercised. Abortion is legal in order to save the life, physical health, or mental health of the woman. Legal interpretation generally allows abortion in cases of rape, incest, and fetal impairment.

Brazil
Article 5 of Brazil's constitution protects religious freedom, provides for "the protection of places of worship and their rites," and states that religious belief

does not exempt people from obligations placed on all citizens but does allow for "an alternative obligation established by law." Article 143 requires the military to provide alternative service options for conscientious objectors and exempts clergy from military service in times of peace. Article 19 forbids the government from "establishing religious cults or churches, subsidizing them, hampering their operation or maintaining with them or their representatives relations of dependency or alliance, with the exception of cooperation for the public interest, as set forth in the law." Article 201 includes a Christmas bonus in the country's social security plan. Article 210 provides for optional religious education in public schools. Article 213 allows the funding of religious schools. Article 226 recognizes religious marriages as having "civil effects." The preamble includes religious imagery.

The law prohibits discrimination on the basis of religion and there is a hate crime law that includes religious hate. There are limitations on missionaries in official indigenous areas. Abortion is legal only to save the life of the woman or in cases of rape.

Trinidad & Tobago

Article 4 of the country's constitution guarantees religious freedom and bans discrimination on the basis of religion. The preamble includes religious imagery.

Religions must register in order to obtain benefits including tax exemptions, but registration is not obligatory. Religious education is available on a voluntary basis in public schools by instructors provided by religious organizations. The government also subsidizes religious schools. The government gives financial grants to religious organizations and subsidizes religious festivals and celebrations. It is illegal to commit acts that insult another person or group on the basis of religion or that would incite religious hatred. Foreign missionaries are allowed to act freely but they are limited to 35 per denomination. The only group to maintain the maximum number of missionaries is the Mormons. The government monitors the Jamaat al Muslimeen, a radical Muslim organization, due to its participation in a 1990 coup. It also monitors other radical Muslim organizations. Abortion is legal only in order to preserve the life, physical health, or mental health of the woman.

NEAR FULL SEPARATION

All of the countries in this category engage in either no restrictions on minority religions or low levels of restrictions.

Barbados

Article 19 of Barbados' constitution includes detailed guarantees for religious freedom. It guarantees that no one attending a place of education will be required to "receive religious instruction or to take part in or attend any religious ceremony or observance of that instruction, ceremony or observance relates to a religion other than his own." It guarantees religious institutions the right to educate without interference regardless of whether they receive financial support from the government. It prohibits requiring anyone to take an oath contrary to their religious beliefs. Finally, it states that these protections cannot be contrary to "defense, public safety, public order, public morality or public health; or for the purpose of protecting the rights and freedoms of other persons." Article 36 provides for the appointment to the senate of "religious, economic or social interests or such other interests as the Governor-General considers ought to be represented." Article 44 disqualifies clerks in holy orders and other ministers of religion from membership in the national assembly. The preamble acknowledges the "supremacy of God." The oaths contained in the constitution include the phrase "so help me God."

Religious education is included as "values education" in the public school curriculum and focuses on Christianity, but speakers from other religions are also invited. Registration is required only in order to gain tax benefits. Abortion is legal to save the life, physical health, or mental health of the woman, as well as in cases of rape, incest, and fetal impairment. It is also allowed for economic or social reasons, but is not available on request. For the first 12 weeks of gestation the procedure must be authorized by 1 physician, between 12 and 20 weeks, 2 physicians, and, after 20 weeks, 3 physicians. The woman must also receive counseling before the procedure.

Ecuador
Article 19 of Ecuador's constitution provides for religious freedom, with the exception of restrictions "proscribed by law to protect and respect the diversity, plurality, security, and rights of others." Article 27 declares that public education is secular. The constitution also prohibits discrimination on the basis of religion.[15] There is no registration requirement for religions unless they engage in commercial activity or wish to obtain the status of a legal entity. Religious education is prohibited in public schools but allowed in private ones. Ministers of religion may not run for president or congress. The Papal Nuncio is, according to custom, the dean of the country's diplomatic corps. Abortion is legal only in order to preserve the life or health of the woman. The law is unclear as to whether this includes mental health. It is also legal in cases of rape or incest, when the woman is considered insane or an "idiot."

Guyana
Article 1 of Guyana's constitution declares Guyana a secular state. Article 145 includes detailed guarantees for religious freedom. Article 145 also states that students cannot be forced to take religion classes or participate in religious ceremonies in a religion other than their own and no one can be forced to take

[15] I was unable to obtain an English-language version of Ecuador's constitution so this description may be incomplete.

an oath contrary to his religious beliefs. These rights can be limited "in the interests of defense, public safety, public order, public morality or public health; or for the purpose of protecting the rights and freedoms of other persons." Article 149 prohibits discrimination on the basis of creed. Article 40 protects a number of basic rights regardless of creed.

All religious organizations are required to register. There are no instances of such registration being refused. Advocacy groups claim that despite constitutional guarantees, non-Christians are forced to receive religious instruction in public schools under the guise of moral education and, in some cases, are required to attend religious ceremonies.[16]

HOSTILITY

No Restrictions on Minorities Religions

Mexico

Article 3 of Mexico's constitution requires that education not include any religious doctrine and that clergy and religious institutions "shall not in any way participate" in educational institutions. Article 5 forbids the establishment of monastic orders. Article 24 provides religious freedom "provided [acts] do not constitute an offense punishable by law." Article 24 also restricts all public worship to places of worship, "which shall at all times be under governmental supervision." Article 27 forbids religious institutions from owning property and orders the nationalization of all religious properties, though the government is allowed to let the religious organizations continue using the property. Article 27 also declares that "all places of public worship hereafter erected shall be the property of the Nation." Article 55 forbids clergy from being elected to congress. A 2001 amendment prohibits discrimination on the basis of religion.

Article 130 includes detailed instructions for the regulation of religion in Mexico. It declares the authority of the federal government to regulate religion and that churches cannot exist as legal entities. Local legislatures may limit the number of clergy. All clergy must be Mexican citizens. Clergy may not criticize the state or participate in politics. Religious periodicals may not comment on political or public issues. Places of worship may not be built without government consent. All places of worship must have an official who assures compliance with government regulations. Political organizations may not be in any way associated with a religion. Political meetings may not take place in places of worship. However, Article 130 also places some limits on governmental regulation of religions. For example, "congress cannot enact laws establishing or prohibiting any religion." The government may not interfere in programs for training clergy.

---

[16] Swami Aksharananda, "Christian Hegemony Continues in Guyana," *Tabroek News*, September 11, 1999.

A 1992 law changed some of these constitutional restrictions. Places of worship built after 1992 belong to the religious organizations that built them. Religious meetings can be held outside places of worship, but only with government approval. The law lifts the limits on the number of clergy. It also requires religions to register with the government in order to operate legally and establishes the Director for Religious Affairs of the Federal Secretariat of Government.

Religious education is not permitted in public schools but private religious schools are legal. Religious organizations may not own or operate television or radio stations and government permission is required to transmit religious programming. This permission is generally granted. The Catholic Church operates a national cable channel. There are multiple reports of harassment and attacks against non-Catholics in some rural areas. The national government tries to prevent this type of behavior with mixed success. Federal law allows abortion only to save the life of the woman, or in cases of incest. However, this applies only in the federal district. Abortion laws are determined at the state level. While some state laws are less restrictive than the federal law, none allows abortion on demand.

Uruguay

Uruguay's constitution declares that the state supports no religion. It guarantees religious freedom and prohibits discrimination on the basis of religion.[17] Religious education in public schools is prohibited. Religious bodies must register as a religion every five years in order to obtain tax exemptions. The Catholic Church has been denied the right to a radio frequency on the grounds that "giving in to the wishes of the Catholic Church would be against the traditions of the Uruguayan people." Abortion is legal in order to preserve the life, physical health, or mental health of the woman. "The penalty for undergoing an abortion may be reduced or waived if the pregnancy results from rape or when there is economic hardship."[18]

High Restrictions on Minorities

Cuba

Article 10 of Cuba's 1992 constitution protects against discrimination on the basis of religion. Article 35 declares SRAS and protects the freedom of religion and worship "without other limitation than respect for Christian morality and public order." Article 55 declares that "official instruction shall be laic" but preserves the right to private religious education. Article 54 of the pre-1992 constitution contained references to atheism and scientific materialism.

---

[17] I was unable to obtain an English-language version of Uruguay's constitution so this description may be incomplete.

[18] "The Catholic Church Out To Woo Back the Faithful," *Inter Press Service*, July 22, 1992.

All religions must register with the government. In practice registration of new religions has been halted, but several unregistered religions are allowed to practice. As registered religions are the only legal associations outside of the government and Communist Party, unregistered religions are open to charges of being illegal associations. Only registered religions are allowed to import and distribute religious literature. Also, only they can obtain official permission to travel abroad and receive official visitors. The government has in practice restricted the number of foreign Catholic clergy who can enter the country. Since 1992, the Communist Party has allowed members who profess a religious faith. The government does not allow any private schools, including religious ones. The government restricts permits to build churches but generally allows registered groups to meet in private homes. Religious ceremonies and processions outside of official religious buildings require a government permit. Religious organizations must buy their office equipment, such as computers and photocopiers, from the government, which charges exorbitant prices. Most religious organizations are denied access to the Internet.

The government monitors all houses of worship and harasses private houses of worship. This includes police visits to clergy and monitors sent to religious services. While some private houses of worship have been allowed to operate without harassment, others have been subject to severe harassment, including closure. This harassment is targeted especially at Evangelical religions. The Jehovah's Witnesses are officially considered enemies of the revolution. However, in practice the government has eased restrictions on them and they are allowed to operate with only minor harassment from local officials. Members of the military are prohibited from allowing anyone in their family to observe religious practices, with the exception of elderly family members whose actions do not harm the revolution.

SOME GENERAL OBSERVATIONS

The major basis of diversity in GIR in Latin America is whether or not the state is Catholic. Catholic states tend to support Catholicism and non-Catholic states tend to have lower levels of GIR. On the RAS measures, this remained largely static between 1990 and 2002 though there have been some minor shifts, which are discussed in more detail in Chapter 11.

Perhaps the most important changes occurring in Latin America do not register on the RAS codings. People are converting away from Catholicism to Evangelical Christianity in large numbers. In the long term this is likely to influence the RAS codings as well as the basic relationship between the Catholic Church and the states where this demographic shift is occurring. In such situations there are three potential reactions. The government may choose to make no changes maintaining the status quo. Pressure from the Catholic Church and the remaining Catholics may cause the government to actively support the religion in order to preserve it. Or the government may recognize the reality of the situation and begin to distance itself from the Catholic Church.

Another interesting dynamic, documented by Anthony Gill, is the reaction of the Catholic Church to its loss of congregants. Gill argues that the Catholic clergy are more likely to support the opposition in countries where large numbers of people are converting away from Catholicism. This is because many feel that those leaving the Church are disaffected from the government and see the Catholic Church as supporting the government. Thus, challenging the government is a good tactic to prevent this loss of membership and, perhaps, to get some former members to return.[19] If this is true, it is likely that sustained Catholic opposition to a government may cause that government to reassess its support for the Catholic Church.

Given all of this, the relationship between religion and state in Latin America is potentially at a crossroads and is likely to change significantly in the next few decades.

---

[19] Gill (1998).

Patterns and Trends

As Chapters 5 to 10 have demonstrated in considerable detail, the relationship between religion and state is complex. Furthermore, the perspective from which one views this relationship influences one's conclusions regarding its nature. Chapter 4 provides a macro-level analysis that depicts a number of global trends. First, there has been little change in the basic structure of world government involvement in religion (GIR) – as measured by a state's official relationship with religion and the larger pattern of state treatment of religion. But there has been a shift toward more GIR when examining more specific manifestations of GIR, such as *religious discrimination* against minorities, regulation of the majority religion (*religious regulation*), and *religious legislation*. Second, there is a clear difference in the patterns of GIR between different religious traditions. Third, few states have separation of religion and state (SRAS), even when using relatively lax definitions of SRAS. Fourth, economic modernization is linked to higher GIR. Fifth, democracies are shown to have less GIR, on average, than nondemocracies.

However, the finer perspective employed in the regional and country breakdowns in Chapters 5 through 10, show that the macro-perspective does not present the entire picture. There are exceptions to each of the general trends revealed by the macro-level analysis. Some democracies have considerable levels of GIR. One of the world's most economically developed states, the USA, has a lower GIR score than any other state in the RAS database. While for the majority of states their 2002 GIR scores were higher or at the same level as their 1990 scores, many had lower scores than in 1990. The regional analyses showed considerable diversity within religious traditions. For example, the relationship between religion and state in former Soviet bloc Muslim majority states is very different from the relationship between religion and state in the Middle East.

The purpose of this chapter is to expand the perspectives from which this study examines the RAS data. This is accomplished through an intermediate level analysis, which sheds light on several important trends which the macro and micro analyses did not fully uncover. Specifically, it focuses on three aspects of the religious economy which fall between the micro and macro. First, it examines shifts between 1990 and 2002 in the 60 individual components of the *religious discrimination*, *religious regulation*, and *religious legislation* variables. Chapter 4 documented an overall rise in these variables but did not examine what aspects of these forms of GIR increased. Second, it examines the link between GIR and individual religiosity. As discussed in Chapters 2 and 3, many scholars believe these two factors are causally linked. In fact the debate over this issue has been one of the major debates among sociologists of religion and a major focus of research on the religious economy. Third, it examines the relationship between democracy and GIR. The global analysis shows that democracies have less GIR than nondemocracies but the micro-level analysis shows that many democratic states have substantial levels of GIR. This implies a more complicated relationship between religion and state in democracies that requires further examination.

The first of these issues is clearly central to the basic questions posed by this study and not including such an analysis in this study would make it incomplete. However, the second two issues are just two among many that could be included in this context to flesh out the various interrelationships between GIR and other parts of the political and social systems. I chose these two because they address issues that are central to their respective disciplines and also overlap with the more central questions posed by modernization-secularization theory. If religiosity and GIR, in fact, do not monolithically drop at the same time, as predicted by modernization-secularization theory, this would go a long way toward falsifying these theories. Also, the political science version of modernization theory not only links the decline of religion to modernization but also predicts that modernization will promote democratization. Thus, the link between democracy and GIR is particularly relevant to the questions posed in this study.

CHANGE IN GIR BETWEEN 1990 AND 2002

This section is intended to answer three basic questions. First, is the global rise in GIR documented in Chapter 4 mainly due to a limited number of the 60 specific types of GIR measured by the RAS dataset or is it more or less common to all of them? Second, have some types of GIR become less common while others have become more common? Both of these questions essentially examine whether the rise in GIR is uniform to all types of GIR or whether a more complicated pattern exists. Third, controlling for the influence of world region and religious tradition, are these shifts in GIR a general phenomenon or are they found mostly in specific clusters of states? For example, the analysis in Chapter 4 shows that GIR has increased significantly in Muslim and Orthodox states. Is this rise common to all of these states or does it exist in only some of them? If so, is there some common trait that these states share which differentiates them from the states in which GIR did not increase? Also, among those states within a specific tradition or world region where GIR did increase, are the increases in the same specific types of GIR? In short, there is clearly a large amount of diversity in the extent of GIR. This section of the study examines whether there is some pattern to this diversity. To paraphrase Shakespeare, is there a method to this madness?

A good place to begin to answer these questions is with the examination of the specific types of GIR that increased and decreased between 1990 and 2002. All of the tables in this portion of the analysis show, for each specific type of GIR, the number of states in which GIR increased and the number in which it decreased. This analysis controls both for world region and religious tradition, as both have been shown to be important influences on GIR.

The shifts in the 16 types of *religious discrimination* included in the RAS dataset are presented in Table 11.1 and show that some forms of *religious discrimination* are increasing more than others. Two factors can explain this. First, all those types of *religious discrimination* that are not increasing significantly can be described as limitations on the practice of religion itself: forced observance of the religious laws of the majority group; limitations on religious schools and education; restricted access to materials for religious ceremonies and rites; restrictions on the observance of religious laws concerning personal status; limitations on the ordination of or access to clergy; restrictions on conversions; and forced conversions.

In contrast, many of the types of *religious discrimination* that have increased significantly involve efforts by governments to restrict or monitor religious *organizations* as opposed to restricting religious *practices*. Formal restrictions on religious organizations and registration requirements are only the most obvious of such discriminatory acts. The restrictions on places of worship fit into this category because places of worship are often locales for organizing. Government arrest, detention, and/or harassment of religious minorities is often motivated not by hostility to religion itself but as preemptive attacks on religious leaders or members of religious groups who either have political agendas or are in some other way seen as a threat to the state.

A second type of growing *religious discrimination*, defense of local culture, targets religious practices that have the potential to impinge on the religious culture of the majority religion in the state. Proselytizing does this by trying to convert members of the majority religion. Missionaries often do this by handing out religious texts. Finally, the public celebration of minority religious festivals can be considered by some to impinge upon the religious character of their state. Other than limitations on conversions, all of the types of *religious discrimination* that have not risen significantly are more strongly associated with the practice of religion within a group that does not impinge upon others, or are ways the majority group might try to enforce their religion on the minority.

Nearly half the increases in religious discrimination occurred in the former Soviet bloc. This finding is not particularly surprising since the former Soviet bloc was in a state of flux between 1990 and 2002. Nevertheless, there are

TABLE 11.1. Changes in Religious Discrimination, 1990* to 2002

	Region											
	Western democ.		Former Soviet		Asia		Middle East & N. Africa		Sub-Saharan Africa		Latin America	
	−	+	−	+	−	+	−	+	−	+	−	+
Public observance	—	—	—	7	1	3	—	1	3	2	1	1
Build, repair, maintain places of worship	1	—	2	6	1	3	1	—	3	4	—	—
Access to places of worship	1	—	2	5	—	1	—	1	1	4	—	—
Forced observance of religious laws	—	—	—	—	1	—	—	—	1	2	—	—
Formal religious organizations	—	1	—	6	—	3	—	—	3	1	—	—
Religious schools and education	—	—	—	2	—	—	—	—	2	2	—	—
Arrest, detention, & harassment	—	—	—	6	—	4	—	1	3	8	1	—
Materials for religious rites & ceremonies	—	—	—	1	—	—	—	—	1	—	—	—
Religious publications	—	—	—	6	—	—	—	—	1	1	—	—
Personal status	—	—	—	2	1	—	1	—	—	1	—	—
Ordination or access to clergy	—	—	—	—	—	—	—	—	—	—	—	1
Conversion to minority religions	—	—	—	—	—	—	—	—	—	1	—	—
Forced conversions	—	—	—	—	—	—	—	—	—	—	—	—
Proselytizing	—	1	1	6	1	1	—	—	1	2	1	1
Registration	—	2	—	10	—	3	—	1	2	4	—	—
Other	—	1	—	1	—	1	—	1	—	1	—	1
TOTAL	2	5	5	58	6	19	2	5	21	33	3	4

	Catholic		Orthodox		Other Christian		Muslim		Other		Total	
	−	+	−	+	−	+	−	+	−	+	−	+
Public observance	1	1	—	5	1	1	1	4	2	3	5	14
Build, repair, maintain places of worship	—	1	2	4	1	2	2	3	3	3	8	13
Access to places of worship	1	1	1	3	—	2	—	3	2	2	4	11
Forced observance of religious laws	—	—	—	—	1	—	1	2	—	—	2	2
Formal religious organizations	—	—	—	4	2	2	—	1	1	4	3	11
Religious schools and education	—	—	—	1	1	—	—	3	1	—	2	4
Arrest, detention, & harassment	1	1	1	3	1	3	1	6	1	6	5	19
Materials for religious rites & ceremonies	—	—	—	1	—	—	—	—	2	—	2	1
Religious publications	—	—	—	4	—	1	—	1	1	1	1	7
Personal status	—	1	—	1	—	1	1	—	1	—	2	3
Ordination or access to clergy	—	1	—	—	—	—	—	—	—	—	—	1
Conversion to minority religions	—	—	—	—	—	—	—	1	—	—	—	1
Forced conversions	—	—	—	—	—	—	—	—	—	1	—	1
Proselytizing	1	2	1	5	—	1	—	2	2	2	4	12
Registration	1	4	—	4	1	5	—	3	—	4	2	20
Other	—	1	—	2	—	1	—	2	—	—	—	6
TOTAL	5	13	5	37	8	19	6	31	16	26	40	126

* For countries where data was not available for 1990, the first available year was used.

a number of specific patterns that help to explain this finding as well as other aspects of the shifts in *religious discrimination*, but these patterns are better understood when combining the findings for *religious discrimination* with those for *religious regulation* and *religious legislation*. Accordingly, they are discussed later in this section.

Like *religious discrimination*, the shifts in *religious regulation*, presented in Table 11.2, are linked to whether a specific type of regulation applies to the practice of religion or religious organizations. The largest increases in *religious regulation* were on political parties, religious organizations, and the arrest, detention, and/or harassment of religious leaders. There were also significant increases in limitations on public speech by clergy, usually political speech. All of these can be said to focus on the political and organizational side of religion. There were few shifts in this type of GIR in Western democracies and Latin America, but shifts did occur in other world regions. In this case, religious tradition provides a strong explanation. Of the 81 increases in *religious regulation*, 50 (61.7 percent) occurred in Muslim states and almost none occurred in Catholic and Orthodox states.

While there were a total of 113 increases in *religious legislation*, as shown in Tables 11.3a and 11.3b, there is a much more even distribution of changes between the 33 specific types of legislation. Only 5 types of religious legislation increased in more than 5 states. Two of them involve religious education – the funding of religious education and the inclusion of optional religious education in public schools. The requirement of all religions to register was implemented in 11 new states during this period. Nine governments began to monitor "sects." Finally, 7 increased their funding of religion. Shifts in *religious legislation* were less common in the Middle East-North Africa region, Western democracies, and Latin America. Interestingly, in Western democracies, there was an overall drop in *religious legislation*.

Many of the shifts in these 3 variables can be attributed to several trends that are specific to particular categories or groupings of states. Chapters 5 through 10 demonstrate that each world region has its own character and idiosyncrasies with regard to GIR and the analysis in Chapter 4 shows that religious tradition has a significant impact on GIR. Accordingly, it is not surprising that combining these two factors helps to define specific groupings of states that display unique patterns of change in the extent of GIR.

For example, the 10 Orthodox Christian states of the former Soviet bloc, which constitute less than 6 percent of all states in this study, account for about 29 percent of the increases in *religious discrimination*. Other than Russia, all of these states can be said to have had their local culture repressed by a foreign power – the Russian-controlled Soviet Union. In response, since the fall of the Soviet Union, many of these states have developed policies to reinvigorate their indigenous cultures. This has included the conscious cultivation of nationalism and the revival of national languages. It has also resulted in restrictions on minority religions that are considered nonindigenous. Russia also fits well into this pattern, though the reasons for this protection of indigenous culture are likely motivated by historical factors that are in some ways similar to the other Eastern European Orthodox states but also in some ways are different.

All of the Orthodox former Soviet bloc states had restrictions on these non-indigenous religious minorities in place from the time of their independence, and many of them increased these restrictions over time. Registration of a religion is often conditional on a minimum time of presence in the country, a minimum numbers of adherents, and sometimes a minimum number of separate religious communities in different locations. Much of the discrimination against religious minorities in these states is against religious groups that are unable to register.[1]

This trend is common to all of the former Soviet bloc Orthodox majority countries, as all of them added at least one type of *religious discrimination* between 1990 and 2002, and it is strongest in Georgia, Bulgaria, and Russia. Interestingly, this is not the case for non-Orthodox Christian states in this region. There have been few changes in the level of *religious discrimination* in these states and, other than Poland and Slovakia, none of them have high levels of *religious discrimination*. The Muslim states of this region follow the pattern of Orthodox states in this respect, but to a lesser extent.

Thus, the pertinent question is not why these Orthodox states seek to protect and reinvigorate their indigenous cultures through *religious discrimination*, but, rather, why the non-Orthodox Christian states of the region are not doing so. A simple answer is that all of these countries but Croatia and Bosnia have joined the European Union, which precludes high levels of *religious discrimination*. In addition, Croatia is seeking to become a member of the EU and Bosnia is to a great extent under the supervision of NATO. In contrast, none of the Orthodox states of Eastern Europe that engage in high levels of religious discrimination had joined the EU by 2002.

Of course, it is possible to argue that the divide in European Christianity between Orthodox Christianity on one hand and the Catholic and Protestant traditions on the other also represent cultures with very different histories. That is, excluding the Cold War era, the historical and cultural experiences of the non-Orthodox Christian states of Eastern Europe is arguably more similar to that of Western Europe than those of Eastern Europe's Orthodox states and, as a result, these countries are more open to the concepts of civil rights and religious freedom.[2] It is also likely that this divide was a factor in determining which Eastern European countries were deemed most suitable to join the EU.

---

[1] The absolute level of restrictions on religious minorities in the former Soviet bloc is generally less than it was during the communist era. However, the data show a rise in religious discrimination for two reasons. First, the communist era repression of religion was a general repression of religion that applied to all religions, not just minority ones. The *religious discrimination* variable focuses on restrictions placed on minority religions that are not placed on the majority religion. Second, many of the states included in this region are former Soviet republics. The codings for them begin at independence so do not include the Soviet era and even for those countries that did exist independently, the codings begin in 1990, which is just after the fall of the Soviet Union.

[2] Huntington (1996).

TABLE 11.2. *Changes in Religious Regulation, 1990* to 2002*

	Region											
	Western democracies		Former Soviet		Asia		Middle East & N. Africa		Sub-Saharan Africa		Latin America	
	−	+	−	+	−	+	−	+	−	+	−	+
Political parties	—	—	1	1	1	2	—	3	—	13	—	—
Arrest, detention, & harassment of leaders	—	—	—	5	—	2	—	2	1	5	—	—
Formal organizations	—	—	—	3	—	6	—	6	2	—	—	—
Public observance	—	—	—	—	2	—	—	—	—	1	2	—
Speech & sermons	—	—	—	1	—	3	—	—	—	3	—	—
Access to places of worship	—	—	—	2	2	—	—	—	1	1	—	—
Publication or dissemination of religious writings	—	—	—	3	—	—	—	—	1	—	—	—
Arrest, detention, & harassment of nonleaders	—	—	—	2	—	1	—	—	1	—	—	—
Public gatherings	—	—	—	—	—	—	—	—	—	—	—	—
Public display of religious symbols	—	—	—	1	—	—	—	—	—	—	—	—
Other	1	—	—	4	—	4	1	2	1	4	—	1
TOTAL	1	0	1	22	5	18	1	13	7	27	2	2

	Religion										Total	
	Catholic		Orthodox		Other Christian		Muslim		Other			
	−	+	−	+	−	+	−	+	−	+	−	+
Political parties	—	1	—	—	—	6	2	9	—	3	2	18
Arrest, detention, & harassment of leaders	—	—	—	—	—	2	—	10	1	2	1	14
Formal organizations	—	—	—	—	2	1	—	11	—	4	2	16
Public observance	2	—	—	—	—	1	1	—	1	—	4	1
Speech & sermons	—	—	—	—	—	1	—	5	—	1	—	7
Access to places of worship	—	—	—	—	—	1	—	2	3	—	3	3
Publication or dissemination of religious writings	—	—	—	—	—	—	—	2	1	1	1	3
Arrest, detention, & harassment of nonleaders	—	—	—	—	—	—	—	3	1	—	1	3
Public gatherings	—	—	—	—	—	—	—	—	—	—	—	—
Public display of religious symbols	—	—	—	—	—	—	—	1	—	—	—	1
Other	—	2	—	2	2	3	—	7	—	—	2	15
TOTAL	2	3	0	2	4	15	3	50	7	11	16	81

* For countries where data was not available for 1990, the first available year was used.

TABLE 11.3a. *Changes in Religious Legislation by Region, 1990* to 2002*

	Region											
	Western democracies		Former Soviet		Asia		Middle East & N. Africa		Sub-Saharan Africa		Latin America	
	−	+	−	+	−	+	−	+	−	+	−	+
Dietary laws						1						
Alcohol										1		
Personal status defined by clergy					1				1			
Laws of inheritance defined by religion												
Restrictions on conversions				1								
Restrictions on interfaith marriages	1											
Restrictions on public dress		1		1		1				2		
Blasphemy laws				1		1				2		
Censorship				1	1				1			
Close businesses on Sabbath or holidays					1					2		
Blue laws					1							
Optional religious education in public schools				7						3		2
Mandatory religious education in public schools				1		2			1		1	1
Fund religious education				7		2						
Fund religious charitable organizations				1								
Religious taxes						1		2				

Positions, salaries, or funding for clergy	1	—	—	3	—	—	—	—	—	1	—	—
Other funding	—	—	—	2	1	2	—	—	—	3	—	—
Government approval for clergy or speeches	—	—	—	1	—	1	—	—	—	1	—	—
Government appoints some clergy	2	—	—	1	1	—	—	—	1	—	—	—
Government religious department of ministry	1	1	—	4	—	1	—	—	1	3	—	1
Religious position for government official	1	—	—	—	—	—	—	—	—	1	—	—
Government position for religious official	1	—	—	—	—	—	—	—	—	—	—	—
Religious requirements for government position	1	—	—	—	—	—	—	—	—	1	2	—
Religious courts	—	—	—	—	—	—	—	—	—	—	—	—
Religious apportionment of cabinet or legislature	—	—	—	—	1	—	—	—	—	2	—	1
Prohibitive restrictions on abortion	—	2	—	1	—	—	—	—	1	—	1	—
Religious symbol on state flag	—	—	—	—	—	—	—	—	—	—	—	—
Religion listed on state identity card	1	—	—	—	1	1	1	—	—	—	—	—
Registration	—	—	—	4	—	3	—	1	1	2	—	1
Monitoring of "sects"	—	3	1	3	—	1	—	—	—	1	—	1
Restrictions on women	—	—	—	1	1	—	—	—	—	1	—	—
Other	—	—	—	—	1	1	—	—	—	2	—	1
TOTAL	9	4	4	38	9	18	1	3	7	28	4	8

* For countries where data was not available for 1990, the first available year was used.

TABLE 11.3b. *Changes in Religious Legislation by Religion, 1990* to 2002*

| | Religion | | | | | | | | | | Total | |
| | Catholic | | Orthodox | | Other Christian | | Muslim | | Other | | | |
	−	+	−	+	−	+	−	+	−	+	−	+
Dietary laws								1				1
Alcohol								1				1
Personal status defined by clergy							2				2	
Laws of inheritance defined by religion												
Restrictions on conversions								1				1
Restrictions on interfaith marriages			1								1	
Restrictions on public dress						2		2		1		5
Blasphemy laws				1				2		1		4
Censorship				1			2				2	1
Close businesses on Sabbath or holidays					1					2	1	2
Blue laws					1						1	
Optional religious education in public schools		4		5		2		1				12
Mandatory religious education in public schools	1	1		1	1			1		1	2	4
Fund religious education		3		4		2		2		1		12
Fund religious charitable organizations						1						1
Religious taxes								3				3

											Total
Positions, salaries, or funding for clergy	—	—	—	—	1	2	—	1	—	—	1	4
Other funding	—	—	—	1	—	3	—	2	1	1	1	7
Government approval for clergy or speeches	—	—	—	—	—	—	—	2	—	1	—	2
Government appoints some clergy	—	—	—	—	2	—	1	1	1	—	4	1
Government religious department of ministry	2	—	—	1	1	2	—	4	2	—	3	9
Religious position for government official	—	—	—	1	—	—	—	1	—	—	1	1
Government position for religious official	—	—	—	1	—	—	—	—	—	1	—	—
Religious requirements for government position	2	—	—	1	—	1	—	1	—	—	3	1
Religious courts	—	1	—	—	—	1	—	—	—	1	—	—
Religious apportionment of cabinet or legislature	—	1	—	—	—	1	1	—	1	1	1	3
Prohibitive restrictions on abortion	—	1	1	2	—	—	1	—	—	—	4	1
Religious symbol on state flag	—	—	—	—	—	—	—	—	—	—	—	—
Religion listed on state identity card	—	—	1	—	—	—	—	—	2	1	3	1
Registration	—	2	—	1	1	2	—	4	—	2	1	11
Monitoring of "sects"	5	—	—	1	—	1	—	—	1	2	1	9
Restrictions on women	1	—	—	—	—	—	—	1	—	—	—	2
Other	1	—	—	—	1	1	—	1	1	1	1	4
TOTAL	3	22	3	16	13	19	7	32	8	14	34	113

* For countries where data was not available for 1990, the first available year was used.

A second important set of patterns involves Muslim states, which collectively accounted for the majority increases in *religious regulation*, the greatest number of increases in *religious legislation*, and the second largest number of increases in *religious discrimination*. Yet these increases did not occur equally in all Muslim states.

One thing that the Muslim states of all world regions do have in common is an increase in *religious regulation*. Of the Muslim states in this study, 38 (81 percent) engage in *religious regulation* and 22 (47 percent) increased the extent of *religious regulation* between 1990 and 2002. These numbers are much higher than those for all other states – 44 percent of the world's non-Muslim states engage in *religious regulation* and 14.8 percent increased the extent of *religious regulation*. This tendency is consistent across regions, as about half of the Muslim states in each region have increased *religious regulation*.

The probable explanations for this phenomenon are the political power of Islam and the rise of militant Islamic fundamentalism. Islam has always been disposed to see continuity rather than separation between religion and state, a tendency manifest in the high levels of all aspects of GIR in Muslim states. *Religious regulation* is disproportionally high in these states because of fears that Islam may co-opt a state that does not co-opt or otherwise regulate and control Islam.

Yet this aspect of Islam's relationship with the state has been constant for a considerable amount of time, so it does not explain the large-scale increase in *religious regulation* in Muslim states between 1990 and 2002. One explanation for this increase is the growing challenge to regimes from Muslim integralists who wish to bring the world, and especially Muslim majority states, under the rule of Islamic law. Militant fundamentalists have violently challenged the governments of even some of the most conservative Muslim states, including Saudi Arabia, which scores higher on the measures of GIR than any other state in the world. Accordingly, upon careful inspection, most increases in *religious regulation* in Muslim states reflect government activities directed specifically against religious groups that are seeking either to replace the state government with an Islamic one or otherwise to push the state more in line with Islamic law.

Aside from *religious regulation*, the behavior of Muslim states with regard to changes in GIR differs between the Middle East–North Africa region and elsewhere. In the Middle East–North Africa region there has been little change. Of the 19 such states, only 4 (21 percent) increased the extent of *religious discrimination*, with 1 reducing it, and 3 (16 percent) increased the extent of *religious legislation*. All of these increases were small ones. This is likely because the Muslim states in this region are mostly stable states with long-established regimes with regard to GIR, and because most of them already have high levels of GIR.

In the rest of the world there has been a moderate to extensive increase in GIR depending on the region. The extent of GIR increased in 4 of 6 Muslim states in the former Soviet bloc.[3] While Albania and Azerbaijan did not make any changes to their *religious discrimination* and *legislation* policies during this period, the other 4 states did. Kyrgyzstan, Tajikistan, and Uzbekistan slightly increased the extent of *religious legislation*. Uzbekistan and Turkmenistan made large increases in the extent of *religious discrimination*.

GIR increased in 4 of 7 of the Muslim states in Asia, though it dropped in 1 – Afghanistan. This drop in Afghanistan was artificially imposed by the fall of the Taliban regime. Despite this drop, the extent of GIR remains high in that country as it does in all Muslim states in the region, with the lowest scoring country, Bangladesh, scoring about 33 on the *general GIR* variable in 2002 and the others scoring 49 or higher. Other than Pakistan and Bangladesh, which remained at the same level, either *religious discrimination* or *religious legislation* increased between 1990 and 2002 in these states. In sub-Saharan Africa, GIR increased in 8 of the 14 Muslim states in the region. It dropped slightly in Djibouti and Mali. Burkina Faso, Gambia, Mauritania, and Somalia showed no change.

A third pattern involves stasis in GIR in Latin America and Western democracies between 1990 and 2002. Of the 27 countries in Latin America, GIR did not change at all in 14 and dropped in 4. It rose in nine states but none of these increases were large. The only large drop was in Paraguay, due mostly to a new constitution in 1992 that removed the state's official religion. Overall, GIR in Latin America was stable between 1990 and 2002 to the extent that the mean levels of *religious regulation* and *religious discrimination* did not change at all and the mean level of *religious legislation* rose slightly from 4.15 to 4.41.

Of the 27 countries considered Western democracies, GIR did not change in 17 of them, dropped in 5 and rose in 2. *General GIR* rose slightly in Belgium, by 1.04 points, and by 11.04 points in France. This increase in GIR in France is due mostly to a 2001 law that allows for the dissolution of religious groups. General GIR dropped significantly in Sweden because in 2000 the Swedish government formally separated itself from its state church. Overall the mean level of GIR in Western democracies did not change much between 1990 and 2002. It decreased slightly for *religious regulation* and *religious legislation* but increased slightly for *religious discrimination*.

The final group of states to examine are the non-Muslim states in Asia and Africa. Theses states are in a state of flux – meaning that a clear majority of them have changed their GIR policies, with some increasing GIR and some decreasing it. In sub-Saharan Africa, the general tendency is to increase GIR. Among the 32 non-Muslim states in the region 18 increased GIR, 6 decreased it, and 8 did not change their policy. This pattern remains consistent across religious traditions.

In Asia the changes in GIR are more balanced with GIR decreasing in 7 states, increasing in 8 and staying the same in 6. The Buddhist states in the

---

[3] Kazakstan is not included in these states because it does not have a Muslim majority, though Muslims are clearly the largest religious group in the state.

region tend to be lowering GIR. Four of the eight Buddhist states reduced GIR between 1990 and 2002 and two increased GIR. GIR increased in both Hindu states, India and Nepal, though only slightly, with *general GIR* increasing by 2.88 in India and 0.42 in Nepal. The extent of change was balanced for Christian states and for states of all other religious traditions that are not Muslim, Buddhist, or Hindu.

In all, the increases in GIR from 1992 to 2002 can be partially attributed to two trends. First, many states are trying to protect their indigenous religion and cultures from outside influences. This explains much of the increase in *religious discrimination*, especially increases in registration requirements and limits on proselytizing. It also explains the increased government support for religious education. While this trend is strongest in the former Soviet bloc, it can be found elsewhere.

The second trend is a fear of religious challenges to the state. This trend is present in many Muslim states as well as states with significant Muslim minorities. This trend is associated with much of the increased *religious regulation* in Muslim states and some of the increased *religious discrimination* in states with Muslim minorities. This trend is similar to the previous one in that the changes between 1990 and 2002 make it more obvious with regard to Islam but it has been present in many states since before 1990, not just Muslim states or states with Muslim minorities. The rise of political Islam has been an important trend since the 1980s so it is natural that states have been reacting to it. Yet the fear of religion's political power existed before 1990. For example in 1990, 39 states restricted religious political parties and 34 restricted public speech by clergy.

Thus, the increases in GIR are the result of religion's strength in some parts of the religious economy and its weakness in others. On one hand many states seem to be protecting and nurturing indigenous religious culture that has been weakened. On the other hand, those states feel the need to regulate and control those strains of religion that are seen as a potential political threat.

GIR AND INDIVIDUAL RELIGIOSITY

As discussed in Chapter 2, the supply-side theory of religion links religious monopolies and individual religiosity.[4] It predicts that religious monopolies will result in lower formal affiliation with religion and attendance at religious services but will not substantially influence belief. While individual religiosity is not the focus of the RAS study, the potential link between GIR and individual religiosity warrants a brief examination of this theory. More importantly, if the supply-side theory is correct, it is unlikely that both religiosity and GIR will be low in the same place at the same time. This dynamic reflects a religious economy where sacralization and secularization are occurring simultaneously rather

---

[4] See, for example, Stark & Finke (2000), and Stark & Iannaccone (1994).

than the monolithic drop in religion's influence predicted by modernization-secularization theory.

The supply-side theory is in some ways counter-intuitive. One would expect that states with more religious populations would have more GIR. Religion would be a less contentious issue in homogeneous states obviating the need for SRAS. Intuition would also tell us that religious populations would have a desire for that religiosity to be expressed through the state. The supply-side theory predicts the opposite in two ways. First, the predicted direction of causation is different, with government policy influencing religiosity rather than the other way around. Second, rather than a positive relationship between the two, the relationship is inverted with one factor rising as the other falls. The prediction rests on the assumption that established religions, lacking incentives to proselytize, will act as lazy monopolies and religious behavior will thus decline.

Previous empirical tests of this theory have almost exclusively used religious pluralism as the measure for religious monopolies[5] and the overall results differ from one study to the next.[6] Many of these studies tend to support the theory, but most of them are limited to a few states. Many of them look at a single country and focus on differences between towns or counties in those countries.[7] A few focus on 15 to 76 states.[8]

For three reasons, the RAS database allows us to improve on these studies. First, religious pluralism, a demographic variable, is not the optimal measure of a religious monopoly, a legal status conferred by government.[9] While religious homogeneity can be said to be an indirect indicator of religious monopolies and is correlated with legal statutes (Chapter 4), the two indicators are not the same. The RAS measures of government support for religion are better suited for testing this theory than is religious pluralism. Second, the religious pluralism variable generally used in these studies, the Herfindahl index, has its own shortcomings. This variable measures the probability that any two individuals selected randomly will belong to different denominations. Some argue that there is a mathematical relationship between the Herfindahl index and religiosity.[10] This covariance confounds religious pluralism with religious participation, undermining the use of the index as a predictor of religiosity. Third, in the few studies that have tested the impact of various GIR variables on aspects of religiosity, the authors rely on a much more limited set of GIR variables than those available in the RAS dataset.[11]

---

[5] For a review of this literature, see Chaves & Gorski (2001), Norris & Inglehart (2004), and Sherkat & Ellison (1999).

[6] See, for example, Chaves & Gorski (2001), and Olson & Hadaway (1999).

[7] Finke, Guest, & Stark (1996), Finke & Stark (1998), Hamberg & Pettersson (1994), Pettersson & Hamberg (1997), Stark, Finke, & Iannaccone (1995).

[8] Greeey (1994), Iannaccone (1991), Norris & Inglehart (2004).

[9] Chaves & Cann (1992) makes similar arguments.

[10] Voas, Olson, & Crockett (2002).

[11] Chaves & Cann (1992), Gill (1999), McCleary & Barro (2006b), Norris & Inglehart (2004).

Research Design

This study tests the supply-side theory of religion using OLS regressions with three religiosity variables as dependent variables. The religiosity data used in this study are an updated version of the data used by Barro and McCleary.[12] Barro and McCleary drew their data from the World Value Survey (WVS) for 1990–1993, 1995–1997, and 2000–2003 and the International Social Survey Program (ISSP) for 1990–1993, and 1998–2000.[13] The dependent variables are whether respondents attend religious services at least once a month (*monthly attendance*); whether the respondents consider themselves religious people (*religious people*); and whether the respondents have a belief in God (*belief*). Barro and McCleary converted each of the items asked of individuals to a variable for each country that expresses the proportion of people who answered yes to these questions as a value between 0 and 1.

The details of which countries are included in the problem set and for which years are presented in Table 11.4. There are 205 observations but not all of the dependent variables are available for all of the cases. Also, a single country may be included between 1 and 5 times in this study, once for each survey with a total of 81 different countries represented. While Western Christian countries are overrepresented, as is commonly the case with studies based on the WVS and ISSP, a number of non-Western and non-Christian countries are included in the study. This selection of states is subject to several criticisms of selection bias, which are discussed in detail in Chapter 3.

For all the potential problems of selection bias, this study includes as many or more states than the vast majority of previous studies that tested the supply-side theory of religion. This is by far the most comprehensive data available on religiosity. Especially in the more recent rounds of the survey, the WVS project has made an intensive effort to include non-Western countries in the survey. While there is more to do in the future, these data are the most suitable we have to test the supply-side theory.

In order to test the impact of GIR on religiosity, the six RAS variables used in Chapter 4 as dependent variables – *official support, general restrictions, religious discrimination, religious regulation, religious legislation,* and *general GIR* – are used here as independent variables. In order to test both the individual and combined impact on religiosity of each of these factors, seven regressions – labeled as models one through seven – are performed for each dependent variable. Models one through five test the individual impact of each of the first five GIR variables. Model six tests the combined impact of these five variables. Model seven tests the impact of *general GIR. General GIR* must be

---

[12] Barro & McCleary (2003), McCleary & Barro (2006b). The data were obtained directly from Robert Barro. I thank him for the use of the data. This version of the data also includes data from the 2001–3 round of the WVS survey.

[13] Barro & McCleary (2003) also used the 1981–4 WVS, but this is not used in this study because the RAS variables are not available before 1990.

TABLE 11.4. *Countries Included in the Study*

	1990 WVS	1991 ISSP	1995 WVS	1998 ISSP	2000 WVS	Times in study
Albania					x	1
Algeria					x	1
Argentina	x		x		x	3
Armenia			x			1
Australia		x	x	x		3
Austria	x	x		x	x	4
Azerbaijan			x			1
Bangladesh			x		x	2
Belarus	x		x		x	3
Belgium	x				x	2
Bosnia Herz.			x		x	2
Brazil	x		x			2
Bulgaria	x	x	x	x	x	5
Canada	x	x		x	x	4
Chile	x		x	x	x	4
China	x				x	2
Colombia					x	1
Croatia			x		x	2
Cyprus, Greek				x		1
Czech Republic	x	x		x	x	4
Denmark	x			x	x	3
Dominican Rep.			x			1
Egypt					x	1
El Salvador					x	1
Estonia	x		x		x	3
Finland	x		x		x	3
France	x			x	x	3
Georgia			x			1
Germany	x	x	x	x	x	5
Ghana			x			1
Greece	x				x	2
Hungary	x	x		x	x	4
Iceland	x				x	2
India	x		x		x	3
Indonesia					x	1
Iran					x	1
Ireland	x	x		x	x	4
Israel		x		x		2
Italy	x	x		x	x	4
Japan	x	x	x	x	x	5

(continued)

TABLE 11.4 (*continued*)

	1990 WVS	1991 ISSP	1995 WVS	1998 ISSP	2000 WVS	Times in study
Jordan					x	1
Latvia	x		x	x	x	4
Lithuania	x		x		x	3
Luxembourg					x	1
Macedonia			x		x	2
Malta					x	1
Mexico	x		x		x	3
Moldova			x		x	2
Morocco					x	1
Netherlands	x	x		x	x	4
New Zealand		x		x	x	3
Nigeria	x		x		x	3
Norway	x	x	x	x		4
Pakistan					x	1
Peru			x		x	2
Philippines		x	x	x	x	4
Poland	x	x	x	x	x	5
Portugal	x			x	x	3
Romania	x				x	2
Russia	x	x	x	x	x	5
Saudi Arabia					x	1
Singapore					x	1
Slovakia	x			x	x	3
Slovenia	x	x	x	x	x	5
South Africa	x		x		x	3
South Korea	x		x		x	3
Spain	x	x	x	x	x	5
Sweden	x	x	x	x	x	5
Switzerland	x		x	x		3
Taiwan			x			1
Tanzania					x	1
Turkey	x		x		x	3
Uganda	x	x		x	x	4
UK					x	1
Ukraine			x		x	2
USA	x	x	x	x	x	5
Uruguay			x			1
Venezuela			x		x	2
Vietnam					x	1
Yugoslavia			x		x	2
Zimbabwe					x	1
TOTAL	42	22	43	30	68	205

tested separately because it is a composite variable based on the first five variables.

In order to control for other factors that may influence religiosity, the regressions also include variables for the religious identity of the state – whether the state is Catholic, Orthodox Christian, other Christian, or Muslim – the two polity measures, infant mortality,[14] the two religious demographics variables, and the log of the country's population.[15] As the survey data is taken from multiple years, a variable measuring time is also included, which measures the number of years after 1990. The year 1990 is set as 0 and the value for each year after that is the result of the formula: year – 1990.

Data Analysis

The results for *monthly attendance*, presented in Table 11.5, are consistent with the supply-side theory. *Religious discrimination, religious regulation*, and *general GIR* all individually suppress *monthly attendance* in a statistically significant manner. All of the other regressions show the same relationship but it is not statistically significant. However, a number of other factors have a greater impact on *monthly attendance*. These include if the state has a Catholic or Muslim majority, a stable regime, and low economic development. States with "other Christian" populations and larger populations are also more likely to have populations that attend religious services. Also, people were more likely to attend religious services later in the survey period than they were earlier in the survey period.

The results for *religious people*, presented in Table 11.6, produces similar results. All of the regressions show GIR to be negatively associated with *religious people* but this relationship is statistically significant only for model seven. The results show that countries of all denominations of Christianity and Islam are more likely to have people who consider themselves religious. This means that non-Christian, non-Muslim countries tend to have fewer people who consider themselves religious. Countries with lower levels of economic development and more homogeneous populations are more likely to have more people who consider themselves religious. Also, people were more likely to consider themselves religious later in the survey period than they were earlier in the survey period.

The results presented in Table 11.7 show no significant correlation between GIR and *belief*. This is also as one would expect based on the supply-side theory. However, several of the other variables are significantly correlated with *belief*.

---

[14] The log-per-capita GDP variable was not included because the infant mortality variable was shown in Chapter 4 to be the more influential of the economic variables. In regressions not presented here that use the log-per-capita GDP variable in place of the infant mortality variable, the results were similar.

[15] These variables are described in more detail in Chapter 4.

TABLE 11.5. *GIR and Whether People Attend Services at Least Once a Month*

Variable	Model 1	Model 2	Model 3	Model 4	Model 5	Model 6	Model 7
Official support	-.007	—	—	—	—	-.046	—
Religious restrictions	—	-.115	—	—	—	-.043	—
Religious discrimination	—	—	-.146*	—	—	-.089	—
Religious regulation	—	—	—	-.149*	—	-.110	—
Religious legislation	—	—	—	—	-.035	.059	—
General GIR	—	—	—	—	—	—	-.192**
Majority Catholic	.671***	.637***	.622***	.594***	.666***	.573***	.593***
Majority Orthodox Chr.	.034	.038	.049	.005	.030	.038	.035
Majority Other Christian	.209*	.176	.164	.146	.214*	.130	.198*
Majority Muslim	.152	.184*	.209**	.168*	.173	.185*	.227**
% Majority religion	.005	.033	.026	.030	.014	.059	.119
# of Minority religions	-.051	-.018	-.031	-.035	-.051	-.020	-.027
Polity	-.085	-.091	-.095	-.083	-.086	-.092	-.101
Regime stability	.207**	.184**	.199**	.197**	.205**	.182**	.168**
Log population	.126*	.127*	.144*	.145*	.126*	.146*	.124*
Infant mortality	.588***	.566***	.549***	.608***	.581***	.578***	.552***
Years after 1990	.124*	.130**	.134**	.134**	.126**	.137**	.133**
df	198	198	198	198	198	198	198
Adjusted r-squared	.540	.549	.553	.554	.540	.552	.558

* = Significance < .05
** = Significance < .01
*** = Significance < .001

TABLE 11.6. *GIR and Whether Respondents Consider Themselves Religious*

Variable	Model 1	Model 2	Model 3	Model 4	Model 5	Model 6	Model 7
Official support	-.105	—	—	—	—	-.101	—
Religious restrictions	—	-.020	—	—	—	.126	—
Religious discrimination	—	—	-.146	—	—	-.144	—
Religious regulation	—	—	—	-.117	—	-.105	—
Religious legislation	—	—	—	—	-.162	-.082	—
General GIR	—	—	—	—	—	—	-.213*
Majority Catholic	.745***	.770***	.711***	.702***	.729***	.639***	.641***
Majority Orthodox Chr.	.377***	.368***	.368***	.337**	.343**	.338**	.336***
Majority Other Christian	.580***	.544***	.491***	.489***	.554***	.510***	.495***
Majority Muslim	.413***	.396***	.440***	.393***	.485***	.480***	.451***
% Majority religion	.312*	.244*	.259*	.260*	.296*	.346*	.363**
# of Minority religions	.003	.022	.034	.027	-.008	-.008	.044
Polity	-.076	-.073	-.084	-.072	-.080	-.083	-.089
Regime stability	.056	.074	.064	.066	.072	.057	.025
Log population	.007	.028	.050	.044	.012	.033	.024
Infant mortality	.474***	.481***	.446***	.500***	.464***	.461***	.446***
Years after 1990	.137*	.141*	.147*	.147*	.143*	.146*	.147*
df	149	149	149	149	149	149	149
Adjusted r-squared	.426	.421	.434	.429	.433	.434	.443

* = Significance < .05
** = Significance < .01
*** = Significance < .001

TABLE 11.7. *GIR and Whether Respondents Believe in God*

Variable	Model 1	Model 2	Model 3	Model 4	Model 5	Model 6	Model 7
Official support	.090	—	—	—	—	.017	—
Religious restrictions	—	.001	—	—	—	.043	—
Religious discrimination	—	—	-.072	—	—	-.078	—
Religious regulation	—	—	—	-.135	—	-.115	—
Religious legislation	—	—	—	—	.034	.048	—
General GIR	—	—	—	—	—	—	-.084
Majority Catholic	.411***	.388**	.372*	.325*	.398**	.347*	.352*
Majority Orthodox Christian	-.051	-.040	-.023	-.061	-.034	-.036	-.039
Majority Other Christian	.202	.230	.216	.180	.226	.175	.224
Majority Muslim	.195*	.214*	.250*	.235*	.195	.227*	.248*
% Majority religion	.323*	.386***	.393***	.405***	.371**	.368**	.433***
# of Minority religions	.218*	.205*	.208*	.210*	.205*	.206*	.210*
Polity	-.043	-.047	-.051	-.044	-.046	-.044	-.052
Regime stability	.142	.124	.118	.112	.127	.124	.104
Log population	.152*	.139	.143*	.151*	.140*	.159*	.134
Infant mortality	.285***	.275**	.257**	.296***	.282**	.293**	.259**
Years after 1990	.171**	.171**	.177**	.183**	.169**	.181**	.177**
df	184	184	184	184	184	184	184
Adjusted r-squared	.325	.322	.325	.333	.322	.320	.325

* = Significance < .05

** = Significance < .01

*** = Significance < .001

These include: Catholic majority states; Muslim majority states; states with large religious majorities but several large religious minorities; more populous states; and states with low levels of economic development. Also, people were more likely to believe in God later in the survey period than they were earlier in the survey period.

These results have several implications. In the main, they are consistent with the supply-side theory of religion. Religious monopolies, as measured by the RAS variables, do exert a negative impact on religious participation and religious identity but not on religious belief. All other things being equal, people are more likely to attend religious services or consider themselves religious people in states with a free religious economy. However, the level of GIR does not significantly affect basic elements of religious belief, like the belief in God.[16]

Yet, while the supply-side theory appears to be correct based on this analysis, a number of factors other than GIR have a greater impact on religious participation. The religious tradition of a state, the size of its population, the stability of its regime, religious homogeneity and a lack of economic development all have greater impact on religious participation than does GIR. Thus, if one is looking for the macro-level factors which *most* influence religious participation, a religious monopoly may be among the least influential of the significant influences.

Finally, these results undermine some of the predictions of modernization-secularization theory in two ways. Scholars expected a simultaneous decline in both religiosity and GIR. All of the regressions show that people have become more religious since 1990. This result is consistent with the work of Norris and Inglehart, who analyzed the same data but used different independent variables.[17] Results presented in Chapter 4 show that GIR also rose between 1990 and 2004. Thus these predictions did not come to fruition.

Interestingly, the results presented here also show an inverse relationship between GIR and religiosity. This implies that if one facet of religion becomes weaker, another becomes stronger, and from the perspective of the larger religious economy, religion, in one form or another, maintains a presence. In fact, as is discussed in more detail in Chapter 12, religion can be said to be a phenomenon that evolves and adjusts in order to survive and even thrive in changing social and political environments.

Yet these two observations are seemingly inconsistent. How can there be an inverse relationship between religiosity and GIR while both rise at the same time? One likely explanation is that the impact of GIR on the religiosity variables is weaker than other factors. Thus, increased GIR does lower the relative levels of religiosity but shifts in other factors, such as economic modernization, outweigh the impact of this influence.

---

[16] In results not presented here, this is also true of variables that measure whether respondents believe in an afterlife, Heaven, and Hell.

[17] Norris & Inglehart (2004).

GIR AND DEMOCRACY

The multivariate analysis presented in Chapter 4 shows that democratic states tend to have less GIR than do nondemocratic states.[18] However, the analysis presented here, which examines the link between GIR and democracy, shows that the relationship is more complicated than this simple correlation.

The debate in the academic literature on whether SRAS is an essential element of democracy also reflects this complex relationship. The argument that SRAS is an inseparable element of democracy is for many an assumption that is never rigorously questioned.[19] Others argue that there is a structural incompatibility between democracy and religion in that religion does not tolerate dissent. For example, Grotius argues that in order to maintain pluralism and liberalism, religious pluralism needs to be kept within certain bounds.[20] Rawls makes a normative version of this argument, asserting that we must "take the truths of religion off the political agenda."[21]

This argument is complemented by a set of arguments that posit that democracies can also be intolerant of dissent. One form of this argument is that democracy is difficult to implement in heterogeneous societies. For instance, John Stuart Mill argued that democracy is almost impossible in states with multiple nationalities.[22] There is no shortage of more recent scholarship that concurs with this assessment. Donald Horowitz in his seminal work on ethnic conflict argues that a major contributor to the decline of democracy in Africa, Asia, and the Caribbean is precisely this weakness of democracy and liberalism.[23] The literature on consociationalsim also assumes the inherent inability of multiethnic and multireligious societies to maintain democracy by implying that only complicated power-sharing arrangements and coalition politics can preserve democracy in these states.[24]

Another form of this argument is that liberal democracies are by their nature intolerant of religion. This is because when a state embraces the ideal that a government should not in any way support religion, this results in a bias against religion. Put differently, the ideal of SRAS results in a preference for secular beliefs and institutions over religious ones.[25] Bader takes this a step further arguing that the concept of neutrality toward religion is actually a cover for a bias in favor of the dominant religion and that democracies often put significant constraints on religious minorities.[26]

---

[18] Another version of the analysis presented in this section is published in Fox (2007).
[19] Stepan (2000: 40).
[20] Shah (2000: 122).
[21] Rawls (1993: 151). See also Beit-Hallahmi (2003: 32), and Demerath (2001: 2).
[22] Mill (1951: 46).
[23] Horowitz (1985: 86–7) .
[24] Esman (1973), Lijphart (1977), Nordlinger (1972).
[25] Kekes (1993), Monsma & Soper (1997).
[26] Bader (1999).

The argument that democracy and religion are incompatible is not uncontested. In practice, we see numerous examples of religion and democracy coexisting. Chapter 5 shows that many Western democracies have state religions and substantial levels of GIR.[27] Anthony Smith links many particular nationalist ideologies in democratic states to religious origins. This includes the national ideologies of France, Greece, Ireland, the USA, and the UK.[28] Several studies that focus on the rise of democracy in Belgium and a number of other Catholic states suggest that religious groups often support democracy for strategic reasons.[29] Liberation theology has been credited with increasing democratic participation throughout Latin America.[30]

Others make a more structural version of this counter-argument. For example, Greenwalt argues that liberal democracy tolerates people who want to impose their religious convictions on others, "just as it tolerates people who wish to establish a dictatorship of the proletariat."[31] Tocqueville takes this a step further by arguing that democracy needs religion because "successful political democracy will inevitably require moral instruction grounded in religious faith."[32]

Mazie engages in a particularly nuanced treatment of religion and democracy. Rather than dealing in absolutes, he argues that some elements of religion are compatible with democracy while others are not. National religious holidays are acceptable as long as observance is not mandatory and religious minorities can observe their own holidays.[33] Anecdotal evidence supports this contention in that this practice is so common that the RAS project did not code whether states declare religious holidays and Sabbaths official holidays.

Using religious symbols on state flags and other state symbols, in Mazie's view, also should be subject to minimal scrutiny. While this practice can alienate minorities, refusing this right "would transform liberalism into a doctrine denying independent states the moral right to even the most rudimentary form of political culture."[34] Of course it is important to assure that the particular religious symbol not be offensive to a minority for some reason beyond the fact that it is a symbol that is not theirs. Funding of religion is possible because democratic checks and balances and an effective judicial system can prevent reasonable levels of support for religion from turning into religious tyranny. However, imposing religious values or behavior is in most cases incompatible with democracy.

While it is possible to quibble with the specifics of Mazie's arguments, the general principle that some types of GIR are more compatible than others with

---

[27] See, for example, Stepan (2000: 41–2).
[28] A. Smith (1999).
[29] Kalyvas (1998; 2000), Linz (1978), C. Warner (2000).
[30] Berryman (1987), Roelofs (1988).
[31] Greenwalt (1988: 55).
[32] Fradkin (2000: 90–1).
[33] Mazie (2004).
[34] Mazie (2004: 6).

democratic principles is sound. This is a reasonable middle ground between the argument that religion is incompatible with democracy and the one that GIR does not undermine democracy. Those who argue that religion is compatible with democracy seem to acknowledge that while religion can be compatible with democracy, it is not always so. They recognize that there are intolerant forms of religion that are not compatible with the concept of pluralism and some that are not even tolerant of any diversity within their own traditions. Democracy can be compatible only with manifestations of religion that are either willing to tolerate democracy or whose followers do not have the ability to oppose it.

This debate over the compatibility of religion and democracy has also taken place within the context of the debate over whether democracy is compatible with Islam. The arguments positing that the two are incompatible are not new. There are two such arguments. First, there is no recognition of SRAS in Islam. Religious Muslims consider Islamic law the divinely decreed law of the land, leaving no room for public participation in lawmaking. Second, in Muslim states, citizens do not have equal rights. Muslims have more rights than non-Muslims and men have more rights than women.[35] This contention is consistent with the results presented in Chapter 4 where states with a Muslim majority are shown to have the highest average level of *religious discrimination* against minority religions. A common explanation for this situation is that "the Islamic world never experienced the Enlightenment or had its own Reformation out of which the Islamic equivalent of Western concepts of democracy, human rights, and civil liberties could have developed."[36]

The argument that Islam is compatible with democracy, tends to describe a form of democracy that many in the West would not consider a full democracy because, among other things, it is more democratic for Muslims than non-Muslims. Islam, like many religions, has a rich and diverse tradition which includes many possible interpretations. Thus, it is possible to interpret such Islamic principles as consultation, consensus, the equality of all men, the rule of law, and independent reasoning in a way that allows one to build a democracy based on an Islamic rationale. However, in such a democracy, non-Muslims would be at best second-class citizens and elements of Islamic law regarding women and family life would make it difficult to grant women equal rights.[37]

Many also note that Islam in theory and Islam in practice are not always the same thing and this allows some room for democracy. For instance, although there are no democracies within the Arab world, about half of all Muslims live in democratic and semi-democratic states.[38] Islamic parties have successfully used parliamentary systems to their benefit and have even pushed for

---

[35] Dalacoura (2000: 879), Lewis (1993: 96–8), Stepan (2000: 46–8).
[36] An-Na'im (2002: 31).
[37] Esposito & Piscatori (1991), Esposito & Voll (2000), Feldman (2003), Fuller (2002).
[38] Stepan (2000: 48–9).

democratic reforms.[39] Finally, some would argue that although Islamic doctrine has a tendency to inhibit democracy, in practice there has rarely, if ever, been true unity between Islam and state authority.[40]

Previous quantitative studies on religion and democracy are mixed. Several found that Islamic states tend to be more autocratic.[41] However, one found that Islam neither undermines or supports democracy and human rights.[42] Leak and Randall found that religiosity is correlated with individual authoritarian attitudes.[43] Chaves and Cann, as well as this study, show that many Western European states regulate religion.[44] These studies all have at least one of three failings. First, they look only at the link between a particular religion and democracy. Second, they focus on only one or two aspects of GIR in a limited context. Third, they look only at a limited number of states. The RAS permits covering the entire world with a more detailed set of measures for GIR.

Research Design

This study examines the intersection between the RAS variables and two democracy variables. The first is the Polity indicator (see Chapter 4) to measure the procedural aspects of democracy. The variable ranges from -10 (the most autocratic states) to $+10$ (the most democratic states). The second measure is the Freedom House indicator based on "a checklist of 10 political rights questions and 15 civil liberties questions."[45] Thus this measure focuses on the human and civil rights aspects of democracy or, perhaps more properly, liberal democracy. This is distilled into two indicators – one for political rights and one for civil liberties – each measuring one through seven with seven being the least democratic. This study combined them into a single measure by addition. In order to simplify comparisons with the Polity measure, this combined Freedom House measure was rescaled so that it ranges from 0 to 12, with 12 being the most democratic. Both measures now assign the highest value to the most democratic states.

In order to test the intersection between democracy and the RAS variables, the democracy variables and some of the RAS variables were truncated in a manner similar to what was done in Chapter 4 in the analysis of the impact of religious traditions on GIR. As was the case in that portion of the analysis, this was done here in order to assure that there would be a sufficient number of cases in each category to make meaningful comparisons.

---

[39] Esposito & Piscatori (1991).

[40] Haynes (1998: 128–9), Hefner (2001: 494).

[41] Fisch (2002), Midlarsky (1998).

[42] Price (1999; 2002).

[43] Leak & Randall (1995).

[44] Chaves & Cann (1992).

[45] Freedom House website, at http://www.freedomhouse.org/research/freeworld/2005/methodology.htm.

TABLE 11.8. *Democracy and Official GIR*

	One or more official religions (%)	Civil religion (%)	Official separation score					
			Cooperation (%)	Supportive (%)	Accom (%)	Separationist (%)	Inadvertent insensitivity (%)	Hostile
Polity score								
10 (most dem.)	21.9	12.5	40.6	0.0	21.9	3.1	0.0	0.0
7 to 9	7.3	43.9	22.0	2.4	19.5	4.9	0.0	0.0
0 to 6	22.5	12.9	19.4	0.0	41.9	3.2	0.0	0.0
−6 to −1	34.6	11.5	11.5	0.0	30.8	11.5	0.0	0.0
−10 to −7	46.2	19.2	0.0	0.0	7.7	7.7	15.4	3.8
Freedom House score								
12 (most dem.)	33.4	12.5	25.0	0.0	25.0	4.2	0.0	0.0
11	9.0	13.6	45.5	4.5	22.7	4.5	0.0	0.0
9 to 10	16.0	28.0	20.0	4.0	28.0	4.0	0.0	0.0
6 to 8	12.9	41.9	12.9	0.0	29.0	3.2	0.0	0.0
3 to 5	39.5	7.9	23.7	0.0	21.1	7.9	0.0	0.0
0 to 2	35.3	20.6	2.9	2.9	17.6	5.9	11.8	2.9

Each of the five major RAS variables as well as the *general GIR* composite variable is compared to each of the democracy variables. Then both democracy variables are examined to see whether democracies tend to meet the seven operationalizations of SRAS developed in Chapter 4.

Data Analysis

Overall the results show that the correlation between democracy and SRAS depends to a great extent on the type of RAS variable being examined.

The results presented in Table 11.8, show that *official GIR* is not strongly correlated with democracy. Specifically, democracies are not appreciably more likely to accommodate religion. That honor (on the Polity dependent variable) is reserved for states that score between 0 and 6 and then states that score between −1 and −6. The pattern for the Freedom House variable is similar but less pronounced. That is, the states in many of the categories between the most autocratic and the most democratic are more likely to be coded as having "accommodation" on the *official GIR* score, but the differences between the categories of regime are small.

While they are not overwhelmingly accommodationist, democratic states are unlikely to show much hostility to religion based on the *official GIR* measure. On the Polity score, the most democratic states are the least likely to be coded

TABLE 11.9. *Democracy and General Restrictions*

	General restrictions score				
	None (%)	Practical limitations (%)	Legal limitations (%)	Some (Other) religions illegal (%)	All (Other) religions illegal (%)
Polity score					
10 (most dem.)	50.0	34.4	15.6	0.0	0.0
7 to 9	24.4	56.1	14.6	4.9	0.0
0 to 6	45.2	38.7	9.7	6.5	0.0
−6 to −1	15.4	19.2	42.3	23.1	0.0
−10 to −7	3.8	3.8	65.4	23.1	3.8
Freedom House score					
12 (most dem.)	62.5	29.2	8.3	0.0	0.0
11	40.9	49.5	13.6	0.0	0.0
9 to 10	32.0	56.0	12.0	0.0	0.0
6 to 8	35.5	41.9	19.4	3.2	0.0
3 to 5	13.2	31.6	36.8	15.8	2.6
0 to 2	14.7	8.8	44.1	29.4	2.9

as "separationist." On the Freedom House score, the most democratic states are not the least likely to be coded as "separationist," but the differences between the various categories are small. Also, on both variables only the least democratic states are coded as having the higher levels of hostility toward religion. This, combined with the fact that the percentage of states coded as "separationist" is small between regime types, implies that this aspect of SRAS is better described as lacking among some of the most autocratic states rather than something unique to the most democratic states.

The results for *general restrictions*, presented in Table 11.9, show a strong link between democracy and SRAS. This is not unexpected with regard to the Freedom House variable because the Freedom House variable measures the extent of political freedom and civil liberties in a state. This is likely covariant with the *general restrictions* variable, which is based in part on the extent of religious restrictions placed on minorities, an aspect of political rights and civil liberties. This is not the case with the Polity variable, which is based on the procedural aspects of democracy. Thus, the conclusion that democracies are less likely to give different legal and practical statuses to different religions is sound. However, it is important to point out that half of the most democratic states do give different legal and practical statuses to different religions. Even on the Freedom House measure of democracy over a third of states score higher than 0 on the *general restrictions* measure. Thus, despite a correlation between democracy and *general restrictions*, a large portion of democratic states do not have full SRAS on this measure.

TABLE 11.10. *Democracy and Religious Discrimination*

	Religious discrimination score					
	0 (%)	1 (%)	2 (%)	3 to 4 (%)	5 to 10 (%)	11 or higher (%)
Polity score						
10 (most dem.)	28.1	21.9	15.6	18.8	15.6	0.0
7 to 9	22.0	17.1	14.6	14.6	24.4	7.3
0 to 6	38.7	9.7	19.4	19.4	3.2	9.7
−6 to −1	23.1	11.5	3.8	15.4	11.5	34.6
−10 to −7	0.0	0.0	7.7	7.7	23.1	61.5
Freedom House score						
12 (most dem.)	54.2	20.8	4.2	12.5	8.3	0.0
11	22.7	27.3	18.2	13.6	18.2	0.0
9 to 10	28.0	12.0	16.0	24.0	16.0	4.0
6 to 8	25.8	16.1	19.4	12.9	16.1	9.7
3 to 5	15.8	2.6	13.2	21.1	13.2	34.2
0 to 2	14.7	8.8	2.9	8.8	14.7	50.0

The results for *religious discrimination*, presented in Table 11.10, also show a correlation between SRAS and democracy. This is especially true of the Freedom House measure but this measure is covariant with the *religious discrimination* measure for the same reasons it is covariant with the *general restrictions* measure. Even so, over 45 percent of states that are in the most democratic category of the Freedom House measure still engage in *religious discrimination*. Thus, even on a measure that is in theory biased in favor of showing that democracies do not engage in discrimination, many do so.

The correlation between the Polity measure of democracy and *religious discrimination* is weaker. The more democratic states are less likely to engage in the higher levels of *religious discrimination* than are the more autocratic states. However, if one examines how many states score at the lower end of the range, states in the "0 to 6" category are more likely to have low levels of *religious discrimination* than are states in the most democratic category. This is true of states that score 0, states that score 2 or less and states that score 4 or less. However, states in the "0 to 6" category are more likely to score 11 or higher on the *religious discrimination* measure than are the most democratic states.

The results for *religious regulation*, presented in Table 11.11, show a clear correlation between democracy and SRAS. On both the Polity and Freedom House measures, the more democratic a state the more likely it is to have more SRAS. Furthermore, this is the only one of the RAS variables where a majority of the most democratic states have full SRAS on both measures of democracy.

The results for *religious legislation*, presented in Table 11.12, show a more complicated relationship between SRAS and democracy. First, it is important to

TABLE 11.11. *Democracy and Religious Regulation*

	Religious regulation score				
	0 (%)	1 to 2 (%)	3 to 4 (%)	5 to 8 (%)	9 or higher (%)
Polity score					
10 (most dem.)	75.0	15.6	9.4	0	0.0
7 to 9	53.7	17.1	17.1	7.3	4.9
0 to 6	38.7	16.1	32.3	12.9	0.0
−6 to −1	23.1	19.2	7.7	23.1	26.9
−10 to −7	15.4	15.4	3.8	30.8	34.6
Freedom House score					
12 (most dem.)	87.5	8.3	4.2	0.0	0.0
11	68.2	18.2	9.1	4.5	0.0
9 to 10	56.0	16.0	20.0	4.0	4.0
6 to 8	48.4	19.4	19.4	12.9	0.0
3 to 5	23.7	13.2	23.7	18.4	21.1
0 to 2	20.6	17.6	5.9	26.5	29.4

TABLE 11.12. *Democracy and Religious Legislation*

	Religious legislation score					
	0 (%)	1 to 2 (%)	3 to 4 (%)	5 to 6 (%)	7 to 10 (%)	11+ (%)
Polity score						
10 (most dem.)	3.1	9.4	15.6	31.3	37.5	3.1
7 to 9	0.0	9.8	39.0	29.3	17.1	4.9
0 to 6	0.0	16.1	32.3	25.8	16.1	9.7
−6 to −1	0.0	30.8	23.1	7.7	3.8	34.6
−10 to −7	0.0	7.7	19.2	11.5	15.4	46.2
Freedom House score						
12 (most dem.)	4.2	8.3	33.3	29.2	25.0	0.0
11	0.0	13.6	22.7	36.4	27.3	0.0
9 to 10	0.0	16.0	24.0	24.0	32.0	4.0
6 to 8	0.0	16.1	35.5	25.8	19.4	3.2
3 to 5	0.0	13.2	28.9	13.2	2.6	42.1
0 to 2	0.0	14.7	23.5	11.8	11.8	38.2

reiterate that only the USA lacks any of the 33 types of legislation included in the *religious legislation* measure. That being said, democracies do not score particularly low on *religious legislation* even relative to less democratic states. On the Polity measure, only 12.5 percent of democracies score 2 or lower on the *religious legislation* measure. While this is a higher proportion than the next most-democratic category, states in the "0 to 6" and "−6 to −1" categories are more likely to score 2 or lower on the *religious legislation* measure than are the most democratic states. Furthermore, every category of regime based on the Polity measure, other than the most autocratic category, has a higher proportion of states that score 4 or less on the *religious legislation* measure, and this is also true if one uses a score of 6 or less on the *religious legislation* measure. The results are similar with the Freedom House measure of democracy: democratic states have substantial levels of GIR, even when compared to other types of regimes.

However, both on the Polity, and Freedom House measures, the more democratic a state, the less likely it is to be among the highest scores on the *religious legislation* measure. That is, on the Polity scale, few democratic states score 11 or higher and on the Freedom House scale, none of the most democratic states score 11 or higher. As states become more autocratic, they are more likely to be among the high scorers on the *religious legislation* measure.

This implies that while *religious legislation* is not a foreign concept in most democracies, there is a limit to the extent of *religious legislation* that democracies will tolerate. Thus, as many as 10 of the items on the list of 33 types of religious legislation may exist in a fair number of democracies, but there are few democracies that go beyond this.

The results for *general GIR*, presented in Table 11.13, are similar to those for *religious legislation*. On the Polity measure, only 25 percent of the states in the most democratic category score below 10, but none score among the higher levels of *general GIR*. Also, a larger proportion of states in the "0 to 6" category score lower than 10 than do states in the most democratic category. On the Freedom House measure, 29.2 percent of states in the most democratic category score lower than 10. This is the highest proportion of all categories of regime based on the Freedom House measure, but the proportion of states in several of the other categories of regime that score lower than 10 on the *general GIR* measure are nearly as high. Also, none of the most democratic states on the Freedom House measure score at the highest levels of the *general GIR* measure.

Based on all of this, the question of whether democracies have more SRAS than nondemocracies depends on the type of GIR in question. Democracies clearly are less likely to engage in *religious discrimination*, are less likely to treat different religions differently, and are less likely to regulate the majority religion than are nondemocracies.

However, democracies are nearly as likely to legislate religious laws as non-democracies. The major difference between democracies and nondemocracies in this respect is not a question of willingness to legislate on religious matters but a question of how much religious legislation they will place on the books. Thus, the average democracy legislates several types of religious laws, but the mean level of *religious legislation* is higher among nondemocracies than it is among democracies. The results for *official GIR* are difficult to evaluate in

TABLE 11.13. *Democracy and General GIR*

	General GIR score						
	0 to 9.99 %	10 to 19.99 %	20 to 29.99 %	30 to 39.99 %	40 to 49.99 %	50 to 59.99 %	60 + %
Polity score							
10 (most dem.)	25.0	34.4	28.1	12.5	0.0	0.0	0.0
7 to 9	22.0	24.4	36.6	12.2	4.9	0.0	0.0
0 to 6	35.5	25.8	19.4	12.9	3.2	0.0	3.2
−6 to −1	15.4	26.9	19.2	3.8	7.7	19.2	7.7
−10 to −7	3.8	3.8	3.8	23.1	46.2	15.4	3.8
Freedom House score							
12 (most dem.)	29.2	20.8	45.8	4.2	0.0	0.0	0.0
11	27.3	40.9	27.3	4.5	0.0	0.0	0.0
9 to 10	28.0	24.0	28.0	20.0	0.0	0.0	0.0
6 to 8	29.0	29.0	19.4	16.1	6.5	0.0	0.0
3 to 5	10.5	23.7	21.1	13.2	10.5	15.8	5.3
0 to 2	14.7	8.8	11.8	8.8	32.4	14.7	8.8

terms of relative SRAS, but they certainly do not support a conclusion that democratic states have more SRAS than nondemocratic states.

Another interesting finding is that on several of the measures, the states that score the closest to 0 on the GIR measures are not democracies. As noted above, this is true of the *official GIR* measure. What is particularly interesting is that in some measures those states that fall toward the middle of the autocracy-democracy continuum have the highest levels of SRAS. This is true of *religious regulation* and *religious legislation*.

One possible explanation for this is that there is a u-shaped relationship between democracy and economic development. That is, the most developed countries tend to be either on the autocratic or democratic ends of the autocracy-democracy continuum and the less developed countries tend to be in the middle of the scale. This is important because, as will be recalled, the results in Chapter 4 show that economically developed countries tend to have higher levels of GIR. Figure 11.1 shows a scatterplot for the Polity variable and the log-per-capita-GDP variable described in Chapter 4 with a best-fit line created using a quadratic regression to display the u-shaped relationship between these two variables.

The reason the relationship between democracy and economic development is important is because less developed states tend to be weaker states. Weak states have less ability to enforce laws generally, which includes less capacity to

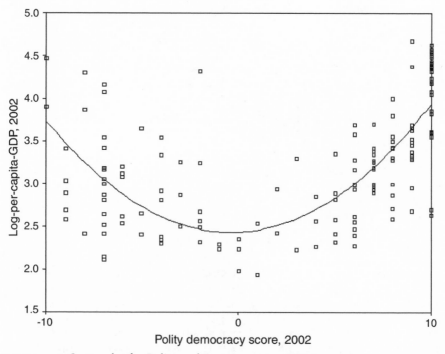

FIGURE 11.1. Scatterplot for Polity and Log-per-capita-GDP in 2002

engage in GIR. Thus the reason that the states in the middle of the autocracy-democracy continuum have less GIR in many of the 60 specific types of GIR examined here may be because they tend to be weaker states, which have less of an ability to engage in GIR.

None of this is to imply that SRAS is standard among democracies. On four of the six measures examined here, *official GIR*, *religious discrimination*, *religious legislation*, and *general GIR*, the majority of states in the most democratic category do not have absolute-SRAS and, on the other two variables, a significant number of democracies do not have absolute-SRAS.

This is confirmed when examining whether regime influences those states that can be considered to have SRAS based on the seven operationalizations of SRAS developed in Chapter 4 (Table 11.14). Based on the Polity measure, the most democratic states are most likely to have SRAS on two of the operationalizations but on the other operationalizations the "0 to 6" category is most often coded as having SRAS. On the Freedom House measure, the most democratic states are more likely to have SRAS based on all of the operationalizations except the one for the exclusion of ideals standard for SRAS.

Depending on the democracy variable and the operationalization of SRAS in question, between 3.1 percent and 29.2 percent of countries in the most democratic category have SRAS. Furthermore, the highest score of any category of SRAS on either democracy variable is 35.5 percent. Thus, controlling for

TABLE 11.14. *Democracy and Whether States Have SRAS*

	Percentage of states that meet standard for separation of religion and state						
	Absolute SRAS	Near SRAS 1	Near SRAS 2	Neutral political concern 1	Neutral political concern 2	Neutral political concern 3	Exclusion of ideals
Polity score							
10 (most dem.)	3.1	6.3	18.8	9.4	15.6	21.9	18.8
7 to 9	0.0	9.8	14.6	4.9	22.0	22.0	17.1
0 to 6	0.0	22.6	32.3	19.4	32.3	35.5	6.5
−6 to −1	0.0	11.5	11.5	7.7	14.4	23.1	7.7
−10 to −7	0.0	3.8	3.8	0.0	3.8	3.8	0.0
Freedom House score							
12 (most dem.)	4.2	12.5	29.2	16.7	25.0	29.2	16.7
11	0.0	9.1	18.2	4.5	22.7	27.3	31.8
9 to 10	0.0	12.0	20.0	8.0	24.0	28.0	8.0
6 to 8	0.0	12.9	19.4	9.7	22.6	25.8	9.7
3 to 5	0.0	10.5	10.5	7.9	10.5	13.2	5.3
0 to 2	0.0	9.5	8.8	2.9	14.7	17.6	2.9

democracy does not alter the general finding presented in Chapter 4 that most states do not have SRAS.

This explains the general findings from Chapter 4 that democracies have lower average levels of GIR, and that democracy is correlated with lower levels of GIR. This is true if one looks at average scores. However, the actual dynamics are more complicated. The result that most democracies do not have SRAS, no matter the definition and operationalization of SRAS used, is incompatible with the predictions of modernization-secularization theory.

CONCLUSIONS

While the general trends examined in Chapter 4 show an overall increase in GIR between 1990 and 2002, the results of Chapters 5 through 10, as well as the results in this chapter, show that there is a wide diversity in the relationship between religion and the state. The combination of religious tradition and geographic region helps to explain much of the diversity. Democracy and religiosity are also linked to GIR in complex manners that were not fully revealed in the analysis of global trends.

These factors, while helping to explain the global patterns of GIR, also create some interesting questions. For instance, the supply-side theory predicts that GIR, or religious monopolies, cause people to become less religious. Yet the results of the first section of this chapter imply that many countries are increasing aspects of GIR designed to protect indigenous religions from the perceived threats of secularization or the encroachment of religions considered foreign to the state. It is certainly not hard to find a scenario where the general population of a state is becoming less religious but a segment of its population remains religious or becomes more religious and pressures the government to incorporate aspects of the majority religion into its laws. Thus both analyses predict a negative relationship between GIR and religiosity but do so based on different directions of causality. Most likely the reality is that this causality is not unidirectional and all of these trends are occurring simultaneously. Put differently, there is clearly a negative relationship between GIR and aspects of religiosity, but the direction of causality is more complicated than the supply-side theory would have it.

This dynamic is certainly consistent with other aspects of the findings in this chapter and previous ones. Many states are in fact engaging in policies to protect local culture, including religious culture, which is seen at risk due to past government policies and current outside influences. It is also consistent with the large literature on fundamentalism briefly discussed in Chapter 2. This literature defines fundamentalism, in part, as a reaction against the encroachments of modernity on religion. That is, modernity causes many people to become more secular, but fundamentalists seek to counter this in a number of ways including pressuring governments to enforce the religion through legislation and policy.

Whatever the interpretation of this result, it clearly contradicts the predictions of modernization-secularization theory. This body of theory, described in more detail in Chapter 2, predicts a monolithic drop in religion's influence in the public sphere. Clearly, this is not happening. This inverse relationship between religiosity and GIR makes a simultaneous and monolithic drop in both religiosity and GIR unlikely. This, combined with the results presented in this chapter and Chapter 4 regarding the general rise in GIR, as well as the results in Chapters 5 through 10, that most states have substantial GIR, paints a picture that is very different from the picture painted by modernization-secularization theory. The extent to which these findings are incompatible with this body of theory is discussed in more detail in Chapter 12.

This one example of the relationship between religiosity and GIR also illustrates a larger point. No study that attempts to compare 175 cases is able to account for all of the nuances of all of those cases. While there are certainly a number of macro-level and intermediate-level trends which can be identified, there are exceptions to every generalization, and crosscutting trends that produce a reality more complex than any quantitative analysis can hope to fully capture.

That being said, the results of this study, including those presented in this chapter, have uncovered trends that could only be uncovered when comparing a large number of cases. Thus, in the end neither the large-n approach used here nor the comparative approach, which focuses on one or a few cases, can uncover all of the complexities of the relationship between religion and state, much less its place in the larger religious economy. Only through the combination of the two approaches can anything approaching full understanding be accomplished.

Conclusions

The religious economy is complicated, interrelated, multifaceted, and has a complex relationship with other political, social, and economic phenomena. At our current level of knowledge, no large-n study can aspire to do more than accurately map a distinct segment of the religious economy and begin to explore the relationship between that segment and other aspects of the religious economy, as well as its relationship to other political, social, and economic factors. This study of 175 governments based on the RAS dataset does this for separation of religion and state (SRAS) and government involvement in religion (GIR).

At the beginning of this study I asked a series of questions: What is the extent of GIR between 1990 and 2002 across the globe? Has the extent or nature of this involvement changed during this period? What social and political factors can explain the variation over place and time in GIR? How is GIR otherwise related to important social and political phenomena? This study has addressed all of these questions.

As is usually the case with this type of study, the answers are in some cases partial and create as many questions as answers. Yet this analysis makes a significant contribution to our knowledge of this particular portion of the religious economy. This contribution is part of the larger effort by social scientists to understand the nature of the religious economy, an effort that is very much a work in progress in which much is unknown and uncharted.

A METHOD TO THE MADNESS

In Act II, scene 2, of *Hamlet*, Polonius utters the famous phrase "though this be madness, yet there is method in it." While Polonius was referring to Hamlet's feigned madness in reaction to the events around him, his observation is also applicable to the patterns of GIR and those of the larger religious economy that have been uncovered by this analysis. It is perhaps more proper to say that there is both method to the madness and madness in the method. Specifically, there are patterns in the extent of GIR and its fluctuations between 1990 and 2002 but there are exceptions to every generalization that can be made about these patterns.

Put differently, there is considerable diversity in the extent and nature of the relationships between governments and religion. Yet, upon examination, patterns emerge. None of these patterns are absolute to the extent that all states that fit into a particular category behave in exactly the same way. The opposite is the case in that within every pattern there is diversity in its application and outright exceptions. Nevertheless these patterns are strong enough to highlight similarities across groups of states and in some cases similarities on a global level, to the extent that using knowledge of these patterns can give one the ability to predict elements of a state's policy toward religion and be correct reasonably more often than one would be incorrect.

One pattern that exemplifies this phenomenon is the tendency of most states to give preference to some religions over others. This manifests through a combination of support for one or more religions, sometimes through the creation of a multitiered system of recognition and benefits for different religions, and restrictions placed on minority religions. In 2002, 117 (66.8 percent) of the 175 states in the RAS dataset supported some religions more than others, and 131 (74.9 percent) engaged in some *religious discrimination* against minorities. Taking the overlap into account, 149 of 175 states (85.1 percent) either support some religions over others, place restrictions on some religions that are not placed on others, or both.

While this pattern clearly exists, these global statistics conceal an amazing level of diversity in approaches to supporting religion. As this book devotes six chapters to only brief descriptions of the religion and state policy for 175 states it is clearly not feasible to discuss the full extent of this diversity in any useful manner at this point in this study. However, it can be said that each state has a unique policy toward religion that is at least a little bit different from that of any other state and in most cases more than a little bit different. Thus, most states treat different religions differently, but this pattern manifests uniquely in each state. Furthermore, it is arguable that there is diversity in the motivations behind this commonality in state policy.

Uncovering all of the motivations for this differential treatment by state governments is not a realistic goal, but some common motivations can be listed. There is some overlap between these categories of motivations, but each of them highlights an important trend that deserves to be examined individually. First, many states wish to protect their indigenous culture from outside influences. This pattern is particularly prominent in the Orthodox Christian states of Eastern Europe. The indigenous religious cultures of these states were eroded by the policies of past communist governments, but since the early 1990s most of these states are following policies of reestablishing indigenous cultures. They tend to support Orthodox Christianity and have policies that vary from tolerance to support of other religions with a historical presence in the state, but they often severely restrict religions considered new to the state.

Second, many states see the need to protect their citizens from religions they consider dangerous. This pattern is distinct from the previous one in that certain religions are often singled out as particularly dangerous. This pattern, which often manifests as an anti-sect or anti-cult policy, is particularly common in Western and Eastern Europe, where nearly one-fourth of states were coded in 2002 as having anti-sect legislation, but it can be found elsewhere. This type of policy presumes that some religions are somehow dangerous to citizens or society. While this diagnosis appears true of such sects as Japan's Aum Shinrikyo sect, these policies may also target nonviolent groups, such as Sung Yung Moon's Unification Church and the Church of Scientology. The perception of the German government that Scientology is actually a business or con game that exploits vulnerable citizens and manipulates them into turning over their money, illustrates this type of government attitude. When countries compile lists of sects and cults, they often include religions that are considered mainstream elsewhere like Seventh Day Adventists, Mormons, Quakers, Jehovah's Witnesses, Hasidic Judaism, and Pentecostalism. In practice, "cult" and "sect" often seem to be applied to religions that are new to a state.[1]

Third, in many states religion is linked to national identity. This is particularly common in states with Muslim majorities. Of all such states, 57.4 percent declare Islam their official religion, which is over three times as often as any other religious tradition. Furthermore, all but 19.2 percent of Muslim majority states support some religions, including Islam, more than others. However, the association between a religious tradition and national identity is not at all limited to Muslim states or states that declare official religions. For instance, even though India has no official religion, many Hindus in India strongly associate Hinduism with national identity. This is part of the platform of one of India's major political parties, the BJP, and a strong part of the government's policy when the BJP is in power. Another manifestation of this tendency is hostility toward those who convert from the national religion. In a number of Asian states, including Bangladesh, India, Indonesia, Laos, and Vietnam, restrictions are placed on conversion from the national religion and converts suffer from considerable harassment intended to encourage them to renounce their conversion. Restrictions on conversion also exist in 14 of 20 Middle Eastern states, and several states in the former Soviet bloc and Africa. Interestingly, no Christian states place restrictions on conversion away from Christianity. Of the 29 states that are coded as restricting conversions away from the majority religion, 24 are Muslim majority states, 3 are Buddhist majority states, 1, Nepal, is Hindu, and the last is China.

Fourth, religions, and religious institutions and elites often have a symbiotic relationship with the state with each supporting the other. This is a classic relationship, noted by many in the literature on religion and state,[2] where religious elites and institutions support the state's legitimacy and in return the

---

[1] See also Bromley & Shupe (1985).
[2] See, for example, Lincoln (2003), and Stark & Bainbridge (1985: 506–30).

state supports the religion. Legislating aspects of the religion, and preferred access to state educational institutions are among the more common manifestations of this support. It can also manifest in the form of restricting or repressing other religions. In an extreme example of this phenomenon, in many Middle Eastern states citizenship is linked to religion. In Saudi Arabia all citizens must be Muslims and in Iran, Kuwait, and the UAE citizenship is strongly linked to Islam. In Israel, any Jew born anywhere can claim citizenship.[3] While most states with official religions can be said to fit into this category, most do not take the extreme step of directly linking religion and citizenship.

Fifth, religious doctrine can play a role. An obvious example is the hierarchy of religions in Islam. Islam is considered the superior religion and is expected to be given the dominant status in a Muslim state. Members of such religions as Judaism and Christianity are "peoples of the book," and Muslims believe these religions are based on authentic revelations that have become corrupted. These religions are to be tolerated, but are given second-class status. For instance, the places of worship of these religions cannot be built taller than mosques and the members of these religions are classically expected to pay a tribute to their Muslim rulers. The actual application of this principle varies considerably. The next rung is occupied by religions whose members are not considered "peoples of the book." There is no doctrinal tolerance for such religions but they are often given some level of toleration. The lowest rung is religions that are considered to be apostate religions, those that evolved from Islam into something else, making them heretical Muslim sects. These religions include the Bahai, Sikhs, Allowites, and Druze. These religions, especially the Bahai, tend to be subject to the highest level of *religious discrimination* in Muslim majority states. There are many other examples of how doctrine influences state policies, giving preference to some religions over others. Doctrine can be the source of legislation. A religious doctrine that is commonly legislated is the banning of abortions.

Sixth, in some states the support for a particular religion is to a great extent the result of historical inertia. In the state by state analyses in Chapters 5 through 10, eight states are listed as having a historical or cultural state religion. This relatively small number of states is likely the tip of the iceberg with regard to historical influence on GIR and state support for a religion. For example, it is true for many states that support for a religion is at least partially dependent on whether that religion has had a historical presence in that state. In the example of Greece and Turkey, certain religious minorities are given special privileges based on a historical agreement.

While these six motivations and causes for the pattern of most states giving different religions different treatment is not exhaustive, it does arguably cover a large proportion of the motivations for this trend across states. Of course, each state has a distinct history and unique set of motivations. Also, in most, if

---

[3] Israel also allows citizenship to non-Jews.

not all, cases the motivations and causes for the policies that fit this pattern of GIR are complicated and include multiple items from this list, as well as others.

Yet, these six motivations and causes are sufficient to demonstrate that similar policies can have dissimilar sources. For example, consider one of the more common forms of *religious discrimination*. In 2002, there were 77 states that placed limits on proselytizing. This certainly fits the pattern of protecting indigenous religions, as this would limit citizens' exposure to different religions. In some states these limits are placed mostly on religions the state considers dangerous. For instance Honduras' government has declared the Unification Church a dangerous sect and does not allow entry of its missionaries. It has also expelled numerous members of that Church. Honduras does not place similar restrictions on the missionaries of any other religion. Panama and Venezuela similarly single out the Unification Church. Proselytizing can easily be seen as an effort to undermine national identity in states where national identity is linked to religion. It can also be seen as an effort to undermine a religious monopoly by changing the religious demographics of a population. Also, most religious doctrines tend to convey a negative attitude toward missionaries who try to convert members away from their religion.

A second pattern that deserves attention is the overall increase in GIR between 1990 and 2002. This change was not seen in the structural variables from the RAS dataset – *official GIR* and *general restrictions*. However, the variables that examine 60 different government policies – *religious discrimination*, *religious regulation*, and *religious legislation* – showed a general shift to more GIR. Thus, during the 13-year period covered by the RAS data, the basic structure of GIR has not changed significantly but within that structure governments have been engaging in more GIR.

The shift to more GIR has not been monolithic. The states that have increased GIR greatly outnumber those that have decreased GIR, but GIR has dropped in a significant number of states. *Religious discrimination*, *religious regulation*, and *religious legislation* increased respectively in 55, 41, and 43 states, but dropped respectively in 17, 8, and 14 states. *General GIR*, which measures the overall level of GIR in a state, rose in 86 states, just short of half of the states in the RAS dataset, but dropped in 29 states.

As discussed in more detail in Chapter 11, a good proportion of these shifts in GIR can be explained by world region and religious tradition. Each world region has its own distinct pattern of GIR, as does each religious tradition. When combined, these two factors allow us to predict patterns of change in GIR with reasonable accuracy. Yet, for each general rule there are exceptions. Also, even for states that fit the pattern, there are diverse manifestations of that pattern. For instance, Orthodox Christian states in the former Soviet bloc have been increasing *religious discrimination*. The results, presented in Table 12.1, show that both the extent and nature of these changes in *religious discrimination* vary from state to state. Georgia is the most extreme case. Its score on the variable has increased 12 points and includes increases in 10 of the 16 categories of *religious discrimination* coded by the RAS project. On the other side of

TABLE 12.1. *Changes in Religious Discrimination in Former Soviet Orthodox Christian States, 1990* to 2002*

	Public observance	Build or repair places of worship	Access to places of worship	Formal orgs.	Education	Arrest, detention, harassment	Materials	Publications	Personal status	Proselytizing	Registration	Other
Armenia	i									i		i
Belarus		i	i	i				i				
Bulgaria	i	i	i	i		i		i			i	
Georgia		i	i	i	i	i	i			i	i	
Macedonia	i											
Moldova						i				d		
Romania	i	d						i	i			
Russia	i	i		i						i	i	
Ukraine								i		i	i	
Yugoslavia		i								i		

* In cases where data was not available for 1990, the first available year was used.

i = This form of religious discrimination increased between 1990 and 2002.

d = This form of religious discrimination decreased between 1990 and 2002.

the spectrum, Moldova decreased restrictions on proselytizing but increased arrests and harassment of minority religions, and this resulted in no overall change between 1990 and 2002 in the composite *religious discrimination* variable. In all these states other than Moldova, *religious discrimination* increased more than it decreased. Thus, there is a common pattern, but the exact manifestation of that pattern in each state is unique.

A third pattern that deserves further discussion is the high and growing level of GIR in Muslim states. While a complete evaluation of the causes of this trend is beyond the scope of this study, a number of factors worthy of note likely contribute to this trend. Many note that SRAS is a concept that is foreign to Islam. Many religious Muslims consider Islamic law the divinely decreed law of the land, leaving no room for public participation in lawmaking.[4] While this can also be said to be true of Christianity or Judaism, Islam has not undergone processes similar to the Reformation and the Enlightenment where society as a whole reassessed the role religion should play in society.[5] Interestingly, this can also be said to be true of Orthodox Christianity, which also has high levels of GIR.

There is, however, currently an important debate occurring among Muslims about Islam's public role. Militant Muslim fundamentalists seek an absolutist version of Islam, which aims to unite all Muslims within a single Muslim state and, in the interim, assures that states with Muslim majorities base rule on the principles of Islam. Movements advocating such views exist in nearly every Muslim majority state included in this study and many of these movements are actively pursuing their goal of making the state more Islamic. This is true even of such states as Saudi Arabia, which has the highest levels of GIR as measured by the RAS dataset.

These movements have resulted in increased GIR in several ways. First, they often gain influence in states and use that influence to get the state to legislate aspects of Islam. Sometimes the focus of these efforts is at the local or regional government level. Second, states often feel threatened by the political power of these movements and legislate aspects of Islam in order to preempt these movements. Third, states often seek to regulate and restrict these movements. This also results in an increase in GIR, especially in the *religious regulation* category. The tendency of some Muslim majority states to create state-controlled Islamic organizations and restrict all other Islamic organizations fits into the second two of these paths toward higher GIR. These organizations are intended to both bolster the claim that the government supports Islam and to reduce the influence of these militant Islamic movements. Even Saudi Arabia, which has given a considerable amount of influence to one of the more radical and absolutist versions of Islam, still needs to use its official institutions in order to protect it from even more radical and absolutist versions of the religion.

This third pattern is related to a fourth in which religious tradition is linked to the extent of GIR in a state. While there is certainly variation within religious

---

[4] Dalacoura (2000: 879), Lewis (1993: 96–8), Stepan (2000: 46–8).
[5] Huntington (1996).

traditions, each religious tradition can be said to have a pattern of GIR that is distinct from other traditions. As there was in the context of Orthodox Christianity, there are exceptions to these patterns and the pattern associated with a religious tradition manifests differently in different states. While this diversity is influenced by the factors identified in this study, it is also influenced by factors unique to each state's history and culture.

A fifth pattern is the globalization of religion. Religion is crossing borders in a number of ways. While this has perhaps been true for some time, the increasing globalization of the world is accelerating this process. Two phenomena that fit this pattern are international missionary movements and the spread of radical Islamic fundamentalism. Missionaries, especially from Christian and Muslim groups, are becoming increasingly common. The desire to spread one's religion is an old one but modern technology and the process of globalization has made doing so on an international level both logistically and financially easier. This is likely one of the reasons that limits on proselytizing are among the more common forms of *religious discrimination* and have increased considerably between 1990 and 2002.

The impact of militant Islamic fundamentalist movements in Islamic states has already been discussed in this chapter, though it is worth restating that such movements are ubiquitous in Muslim majority states. Such movements are also common in states with non-Muslim majorities, especially those with significant Muslim minority populations. In such states these movements tend to pursue a four-pronged agenda. First, they try to convert Muslims to their form of Islam. Second, they try to convert non-Muslims to Islam. Both of these goals are often pursued through providing social welfare to those who do not receive sufficient help from the state, though this tactic is common to many religious groups, not just Muslim ones. Third, they act as advocates for the Muslim community in the state. This can mean opposing perceived or real oppression or injustices perpetrated against Muslims. It can also mean pursuing a goal of trying to gain some form of preferential treatment for Islam. Fourth, a portion of these radicals, though certainly not all of them, fight what they consider to be a holy war against the state with the goal of turning it into a Muslim state. This goal is often pursued violently.

A sixth important pattern is that few states have SRAS. This is true no matter which of the seven operationalizations of the concept of SRAS is used. In fact, with the exception of the strictest definition of SRAS, absolute-SRAS, exemplified only by the United States of America, the proportion of states that have SRAS ranges between 8 percent and 22.3 percent of the 175 states in this study depending on the definition and operationalization of the concept. Thus, no matter how it is measured most states do not separate religion and state.

A seventh pattern is the link between democracy and GIR. On average, democracies are associated with lower levels of GIR. However, democracies are not substantially more likely than non-democracies to have SRAS. What differentiates democracies from nondemocracies is not whether they are willing to engage in substantial levels of GIR, but rather that there appears to be a line they will not cross. That is, there is an upper limit to the extent of GIR found in democracies that does not seem to apply to nondemocracies. This finding has significant implications for our conceptions of the nature of democracy.

Eighth, in a number of states the behavior of local and national governments differ. In nearly every case where this occurs it is because the local government engages in more GIR than does the national government. In some extreme cases, Nigeria for example, the national government is trying to pursue a policy of SRAS while local governments are trying to implement the religious laws of the majority religion in the region. There are numerous states in the former Soviet bloc and Asia where local governments are responsible for much of the *religious discrimination* against minorities, often in a manner that is in contrast to national policy or at least in a manner that can be considered as embellishing upon the national policy. In some cases the national government steps in to limit this practice but more often it does not. This pattern is particularly prominent in Afghanistan, Azerbaijan, Bangladesh, Belarus, Bhutan, Bulgaria, Georgia, India, Indonesia, Laos, Malaysia, Kazakhstan, Romania, Russia, Tajikistan, Ukraine, Uzbekistan, and Vietnam. Assuming that local governments are more aware of the desires of common citizens, this pattern implies that support for SRAS is weaker among the citizenry than among national policy makers.

Ninth, clauses in constitutions protecting religious freedom and rights are common. In fact, states that have these clauses in their constitution are far more common than states that respect the right to religious freedom. Of the 148 states for which there is sufficient information on the content of their constitutions, 133 promise some form of freedom of worship, 92 promise no discrimination on the basis of religion or equality for all religions, and 52 declare the state secular or prohibit the establishment of a religion. Yet, all but 44 of the 175 states in the RAS dataset engage in at least some *religious discrimination* and all but one enact at least some *religious legislation*. Thus, there is a large discrepancy between the principles enshrined in the states' constitutions and an examination of actual government behavior.

There are a number of additional patterns that emerged from the analysis of the RAS data. These include:

- GIR is inversely linked to individual religiosity.
- GIR is higher in states with higher levels of economic development.
- Aspects of GIR are higher in more populous states.
- Aspects of GIR are higher in states with more homogeneous populations.
- Individual religiosity has been increasing over time.
- Religious tradition, religious demography, population size, and economic development are all linked to the extent of individual religiosity.
- The Middle East has the highest levels of GIR in the world, even when compared to non–Middle Eastern Muslim states.

- Many of the states with the lowest GIR scores are in Africa and Latin America.
- The increases in *religious discrimination* between 1990 and 2002 tend to fit into one of two categories: restrictions on minority religious organizations and restrictions on efforts to spread minority religions or otherwise alter the religious character of the state.
- Increases in *religious regulation* tend to be mostly increases in the restrictions on religious organizations rather than religious practices.

In all, a considerable amount of method emerges from the madness and there are a number of identifiable trends that help to predict and explain the extent of GIR in individual states. Yet there remains a certain amount of madness within the method in that all of these patterns combined cannot explain the full extent of the diversity in the patterns of GIR.

It is likely that no large-n study such as this one can provide a complete explanation. While there are clearly international and regional trends as well as trends within other subgroups of states based on religious tradition, economic development, regime type, or some other basis for grouping states, local factors and history also play an important role. The strength of a study such as this one is its ability to assimilate large amounts of standardized information into a comprehensible framework that can discern larger patterns. Such a study can often uncover patterns that probably would not have been uncovered using more traditional comparative methodology. It can also settle debates where those using comparative methodology often argue that two opposite propositions are true, with each side able to find anecdotal evidence to support their contention. Large-n methodology can include all of the relevant anecdotes in the study and in doing so can often settle such debates.

The drawback of large-n methodology is that it often misses the local nuances and details that are critical for understanding a phenomenon. Social scientists seek to better understand the extent of GIR in each particular political and social setting. Thus, these local historical, political, and cultural factors are critical. It is my hope that those examining GIR in particular contexts will be able to integrate the insights from this study into their understanding of the unique local and regional histories and cultures of these particular contexts. These new understandings can then be the basis for future large-n studies. In short, the interaction between the large-n method and the comparative method is likely to produce a far deeper understanding of the extent and nature of GIR than either method could achieve on its own.

ALL PATHS LEAD TO RELIGION

The results presented here speak to an aspect of the seemingly endless secularization-modernization debate in a new way. As noted, the analysis documents a statistically significant rise in GIR between 1990 and 2002 that is mostly consistent across world regions and religious traditions. It also documents the finding that economic development is linked to higher levels of GIR, even when controlling for other relevant factors. All of this is inconsistent with the predictions of modernization-secularization theory.

Yet this evidence alone, despite its merits, cannot warrant a complete rejection of modernization and secularization theory. There are three reasons for this. First, its time-scope is limited. It covers only a 13-year segment of a process said to have been taking place for centuries. Second, GIR is only one aspect of the religious economy. Any rejection of the predictions of secularization and modernization theory would need to be based on more than one segment of the religious economy. For example, GIR is shown to have an inverse relationship with religiosity so it is arguable that this rise in GIR is merely a compensation for people becoming less religious and that overall the influence of religion in the larger picture has weakened.

Third, even if one were to look only at this aspect of the religious economy in isolation, it is not clear that the increase in GIR is really due to an increase in the influence of religion. As discussed earlier, a government's actions can have many motivations. Increasing GIR can mean that the government wants to increase its support for religion, but it can also mean that it wants to restrict or control religion. Even when a government intends to increase GIR the motivations for this can be diverse. For instance, a policy that gives preference to some religions over others can be motivated by any combination of the motivations discussed earlier in this chapter.

Despite all of this it is arguable that the evidence presented here is sufficient to call into question the predictions of modernization-secularization theory. No matter how one interprets these results, the interpretation leads to the conclusion that an aspect of religion remains a significant influence on government behavior or on some other important aspect of society.

There are several possible interpretations of the finding that GIR has risen between 1990 and 2002. The first is the simple explanation – that this is part of a larger rise in the influence of religion. This is consistent with the finding of Norris and Inglehart that, overall, religiosity is rising in the world, though it is dropping in postmodern societies.[6]

Another possible explanation is that GIR is increasing in order to compensate for a drop elsewhere in the religious economy. The most likely culprit for this drop elsewhere in the religious economy, based on the supply-side theory of religion, is a drop in religiosity. Religiosity is dropping in more developed societies where people no longer need to worry about their physical needs being met[7] and these states are precisely where, according to the multivariate analysis in Chapter 4, GIR is increasing the most.

Assuming for the moment that this description of the religious economy is accurate, this does not necessarily represent a drop in religion's influence. Rather, it can be seen to represent religion's ability to evolve and compensate

---

[6] Norris & Inglehart (2004).
[7] Norris & Inglehart (2004).

in a new environment. If secularization-modernization theory were correct, we would expect a drop in religion's influence in all aspects of the religious economy, or at least in most major aspects. Yet what we find is an inverse relationship where when religion's influence drops in one aspect of the religious economy, it becomes stronger in another. When viewed from this perspective, religion is a strong and dynamic sociopolitical phenomenon that adapts to changing environments in order to remain relevant. The nature and manifestation of that relevance may change with the times but the fact of that relevance remains constant.

Of course, it is arguable that this interpretation of the religious economy is inaccurate. One reason for this is that while religiosity is dropping in some states, especially developed ones, overall, according to the most comprehensive study to date on the topic, the number of religious people in the world is increasing.[8] Also, as discussed in more detail in Chapter 11, it may be that it is decreased religiosity that is causing the rise in GIR, rather than a rise in GIR causing decreased religiosity. Religious conservatives do lobby governments to legislate aspects of religion, especially in cases where social norms are no longer sufficient to regulate behavior in the desired manner. Also, as discussed in more detail in Chapter 2, religious fundamentalism is believed to be in part a reaction to protect religion against the encroachments of modernity and it is precisely religious fundamentalists who are among the most active in trying to get governments to become more religious.

A third possible interpretation of the results is that the rise in GIR represents a concerted effort by governments to restrict and control religion. That is, governments do not support religion. They fear it and wish to keep it under control. One could argue that this means that religion's influence on governments is waning. From the narrow point of view of whether governments are trying to support religion, this interpretation would be correct. However, when looking at the larger picture, this interpretation of the findings also supports the argument that religion remains relevant. If governments truly fear religion's political and social power to the extent that they see a need to restrain it, this would imply that this political and social power exists. Thus, based on this scenario, governments may not be guided by religion, but they are certainly influenced by it. The political power of religion in other parts of the religious economy is perceived by the government as sufficiently strong that measures to co-opt, control, or repress it are necessary.

Given this, whatever one's interpretation of the reasons for the rise in GIR documented in this study, all of these interpretations require that some aspect of the religious economy remains strong and influential. Thus, so to speak, all paths lead to religion.

Whether this evidence when viewed from this "all paths" perspective is sufficient to reject modernization and secularization theory depends on how

---

[8] Norris & Inglehart (2004).

one interprets the predictions of these theories. If one requires a measurable drop in religion's influence in the religious economy as a whole, these results cannot really address the issue. As discussed in Chapters 1 and 3, comprehensive data does not exist. Furthermore, even assuming we had accurate and detailed data on every aspect of the religious economy, it would be difficult if not impossible to find a way to combine these measures in a way that accurately measures the entire religious economy.

However, if one takes the position that secularization-modernization theory predicts a decline in religion's influence to the extent that it is no longer a significant sociopolitical factor, it is arguable that the evidence presented here contradicts this. All possible interpretations of the result lead to the conclusion that an aspect of the religious economy, though not necessarily its influence on government, remains significant in the public sphere. When looking at the data and secularization-modernization theory from this perspective, the fact that this study has data from only a limited time period becomes irrelevant.

On balance, this study emphasizes the persistence of a vibrant religious economy where religion adjusts to an ever-changing environment to remain strong and influential. Of course, this entails a reduction of religion's influence in some aspects of the religious economy, but this is countered by a rise in its influence in other facets of that economy. This description does not fit well with the prediction of a unidirectional drop in religion's influence. Secularization and modernization theory's description of modernity's influence in religion is in many ways accurate but presents only part of the picture. The decline in some manifestations of religion's influence are complemented by reactions in other parts of the religious economy that increase other manifestations of its influence.

Two things are becoming increasingly clear. All paths, in a sense, lead to religion. No matter how one views the larger picture, some aspect of religion remains a significant influence on at least some aspects of society and politics. Likely many aspects of religion are influential on many aspects of society and politics. Second, we do not have sufficient information to properly evaluate the true impact of religion in its full multifaceted splendor on politics and society. The data on religion is less developed than it is in other areas studied by social scientists such as conflict, economics, political parties, voting patterns in legislatures, judiciary policy, and electoral behavior to name a few.

Fortunately, many young scholars, strongly influenced by the events of 9/11, are making religion the focus of their work. Many of them are interested in the quantitative aspects of the profession and, in time, will hopefully fill in many of the gaps in the data. Perhaps this particularly blatant and abhorrent manifestation of the power of religion, through reminding us of religion's potential, will have the positive influence of increasing our understanding of religion's role in society and politics.

Appendix

Data Collection and Reliability

All of the RAS variables were collected as follows. A research assistant wrote a report on each country based on general sources, such as the US State Department Religious Freedom reports and the *World Christian Encyclopedia* (*WCE*),[1] journalistic sources from the Lexis/Nexis database, and country-specific academic sources including journal articles and books. A more complete listing of the sources used can be found in the notes for Chapters 5 through 10. After I approved the report, the same research assistant filled out a codesheet, which I reviewed in tandem with the report. The primary purpose of the second review was to ensure consistency in codings between coders.

While clearly there was more information available for some countries than others, I am confident that the data closely reflects reality for two reasons. First, the general sources, including the US State Department and the *WCE*, contain good information for most states. However, these sources, while nearly always accurate, did often omit information. Second, even in the less covered third-world states, including many African states, religious issues drew considerable attention by human rights groups and the media. Thus, when the general sources indicated that religious issues were relevant in a country, the additional sources usually provided further detail. While it is certainly possible, and even likely, that the dataset is missing some information, I am confident that the data very closely resembles the reality on the ground as well or better than do other datasets that focus on similar topics. See, for example, the Minorities at Risk project's dataset on ethnic conflict.[2]

In order to assure inter-coder reliability, approximately 25 percent of the cases were recoded. I selected these cases so that about 25 percent of cases from each region and 25 percent of cases from each coder were recoded. The cases were also selected so that there would be a reasonable distribution based on

---

[1] Barret, Kurian, & Johnson (2001).
[2] A full description of the Minorities at Risk dataset as well as a copy of the dataset is available at www.cidcm.umd.edu/.

TABLE A.I. *Countries Included in Backup Codings*

Country	Region	Majority religion	Country	Region	Majority religion
Afghanistan	Asia	Sunni Islam	Latvia	Former USSR	Christian
Albania	Former USSR	Sunni Islam	Lesotho	Sub-Saharan Africa	Christian
Algeria	Middle East & N. Africa	Sunni Islam	Liberia	Sub-Saharan Africa	Mixed
Angola	Sub-Saharan Africa	Christian	Malaysia	Asia	Sunni Islam
Austria	Western democracies	Catholic	Malta	Western democracies	Catholic
Azerbaijan	Former USSR	Shi'i Islam	Mauritius	Sub-Saharan Africa	Mixed
Brazil	Latin America	Catholic	Nicaragua	Latin America	Catholic
Cambodia	Asia	Buddhist	Pakistan	Asia	Sunni Islam
Cameroon	Sub-Saharan Africa	Mixed	Peru	Latin America	Catholic
Colombia	Latin America	Catholic	Poland	Former USSR	Catholic
Finland	Western democracies	Christian	Qatar	Middle East & N. Africa	Sunni Islam
France	Western democracies	Catholic	Saudi Arabia	Middle East & N. Africa	Sunni Islam
Gabon	Sub-Saharan Africa	Christian	Senegal	Sub-Saharan Africa	Islam
Georgia	Former USSR	Orthodox Christian	South Korea	Asia	Mixed
Ghana	Sub-Saharan Africa	Christian	Spain	Western democracies	Catholic
Guinea-Bissau	Sub-Saharan Africa	Mixed	Thailand	Asia	Buddhist
Haiti	Latin America	Catholic	Turkey	Middle East & N. Africa	Sunni Islam
Iceland	Western democracies	Christian	Turkmenistan	Former USSR	Sunni Islam
Iran	Middle East & N. Africa	Shi'i Islam	UK	Western democracies	Christian
Iraq	Middle East & N. Africa	Shi'i Islam	Uganda	Sub-Saharan Africa	Christian
Ivory Coast	Sub-Saharan Africa	Mixed	Uruguay	Latin America	Catholic
Japan	Asia	Other (Shinto)			

TABLE A.2. *Correlations between RAS Data and Backup Codings*

Year	Official GIR	General restrictions	Religious discrimination	Religious regulation	Religious legislation
1990	.888	.805	.985	.848	.990
1991	.887	.809	.985	.848	.990
1992	.892	.821	.985	.882	.990
1993	.892	.918	.985	.884	.990
1994	.892	.922	.985	.883	.990
1995	.892	.912	.985	.883	.990
1996	.892	.943	.986	.881	.990
1997	.892	.943	.991	.885	.990
1998	.892	.943	.986	.884	.990
1999	.892	.943	.982	.896	.990
2000	.892	.943	.982	.900	.991
2001	.892	.939	.961	.907	.984
2002	.892	.939	.979	.916	.987

Significance (p-value) for all correlations in table = .000

majority religion and country size. Forty-three of the cases included in this study were recoded. These are listed in Table A.1. The recoders were all research assistants from the project who had coded other cases. I did not review these codings in order to avoid any bias.

The reliability tests are presented in Table A.2. The results show that all of the codings by the backup coders have acceptable levels of correlation and all of these correlations have high levels of statistical significance. The correlations are particularly high for *religious discrimination, religious regulation*, and *religious legislation*. This is because determining whether a particular form of discrimination, regulation, or legislation existed in a state was relatively straightforward.

The correlations for *official GIR* and *general restrictions* are somewhat lower because these variables are based on broader categories. It sometimes occurred that a state could fit into either of two categories and a judgement call had to be made as to which category to choose. For the official GIR variable, these differences in codings were only among states that did not have official religions. That is, the coders are in complete agreement as to which states had official religions and which did not. Similarly, there were no disagreements on the coding of the *general restrictions* variable for the categories of "some religions are illegal" and "all religions are illegal."

Finally, the *religious discrimination, religious regulation, religious legislation*, and *general GIR* variables are composite variables. Accordingly, it is important to assess whether the components are measuring the same thing. The Crombach's Alpha for these variables are 0.90, 0.76, 0.87, and 0.71

respectively. As a score of 0.70 or higher is generally considered to mean that the component variables measure similar phenomena, this confirms the appropriateness of the design of these composite variables.

Overall, these results are well within the bounds considered acceptable within the field of events data coding.

Bibliography

Abu-Nimer, Mohammed, 2001, "Conflict Resolution, Culture, and Religion: Toward a Training Model of Interreligious Peacebuilding," *Journal of Peace Research*, 38 (6): 685–704.

Aldridge, Alan, 2000, *Religion in the Contemporary World*, Cambridge: Polity Press.

Almond, Gabriel, 1960, "Introduction: A Functional Approach to Comparative Politics," in Almond and James C. Coleman, eds., *The Politics of the Developing Areas*, Princeton: Princeton University Press.

Almond, Gabriel, R. Scott Appleby, and Emmanuel Sivan, 2003, *Strong Religion: The Rise of Fundamentalism Around the World*, Chicago: University of Chicago Press.

Amor, Abdelfattah, 1995, "Implementation of the Declaration on the Elimination of All Forms of Intolerance and of Discrimination Based on Religion or Belief: Austria," United Nations Economic and Social Council Commission on Human Rights.

An-Na'im, Abdullahi Ahmed, 2002, "The Islamic Counter-Reformation," *New Perspectives Quarterly*, 19 (1): 29–35.

Appleby, R. Scott, 2000, *The Ambivalence of the Sacred: Religion, Violence, and Reconciliation*, New York: Rowman & Littlefield.

Apter, David, 1965, *The Politics of Modernization*, Chicago: University of Chicago Press.

Argyle, Michael, 1959, *Religious Behavior*, Glencoe, IL: Free Press.

Arjomand, Said Amir, ed., 1993, *The Political Dimensions of Religion*, New York: State University of New York Press.

Bader, Viet, 1999, "Religious Pluralism; Secularism or Priority for Democracy," *Political Theory*, 27 (5): 597–633.

Barret, D. B., G. T. Kurian, and T. M. Johnson, 2001, *World Christian Encyclopedia*, 2nd edn., Oxford: Oxford University Press.

Barro, Robert J., and Rachel M. McCleary, 2003, "Religion and Economic Growth Across Countries," *American Sociological Review*, 68 (5): 760–81.

Barro, Robert J., and Rachel M. McCleary, 2005, "Which Countries Have State Religions," *Quarterly Journal of Economics*, 104 (4): 1331–70.

Batson, C. Daniel, and Patricia A. Schoenrade, 1991, "Measuring Religion as Quest: 2 Reliability Concerns," *Journal for the Scientific Study of Religion*, 30 (4): 430–47.

Beckford, James A., 1985, "The Insulation and Isolation of the Sociology of Religion, *Sociological Analysis*, 46 (4): 347–54.

Beit-Hallahmi, Benjamin, 2003, "The Return of Martyrdom: Honour, Death, and Im-
mortality," *Totalitarian Movements and Political Religions*, 4 (3): 11–34.

Bellah, Robert N., 1978, "Religion and Legitimation in the American Republic,"
Society, May–June: 16–23.

Ben-Dor, Gabriel, and Ami Pedahzur, 2003, "The Uniqueness of Islamic Fundamentalism and the Fourth Wave of International Terrorism," *Totalitarian Movements and
Political Religions*, 4 (3): 71–90.

Berryman, Phillip, 1987, *Liberation Theology*, Philadelphia: Temple University.

Beyer, Peter, 1999, "Secularization from the Perspective of Globalization: A Response to
Dobbelaere," *Sociology of Religion*, 60 (3): 289–301.

Beyerlein, Kraig, and Mark Chaves, 2003, "The Political Activities of Religious Congregations in the US," *Journal for the Scientific Study of Religion*, 42 (2): 229–46.

Boyle, Kevin, and Juliet Sheen, 1997, *Freedom of Religion and Belief: A World Report*,
London: Routledge.

Bromley, David, and Anson Shupe, 1985, *A Documentary History of the Anti-Cult
Movement*, Arlington, TX: Center for Social Research.

Bruce, Steve, 1992, *Religion and Modernization*, Oxford: Clarendon Press.

Campbell, Robert A., and James E. Curtis, 1994, "Religious Involvement Across Societies: Analysis for Alternative Measures in National Surveys," *Journal for the Scientific Study of Religion*, 33 (3): 217–29.

Canetti-Nisim, Daphna, 2003, "Two Religious Meaning Systems, One Political Belief
System: Religiosity, Alternative Religiosity, and Political Extremism," *Totalitarian
Movements and Political Religions*, 4 (3): 35–54.

Chaves, Mark, 1994, "Secularization as Declining Religious Authority," *Social Forces*,
72 (3), March: 749–74.

Chaves, Mark, and David E. Cann, 1992, "Religion, Pluralism and Religious Market
Structure, *Rationality and Society*, 4 (3): 272–90.

Chaves, Mark, and Phillip S. Gorski, 2001, "Religious Pluralism and Religious Participation," *Annual Review of Sociology*, 27: 261–81.

Chaves, Mark, Peter J. Schraeder, and Mario Sprindys, 1994, "State Regulation of Religion and Muslim Religious Vitality in the Industrialized West," *Journal of Politics*,
56 (4): 1087–97.

Chiozza, Giacomo, 2002, "Is There a Clash of Civilizations? Evidence from Patterns of
International Conflict Involvement, 1946–97," *Journal of Peace Research*, 39 (6):
711–34.

Cox, Harvey, 1965, *The Secular City*, London: SCM Press.

Cunradi, Carol B., Raul Caetano, and John Schafer, 2002, "Religious Affiliation,
Denominational Homogamy, and Intimate Partner Violence Among US Couples,"
Journal for the Scientific Study of Religion, 41 (1): 139–51.

Dalacoura, Katrina, 2000, "Unexceptional Politics? The Impact of Islam on International Relations," *Millennium*, 29 (3): 879–87.

Demerath, N. J. III, 1995, "Rational Paradigms, A-Rational Religion, and the Debate
over Secularization," *Journal for the Scientific Study of Religion*, 34 (1): 105–12.

Demerath, N. J. III, 2001, *Crossing the Gods: World Religions and Worldly Politics*, NJ:
Rutgers University Press.

Deutsch, Karl, 1953, *Nationalism and Social Communication*, Cambridge, MA: MIT
Press.

Deutsch, Karl W., 1963, "The Limits of Common Sense," in Nelson Polsby, ed., *Politics and Social Life*, Boston: Houghton Mifflin, 51–7.

Dobbelaere, Karel, 1999, "Towards an Integrated Perspective of the Processes Related to the Descriptive Concept of Secularization," *Sociology of Religion*, 60 (3): 229–47.

Durham, W. Cole Jr., 1996, "Perspectives on Religious Liberty: A Comparative Framework," in John D. van der Vyver and John Witte Jr., *Religious Human Rights in Global Perspective: Legal Perspectives*, Boston: Martinus Njhoff, 1–44.

Durkheim, Emile, 1964, *The Elementary Forms of Religious Life*, trans. Joseph Ward Swain, London: George Allen & Unwin.

Ebaugh, Helen R., 2002, "Return of the Sacred: Reintegration Religion in the Social Sciences," *Journal for the Scientific Study of Religion*, 41 (3): 385–95.

Eisenstadt, S. N., 2000, "The Reconstruction of Religious Arenas in the Framework of 'Multiple Modernities,' " *Millennium*, 29 (3): 591–611.

Elazar, Daniel J., 1986, *Israel: "Building a New Society,"* Bloomington: Indiana University Press.

Ellingsen, Tanja, 2000, "Colorful Community or Ethnic Witches' Brew? Multiethnicity and Domestic Conflict During and After the Cold War," *Journal of Conflict Resolution*, 44 (2): 228–49.

Ellingsen, Tanja, 2002, "The Relevance of Culture in UN Voting Behavior," paper presented at the International Studies Association 43rd annual conference in New Orleans, March.

Ellison, Christopher G., 1995, "Rational Choice Explanations of Individual Religious Behavior: Notes on the Problem of Social Embeddedness," *Journal for the Scientific Study of Religion*, 34 (1): 89–97.

Ellison, Christopher G., and Kristin L. Anderson, 2001, "Religious Involvement and Domestic Violence Among US Couples," *Journal for the Scientific Study of Religion*, 40 (2): 269–86.

Ellison, Christopher G., John P. Bartkowski, and Kristin L. Anderson, 1999, "Are There Religious Variations in Domestic Violence," *Journal of Family Issues*, 20 (1): 87–113.

Erickson, Joseph A., 1991, "Adolescent Religious Development and Commitment: A Structural Equation Model of the Role of Family, Peer Group, and Educational Influences," *Journal for the Scientific Study of Religion*, 21 (2): 131–52.

Esman, Milton, 1973, "The Management of Communal Conflict," *Public Policy*, 21, 49–78.

Esmer, Yilmaz, 2002, "Is There an Islamic Civilization?" *Comparative Sociology*, 1 (3–4): 265–98.

Esposito, John L., and James P. Piscatori, 1991, "Democratization and Islam," *Middle East Journal*, 45 (3): 427–40.

Esposito, John L., and John O. Voll, 2000, "Islam and the West: Muslim Voices of Dialogue," *Millennium*, 29 (3): 613–39.

Fearon, James D., and David D. Latin, 2003, "Ethnicity, Insurgency, and Civil War," *American Political Science Review*, 97 (1): 17–32.

Feldman, Noah, 2003, "Muslim Democrats? Why Not!" *Wall Street Journal*, April 8: A. 14.

Fergusson, D. M., L. J. Horwood, K. L. Kershaw, and F. T. Shannon, 1986, "Factors Associated with Reports of Wife Assault in New Zealand," *Journal of Marriage and the Family*, 48: 407–12.

Finke, Roger, 1990, "Religious Deregulation: Origins and Consequences," *Journal of Church and State*, 32 (30): 609–26.

Finke, Roger, Avery M. Guest, and Rodney Stark, 1996, "Mobilizing Local Religious Markets: Religious Pluralism in the Empire State, 1855 to 1865," *American Sociological Review*, 61 (2): 203–18.

Finke, Roger, and Laurence R. Iannaccone, 1993, "Supply-Side Explanations for Religious Change,"*Annals of the American Association of Political and Social Sciences*, 527, May: 27–39.

Finke, Roger, and Rodney Stark, 1998, "Religious Choice and Competition (Reply to Olson)," *American Sociological Review*, 63 (5): 761–6.

Fisch, M. Steven, 2002, "Islam and Authoritarianism," *World Politics*, 55 (1): 4–37.

Foster-Carter, A., 1985, "The Sociology of Development," in M. Haralambos, ed., *Sociology: New Directions*, Ormskirk: Causeway.

Fox, Jonathan, 2002, *Ethnoreligious Conflict in the Late Twentieth Century: A General Theory*, Lanham, MD: Lexington Books.

Fox, Jonathan, 2004, *Religion, Civilization and Civil War: 1945 Through the New Millennium*, Lanham, MD: Lexington Books.

Fox, Jonathan, 2006, "World Separation of Religion and State into the Twenty-first Century," *Comparative Political Studies*, 39 (5): 537–69.

Fox, Jonathan, 2007, "Do Democracies Have Separation of Religion and State?" *Canadian Journal of Political Science*.

Fox, Jonathan, and Shmuel Sandler, 2003, "Quantifying Religion: Toward Building More Effective Ways of Measuring Religious Influence on State-Level Behavior," *Journal of Church and State*, 45 (3): 559–88.

Fox, Jonathan, and Shmuel Sandler, 2004, *Bringing Religion into International Relations*, New York: Palgrave-Macmillan.

Fradkin, Hillel, 2000, "Does Democracy Need Religion?" *Journal of Democracy*, 11 (1): 87–94.

Froese, Paul, 2004, "After Atheism: An Analysis of Religious Monopolies in the Post-Communist World," *Sociology of Religion*, 65 (1): 57–75.

Fuller, Graham E., 2002, "The Future of Political Islam," *Foreign Affairs*, 81 (2): 48–60.

Funk, Ruth A., 1967, "A Survey of Attitudes Toward Religion and Philosophy of Life," in Marvin E. Shaw and Jack M. Wright, eds., *Scales for the Measurement of Attitudes*, New York: McGraw-Hill.

García-Montúfar, Guillermo, Moisés Arata Solís, and Scott E. Isaacson, 2004, "Advances in Religious Liberty in Peru," *Brigham Young University Law Review*, Summer.

Gellner, Ernest, 1992, *Postmodernism, Reason and Religion*, London: Routledge.

Gill, Anthony, 1998, *Rendering Unto Caesar: The Catholic Church and the State in Latin America*, Chicago: University of Chicago Press.

Gill, Anthony, 1999, "Government Regulation, Social Anomie and Religious Pluralism in Latin America: A Cross-National Analysis,"*Rationality and Society*, 11 (3): 287–316.

Gill, Anthony, 2001, "Religion and Comparative Politics," *Annual Review of Political Science*, 4: 117–38.

Girard, Rene, 1977, *Violence and the Sacred*, trans. Patrick Gregory, Baltimore: Johns Hopkins University Press.

Gjuraj, Tonin, 2000, "A Stable Ecumenical Model? How Religion Might Become a Political Issue in Albania," *East European Quarterly*, Spring.

Glasner, Peter E., 1977, *The Sociology of Secularization: A Critique of a Concept*, London: Routledge & Kegan Paul.

Gopin, Marc, 2000, *Between Eden and Armageddon: The Future of World Religions, Violence, and Peacemaking*, Oxford: Oxford University Press.

Gopin, Marc, 2002, *Holy War, Holy Peace: How Religion Can Bring Peace to the Middle East*, New York: Oxford University Press.

Greeley, Andrew, "A Religious Revival in Russia?" 1994, *Journal for the Scientific Study of Religion*, 33 (3): 253–72.

Greenwalt, Kent, 1988, *Religious Convictions and Political Choice*, Oxford: Oxford University Press.

Grim, Brian J., and Roger Finke, 2006, "International Religion Indexes: Government Regulation, Government Favoritism, and Social Regulation of Religion," *Interdisciplinary Journal of Research on Religion*, 2 (1): 1–40.

Gurr, Ted R., 1993, *Minorities at Risk*, United States Institute of Peace.

Gurr, Ted R., 2000, *Peoples versus States: Minorities at Risk in the New Century*, Washington, DC: United States Institute of Peace Press.

Haddad, Mohanna, 1998, "Culture and State in Jordan: Religious Freedom and Citizenship,"*Ecumenical Review*, (Geneva) Oct.

Hadden, Jeffrey K., 1987, "Toward Desacralizing Secularization Theory," *Social Forces*, 65 (3): 587–611.

Halpern, 1964, "Toward Further Modernization of the Study of New Nations," *World Politics*, October (17): 157–81.

Hamberg, Eva M., and Thorleif Pettersson, 1994, "The Religious Market: Denominational Competition and Religious Participation in Contemporary Sweden," *Journal for the Scientific Study of Religion*, 33: 205–16.

Harris, Fredrick C., 1994, "Something Within: Religion as a Mobilizer of African-American Political Activism," *Journal of Politics*, 56 (1): 42–68.

Hayes, Bernadette C., 1995, "The Impact of Religious Identification on Political Attitudes: An International Comparison," *Sociology of Religion*, 56 (2): 177–94.

Haynes, Jeff, 1997, "Religion, Secularisation, and Politics: A Postmodern Conspectus," *Third World Quarterly*, 18 (4): 709–28.

Haynes, Jeff, 1998, *Religion in Global Politics*, New York: Longman.

Haynes, Jeff, 1994, *Religion in Third World Politics*, Boulder: Lynne Rienner.

Hefner, Robert H., 2001, "Public Islam and the Problem of Democratization," *Sociology of Religion*, 62 (4): 491–514.

Henderson, Errol A., 1997, "Culture or Contiguity: Ethnic Conflict, the Similarity of States, and the Onset of War, 1820–1989," *Journal of Conflict Resolution*, 41 (5), October: 649–68.

Henderson, Errol A., 1998, "The Democratic Peace Through the Lens of Culture, 1820–1989," *International Studies Quarterly*, 42 (3), September: 461–84.

Henderson, Errol A., 2004, "Mistaken Identity: Testing the Clash of Civilizations Thesis in Light of Democratic Peace Claims," *British Journal of Political Science*, 34: 539–63.

Henderson, Errol A., 2005, "Not Letting the Evidence Get in the Way of Assumptions: Testing the Clash of Civilizations with More Data," *International Politics*, 42 (4): 458–69.

Henderson, Errol A., and J. David Singer, 2000, "Civil War in the Post-colonial World, 1946–92," *Journal of Peace Research*, 37 (3): 275–99.

Henderson, Errol A., and Richard Tucker, 2001, "Clear and Present Strangers: The Clash of Civilizations and International Conflict," *International Studies Quarterly*, 45 (2): 317–38.

Hendon, David W., and James M. Kennedy, 1995, "Notes on Church-State Affairs: Armenia," *Journal of Church and State*, 37 (4).

Horowitz, Donald L., 1985, *Ethnic Groups in Conflict*, Berkeley: University of California Press.

Hunsberger, Bruce, 1989, "A Short Version of the Christian Orthodoxy Scale," *Journal for the Scientific Study of Religion*, 28 (3): 360–5.

Huntington, Samuel P., 1993, "The Clash of Civilizations?" *Foreign Affairs*, 72 (3): 22–49.

Huntington, Samuel P., 1996, *The Clash of Civilizations and the Remaking of the World Order*, New York: Simon & Schuster.

Hurd, Elizabeth S., 2004, "The Political Authority of Secularism in International Relations," *European Journal of International Relations*, 10 (2): 235–62.

Iannaccone, Lawrence R., 1991, "The Consequence of Religious Market Structure," *Rationality and Society*, 3: 156–77.

Iannaccone, Lawrence R., 1995a, "Second Thoughts: A Response to Chaves, Demerath, and Ellison," *Journal for the Scientific Study of Religion*, 34 (1): 113–20.

Iannaccone, Lawrence R., 1995b, "Voodoo Economics? Reviewing the Rational Choice Approach to Religion," *Journal for the Scientific Study of Religion*, 34 (1): 76–89.

Jaggers, Keith, and Ted R. Gurr, 1995, "Tracking Democracy's Third Wave with the Polity III Data," *Journal of Peace Research*, 32 (4): 469–82.

Jelen, Ted G., 1984, "Respect for Life, Sexual Morality, and Opposition to Abortion," *Review of Religious Research*, 25: 220–31.

Jelen, Ted G., 1993, "The Political Consequences of Religious Group Attitudes," *Journal of Politics*, 55 (1): 178–90.

Jelen, Ted G., and Clyde Wilcox, 1990, "Denominational Preference and the Dimensions of Political Tolerance," *Sociological Analysis*, 51 (1): 69–81.

Juergensmeyer, Mark, 1991, "Sacrifice and Cosmic War," *Terrorism and Political Violence*, 3 (3): 101–17.

Juergensmeyer, Mark, 1993, *The New Cold War?* Berkeley: University of California Press.

Kalyvas, Stathis N., 1998, "Democracy and Religious Politics: Evidence from Belgium," *Comparative Political Studies*, 31 (3): 292–320.

Kalyvas, Stathis N., 2000, "Commitment Problems in Emerging Democracies: The Case of Religious Parties," *Comparative Politics*, 22 (4): 379–98.

Kaplan, Jeffrey, 2002, "Introduction," *Terrorism and Political Violence*, 14 (1): 1–24.

Karpov, Vycheslav, 2002, "Religiosity and Tolerance in the United States and Poland," *Journal for the Scientific Study of Religion*, 41 (2): 267–88.

Kautsky, J., 1972, *The Political Consequences of Modernization*, New York: John Wiley.

Keddie, Nikki R., 1985, "Shiism and Revolution," in Bruce Lincoln, ed., *Religion, Rebellion and Revolution,* London: Macmillan.

Kekes, J., 1993, *The Morality of Pluralism*, Princeton, NJ: Princeton University Press.

Kimball, Charles, 2002, *When Religion Becomes Evil*, San Francisco: Harper Collins.

Kuran, Timur, 1991, "Fundamentalism and the Economy," in Martin E. Marty and R. Scott Appleby, eds., *Fundamentalisms and the State: Remaking Politics, Economies and Militance*, Chicago: University of Chicago Press, 289–301.

Lai, Brian, 2006, "An Empirical Examination of Religion and Conflict in the Middle East, 1950–1992," *Foreign Policy Analysis*, 2 (1): 21–36.

Lambert, Yves, 1999, "Religion in Modernity as a New Axial Age: Secularization or New Religious Forms," *Sociology of Religion*, 60 (3): 303–33.

Laitin, David, 2000, "Language Conflict and Violence: The Straw that Strengthens the Camel's Back," *Archives Europennes de Sociologie*, 41 (1): 97–137.

Leak, Gary K., and Brandy A. Randall, 1995, "Clarification of the Link Between Right-Wing Authoritarianism and Religiousness: The Role of Religious Maturity," *Journal for the Scientific Study of Religion*, 34 (2): 245–52.

Lechner, Frank A., 1991, "The Case Against Secularization: A Rebuttal," *Social Forces*, 69 (4), June: 1103–19.

Leng, Russel J., and Patrick M. Regan, 2002, "Social and Political Cultural Effects on the Outcome of Mediation in Militarized Interstate Disputes," *International Studies Quarterly*, 47 (3): 431–52.

Lewis, Bernard, 1993, *Islam and the West*, Oxford: Oxford University Press.

Lewy, Gunther, 1974, *Religion and Revolution*, New York: Oxford University Press.

Lijphart, Arend, 1997, *Democracy in Plural Societies*, New Haven: Yale University Press.

Lincoln, Bruce, 2003, *Holy Terrors: Thinking About Religion After September 11*, Chicago: University of Chicago Press.

Linz, Juan J., 1978, *Crisis, Breakdown, and Reequilibration*, Baltimore, MD: Johns Hopkins University Press.

Luttwak, Edward, 1994, "The Missing Dimension," in Douglas Johnston and Cynthia Sampson, eds., *Religion, the Missing Dimension of Statecraft*, Oxford: Oxford University Press, 8–19.

Madeley, John T. S., 2003a, "European Liberal Democracy and the Principle of State Religious Neutrality," *West European Politics*, 26 (1): 1–22.

Madeley, John T. S., 2003b, "A Framework for the Comparative Analysis of Church-State Relations in Europe," *West European Politics*, 26 (1): 23–50.

Marshall, Paul, 1998, "Religion and Global Affairs: Disregarding Religion," *SAIS Review*, Summer–Fall: 13–18.

Martin, David A., 1978, *A General Theory of Secularization*, Oxford: Blackwell.

Marty, Martin E., and R. Scott Appleby, eds., 1991, *Fundamentalisms and the State: Remaking Politics, Economies and Militance*, Chicago: University of Chicago Press.

Massimo, Introvigne, 2001, "Religious Minorities and Anti-Cult Opposition: The Italian Situation in Comparative Perspective," paper presented on June 9 at an International Conference at the University of Heidelberg.

Mazie, Steven V., 2004, "Rethinking Religious Establishment and Liberal Democracy: Lessons from Israel," *Brandywine Review of Faith and International Affairs*, 2 (2): 3–12.

McCloskey, Donald, 1987, *The Rhetoric of Economics*, Madison: University of Wisconsin Press.

McCleary, Rachel M., and Robert J. Barro, 2006a, "Religion and Economy," *Journal of Economic Perspectives*, 20 (2): 49–72.

McCleary, Rachel M., and Robert J. Barro, 2006b, "Religion and International Economy in an International Panel," *Journal for the Scientific Study of Religion*, 45 (2): 149–75.

Mendelsohn, Everett, 1993, "Religious Fundamentalism and the Sciences," in Martin E. Marty and R. Scott Appleby, eds., *Fundamentalisms and Society: Reclaiming the Sciences, the Family, and Education,* Chicago: University of Chicago Press, 23–41.

Midlarsky, Manus I., 1998, "Democracy and Islam: Implications for Civilizational Conflict and the Democratic Peace," *International Studies Quarterly,* 42 (3): 458–511.

Mill, John S., 1951 (first published 1861), "Considerations on Representative Government," in John S. Mill, *Utilitarianism, Liberty, and Representative Government,* New York: E. P. Dutton.

Miller, Alan S., 1996, "The Influence of Religious Affiliation on the Clustering of Social Attitudes," *Review of Religious Research,* 37 (3), March: 123–36.

Minkenberg, Michael, 2002, "Religion and Public Policy: Institutional, Cultural, and Political Impact on the Shaping of Abortion Policies in Western Democracies," *Comparative Political Studies,* 35 (2): 221–47.

Monsema, S., and C. Soper, 1996, *The Challenge of Pluralism: Church and State in Five Demorcracies,* Oxford: Rowman & Littlefield.

Monshipouri, Mahmood, 1998, "The West's Modern Encounter with Islam: From Discourse to Reality," *Journal of Church and State,* 40 (1): 25–56.

Morigi, Andrea, Vittorio E. Vernole, and Chiara Verna, 2000, "Report 2000 on Religious Freedom In the World," Aid to the Church in Need, Italian Secretariat.

Nason-Clark, N., 1997, *The Battered Wife: How Christians Confront Family Violence,* Louisville, KY: Westminster/John Knox.

Nason-Clark, N., 2001, "Making the Sacred Safe: Woman Abuse and Communities of Faith," *Sociology of Religion,* 61: 349–68.

Nasr, Vali, 1998, "Religion and Global Affairs: Secular States and Religious Oppositions," *SAIS Review,* Summer–Fall: 32–7.

Nielson, Michael E., and Jim Fultz, 1995, "Further Examination of the Relationships of Religious Orientation to Religious Conflict," *Review of Religious Research,* 36 (4), June: 369–81.

Nordlinger, Eric, 1972, *Contract Regulation in Divided Societies,* Cambridge MA: Harvard University Press.

Norris, Pippa, and Ronald Inglehart, 2004, *Sacred and Secular: Religion and Politics Worldwide,* Cambridge: Cambridge University Press.

Ofeish, Sami A., 1999, "Lebanon's Second Republic: Secular Talk, Sectarian Application," *Arab Studies Quarterly,* 21 (1): 97–116.

Olson, Daniel V. A., and C. Kirk Hadaway, 1999, "Religious Pluralism and Affiliation among Canadian Counties and Cities," *Journal for the Scientific Study of Religion,* 38 (4): 490–508.

Pape, Robert A., 2003, "The Strategic Logic of Suicide Terrorism," *American Political Science Review,* 97 (3): 343–61.

Pearce, Susanna, 2004, "The Double Edged Sword: The Impact of Religion on the Intensity of Political Conflict," Doctoral Dissertation, University of Dublin, Trinity College.

Pettersson, Thorleif, and Eva M. Hamberg, 1997, "Denominational Pluralism and Church Membership in Contemporary Sweden: A Longitudinal Study of the Period 1974–1995," *Journal of Empirical Theology,* 10: 61–78.

Philpott, Daniel, 2000, "The Religious Roots of Modern International Relations," *World Politics,* 52: 206–45.

Philpott, Daniel, 2002, "The Challenge of September 11 to Secularism in International Relations," *World Politics*, 55 (1): 66–95.

Polkinghorn, Brian, and Sean Byrne, 2001, "Between War and Peace: An Examination of Conflict Management Styles in Four Conflict Zones," *International Journal of Conflict Management*, 12 (1): 23–46.

Pollis, Admantia, 2002, "Greece: A Problematic Secular State," in William Safran, ed., *The Secular and the Scared, Nation, Religion and Politics*, London: Frank Cass.

Price, Daniel E., 1999, *Islamic Political Culture, Democracy, and Human Rights*, Westport, CT: Praeger.

Price, Daniel E., 2002, "Islam and Human Rights: A Case of Deceptive First Appearances," *Journal for the Scientific Study of Religion*, 41 (2): 213–25.

Rapoport, David, 1991, "Some General Observations on Religion and Violence," *Journal of Terrorism and Political Violence*, 3 (3): 118–39.

Rawls, John, 1993, *Political Liberalism*, New York: Columbia University Press.

Reynal-Querol, Marta, 2002, "Ethnicity, Political Systems, and Civil Wars," *Journal of Conflict Resolution*, 46 (1): 29–54.

Richardson, James T., 2003, *Regulating Religion: Case Studies from Around the Globe*, Berlin: Springer.

Riphenburg, Carol J., 1999, "Gender Relations and Development in the Yemen: Participation and Employment," *Peacekeeping & International Relations*, May/June 28 (3): 5–13.

Roeder, Philip G., 2003, "Clash of Civilizations and Escalation of Domestic Ethnopolitical Conflicts," *Comparative Political Studies*, 36 (5): 509–40.

Roelofs, H, Mark, 1988, "Liberation Theology: The Recovery of Biblical Radicalism," *American Political Science Review*, 88 (2): 549–66.

Rostow, W., 1959, *The Stages of Economic Growth: A Non-Communist Manifesto*, Cambridge: Cambridge University Press.

Rubin, Barry, 1994, "Religion and International Affairs," in Douglas Johnston and Cynthia Sampson, eds., *Religion, the Missing Dimension of Statecraft*, Oxford: Oxford University Press, 20–34.

Rule, James B., 1988, *Theories of Civil Violence*, Berkeley: University of California Press.

Rummel, Rudolph J., 1997, "Is Collective Violence Correlated with Social Pluralism?" *Journal of Peace Research*, 34 (2): 163–75.

Russett, Bruce, John R. Oneal, and Michalene Cox, 2000, "Clash of Civilizations, or Realism and Liberalism Deja Vu? Some Evidence," *Journal of Peace Research*, 37 (5): 583–608.

Sahliyeh, Emile, ed., 1990, *Religious Resurgence and Politics in the Contemporary World*, New York: State University of New York Press.

Sahliyeh, Emile, Sangeeta Sinha, and Vijayan Pillai, 2002, "Modeling Ethnic Protest: The Case of the Middle East and Central Asia," *African and Asian Studies*, 1 (1): 3–21.

Sambanis, Nicholas, 2001, "Do Ethnic and Nonethnic Civil Wars Have the Same Causes?" *Journal of Conflict Resolution*, 45 (3): 259–82.

Schanda, Balazs, 2002, "Religious Freedom Issues in Hungary," *BYU Law Review*: 405–34.

Seppo, Juha, 1998, "The Freedom of Religion and Conscience in Finland," *Journal of Church and State*, 4 (4), Autumn.

Shah, Timothy S., 2000, "Making the Christian World Safe for Liberalism: From Grotius to Rawls," *Political Quarterly*, 71 (1): 121–39.

Sherkat Daren, E., and Christopher G. Ellison, 1999, "Recent Development and Controversies in the Sociology of Religion," *Annual Review of Sociology*, 25: 363–94.

Shupe, Anson, 1990, "The Stubborn Persistence of Religion in the Global Arena," in Emile Sahliyeh, ed., *Religious Resurgence and Politics in the Contemporary World*, New York: State University of New York Press, 17–26.

Sigelman, Lee, 1977, "Review of the Polls: Multi-Nation Survey of Religious Belief," *Journal for the Scientific Study of Religion*, 16: 289–94.

Smith, Anthony D., 1999, "Ethnic Election and National Destiny: Some Religious Origins of Nationalist Ideals," *Nations and Nationalism*, 5 (3): 331–55.

Smith, Donald E., 1970, *Religion and Political Development*, Boston: Little, Brown.

Smith, Donald E., ed., 1974, *Religion and Political Modernization*, New Haven: Yale University Press.

Stark, Rodney, 1999, "Secularization, R.I.P.," *Sociology of Religion*, 60 (3): 249–73.

Stark, Rodney, and William Bainbridge, 1985, *The Future of Religion: Secularization, Revival and Cult Formation*, Berkeley: University of California Press.

Stark, Rodney, and Roger Finke, 2000, *Acts of Faith: Explaining the Human Side of Religion*, Berkeley: University of California Press.

Stark, Rodney, Roger Finke, and Lawrence R. Iannaccone, 1995, "Pluralism and Piety: England and Wales, 1851," *Journal for the Scientific Study of Religion*, 34: 431–44.

Stark, Rodney, and Lawrence R. Iannaccone, 1994, "A Supply Side Reinterpretation of the 'Secularization' of Europe," *Journal for the Scientific Study of Religion*, 33 (3): 230–52.

Stempel, John D., 2000, "Faith and Diplomacy in the International System," paper presented at the International Studies Association Meeting in Los Angeles (Patterson School of Diplomacy and Intl Commerce), March.

Stepan, Alfred, 2000, "Religion, Democracy, and the 'Twin Tolerations,' " *Journal of Democracy*, 11 (4): 37–56.

Sutton, Frank, 1968, "Social Theory and Comparative Politics," in Harry Eckstein and David Apter, eds., *International Encyclopedia of the Social Sciences*, New York: Macmillan.

Swatos, William H. Jr., and Kevin J. Christiano, 1999, "Secularization Theory: The Course of a Concept," *Sociology of Religion*, 60 (3): 209–28.

Thomas, Scott M., 2005, *The Global Resurgence of Religion and the Transformation of International Relations: The Struggle for the Soul of the Twenty-First Century*, New York: Palgrave-Macmillan.

Tibi, Bassam, 2000, "Post-Bipolar Disorder in Crisis: The Challenge of Politicized Islam," *Millennium*, 29 (4): 843–59.

Turner, Brian S., 1991, *Religion and Social Theory*, 2nd edn., London: Sage.

Tusicisny, Andrej, 2004, "Civilizational Conflicts: More Frequent, Longer, and Bloodier?" *Journal of Peace Research*, 41 (4): 485–98.

Vanhanen, Tatu, 1999, "Domestic Ethnic Conflict and Ethnic Nepotism: A Comparative Analysis," *Journal of Peace Research*, 36 (1): 55–73.

Voas, David, V. A. Daniel Olson, and Alasdair Crockett, 2002, "Religious Pluralism and Participation: Why Previous Research Is Wrong," *American Sociological Review*, 67 (2): 212–30.

Voye, Liliane, 1999, "Secularization in a Context of Advanced Modernity," *Sociology of Religion*, 60 (3): 275–88.

Wald, Kenneth D., 1987, *Religion and Politics in the United States*, New York: St. Martins.

Warner, Carolyn M., 2000, *Confessions of an Interest Group*, Princeton: Princeton University Press.

Warner, R. Stephen, 1993, "Work in Progress toward a New Paradigm for the Sociological Study of Religion in the United States," *American Journal of Sociology*, 98 (5), March: 1044–93.

Wayland, Sarah V., 1997, "Religious Expression in Public Schools: Kirpans in Canada, Hijab in France," *Ethnic and Racial Studies*, 20 (3): 545–61.

Weber, Max, 1930, *The Protestant Ethic and the Spirit of Capitalism*, trans. Talcott Parsons, London: Allen & Unwin.

Weigel, George, 1992, "Religion and Peace: An Argument Complexified," in Sheryl J. Brown and Kimber M. Schraub, eds., *Resolving Third World Conflict: Challenges for a New Era*, Washington, DC: United States Institute for Peace, 172–92.

Weinberg, Leonard B., and William L. Eubank, 1998, "Terrorism and Democracy: What Recent Events Disclose," *Terrorism and Political Violence*, 10 (1): 108–18.

Weinberg, Leonard, William Eubank, and Ami Pedahzur, 2002, "Characteristics of Terrorist Organizations 1910–2000," paper presented at the 25th Annual Meeting of the International Society of Political Psychology in Berlin, Germany, July.

Williams, Rhys H., 1994, "Movement Dynamics and Social Change: Transforming Fundamentalist Ideologies and Organizations," in Martin E. Marty and R. Scott Appleby, eds., *Accounting for Fundamentalisms: The Dynamic Character of Movements*, Chicago: University of Chicago Press, 785–833.

Williamson, Roger, 1990, "Why Is Religion Still a Factor in Armed Conflict?" *Bulletin of Peace Proposals*, 21 (3): 243–53.

Wilson, Bryan R., 1966, *Religion in Secular Society*, Baltimore: Penguin.

Wilson, Bryan R., 1976, "Aspects of Secularization in the West," *Japanese Journal of Religious Studies*, 3 (4): 259–76.

Wilson, Bryan R., 1982, *Religion in Sociological Perspective*, Oxford: Oxford University Press.

Wood, James E., 2005, *Church and State in the Modern World: A Critical Assessment and Annotated Bibliography*, Westport, CT: Praeger.

Zubadia, Sami, 2000, "Trajectories of Political Islam: Egypt, Iran and Turkey," *Political Quarterly*, 71 (Supplement 1): 60–78.

Index